INTERNET, HUMOR, AND NATION IN LATIN AMERICA

Reframing Media, Technology, and Culture in Latin/o America

INTERNET, HUMOR, AND NATION IN LATIN AMERICA

Edited by
Héctor Fernández L'Hoeste
and Juan Poblete

UNIVERSITY OF FLORIDA PRESS

Gainesville

Publication of this work made possible by a Sustaining the Humanities through the American Rescue Plan grant from the National Endowment for the Humanities.

29 28 27 26 25 24   6 5 4 3 2 1

Library of Congress Cataloging-in-Publication Data
Names: Fernández L'Hoeste, Héctor D., 1962– editor. | Poblete, Juan,
    editor.
Title: Internet, humor, and nation in Latin America / edited by Héctor
    Fernández L'Hoeste and Juan Poblete.
Other titles: Reframing Media, Technology, and Culture in Latin/o America.
Description: 1. | Gainesville : University of Florida Press, 2024. |
    Series: Reframing media, technology, and culture in Latin/o America |
    Includes bibliographical references and index.
Identifiers: LCCN 2023020745 (print) | LCCN 2023020746 (ebook) | ISBN
    9781683404033 (hardback) | ISBN 9781683404293 (paperback) | ISBN
    9781683404118 (pdf) | ISBN 9781683404187 (ebook)
Subjects: LCSH: Politics and culture—Latin America—Humor. | Social
    media—Latin America—Politics and government—Humor. | Political
    science—Latin America—Humor. | Politics, Practical—Latin
    America—Humor. | Spanish wit and humor—Political aspects—History and
    criticism. | Portuguese wit and humor—Political aspects—History and
    criticism. | Latin America—Politics and government—Humor. | BISAC:
    POLITICAL SCIENCE / Political Process / Media & Internet | SOCIAL
    SCIENCE / Media Studies
Classification: LCC F1408.3 .I584 2024 (print) | LCC F1408.3 (ebook) |
    DDC 320.98002/07—dc23/eng/20230524
LC record available at https://lccn.loc.gov/2023020745
LC ebook record available at https://lccn.loc.gov/2023020746

University of Florida Press
2046 NE Waldo Road
Suite 2100
Gainesville, FL 32609
http://upress.ufl.edu

CONTENTS

List of Figures   vii

List of Tables   xi

Acknowledgments   xiii

1. Introduction: Internet, Humor, and Nation in Latin America   1

    Héctor Fernández L'Hoeste and Juan Poblete

2. Digital Humor as Cultural Globalization in Latin America   35

    Paul Alonso

3. Hypermediatic Humor: Some Tools for Its Analysis   54

    Damián Fraticelli

4. Satire as the Voice of Resistance in Guillermo Aquino's *El Sketch*   72

    Alberto Centeno-Pulido

5. Political Cartoons and Memes: Artifacts of Discourse Subversion
   through Humor   96

    Alejandra Collado

6. Cutting through Layers of Brazilian Humor: Sampling the Past,
   Commenting on the Present, and Perhaps Creating the Future   117

    Eva Paulino Bueno and Fábio Marques de Souza

7. Humor and Nationalism in Bolsonarist Far-Right WhatsApp Memes in
   Brazil   144

    Viktor Chagas

8. Barbie Votes for Bolsonaro: How an Instagram Account Satirized the
   Brazilian Middle and Upper Classes   176

    Ulisses A. Sawczuk da Silva and Mélodine Sommier

9. "Whatever . . . It's Only a Joke!": Exploring Memes, Racialization, and Discrimination in Puerto Rico during Hurricanes, Earthquakes, and the COVID-19 Pandemic   198

   R. Sánchez-Rivera

10. HolaSoyGermán: On Global Latin American Humor on YouTube   221

   Juan Poblete

11. *La Pulla:* Humor as an Instrument of Intranational Hegemony   239

   Héctor Fernández L'Hoeste

List of Contributors   267

Index   269

FIGURES

3.1. Structure of the hypermediatic social network device   58

3.2. Meme of the conversation between Peter Parker and his Aunt May in which she expresses her unease with his journalism degree   60

3.3. Structure of account system   61

3.4. Meaning circulations diagram   62

3.5. Tweet from Dra. Alcira Pignata: "Is Milagro Sala already in jail?"   63

5.1. Tetrad model of a political cartoon   101

5.2. Tetrad model of the political meme   103

5.3. "Return of the Jedi" meme   105

5.4. "Los 43" (The 43) meme   108

6.1. Satirical caricature of the emperor Dom Pedro as a *manipanso*, an African idol   119

6.2. Satirical representation of an audience with Dom Pedro   120

6.3. Bode Orelana, by Brazilian cartoonist Henfil, is a goat that gets its culture by devouring books   123

6.4. Bode Orelana, named after the Amazonian explorer Francisco de Orellana, complains about the lack of freedom of speech   124

6.5. A freeze-frame of the final image from an episode of the soap opera *Avenida Brasil*   127

6.6. A freeze-frame of Carminha's dismay at the end of an episode of the soap opera *Avenida Brasil*   127

6.7. A sarcastic exchange in Bode Gaiato alluding to misplaced good looks   127

6.8. A meme on who will most likely discover the cure for the coronavirus   128

6.9. A meme mocks the inability to travel as relief from poverty   129

6.10. A meme mocks simplistic understanding of vaccines   130

6.11. An episode of *Tecendo prosa* with Concessa offering advice from the kitchen 132

6.12. An episode of *Tecendo prosa* in which Concessa addresses domestic abuse while pretending to share a recipe 133

6.13. The first edition of *Concessa News*, in which Concessa addresses the US president 135

6.14. A sarcastic coat of arms describing the US/Brazil relationship, according to the first edition of *Concessa News* 136

7.1. Canonical correspondence between functions of memes and Bolsonaro's representations 157

7.2. Canonical correspondence between Bolsonaro's representations and nationalist motives 159

7.3. Bolsonaro's representations and nationalist motives 159

7.4. Historical series 162

7.5. Bolsonaro's representations per week 163

7.6. Antidemocratic values per week 163

7.7. Humor and far-right memes 164

7.8. Humor and far-right memes 165

7.9. Humor and far-right memes 165

7.10. References to pop culture in Bolsonaro memes 166

7.11. References to pop culture in Bolsonaro memes 167

7.12. References to pop culture in Bolsonaro memes 167

7.13. Historical and religious reinterpretations 168

7.14. Historical and religious reinterpretations 168

7.15. Historical and religious reinterpretations 169

8.1. Screenshot of the Barbie Fascionista page with a conservative critique based on meritocratic legitimation 185

8.2. Screenshot of the Barbie Fascionista page displaying the exoticization of racial difference 189

8.3. Screenshot of the Barbie Fascionista page exhibiting a moral double standard 191

9.1. Meme Monkey meme of a man asking for coupons after the hurricane 205

9.2. Radical Cowry meme in the form of a gift label with Governor Roselló willing to do anything to gain state status 207

9.3. Memes de Puerto Rico meme listing the scariest places on Earth, including Guánica, PR   209

9.4. Memes de Puerto Rico meme personifying the island as a distracted boyfriend, caught between the pandemic and earthquakes   210

9.5. Sinophobic memes from Memes de Puerto Rico and El Blogiante, alluding to viral contagion and Chinese cuisine   213

9.6. PR Memes meme of a white man trying to civilize unruly Indigenous people   214

TABLES

5.1. Comparative table: political cartoons and memes   98

7.1. Functions of analyzed memes   157

7.2. Archetypal representations   157

7.3. Nationalist motives   158

7.4. Antidemocratic values   160

ACKNOWLEDGMENTS

This book on the role of humor on the Internet in Latin America explores, from a multi- and interdisciplinary open perspective, the diverse ways in which Internet-based humor is created, produced, consumed, used, circulated, reproduced, and transformed. In the process of editing it, we have had direct experience of the creativity and the cultural translations involved in thinking about humor and the Internet. We have exchanged many emails with our capable and patient contributors, who have done their best to respond, almost always with a smile, to our seemingly endless requests. We really appreciate your work and *las buenas vibras*.

The team at the University of Florida Press—with Stephanye Hunter at its head and Marthe Walters as project editor—has been a godsend, attending to a number of details and aspects of publishing that assure the quality of the end product. Many thanks also go to our anonymous reviewers for their detailed reading and valuable feedback.

Juan: I would like to thank my colleagues (some of them funny, all of them appreciated) in the Department of Literature at the University of California at Santa Cruz for more than twenty-five years of collective work. Thanks are due to my kids—Samson, Miguel, Esther, and Natalia—and to my wife, Micah Perks, who have over many years put up with both my not-always-spectacular humor and my questions about their use and experience of digital culture.

Héctor: I would like to thank the Office of the Dean of the College of Arts & Sciences at Georgia State University for its continuous support of this work. Thanks also go to many friends and colleagues who listened patiently about many aspects of this project—you know well who you are—in turn offering precious advice and many worthwhile suggestions. Endless gratitude goes to my sisters in Denver, who many times put up with my reclusive inclinations, even during the pandemic. As always, special thanks go to my son Sebastián for bearing with Dad and sharing his enthusiasm for many things on the Internet (and on not few occasions educating me about Gen Z-ers' cultural preferences and distinct sense of irony). *Hijo,* you always allow me to see things in a different way. Lastly, many thanks also go to Los Andes and Stony Brook, two institutions that have informed my views with respect to the relationship between the humanities and technology.

Juan dedicates his work in this book to his family, *los amigos del 4C en el Instituto Nacional* and Henry, who, with humor and constancy, have remained close through the distance.

Héctor dedicates his work in this book to Bubu, so he may always remember the importance of laughter—especially when life is challenging—and the family and friends in Auckland, Bogotá, Katonah, Medellín, Miami, and Naperville, who, many years later, fortunately, keep saying *hueseras*.

1

Introduction

Internet, Humor, and Nation in Latin America

Héctor Fernández L'Hoeste and Juan Poblete

The Internet and humor are fine examples of forms of participatory culture. A notable portion of what circulates on the web is humor, produced and consumed by private citizens. These are participants, who, along with consuming the corporate diet on offer, also respond creatively and productively to commercial and social invitations to participate, moving from consumer to prosumer. Humor is one of the central ways in which such Internet-based capture and participation mechanisms are successfully presented and enacted.

The Internet is both a medium, the latest in a long line of mass media, and a space of trans-individuation, in other words, collective or social cocreation. As a media space often organized in a limited variety of formats, it tends to favor certain forms, lengths, and affects. As a commons, it is nurtured by all participants and shapes their affects and subjectivities in ways that have deep cultural, economic, and political corollaries inside and outside the nation, constituting a key space for the definition of identity. As a relatively deterritorialized space, it interacts in myriad ways with the forms of cultural and political territorialization of the nation. Lastly, as a part of the communication infrastructure, the Internet is associated in more conventional ways with the geopolitics of information production and circulation.

Humor, on the other hand, is often based on mechanisms of superiority, relief, or incongruity, while its effects also contribute to the formation of community and identity. As theorized by British critic Simon Critchley, ethnic humor in a national context is an instance of superiority-based humor. It functions like "a secret code" that is shared by all those who belong to the *ethnie*, producing a context and community-based ethos of superiority. This superiority is expressed in two ways: first, foreigners do not share our sense of humor or simply lack a sense of humor. Second, foreigners are themselves funny and worth laughing at. Thus, humor plays a strategic role in the signaling of the boundaries of identity—who stands inside or outside significant communities. If the Internet seems to have universal reach and may tend to de-territorialize the availability of cultural production, humor is based both on a series of references (contents, figures, processes) of global circulation (what Renato Ortiz calls an international popular culture) and on much more specific territorializing processes that pertain to the world as lived within a geocultural space (what Ortiz terms concrete *mundializações*), in other words within a shared territory demarcated by a language, and cultural, historical, and political references (often a nation-state, sometimes a world-region, following John Sinclair).

When we began the work for this book on the Internet and humor in Latin America, we developed a series of bold questions that were meant to outline a broader agenda-setting paradigm that our volume could contribute to but, given the state of research on these topics in Latin America, could not truly hope to answer: If Internet-based humor provides relief, what is it a relief from or of? What are the semantics and syntactics specific to Internet humor? What is the distinctive logic of Internet-based humor? In the context of the Internet, what is incongruous? When it comes to humor, what relationships does the audiovisual aspect of the Internet bring about with its written side? What kinds of humor go viral and which do not, and why? What role does humor itself play in the affective and economic structure of the Internet? In sum, how does the Internet alter, confirm, enhance, or deflate the dynamics of humor?

At stake here was the possibility that new forms of theorizing humor and its cultural role in our contemporary life may be needed to account for the actual intersections of humor and the Internet in an area that years ago a group of distinguished Latin American scholars envisioned as the Latin American cultural space of the twenty-first century (Garretón et al.). One of the best-known forms of this alternative theorizing of humor in direct connection with the culture of the Internet is the work of Sianne Ngai on the gimmick and what she calls "our aesthetic categories": the zany, the cute, or the interesting (*Our Aesthetic* 1). Indeed, humor may be one of the central gimmicks of Internet-based culture. While the conventional acceptation of "gimmick," according to Oxford Languages, is "a trick or device intended to attract attention, publicity, or business," Ngai explains the gimmick as a specifically modern labor- and time-saving device that, in calling attention to itself and grabbing our attention, often irritatingly but also always effectively passes itself off as a full aesthetic object worthy of our consideration when it is, in fact, only "an instrumental part-object" (*Theory* 52). Hence, the gimmick is both a trick and a wonder—"It is a form we marvel at and distrust, admire and disdain, whose affective intensity for us increases precisely because of this ambivalence" (54). In her work, Ngai begins to think about aesthetics in direct connection with the cultures of production, circulation, and consumption for which the Internet is both a major medium and vehicle. While our volume will not be the place to significantly develop such an agenda in its connection to humor, we envision it as one of the first steps in the proper direction in the Latin American-related area by focusing empirically and theoretically, within the humanities and the social sciences, on a few formats and platforms that are important in the production, circulation, and consumption of humor on the web within this world-region.

With the nature of the Internet and humor in mind, we originally asked our contributors: If what we described above is the case for humor in a nation-based context, could they produce empirically based chapters discussing concrete examples of Latin American-produced and -consumed Internet-based humor in any of its multiple manifestations? Within the broader context, we mentioned recent precedents on the topic of humor in modern media, such as Jody Baumgartner and Jonathan Morris's *Laughing Matters: Humor and American Politics in the Media Age*, which examines the role of humor in US politics—along with David Thorne's *The Internet Is a Playground*, exemplifying a performative disposition—and resources like Luis Loya García's bibliography, *Latino Humor in Comparative Perspective*. In the spirit of *Cualca* (AR), the web series starring Malena Pichot; *País de Boludos* (AR), the political humor YouTube channel; *Greg News* (BR), the John Oliver–styled satire show; *Porta dos Fundos* (BR), the massively popular YouTube channel; *El Boletín del Gomelo* (CO), the political satire Internet show; *La Pulla* (CO), the YouTube political news team; *Upsocl* (CL), the quirky humor website; *ElDeforma* (MX), the entertainment, news, and satire website; *El Pulso de la República* (MX), Chumel Torres's YouTube channel; *Gente Como Uno* (PE), the "real-life" TV series; or *Remezcla* (US), the Latin American culture–based website and media company, we then set out to contribute to the study of the interaction among the Internet, humor, and nation.[1] While much work to date in this field has focused on satire—see Paul Alonso's *Satiric TV in the Americas*, which discusses how cultural globalization and hybridity operate in today's transnational entertainment and commercial critical humor thanks to the impact of streaming—we were interested in all types of Internet-based humor practices (cutting across formats and media).

Our volume, then, aims to explore, from a multi- and interdisciplinary open perspective, the many ways in which Internet-based humor is created, produced, consumed, used, circulated, reproduced, transformed, and answered. On the whole, we are interested in the significance of web-based discourses and narratives in the context of local, national, regional, transnational, and global cultural production, commercial ventures, material culture, audiences, education, government policy, and community practices. If the Internet has been an extraordinarily effective medium for social interactions and even for a redefinition of what counts as a social interaction, then, we have come to conclude, humor is one of the things that circulates the most in such interactions. This is true both for online and off-line interaction. In the context of off-line, a recent psychology textbook clarifies, "Humor is a universal human activity that most people experience many times over the course of a typical day and in all sorts of social contexts" (Martin and Ford 37). Online, businesses and advertising agencies, to name some actors in this arena, discovered early on that humor is one of the fundamentals of viral advertising. An early article on the then still relatively new form stated in 2006, "Humor was employed at near unanimous levels for all viral advertisements. Consequently, this study identified humor as the universal appeal for making content viral" (Porter and Golan n.p.) For this reason, our main contention is that humor increasingly plays a critical role in the way social media articulate negotiations within the culture, often between the overall population—an expanded civil society embodying the nation—and the characters and/or institutions associated with the cultural/political establishment, which personify the state, effectively leading to new modes of imagining interactions between both while addressing a wide variety of issues and topics, from the daily impact of inflation to gender disparity. To a great extent, then, many of these social interactions are amusing and much of the humor that circulates the most does so via the Internet or social media, so much so that one of the pioneers in the study of web-based humor, Limor Shifman, has proposed a method, web memetics, to study how jokes circulate (and change as they do) through the Internet (Shifman and Thelwal 2567). A different set of web-based humor quantitative researchers underscores how the abundant quantity of humor on the web represents the possibility of a new way of studying humor:

> Users of social media, in numbers dwarfing by orders of magnitude the sample sizes of traditional ethnographic studies, incessantly congregate at media aggregation websites to tell other people what they find funny. Given this plethora of Web 2.0 information, it is likely that a new way of

studying the sources of humor may now become feasible. (Mahapatra et al. n.p.)

Then, one can ask, what does humor bring to such social media and Internet-mediated interactions? How does the structure of the different types of humor contribute to shaping social contact? Conversely, how do the Internet and social media influence and transform what comes to be seen as humorous today? What effects do the discursive and technical affordances of new media have on the humor being created, shared, and touched through its channels? This is easily recognizable in all chapters of this volume, though there are texts like the one by Eva Paulino Bueno and Fábio Marquez de Souza—involving the acceptance and circulation of a well-known character in popular culture and videos based on the aesthetics of communitarian advice—that would simply be unimaginable without the gregarious nature and domestic practices of Internet citizens targeted by their objects of study and the impact of technology on their social routines. Their chapter evinces—like many of the others, but to a more acute extent—how the Internet shapes and changes the flow and breakdown of humor. Therefore, we argue for the weight of the role of humor within the new array of practices influenced by technology that define the outlines of cultural, economic, political, and social relationships in Latin America. Thanks to the Internet, Latin American forms of humor are circulating in neoteric ways and reaching previously overlooked audiences on more culturally personalized and value-extracting platforms, generating novel means of interaction with the political sphere as well as greater expectations of accountability.

To advance our contention, we have divided this introduction into four sections. The first part concerns the theorizing of humor as a cultural activity. The second one deals with the Internet as a media space and locus for trans-individuation and social co-creation. Part three brings these issues to the Latin American context, while part four introduces the contents of this volume.

On Theories of Humor

In his edited volume *The Philosophy of Laughter and Humor*, John Morreall divides theories of humor into three different types, depending on which central humor mechanism they emphasize: superiority, relief, or incongruity. Given Morreall's standing as a forerunner in humor studies, his work has been embraced as a template by many authors, including Critchley and Terry Eagleton. Superiority-based theories of humor (dating as far back as Aristotle, Plato, and Hobbes) explain, according to Critchley, a basic functioning of humor, especially of the ethnic variety: "Humor is a form of cultural insider-knowledge, and might, indeed, be said to function like a linguistic defense mechanism. Its ostensive untranslatability endows native speakers with a palpable sense of their cultural distinctiveness or even superiority" (88–89). This type of humor depends on "a secret code" that is shared by all those who belong to the *ethnie,* and it produces a context and collective-based ethos of superiority that separates those who share the code from those who do not and are thus viewed as laughable.

On the other hand, to Critchley, relief-based theories of humor (Herbert Spencer and Sigmund Freud figure among the examples) are about accumulated energy in search of some form of release and relief for its subject, while in incongruity-based theories (examples from the work of Kant, Schopenhauer, and Kierkegaard are mentioned), humor is the result of the incongruity between our structure of expectations and the punch line of the joke that surprises us. Critchley's contribution to this theorizing of humor is to propose that, for the incongruity effect to occur, there has to be a previous basic congruence between the structure of the joke and the cultural presuppositions of a particular society (what he calls a *sensus communis*). If this common sense is affirmed in racist or xenophobic humor, it is also questioned both by a leftover awareness of our own racism that the joke produces and, in other types of humor, by a certain critical detachment from that shared everyday life. In the finest humor, Critchley proposes, the subject, instead of laughing at others, does so at her- or himself. For instance, witness the case of Argentine comedian Guillermo Aquino, discussed by Alberto Centeno-Pulido in this volume, in which, while Aquino criticizes the situation in Argentina, he is most certainly issuing a biting assessment of *argentinidad* (Argentineness or the condition of being Argentinean), and thus including himself within the population not only affected by widespread corruption and political and economic instability but also responsible for it. This is why one of Aquino's favorite mechanisms of representation is to talk to himself, setting himself in the future so he can laugh at his situation in the present. Germán Garmendia, the YouTuber discussed in Juan Poblete's chapter, also replicates this kind of behavior to some extent, as the quick editing of his videos allows him to examine his very own reenactment of Chilean culture and thus poke fun at himself, simultaneously incarnating subject and object of study. Hence, the result is not simply pleasure, but also a critical awareness of the contingency of the subject and her/his circumstance. In this way, humor generates not just a confirmation of our connection to a social group, with all its shared presuppositions, but also an *epoché,* a bracketing of the naturalized belief in those presuppositions. While there is, then, abundantly available reactionary humor, there is also, according to Critchley, the possibility in other forms of humor of a critical distancing from the known, accepted, and expected, which opens up another possible *sensus communis,* based on dissensus different from the hegemonic common sense (Poblete).

British theorist Terry Eagleton borrows a page from Morreall's and Critchley's work and gives both a new twist. In his volume on humor, he offers a more extensive balance of several apposite theories, even if in the end he chooses to focus, once again, on relief, superiority, and incongruity (this is the order that he favors). He commends Christopher Wilson's *Jokes: Form, Content, Use and Function,* a book brimming with graphs and mathematical equations, seeking to analyze and explain humor in a more quantitatively driven fashion—resulting in our awe and delight. Ultimately, Eagleton decides to focus and expand on what he considers to be the three main theories. To him, the release theory incarnates perhaps the most popular conjecture in the theorization of the practice, based on the understanding of humor as a sponsor of relief. According to Eagleton, laughter represents the collapse or disruption of the symbolic realm, while in another sense it never ceases to rely on it (4). Yet laughter, he suggests in a way that echoes Critchley, can be treated as a text or language with so many regional accents (7). Joking, even in regional contexts, may be interpreted as a brief retreat from the mild oppressiveness of everyday meaning, which is itself a form of sublimation (15). Habitually, humor is conceived and celebrated as a form of resistance, especially when it is not at the expense of others, centering on the self rather than on a contrast between parts. Nonetheless, quoting Alexander Bain, Eagleton explains how humor may also be born from the instances of repression embodied by the maintenance of everyday reality (16). In this sense, humor does for adults what play achieves for children: the granting of some unrestricted interplay for the pleasure principle as a result of liberation from the reality principle, echoing Freud. Hence, subjects can attain a demystified perception of their surroundings, occasionally purged of ideological illusion while unmasked as temporary and material (34).

Subsequently, Eagleton centers on the superiority theory, best explained as a convenient construct for environments in which one subject laughs at the expense of another, validating or overturning a hierarchical arrangement. This is the type of humor examined in Ulisses Sawczuk da Silva and Mélodine Sommier's chapter, in which the image of the Barbie doll is simultaneously used by some to critique President Jair Bolsonaro and embraced by others— in all likelihood, his bigoted supporters. At the heart of this theorization is the notion that if humankind cannot be reprimanded into virtue, perhaps it can be satirized into it (41). After all, as Eagleton observes correctly, the term "sarcasm" comes from an ancient Greek verb—*sarkazein*—meaning to tear the flesh like a dog (42). Superiority may even lead to laughter at the expense of oneself, leading to the consideration of self-denigration as a defense mechanism or survival tactic. If one laughs at oneself, it becomes possible to preempt the criticism of others to a certain extent, or even to disqualify their mocking. Eagleton cites Groucho Marx's memorable wisecrack, "I wouldn't join a club that let in people like me" (60), as an incontrovertible example. Even so, like everything, self-denigration has its twists and turns. When we laugh at comedians like Larry David or Ricky Gervais, who excel at making themselves the object of mockery, part of our amusement comes from the clever, adroit way in which they do it—from their performance, aside from the substance of their jokes. And so, within this context, self-denigration or any other practice rooted in the superiority theory conceals a meditation on our valuation of the other, for it is from the perspective of the other that this representation coalesces, given how alterity introduces a game of contrasts. To substantiate his reading, Eagleton quotes Lacan, who claims we love the other insofar as she or he is lacking, allowing us an opportunity to smile at perceiving our defects in others (65).

The third main theory on humor examined by the British critic is the incongruity theory, which, he claims, remains the most plausible account of why we laugh (67). From his standpoint, the incongruity theory involves a breach in the usual order of things, a disruption of widely shared thought processes, or even the violation of conventions or laws (67). From an opposing viewpoint, however, it can be construed as a process of defamiliarization, for that which is well known and recognizable is suddenly represented in a new, less expected manner, leading to glee. This remains especially germane if we are to think of the impact of humor as a transnational practice rooted in deterritorialization. For disruption to work, processes have to apply to an ample segment of the population, regardless of cultural, economic, or political commonality. Then again, given the affinities among the main theories in which all three critics—Morreall, Critchley, and Eagleton—coincide, and once one considers that a sense of relief may emerge from the affirmation of inferiority or the contravention of a pre-established order, it is likely that the combination of these three theories manages to explain the majority of our practices related to humor.

In the end, most theories of humor involve deviation or transgression. That said, as we will see in this volume's chapters, a great deal of humor on the Internet is based on the notion that, while jokes question and/or transgress authority, they ultimately may end up reinstating it, conceivably in a way that is more stable and successful than in its previous inception. Héctor Fernández L'Hoeste's chapter on the work of the Colombian news team behind *La Pulla* is a good illustration of this result: while its actions indict the corruption of the political class, they ultimately condone the hegemonic disposition of Bogotá's cultural and political establishment. In plain terms, humor may have a role to play in the act of creating a long-lasting order or engendering enhanced, more resilient structures of power. After all, humor is an exercise in entropy—in other words a certain relation between order and disorder among or within the elements of a system—trying to optimize its value as a form of restoring balance or equilibrium to a system, metaphorically speaking. Information theory is the discipline involved in the quantification, storage, and communication of digital information. As a field pertinent to many of the examples in this book, it values this tendency to reach balance greatly, centering on the quantification of uncertainty in the value of a random variable or the result of an aleatory process—a course of action in some way akin to the attainment of equilibrium through entropy. This is only sensible, as the principle of maximum entropy in information theory identifies the probability distribution with the highest entropy as the one that best represents the current state of knowledge about a system. Thus, when it comes to issues and public opinion, on many topics, humor serves habitually as a safety valve for information, as a mechanism for reaching stability—cultural, political, social—which, in many cases, may involve engaging and mollifying public opinion, embodying a veritable practice of hegemonic temperament.

In a more recent book theorizing humor, Morreall, this time relying more on cognitive psychology and etiology, revisits his previous efforts and the classical triad of humor theories (superiority, incongruity, and relief), proposing instead:

> The central idea of this book is that in humor we experience a sudden change of mental state—a cognitive shift, I call it—that would be disturbing under normal conditions, that is, if we took it seriously. Disengaged from ordinary concerns, however, we take it playfully and enjoy it. (*Comic Relief* xii)

Conceiving humor in this way, and thus following Aristotle and Thomas Aquinas, Morreall proposes, allows us to understand relaxation and play in a disengaged context as key categories in humor studies, and as the basis of a psychological, aesthetic, and ethical approach to it capable of including both the healthy and unhealthy effects of humor.

Given the nature of the work in this collection, we suggest that humor—or more precisely, certain kinds of humor this book studies—is now one of the most shared forms of communication/information in the new landscape of social media. The expressive and semantic demands of humor and its overall effects on the construction and maintenance of social bonds fit well within the affordances of social media, in other words within their technological limiting and enabling structuration of communication. Thanks to the Internet and to a degree that is perhaps historically unprecedented, humor has become the most favored content of such interactions and one of the key devices for the construction of identities and the exchange of communication lubricating everyday social activity. How does humor affect the dynamics of Internet-mediated engagements and social media, and how is it affected by this technical mediation? What are these mechanisms—affects, effects, and symbolic demands—making possible and marking the broad and massive circulation of humor in social media? In the Latin American context, these are some of the central questions defining the scope and ambition of this volume.

To paraphrase *Networld*, Niall Ferguson's PBS series on networks, in order to discuss what people think about the relationship between humor and technology in the present, it pays to discuss what people think about the relationship between humor and technology in the past. Latin American humor has deep roots in the colonial experience and the nation-forming processes of the nineteenth century, but its modern practice is directly connected to the arrival of modern forms of mass communication in the twentieth century—radio and cinema, and then television and the Internet—as well as the accelerated urbanization of the region.

The printed press sets a distinct precedent in terms of humor and politics. By the late nineteenth century, there is ample evidence throughout the Hispano- and Lusophone Americas of the expansion of graphic and written humor: in Argentina, there are *Don Quijote* (1884–1902) and *Caras y Caretas* (1898–1941); in Chile, Luis Fernando Rojas and *La Revista Cómica* (1895–1915); in Brazil, Angelo Agostini and *Revista Ilustrada* (1876–1898); in Colombia, Alfredo Greñas and *El Zancudo* (1890–1891); in Cuba, Víctor Landaluze and Ricardo de la Torriente, and *La Política Cómica* (1905–1931); in Peru, Marcelo Cabello and Francisco Fierro Palas, and *La Mascarada* (1874); and in Uruguay, *El Negro Timoteo* (1876–1901) and *La Alborada* (1896–1904) (Cerda Catalán; García Moreno; Pini). Since graphic humor frequently incarnated political criticism, it commonly led to harassment, persecution, and even exile, as in the case of the Colombian Greñas.

Many forms of Latin American humor and ways of thinking about it are closely related to the national and/or regional idiosyncrasy of its practitioners. In the twentieth century, with the emergence of the first explicitly nationalist regimes, humor begins to be theorized alongside national imperatives. Two important theorists of the social life and roots of humor in their respective countries are Jorge Mañach in Cuba and Carlos Monsiváis in Mexico.

In *Indagación del choteo,* Mañach produces one of the first modern theorizations of Latin American humor. Conjuring Caribbean idiosyncrasy, he defines *choteo* as "an itch for independence that is externalized in a mockery of all non-imperative forms of authority" (Mañach 41). It embodies selfish, open irreverence and mockery as a habit, in other words as the practice of not taking seriously anything that is usually taken seriously (Mañach 18), which evolves into disdain or lack of recognition for authority. For Mañach, mockery is, by definition, a ruse deployed against power—not to be used against those who are weaker (26). Thus, it focuses on disorder—since to order is to command—as a negation of authority (33). In addition, it exploits the laughable features of authority, pointing out its inner contradictions (27). Choteo, Mañach clarifies, laughs at values that could be emulated by the prankster, were there a desire to do so (37); consequently, resentment is seldom its motivation. It is rooted in lightness (resulting from lack of attention), superficiality (from lack of abstraction), and independence (from Cuban individuality). It can attain many forms: with a negative bent, it can oppose aspirations that are considered too serious just as, with a more constructive inclination, it can aim at institutions that seem dated or no longer valid. Neither intellectual nor based on ingenuity, choteo is founded on the Cuban propensity for bringing things down to earth as well as the obviation of hierarchy. Mañach, Pérez Firmat, and Hidalgo are among its theorists. As a systematic cultural practice, it has proved amazingly resilient, adapting to the changing conditions of Cuban life, both on the island and abroad.

Carlos Monsiváis explores historically how in Mexico *costumbrismo* gradually mixes with nationalism, engendering archetypes such as the *peladito* (a slum vagrant) and practices such as *cantinflismo* (the art of speaking long without saying anything) (*Mexican Postcards* 100). In the wake of the Mexican revolution, says Monsiváis, the prevailing brand of humor was that favored by the rougher sort of theater patron—the *peladitos* who attended performances at small theaters, mixing in the audience with intellectuals, artists, and even members of the state, from the military to bureaucrats ("Notas" 100–102). Humor ensues from the eschatological verborrhea of the audience, merging a variety of registers: on one end, Gallic refinement and untarnished manners, a residue of Porfirian times; on the other, the rude and the profane, thanks to the masses taking over the city. Theater becomes a place to discuss matters like the cost of living or to settle disputes among political adversaries in a veiled fashion. For the new urban masses, aside from the theater, the circus also plays a significant role. This is the point at which Mario Moreno brings the *peladito* to life with failed eloquence and endless improvisation. Cantinflas, of course, gives birth to *cantinflismo*, mocking the powerful, or joking about personal misfortune in a Mexican setting.

Radio and cinema arrive en masse across the Americas in the 1920s and 1930s. Radio, in particular, begins to gestate a humor tradition with a firm national inkling, making the best use of folk culture. Given its nature as the first modern mass-communication technology with national reach, radio's impact is wide-ranging, as explored in the pioneering work of Monsiváis and Jesús Martín-Barbero. In their view, radio played a fundamental role in the adaptation and transformation of folklore and rural culture into an urbanized, more modern-day format, serving as a prelude to film and television. As Monsiváis proposes, just like with radio, Latin Americans went to the movies to learn about their nationalities. Images allowed film directors to engage their public in a more detailed, almost didactic manner. The transition to an audiovisual format, both on the large screen and eventually on TV at home, accelerated the coexistence of cultures with disparate social registers while increasing the degree of cultural penetration from other latitudes. Television arrives in the 1950s, and its influence will remain enormous, thanks to its later transition into streaming.

In this process of modernization and urbanization of the previously rural popular cultures of the continent, each country developed a formula around its idiosyncrasy, progressively settling on a certain ideologically inflected version of national culture. In Mexico, there were *ranchera* comedies and numerous motion pictures with Cantinflas, Capulina, La India María, Tin Tan, etc.; in Brazil, *chanchadas,* musical comedies inspired by Hollywood but based on local carnival and burlesque, starting with comedians like Grande Otelo and Oscarito. With the backing of Televisa, formulaic shows like *El Chapulín Colorado* and *El Chavo del Ocho* became popular across Latin America, whereas lesser-known shows like *Los Polivoces* and *El Show de Los Polivoces,* with Enrique Cuenca and Eduardo Manzano, and *¿Qué nos pasa?,* by Héctor Suárez, demonstrated it was possible to practice enjoyable humor while documenting changes in the culture and ridiculing the government. Given the greater investment demanded by the film and TV industry and the culturally determined nature of national humor, few countries managed to circulate their brand of comedy successfully throughout the region. Most of what was traded were telenovelas, not locally developed sitcoms. Only a few countries like Brazil and Colombia incorporated humor as an integral element of their telenovela production, as in the case of *Yo soy Betty, la fea.* Consequently, when paid television started making inroads in the 1990s, production companies like Sony favored a collaboration with their equivalents in Argentina, Colombia, and Chile to develop Latin American versions of established US sitcoms, hoping to generate more viable content. This was, according to strategy, a pragmatic way to appeal to Latin American audiences through generic, highly commodified versions of proven US comedic shows. When US giants like Netflix, Disney, Amazon, and Apple started streaming across Latin America, many local TV networks and telecom companies were caught unprepared. From the national to the transnational periods, media, humor, and social groups undergoing significant cultural, economic, and political transformations co-evolved in tight but variable connections.

This new communication scenario, key for the production and consumption of contemporary humor in Latin America, is usefully described in detail by Eli Carter in *The New Brazilian Mediascape*. Just like Televisa in Mexico, Brazilian powerhouse TV Globo had grown complacent with its market domination, rooted in telenovelas. A transition to paid TV service had already started, but when Internet services expanded, the greater availability of choices in terms of topics and representation meant an unexpected challenge for the Brazilian colossus. YouTube in particular became a platform that encouraged scrappy little independents (e.g., *Porta dos Fundos*) to deliver appealing content with acceptable production values at a fraction of the usual cost. By the time Globo launched Globoplay (and Televisa released Blim), the OTT (over the top) video delivery Latin American market was already a reality—"over the top" being the market's designation for media services offering content via the Internet. While Netflix led in the region, aside from the locals, there were US powerhouses like Disney, HBO, Amazon, and Viacom, giving way to hybridity and transculturation. By 2020, Latin America became the second-fastest-growing streaming market in the world, with Netflix taking a remarkable half of the market (LABS). In consequence, the Latin American mediascape loosened dramatically, enabling a greater flow of regional production and increased contact with wider varieties of humor.

Contemporary Latin American research on humor exhibits a great number of lines of inquiry. In Colombia, journalist María Alejandra Medina Cartagena analyzes the emergence of political humor in audiovisual media, also chronicling its transition from television to the Internet. Research psychologist Jacqueline Benavides Delgado has compiled three edited volumes on the study of humor in the region. The first one, in particular, *Humor y política: una perspectiva transcultural*, illustrates the mutual influence between humor and sociopolitical and cultural processes. The volume includes chapters on the role of humor in the formation of Colombian individuality in the nineteenth century and a comparative analysis of the use of graphic humor as political resistance in late nineteenth-century Mexican and Argentine newspapers. In

Brazil, journalist Isabela Gama Guandalini explores the limits of humor in traditional and more contemporary social media. In her book *O que há por trás do riso?*, following a periodization of the role of humor in Brazilian history, she documents the tensions between free speech and fundamental rights in three recent cases, corroborating how humor in social media ultimately engenders boorish, undemocratic responses.

One clear strand of humor-related and Latin America-based theorizing connects it with its subversive capacity to provide a different angle of consideration of serious social, political, and cultural issues, including oppressive power relations of all kinds, authoritarianism, censorship, and dictatorship. An interesting recent example of this is Caty Borum Chattoo and Amy Henderson Riley's "Comedy as Creative Dissent in Latin America," the product of a collaboration among Univision, the Open Society Foundations, and the Center for Media & Social Impact (CMSI) at American University. The project, which ran for a year between 2017–18, connected three comedy groups, one each in Colombia, Brazil, and Mexico, with "serious social justice advocates and organizations" (4), financial resources, and research help. The goal of the project was "to explore and understand the challenges for comedy groups in Latin America that sought to create original comedy work that spotlights civic and social injustice and that captures public attention to encourage public engagement with serious issues" (4). The premise was that humor should be seriously considered, since "persuasion through positive emotion and entertainment value—comedy's superpowers—is not only powerful but often is more potent for capturing a public's attention and encouraging its civic participation than providing serious information alone" (4). The projects included "Emoteísmo . . . a satirical religion . . . dedicated to the worship of emojis" in Colombia (10), a series of cabaret efforts by six women's organizations in Mexico, and Meme News, translating "boring and complicated political news into memes picked up from the web" (8) in Brazil. Comedy, as it is itself based on creative dissent, was seen in the overall project and the context of polarized media environments as useful in the creation of alternative discursive spaces and ways of lightening the political load. Comedy was described here as "hilari-ouch . . . something that is funny but ouch" (23) or "canibal humor [*sic*]" laughing at "really mean things" (22). The conclusion was that "this type of cultural engagement work incites critical thinking and aims to bring consciousness regarding social issues" (23).

According to Donna M. Goldstein in *Laughter Out of Place. Race, Class, Violence, and Sexuality in a Rio Shantytown*, the favela dwellers of her ethnography used humor to live their lives, as "everywhere I turned I seemed to hear laughter" (2):

This humor was a kind of running commentary about the political and economic structures that made up the context within which the people of Rio de Janeiro's shantytowns made their lives—an indirect dialogue, sometimes critical, often ambivalent, always (at least partially) hidden, about the contradictions of poverty in the midst of late capitalism. (2)

Following scholars such as James C. Scott—who consider humor one of the weapons available to the weak, laughter animated by hidden transcripts of resistance in a form of counter-theater alternative to the publicly dominating displays of the ruling classes—Goldstein proposes that the humor of her *faveladas* "is one of the fugitive forms of insubordination" and reveals "both the cracks in the system and the masked or more subtle ways that power is challenged" (5) because "it does open a discursive space within which it becomes possible to speak about matters that are otherwise naturalized, unquestioned, or silenced" (10). "Their laughter," concludes Goldstein, "contains a sense of the absurdity of the world they inhabit" (13).

Some chapters in this volume agree with Goldstein in thinking of humor as a social tool that provides both a critical angle on reality and tools for living in such a context. On the other hand, a common thread in several other chapters in this book is the notion that humor-developed critical stances are often ultimately based on the validation of underlying prejudice or inequity, thus substantiating a conventional order. R. Sánchez-Rivera's chapter on the assessment of disasters in Puerto Rico (Hurricane Maria, the pandemic, etc.) is a quintessential example of this fact: while the examples discussed contain a critique of power, the author makes plain that forms of racialization, discrimination, and exclusion are operating and being reinforced in many of the memes circulating among islanders with the pretense of criticizing crises, promoting the continued sidelining and exclusion of scapegoat communities and individuals. Within these circumstances, consciously or not, meme content becomes a powerful vehicle for the dissemination of capitalist rationality within the context of world politics. Fueled by the neoliberal economy, globalization terms irrational any difference that may not be incorporated into so-called development—what Greek-French philosopher and social critic Cornelius Castoriadis, another common source for Martín-Barbero, describes as an act of "recovery" by hegemonic logic ("Globalización" 22).

Argentine scholar Damián Fraticelli, the author of a chapter in this volume, has contributed an interesting analysis of how humor and technical nature come together in the new electronic context of social media in Latin America today. In his "La nueva era de la mediatización reidera" (A new age of laughable mediatization), the author proposes distinguishing among three epochs in the analysis of the mediatization of the risible in Argentina. The first, which he calls "mediatic humor," is characterized by a clear separation between the real and its representation, and a strong set of media that institutionally control what and when media products are available. In the postmodern 1980s, secondly, we enter into a time of mediatized humor that multiplies and diversifies what is available in the media. As a result, the unified mass audience is segmented into stylistically specific audiences. The risible at this moment becomes reflexive and parodic, as the full history of media becomes increasingly available as a cultural reference. At this point, rather than a clear separation between the real and representation, the epoch is defined by media that are seen as constructing reality, and the risible is extended, beyond genre specificity, as a general tone of the media, including all programming. The separation between the serious and the non-serious disappears into this generalized humoristic tone for a programming offer that is now available at the discretion of the viewer. The third epoch, what Fraticelli calls hypermediatic humor, corresponds to the new coexistence of two media systems: mass media and social media. At this stage, viewers, collectively and individually, also become producers of mediatized discourse. This results in relative democratization of production, in other words a relative weakening of the institutional strength of media while amateurs gain access to technical capabilities that allow for creative production, appropriation, and transformation of media content. The risible is now generated in wide collective participation and collaboration. These prosumers also gain the ability to avoid some forms of media institutional control over what can be said by playing with the diversity of media available, which allows for the re-posting of media content on different platforms. The diversity of the content grows as new genres and styles appear, and the degree of media rhetoric awareness increases in a 24/7 context. Certain forms of humor, more aggressive and violent—some of which had been relatively controlled by the institutional power of the media before—debut or make a comeback, including cyberbullying and violent political satire. Humor becomes a co-occurrence with important events as users create simultaneous spreading or viral and evolving risible commentary as reality unfolds. Along with his chapter in this volume, Fraticelli's analysis of the mediatization of the risible in Argentina shows that humor and media can combine in ways that can both critique and reproduce unequal structures of power.

An excellent example of this dynamic is Cristian Palacios's analysis of one of the most beloved Argentine comics, *Inodoro Pereyra,* by Roberto Fontanarrosa. Palacios proposes a fundamental distinction between what is comic and what is humorous while stating that both are part of the bigger field of the laughable and contribute in their specific ways to the process constituting a national imaginary. According to Palacios, who could have quoted Critchley on a similar distinction, comic discourse is that which rests on a form of basic commonality between the audience and producers on the shared basis of "what everybody knows" and "cannot not know." Comic discourse then reaffirms the identity of the "we" and its separation from others who do not belong to such a community. Laughing is here a form of belonging and identity confirmation based on shared meanings, and it results in the exclusion of others. Even when it breaks the rules, the comic discourse always ends up reaffirming them. Humoristic discourse, on the other hand, is always already a critical meditation on discourse itself, a separation from the known, and a questioning of its ontological certainties, including national and class identities. For Palacios, *Inodoro Pereyra*, at different moments of its history and in different ways, participates in both these discourses.

Social Media as Digital Culture

In this volume's title, we speak of the Internet in general, but all the examples in the book belong to one historically specific form and stage of Internet development—what theorists have called social media. According to Christian Fuchs, "web 1.0 is a computer-based networked system of human cognition; web 2.0, a computer-based networked system of human communication; web 3.0, a computer-based networked system of human cooperation" (Fuchs 44). As Fuchs makes clear, there is a degree of complexity of functions and interactivity at stake in the movement from cognition to communication to cooperation: one is presupposed by the next, but the latter adds the complexity of human interaction to the process. For Fuchs, the discontinuities—"the rising importance of cooperative sociality . . . the rise of social networking sites [like Facebook] . . . the emergence of blogs [thanks to technologies like WordPress while emulating HuffPost] . . . microblogs (Twitter) and file sharing websites (YouTube)" (Fuchs 46–47)—should not lead us to forget the continuities: in general, except for Wikipedia, all other platforms and the Internet are based on a model that changes to keep its basic capitalist inequity and exploitation structure intact—and perhaps even advance it. Thus, the humor circulated through the Internet, and more specifically, the humor in the Latin American sphere of Internet-based interactions, is simultaneously a form of social exchange and also part of an economic process seeking profits.

In *The Culture of Connectivity. A Critical History of Social Media*, Dutch new media theorist José van Dijck makes clear what is truly at stake in this transformation. In going "from providing a utility [for general access] to providing a customized service" (6), we move in Internet history from websites as "conduits for social activities" to platforms and apps that provide much more structured, easier-to-use but also much-harder-to-tinker-with social media services and spaces. The interpenetration between the social and technology deepens, and co-constitution is now the name of the game for what is also known as "technosociality" (Shah 49): "It is a common fallacy . . . to think of platforms as merely *facilitating* networking activities; instead, the construction of platforms and social practices is mutually constitutive" (6). To make her point, Van Dijck distinguishes between "(human connectedness) and (automated) connectivity" (12), warns us about conflating them, and would prefer to talk about "connective media" as opposed to the now-established "social media." This is important to her because this new culture of connectivity is a culture full of coding technologies whose impact goes well beyond the technical. It is defined by three traits: "it is a culture where the organization of social exchange is staked on neoliberal economic principles [:] . . . hierarchy, competition, and a winner-takes-all mindset" (21). At stake is a dispute about the definitions of "what counts as private or public, formal or informal, collaborative or exploitative, mainstream or alternative" (20). Van Dijck's project is succinctly expressed as "understanding the co-evolution of social media platforms and sociality in the context of a rising culture of connectivity" (33). With her help, we could ask: Is the very significant production and consumption of humor on Internet exchanges predominantly a form of human connectedness or automated connectivity? And how is this human connectedness or automated connectivity properly oiled by the contagious and expansive nature of humor, by its capacity to reproduce itself as it is circulated? More to the point, how is humor contributing to the reconfiguration of social exchange along neoliberal principles? In this process, connecting microsystems (platforms) and the ecosystem of interoperating platforms (25), the author insists that "all kinds of sociality are currently moving from public to corporate space" (37). The tools for such transition are predictive analytics (which mathematically studies data "to capture relations between variables from past occurrences and the likeliness that users will exhibit such behavior in the future" [162]) and real-time analytics ("to explore the potential or real-time sentiments and trends" [162]), hence producing the paradox of affective economics: "Content is spontaneous yet controlled, unmediated yet manipulated" (163), user-generated, yet platform-modulated. And the same can be said for the norms regulating this form of social interaction. What is humor's real contribution to this process—is it a form of social agency for many, a form of resistance or conformity, an already overdetermined practice made more dangerous politically precisely by its seemingly irreverent appearance? More importantly, how and what can we think about this process when we go beyond the dichotomy of resistance and cooptation?

As media scholars Nick Couldry and Andreas Hepp propose in *The Mediated Construction of Reality,* this contemporary co-constitution of the social and the media, what they call deep mediatization, involves a series of important epistemological and methodological changes for research on both. Thus, "It is not a matter of positioning the material against the symbolic, but of grasping both in their interrelatedness" (5). Technology here is not simply an infrastructural means for a social end that is independent of it. Instead, technology (platforms, apps, electronic devices, etc.) becomes "processes of sense-making" (5):

> It means understanding how the social is constructed in an age of *deep mediatization* when the very *elements and building blocks* from which a sense of the social is constructed become *themselves* based in technologically based processes of mediation. As a result, the ways in which we make sense of the world phenomenologically become necessarily entangled with the constraints, affordances and power-relations that are features of media as infrastructures for communication. (7)

With Couldry and Hepp's assistance, we could then ask: What are the traces these technologically based processes of mediation leave in the production, circulation, and consumption of humor through the web? Can we recognize a certain form of machine-generated effect in the kinds of humor we most commonly consume? At stake is an analytical framework or a theory of the social world that "does not any more take face-to-face interaction as its unquestioned centre" (33) and can think of practices of communication as both in direct connection with the social world as well as deeply enmeshed with and "moulded by the long-term processes of institutionalization and materialization we refer to as 'media'" (33).

One of the contentions of Couldry and Hepp's work is that humor may play an outsized role in the process that goes from making the web social (as in social media) to "making sociality technical." As Van Dijck states:

> Sociality coded by technology renders people's activities formal, manageable, and manipulable, enabling platforms to engineer the sociality in people's everyday routines. On the basis of detailed and intimate knowledge of people's desires and likes, platforms develop tools to create and steer specific needs. (Van Dijck 12)

This may be most obvious in the key role of emojis, GIFs, and memes (the last are here the focus of chapters by Viktor Chagas, Alejandra Collado, Damián Fraticelli, and R. Sánchez-Rivera) as part of the bait-and-click economy that engages users in long and unplanned sessions of clicking, from one item to the next, in search of the zany, the cute, or the interesting, as described in Ngai's *Theory of the Gimmick*.

Lastly, it is important to note that, just as technosocial intricacy may be instrumental in new constructions of exchange, with humor playing an integral role, it may also further contrarian epistemologies, sometimes engendering unforeseen outcomes, as documented in An Xiao Mina's *Memes to Movements*.

Culture, Politics, Technology

As a media practice, humor on the Internet presupposes interactions among producers and consumers in a certain geopolitical territory mediated by the cultural, political, and technical affordances of a given technological space, be it a platform, a channel, or a website. In Latin America, the work of Colombian-Spanish scholar Jesús Martín-Barbero concentrated on media and culture long before the Internet, but then, once it arrived, he focused especially on the interface among three factors.

Martín-Barbero served as a precursor to the critical analysis of the impact of new technologies on how the relationship between communities and the nation-state could be construed. In his classic *De los medios a las mediaciones. Comunicación, cultura y hegemonía*, Martín-Barbero divides the issues into three parts: first, the concepts of the people and the masses; second, the forms of mediation the media provided for the encounter between the people and hegemonic social and state projects; and third, the issue of modernity, social identities, and politics from the Latin American nineteenth to the twentieth centuries. Through the specificities of their genres and formats, through the grammar and technical possibilities of each medium and its genres, a mass-mediated culture mediated precisely the becoming mass of the people through the combined effects of media and certain forms of politics. This was a process of mutual constitution between the modern media and the modern masses, and it involved the production of a culture that functioned as the basis of hegemony, and thus, acquired significant political importance in Latin America. Culture—and this is one of Martín-Barbero's most important contributions—is both the place of political struggle and negotiation under modern hegemonic formations and a key site for an understanding of the social and its meanings. To develop such an approach, Martín-Barbero proposes a series of concepts such as cultural matrices (a specific historic-social articulation of culture and media in a given political context), a social imaginary (spaces of identity projection in which what is public and the public itself are constituted), and a sensorium (modes of imagining, seeing, narrating, feeling, sensing, and thinking culture in specific technological and social contexts). These three concepts shared Martín-Barbero's fundamental insight: in modernity, the media play a fundamental role in mediating the connection among the social, the cultural, and the political. This involves an imbrication of reason and imagination in communicative networks that have their grammar and technical possibilities and limitations, and mobilize sociabilities, sensibilities, and identities. From our contemporary perspective, we can see that Martín-Barbero was politicizing the sensible (à la Jacques Rancière) and trying to understand the aestheticization of the political (in Walter Benjamin's terms) through which culture, as mediated by new, "now" electronic technologies, has become immanent to power processes through human/nonhuman assemblages, of which the cases in this book are good examples. The aesthetic is thus expanded to include the sensible in general (reconnecting, in specific ways, the mind and the body, the social and the individual, and society and technologies), and culture becomes crucial for social and political analysis. From this perspective, those sensoria and social imaginaries are the results of the interaction between people (as producers and consumers) and political and social agendas as mediated by the cultural, political, and technical affordances of a given technology or set of technologies. In this way, the sensible, human attention, and social and cultural meanings are articulated through a technical mediation by concrete media (what Martín-Barbero calls a given technical expertise or *tecnicidad*) (*Oficio de cartógrafo* 231).

In *Imaginarios de nación: Pensar en medio de la tormenta*, the volume that Martín-Barbero edited as part of the Colombian Ministry of Culture's *Cuadernos de nación* series, Manuel Castells is quoted as claiming that "now it is that we will see what capitalism is, the worldly calling of capitalism that Marx glimpsed: capitalism becomes a world once it becomes culture, that is what the knowledge or information society points out" ("Colombia" 22). Using Castells, Martín-Barbero points to a deep understanding of the impact of technology on culture. To Martín-Barbero, it is clear that, unlike previous technologies, the computer is not a machine to make objects, but instead sustains a new kind of technical expertise or nature—as mentioned, *tecnicidad* is the term that he favors—that renders feasible the processing of information. When it comes to comparing the impact of the computer on global culture, Martín-Barbero also mentions Roger Chartier's suggestion about comparing the impact of the rise of the computer to the invention of the alphabet, rather than the invention of the printing press, given the extent to which the former holds significance for populations throughout the world ("Colombia" 22–23). Thus, to Martín-Barbero, the computer brings forth a new, distinctive kind of expertise that cultivates the processing of information, and whose main resources are abstractions and symbols, which introduces a new amalgamation of the brain and information, thus replacing the more conventional one of the body and the machine. At the same time, it introduces a new paradigm of thought that reconfigures the relationships between a discursive order (what we could summarize under a prevailing logic) and what is visible (therefore leading to a perception of the form), between intelligibility and sensibility (Castells, "La dimensión" 27; Martín-Barbero, "Globalización" 25). In this sense, it behooves us as academics interested in the effect of technology on the makings of Latin American humor to assimilate the full importance of the media's technical nature as a strategic dimension of culture and society. This is one of the main motivations of this volume.

Following Fernando Broncano, Martín-Barbero reiterates how computer networks manage to escape the binary logic with which we are accustomed to thinking about technology, given they simultaneously integrate and exclude concurrently, de-territorializing and relocating cultural dynamics and people ("Cultura" 27). In other words, at the same time as anything that is informationally valuable is connected, anything that is not informationally worthy to the prevalent logic (neoliberalism, as of late) is immediately devalued— in particular, traditional forms of knowledge that may not be computerizable ("Cultura" 15). Thus, following Castells, technology embodies a new paradigm in which all social processes—world politics, armed conflicts, the economy, etc.—stand to be affected by the capability to process and ubiquitously distribute information within the general context of human activity ("Cultura" 16).

While the Internet is now often conceptualized as constituting a new form of sociality—in which capitalism, technicity, and the traditional social co-evolve with higher and higher degrees of interpenetration as they percolate through the daily lives of billions in social media—it has also been historically thought of, for example, as a new cultural sphere that allowed for novels forms of circulation of cultural production in the traditional sense, that is, culture produced by professionals. In an interesting and early volume, *Latin American Identity in Online Cultural Production,* British academics Claire Taylor and Thea Pitman study the de- and re-territorializing critical and contestatory capacity of "blogging, hypertext fiction, net.art and multimedia art more broadly, and online performance art" (5) to challenge "a series of prominent Latin American(ist) discourses" (1) including Latin America as a geocultural territory, the Lettered City, Macondismo and magical realism, mestizaje, and the dichotomy civilization/barbarism.

The Internet has also been conceptualized as a new technology that recreates in a new guise both the culturally imperialist situation of unequal access in globally distributed digital divides and a new digital inequality of users' practices, skills, and training. An interesting book in this regard is *The Evolution of Popular Communication in Latin America*, edited by Brazilian communication scholar Ana Cristina Suzina. Rather than simply denouncing cultural imperialism, Suzina's volume provides an excellent and up-to-date history, including a chapter on digital media, of the long research and practice tradition of *comunicación popular* (translated here as popular communication) as a Global South–based liberation-seeking epistemology operating in the context of decolonial currents and alternative forms of life or *buen vivir*. Equally interesting is *Media Cultures in Latin America*, a volume edited by anthropologists Ana Cristina Pertierra and Juan Francisco Salazar, which also recuperates what one could call the alternative uses and cultures of communication in the region, as in border studies, citizen media, human rights activism, Zapatismo, and Indigenous communities, and includes a chapter on "Contemporary Social Movements and Digital Media Resistance in Latin America."[2]

Martín-Barbero, using ideas from Martin Hopenhayn, had early on emphasized how virtual cultures mediate between culture and technology, engendering systems of symbolic exchange that result in "new collective meanings and forms of representing reality" ("Cultura" 23–24). For Hopenhayn, virtual cultures—of the kind that we analyze and discuss in this volume—involve a shift in communication practices as the result of the adoption of media that allow interaction from a distance. In turn, these media modify the subjects' sensibility, their way of making sense of the world, their relationships with others, and the categories employed to understand their surroundings ("Cultura" 23). In short, electronic networks weave new ways of being together, of building a collective spirit, within which people not only connect, but also communicate, cooperate, and meet ("Globalización" 22). Many of the chapters in this collection describe and study the impact of a variety of technologies on how people engage and recognize categories like national identity, class, and regional affiliation. So, while on one hand technology is contributing to making a new sense of things, on the other it disrupts the order to which people were accustomed, forcing everyone to pivot and readjust. Now, as a result of the impact of technology, mediation passes from being merely instrumental to becoming structural, in other words thanks to the technical nature of interaction—once again, *tecnicidad*, in Martín-Barbero's words—it begins to embody a structural element in the formation of a novel communicative environment ("Globalización" 25).

While the Internet and the platforms that constitute its social media version may, through their affordances and institutional constraints, structure certain kinds of hegemonic and commercially exploitable audiences, they have also helped develop a different kind of audience segmentation into what is best conceived as counterpublics, such as those studied by Clemencia Rodríguez in *Citizens' Media against Armed Conflict: Disrupting Violence in Colombia* and Elisabeth Jay Friedman in *Interpreting the Internet: Feminist and Queer Counterpublics in Latin America*. Feminist and queer communities in the region have found a useful tool for the development of their counter-public relation to themselves as a group (strengthening of collective identity in safe spaces) and their relations to dominant publics in the public sphere. This line of research is also interesting in our context, and in our volume, when it comes to the proliferation of micro-public spheres such as ultra-right-wing communities and their specific use of crude and hateful humor. This constitutes an interesting counterpart to the subversive effects of humor as theorized by Bakhtin in his ideas about carnival and its celebration of the comic hero as a temporarily liberated underdog endowed with (some) sub-versive potential vis-à-vis dominant ideologies and values. It is also, finally, a good reminder of the need to think beyond the stark dichotomies of re-sistance and cooptation, popular or hegemonic, and socially or corporately generated. It may not be funny, but it may just be the way things happen to be.

A Brief Overview of This Volume

This book contains ten thematic chapters, each of which proposes an ap-proach to the connection between humor and the Latin American Internet, and in particular in Latin American social media. The nature of these ap-proaches is dictated by the object of their research. While in some cases there is a need for thorough quantitative work, in others, it is more a matter of find-ing the right match in terms of theory and object of study. Nonetheless, each case highlights how content on the Internet is playing a key role in the region's relation to democracy—or lack thereof—and civil society.

In his chapter on digital humor as an element of cultural globalization in Latin America, Paul Alonso focuses on two of the best-known online news shows in the hemisphere: Chumel Torres's *El Pulso de la República* (*EPR*) and Malena Pichot's *Cualca*. Both shows are discussed as examples of how cultural globalization and hybridity operate in today's transnational enter-tainment and commercial critical humor. Torres and Pichot rank among the most popular personalities on the Latin American Internet, and their work is not exempt from controversy. Alonso describes their products in detail and explains how they have managed to negotiate a position within national circumstances, managing to stay afloat in the precarious balance involved in communicating with millions via the Internet. In Torres's case, aside from his successful rise as a star on the Internet thanks to his work on *EPR*, there is the cancelation of his show on HBO as the result of criticism on social media; the overbearing presence of Televisa; and Torres's own pivoting to preserve the interest of his followers amid charges of selling out. For Pichot, the situation is even more complicated and dire, given her outspoken demeanor in a country where the debate on gender politics has reached a fever pitch as the result of opposing views. A self-described feminist who does not shy away from debate, Pichot has engaged many Argentine personalities with her criticism, usually on gender-related matters. Her responses, which Alonso discusses as examples of Pichot's outspoken militancy, are representative of the heated nature of discussion in Argentina. Her popularity on social media denotes the generational gap between a population that struggles to dispel the economic and political legacies of the twentieth century and youth who have grown up with access to the Internet, espousing new cultural and political sensibilities.

In his chapter on hypermediatic humor, Damián Fraticelli uses the case of a fake satirical social network account to illustrate the advantages of his research models, used to expose the complexities of this type of humor. Fraticelli's approach denotes the difference between Latin American and US approaches when it comes to communication analysis, as his work is strongly influenced by semiotics and semiology and embodies an academic tradition more influenced by European theories of cognition and communication. Central to the understanding of his chapter is hypermediatic humor, which Fraticelli defines as the device supported by social networks that continuously generates interpretants rendering any social phenomenon laughable. While the concept of interpretant pertains to Peirce's triadic theory of signs, the rest of this chapter's framework reflects a more Latin American approach. Though Fraticelli initially distinguishes between the comical and the humorous, he soon moves on to propose a model for the analysis of the process of enunciation. In addition, Fraticelli shares two models based on the analysis of a social media account and the circulation of its discursivity. The case of Dra. Alcira Pignata, a fictional character who generated widespread controversy in the highly politicized atmosphere of Argentina in the 2010s and whose utterances described her as a supporter of the center-right Macri administration, illustrates the complexities of humor on the Internet, as the accidental discovery of the account's true owner eventually linked its jokes to a political agenda.

In his examination of Guillermo Aquino's *El Sketch*, Alberto Centeno-Pulido discusses the expression of rage in Argentine society according to the theories of Korean-born Swiss-German cultural theorist Byung-Chul Han. Rage, Centeno-Pulido argues, results from the enormous challenges faced by the Argentine population when the economy collapsed as the result of continuous mismanagement and political instability. The current pandemic has only exacerbated some of these issues, increasing the national poverty rate while aggravating Argentina's fiscal deficit. The centerpiece of Centeno-Pulido's work is his analysis of two videos by comedian Guillermo Aquino, who has become increasingly popular on the Internet since the mid-2010s thanks to his vlogging and talent as a scriptwriter. Amid all the commotion, Aquino serves as a sarcastic judge of national idiosyncrasy, bringing the country face to face with its taboos, shortcomings, and prejudices. In this chapter, the videos exemplify how Aquino examines national reality. The first one mocks how the media manage to take all kinds of news and give them a more conformist, even positive spin. The second one is a now-classic video from late 2018, in which Aquino offers a rushed review of the events of the year thanks to a phone call from himself in the future. Centeno-Pulido uses the video to point out how, under Han's theories, Aquino shatters the illusion of freedom internalized by Argentines, seeking to shock his viewers to their senses.

Hopping to Mexico, Alejandra Collado proposes an interesting exercise involving political cartoons and memes, seeking to render explicit the connections between them and suggest that the latter are, to a certain extent, progressively performing the role that the former habitually enacted during earlier periods of national history. To fulfill this task, Collado draws on Mikhail Bakhtin's theory of carnival and Marshall McLuhan's tetradic model. Initially, she applies the tetradic model to political cartoons, so the elements of a transition to a political critique by way of memes become more explicit. Once the shift is described, she moves on to the analysis of the memes, clarifying how they are representative of the aesthetics and sensibilities of new generations. In Collado's case, things have more to do with how well these theories fit in with the examples she has decided to study, showing that, on not a few occasions, it is more a matter of suitably matching theory with praxis than of establishing a regular methodology that may be applied effectively across the board. Collado's orderly examination of how political cartoons are gradually being replaced by memes in the digital age has extensive implications for the practice of democracy and political resistance in Mexico and speaks volumes about how *mexicanidad* is being imagined in the current century.

In "Cutting through Layers of Brazilian Humor," Eva Paulino Bueno and Fábio Marquez de Souza reflect upon the subject using several texts. Their work centers on memes and videos circulating on the web, reflecting the vibrancy of the Lusophone portion of the Latin American Internet. In their chapter, Paulino Bueno and Marquez de Souza clarify just how important cultural competence, media literacy, and the corresponding management of cultural codes happen to be, explaining the context that is necessary to make sense of the memes and videos they discuss. In the first half of their work, to contextualize the memes, they dig into the history of Brazilian comics and touch on the work of renowned cartoonist Henrique de Souza Filho, better known as Henfil. Paulino Bueno and Marquez de Souza also discuss the case of Concessa, a character created by humorist Aparecida Silva Mendez, who, from her rendition of a humble domestic space and in a flawless Caipira (peasant) accent, renders advice on multiple topics, always with a humorous touch. Along the same lines, Cida mockingly alludes to the situation in Brazil by way of dialogue with US culture and politics, hinting at the intimate relationship between the two nations with the highest degree of ethnic and racial diversity in the Americas.

Ulisses Sawczuk da Silva and Mélodine Sommier's piece also contains a pertinent meditation on how contemporary Brazilian culture embraces US cultural products, Brazilianizes them, and subsequently employs them to the benefit of national culture. As they correctly point out, this high level of Americanization is preponderant among the country's privileged sectors. The main character of their chapter is Barbie, the doll made by Mattel, which in Brazilian lands has evolved drastically into Barbie Fascionista—a play on the terms "fascist" and "fashionista." In the eyes of Sawczuk da Silva and Sommier, Fascist Barbie offers insights into the use of memes as a form of political commentary. The pair chooses a period in late 2018 to examine a wide sample of memetic texts through an approach combining semiotic and critical discourse analysis. By analyzing Brazilian cultural appropriation of the doll via memetic texts, Sawzcuk da Silva and Sommier comment on the privileged, prejudiced, and conservative nature of segments of the Brazilian population linked to Brazilian President Jair Bolsonaro. Whereas the doll has been criticized habitually in the US for her commodification of gender, it is riveting to see the sophistication with which her image is used by other nationalities to express views of critical importance within the political arena, and what its corresponding critical dissection says about the current state of Brazilian politics.

The third piece on Brazil, Viktor Chagas's "Humor and Nationalism in Bolsonarist Far-Right WhatsApp Memes in Brazil," confirms the degree of intricacy in current memetic analysis in the South American giant. Initially embracing a sample of 40 groups of Bolsonarist supporters out of 150, Chagas ended with an analysis of 200 memes within which it was possible to determine the various ways in which Jair Bolsonaro was represented on WhatsApp, the function of the respective memes, their connection with nationalist iconography and antidemocratic values, and the degree of correspondence between their functions and Bolsonaro's representations. In this way, Chagas can prove the strong ideological nature of right-wing groups on the Brazilian Internet as a concerted effort toward the recruitment of supporters, to encourage the collective performance of grassroots actions in the digital environment, and to foster a regular process of socialization with politics and debates that, at some other point in time, could have been identified as part of a fringe element (thus normalizing and popularizing discourses initially peripheral in nature). The data tabulated by Chagas demonstrates how quantitative analysis is having an impact on the study of cultural practices on the Internet. His research boils down to digitally oriented studies on media and culture that may serve as a safeguard against the lack of responsibility of Internet platforms when it comes to activist users and as a barrier against the systematic encroachment of political agendas representative of extremist minorities.

In a piece on memes, racialization, and discrimination in Puerto Rico, R. Sánchez-Rivera explains how Internet imagery is being used to contest official narratives by portraying the mismanagement of disasters on the island. While acknowledging the role of colonialism, Sánchez-Rivera goes beyond, seeking to make clear the internal cultural and societal dynamics of Puerto Rico that often pathologize bodies historically construed as Other. Along the way, what becomes apparent is that, while there is a critique of power in these images, forms of racialization, discrimination, and exclusion are also being reinforced and supported, much to the chagrin of marginalized communities and ostracized individuals. It is plain that Sánchez-Rivera views crisis as an opportunity for the critique and reevaluation of society, maybe leading to new ways of imagining nationality. However, this process is sometimes perverted by how critiques rely on old prejudices and continued exclusion. To this extent, memes having to do with recent crises and Puerto Rican society's responses, while playing a significant role in the construction of the public's perception, also serve as accomplices to inequity and intolerance. Overall, what Sánchez-Rivera makes clear is the dark side of humor. While it consolidates belonging, it may do so at the expense of some.

In "HolaSoyGermán: On Global Latin American Humor on YouTube," Juan Poblete visits the case of Germán Garmendia, a hugely successful vlogger. Garmendia's astonishing numbers are substantiated by clever strategies, like a video in which he challenges viewers to restart the clip every single time they laugh. With his phenomenal statistics, the YouTuber typifies the enormous impact that a single individual may now have, as opposed to the conventional media production systems prevailing in the past. Though Garmendia is behind several highly ranked vlogs, Poblete focuses on HolaSoyGermán (HSG) because it illustrates clearly how Garmendia's material combines two key aspects of video production for the Internet: the fact that Internet content usually thrives when its main characters have a certain mainstream, "ordinary guy" quality, while at the same time the piece itself exhibits high production standards. Poblete is adept at showing how Garmendia guarantees a high degree of everydayness in his videos. In addition, Poblete points out how HSG works at various levels: economically, it is located at the point of contact between the conventional model of content production and more contemporary user-generated-content; socio-culturally, it marks the penetration of the logic of cultural production of the self; and politically, it announces the internalization of forms of self-exploitation, profitability, and interest, while blurring the boundaries between leisure and work, what is private and what is political, etc. Basing his argument on the notion that national comedies have the greatest possibility of succeeding against Hollywood's distribution hegemony, Poblete suggests that HSG's success is the result of a similarity in its conditions of production. The ensuing analysis of many of HSG's videos contributes amply to the confirmation of Poblete's assertions.

Finally, in Héctor Fernández L'Hoeste's "*La Pulla:* Humor as an Instrument of Intranational Hegemony," it is possible to see how the team behind an award-winning vlog on Colombian politics embraces the construct of a "country of regions" to gain approval from provincial audiences throughout the country. While the group of research journalists involved in the vlog renders a hypothetical service to the country, denouncing rampant corruption with tangible information and very effective visuals, it also reinforces the capital city's elite's status as a guardian of national identity, seeking consent from the provinces for the cultural and political authority of the central establishment by way of humor. In particular, class prejudice emerges as an especially damning trait of Colombian identity. Fernández L'Hoeste's main analysis centers on the work associated with *La Pulla Regional,* a series of videos dedicated to documenting the clientelist practices of many a provincial political dynasty. The problem, as stated and documented in this final chapter, is how key agents of national identity are managing to adapt to the more effective circulation of information and interpellation of audiences propounded by the Internet and promoting the perpetuation of an advantageous mindset, effectively inhibiting societal change.

Ultimately, we hope you find these chapters to be useful contributions to the exploration of the connection between the Internet and humor in social media. When we first started searching for and compiling a collection of essays that documented how humor on the Internet is contributing to a novel construction of Latin American identities, in a manner that would perhaps offer a more critical view of the ways in which social media influence today's political dialogues, we suspected it would be fertile ground for academic analysis. Yet, what we found defied our expectations and gave us new hope. It shows and proves that, whether research comes from the humanities or the social sciences, the Internet is providing new investigative opportunities for academics across the hemisphere to challenge the dictates of neoliberalism and chip away slowly at superficial understanding of messages on social media platforms. We hope this volume will stimulate interest in the topic and serve as inspiration to the many scholars studying Internet media outlets like Facebook, Twitter, Instagram, and TikTok, to name just a few, which have continued to fill their own pockets while paying scant attention to their duties as cultural actors, unrehearsed members of civil society, and responsible citizens.

Notes

1 Internet abbreviations represent the shows' nationality.
2 In the broader Latin American context of communication studies, a couple of state-of-the-art studies on digital cultures have pointed out some general tendencies. Edgar Gómez Cruz and Ignacio Siles speak of three factors characterizing and determining such a state of affairs in the region: "modest degrees of theorization," which cut both ways—limited theorizing capable of creating a common frame of reference for studies, and a tendency to speculate rather than develop empirical research; "limited methodologies," by which they mean an overreliance on traditional social sciences and communication studies methods, rather than an exploration of new methods such as "social network analysis, digital ethnography, and big data tools" (325); and "the lack of strong ties and research networks" within the region (323).

   Siles is particularly instrumental in analyzing the history of the Internet in Central America from the 1980s to 2000, embracing a transnational approach to posit the Internet's development in the region as an exemplary case of the global south (Siles). In addition, as part of a metahistory of studies of communication technologies in Latin America from 2005 to 2015, and together with Johan Espinoza and Andres Méndez Marenco, Siles identifies 712 articles written in Spanish and published during that decade in ten journals of high impact in the region: *Anagramas, Palabra Clave, Signo y Pensamiento* (Colombia), *Chasqui* (Ecuador), *Comunicación y Medios* (Chile), *Comunicación y Sociedad, Razón y Palabra* (Mexico), *Enl@ce* (Venezuela), *Question/Cuestión* (Argentina), and *Reflexiones* (Costa Rica).

In one of the pioneering efforts to map the new terrain of digital communication, in 1996 Mexican researcher Raúl Trejo Delarbre called the Internet Aladdin's new magic carpet, because it promises discovery and possibilities, but emphasized the lack of digital infrastructure development and planning and the absence of comprehensive governmental policies for regulating and optimizing its growth as structural deterrents (248–249). In a 2013 article summarizing the achievements and challenges of Latin American Internet studies, Trejo highlighted both the deepening of a regional understanding of the nature of the Internet—which could not be reduced skeptically to sheer entertainment or another form of communicational imperialism—and the concomitant and significant growth in the quantity and quality of academic studies on the subject. If in 1995 only two theses studying the Internet were submitted at the National Autonomous University (UNAM) in Mexico, between 2005–2009 there were 495 (Trejo Delarbre, "The Study" 4).

Works Cited

Alonso, Paul. *Satiric TV in the Americas: Critical Metatainment as Negotiated Dissent.* New York: Oxford UP, 2020.

Baumgartner, Jody, and Jonathan Morris. *Laughing Matters: Humor and American Politics in the Media Age.* New York: Routledge, 2008.

Benavides Delgado, Jacqueline, editor. *Humor y política: una perspectiva transcultural.* Bogotá: Universidad Cooperativa de Colombia, 2018.

Borum Chattoo, Caty, and Amy Henderson Riley. "Comedy as Creative Dissent in Latin America." *Center for Media and Social Impact,* a report of the CMSI's Laughter Effect in collaboration with Univision and the Open Society Foundations, n.d., cmsimpact.org/wp-content/uploads/2016/08/ComedyCreativeDissent.pdf.

Broncano, Fernando. *Filosofía del cambio tecnológico.* México: Paidós-UNAM, 2000.

Carter, Eli Lee. *The New Brazilian Mediascape: Television Production in the Digital Streaming Age.* Gainesville, FL: University of Florida Press, 2020.

Castells, Manuel. *El poder de la identidad.* Madrid: Alianza, 1998, trabajosocialucen.files.wordpress.com/2012/05/castells-manuel-la-era-de-la-informacic3b3n-el-poder-de-la-identidad-v-ii.pdf.

———. "La dimensión cultural de Internet." *Debates culturales, sesión 1: cultura y sociedad del conocimiento: presente y perspectivas de future,* Universitat Oberta de Catalunya, 2002, www.uoc.edu/culturaxxi/esp/articles/castells0502/castells0502.html.

———. *La sociedad red.* 2nd ed., translated by Carmen Martínez Gimeno y Jesús Alborés, Madrid: Alianza, 2000, revolucioncantonaldotnet.files.wordpress.com/2018/02/volumen-1-la-sociedad-red.pdf.

Castoriadis, Cornelius. "Reflexiones sobre el desarrollo y la racionalidad." *El mito del desarrollo,* edited by J. Attali and Candido Mendes, Barcelona: Kairos, 1979, pp. 183–223.

Cerda Catalán, Alfonso, and Eugenio Petit Muñoz. *Contribución a la historia de la sátira política en el Uruguay, 1897–1904.* Montevideo: Universidad de la República Oriental del Uruguay, 1965.

Chartier, Roger. *Lecteurs et lectures à l'âge de la textualité électronique.* Paris: Centre Pompidou, 2001.

Couldry, Nick, and Andreas Hepp. *The Mediated Construction of Reality.* Cambridge, UK; Malden, MA: Polity Press, 2017.

Critchley, Simon. *On Humour.* London: Routledge, 2002.

Eagleton, Terry. *Humour.* New Haven and London: Yale UP, 2019.

El Chapulín Colorado. Created by Roberto Gómez Bolaños, Televisa, 1973–1979.

El Chavo del Ocho. Created by Roberto Gómez Bolaños, Televisa, 1973–1975.

El Show de los Polivoces. Created by Mauricio Kleiff, Televisa, 1973–1976.

Fuchs, Christian. *Social Media: A Critical Introduction.* London: Sage, 2014.

Fraticelli, Damián. "La nueva era de la mediatización reidera." *Arruinando chistes. Panorama de los estudios del humor y lo cómico,* edited by Mara Burkart, Damián Fraticelli, and Tomás Várnagy, Buenos Aires: Teseo, 2021, pp.151–170.

Friedman, Elisabeth Jay. *Interpreting the Internet: Feminist and Queer Counterpublics in Latin America.* Oakland, CA: University of California Press, 2017.

Gama Guandalini, Izabela. *O que há por trás do riso: um panorama da relação entre humor, liberdade de expressão e outros direitos fundamentais no Brasil.* Belo Horizonte: Editora Letramento, 2019.

García Moreno, Beatriz, editor. *La imagen de la ciudad en las artes y los medios.* Bogotá: Universidad Nacional de Colombia, 2000.

Garretón, Manuel Antonio et al. *El espacio cultural latinoamericano. Bases para una política de integración.* Santiago: Fondo de Cultura Económica, 2003.

Goggin, Gerard, and Mark McLelland, editors. *The Routledge Companion to Global Internet Histories.* New York: Routledge, 2017.

Goldstein, Donna M. *Laughter Out of Place: Race, Class, Violence, and Sexuality in a Rio Shantytown.* Berkeley: University of California Press, 2003 and 2013.

Gómez Cruz, Edgar, and Ignacio Siles. "Digital Cultures." *The Routledge Handbook to the Culture and Media of the Americas,* edited by Wilfried Rausser, Giselle Liza Anatol, Sebastian Thies, Sarah Corona Berkin, and José Carlos Lozano, London: Routledge, 2020, pp. 319–329.

Hidalgo, Narciso. *Choteo: irreverencia y humor en la cultura cubana.* Bogotá: Siglo del Hombre Editores, 2012.

LABS. "Latin America Surpasses the US and Europe and Is Already the Second Fastest-Growing Streaming Market in the World." *Latin American Business Stories,* 7 Dec. 2021, labsnews.com/en/articles/business/latin-america-surpasses-the-u-s-and-europe-and-is-already-the-second-fastest-growing-streaming-market-in-the-world/.

Los Polivoces. Created by Mauricio Kleiff, Televisa. 1971–1973.

Loya García, Luis. *Latino Humor in Comparative Perspective.* New York: Oxford UP, 2013.

Mahapatra, Amogh, Nisheeth Srivastava, and Jaindeep Srivastava. "Characterizing the Internet's Sense of Humor." 2012 International Conference on Privacy, Security, Risk and Trust (PASSAT), and 2012 International Conference on Social Computing (SocialCom), Sept. 2012, https://doi.org/10.1109/SocialCom-PASSAT.2012.105.

Mañach, Jorge. *Indagación de choteo.* Miami: Mnemosyne Publishing, 1969.

Martin, Rod A., and Thomas E. Ford. *The Psychology of Humor: An Integrative Approach.* London: Academic Press, 2018.

Martín-Barbero, Jesús. "Colombia: ausencia de relato y desubicaciones de lo nacional." *Imaginarios de nación: Pensar en medio de la tormenta,* edited by Jesús Martín-Barbero, Bogotá: Mincultura, 2002, pp. 17–29.

———. "Cultura y nuevas mediaciones tecnológicas." *América Latina: otras visiones desde la cultura,* edited by Jesús Martín-Barbero et al., Bogotá: Convenio Andrés Bello, 2005, pp. 13–38.

———. *De los medios a las mediaciones.* México: Gustavo Gili, 1987.

———. "Globalización y multiculturalidad: notas para una agenda de investigación." *Nuevas perspectivas desde/sobre América Latina,* edited by Mabel Moraña, Santiago: Editorial Cuarto Propio / Instituto Internacional de Literatura Iberoamericana, 2000, pp. 17–29.

———. *Oficio de cartógrafo: travesías latinoamericanas de la comunicación en la cultura.* México City: FCE, 2014.

Medina Cartagena, María Alejandra. *Humor político audiovisual en Colombia: de los gloriosos años noventa en television a Internet como alternativa.* Bogotá: Universidad del Rosario, 2017.

Mina, An Xiao. *Memes to Movements: How the World's Most Viral Media Is Changing Social Protest and Power.* Boston: Beacon Press, 2019.

Monsiváis, Carlos. *Mexican Postcards.* London, New York: Verso, 1997.

———. "Notas sobre cultura popular en Mexico." *Latin American Perspectives,* vol. 5, no. 1, 1978, pp. 98–118, www.jstor.org/stable/2633341.

Morreall, John. *Comic Relief. A Comprehensive Philosophy of Humor.* Malden, MA: Wiley-Blackwell, 2009.

———, editor. *The Philosophy of Laughter and Humor.* Albany: State University of New York, 1986.

Niall Ferguson's Networld. Directed by Adrian Pennink, written and presented by Niall Ferguson, Chimerica Media/Thirteen Productions/PBS, 2020.

Ngai, Sianne. *Our Aesthetic Categories: Zany, Cute, Interesting.* Cambridge, MA: The Belknap Press of Harvard UP, 2012.

———. *Theory of the Gimmick: Aesthetic Judgment and Capitalist Form.* Cambridge, MA: The Belknap Press of Harvard UP, 2020.

Ortiz, Renato. *Mundialização: saberes e crenças.* São Paulo: Brasiliense, 2006.

Palacios, Cristian. "El papel de lo irrisorio en la constitución de las identidades nacionales latinoamericanas." *El rumor del humor: Jornadas de investigación: innovación, rupturas y transformaciones en la cultura humorística argentina,* edited by Ana Beatriz Flores, Córdoba: Universidad Nacional de Córdoba, 2017, pp. 14–37.

Pérez Firmat, Gustavo. "Riddles of the Sphincter: Another Look at Cuban Choteo." *Diacritics,* vol. 14, no. 4 (1984), pp. 67–77.

Pertierra, Ana Cristina, and Juan Francisco Salazar, editors. *Media Cultures in Latin America.* New York: Routledge, 2020.

Pini, Ivonne. *Buscar lo propio: inicios de la modernidad en el arte de Cuba, México, Uruguay y Colombia 1920–1930.* Bogotá: Universidad nacional de Colombia, 2000.

Poblete, Juan. "Introduction: Cinema and Humor in Latin America." *Latin American Film and Humor,* edited by Juan Poblete and Juana Suárez, New York: Palgrave, 2015, pp. 1–28.

Porter, Lance, and Guy J. Golan. "From Subservient Chickens to Brawny Men: A Comparison of Viral Advertising to Television Advertising." *Journal of Interactive Advertising*, vol. 6, no. 2, Spring 2006, pp. 4–33, https://doi.org/10.1080/15252019.2006.10722116.

¿Qué nos pasa? Created by Héctor Suárez, Televisa, 1986–1987, 1998–2000.

Rodríguez, Clemencia. *Citizens' Media against Armed Conflict: Disrupting Violence in Colombia*. Minneapolis: The University of Minnesota Press, 2011.

Siles, Ignacio. *A Transnational History of the Internet in Central America, 1985–2000: Networks, Integration, and Development*. Cham, Switzerland: Springer International Publishing, 2020.

Shah, Nishant. "The State of the Internets: Notes for a New Historiography of Technosociality." *The Routledge Companion to Global Internet Histories*, edited by Gerard Goggin and Mark McLelland. New York: Routledge, 2017, pp. 49–60.

Shifman, Limor. *Memes in Digital Culture*. Cambridge, MA: The MIT Press, 2014.

Shifman, Limor, and Mike Thelwal. "Assessing Global Diffusion with Web Memetics: The Spread and Evolution of a Popular Joke." *Journal of the American Society for Information Science and Technology*, vo. 60, no. 12, 2009, pp. 2567–2576.

Sinclair, John. "Geolinguistic Region as Global Space: The Case of Latin America." *The Television Studies Reader*, edited by Robert C. Allen and Annette Hill, London: Routledge, 2004, 130–138.

Suzina, Ana Cristina, editor. *The Evolution of Popular Communication in Latin America*. New York: Palgrave, 2021.

Taylor, Claire, and Thea Pitman. *Latin American Identity in Online Cultural Production*. New York: Routledge, 2012.

Thorne, David. *The Internet Is a Playground*. New York: Penguin, 2011.

Trejo Delarbre, Raúl. *La nueva alfombra mágica. Usos y mitos de Internet, la red de redes*. Madrid: Fundesco, 1996.

———. "The Study of the Internet in Latin America." *The International Encyclopedia of Media Studies. Volume IV: Media Studies Futures*, edited by Kelly Gates, Blackwell, 2013, pp. 1–29.

Van Dijck, José. *The Culture of Connectivity. A Critical History of Social Media*. Oxford: Oxford UP, 2013.

Wilson, Christopher. *Jokes: Form, Content, Use and Function*. London: Academic Press, 1979.

Yo soy Betty, la fea. Created by Fernando Gaitán, RCN Television, 1999–2001.

2

Digital Humor as Cultural Globalization in Latin America

Paul Alonso

Independent online satire shows have flourished globally, filling a gap for sociopolitical critique left by television and traditional media. In Latin America, a new wave of digital humor has become an increasingly relevant site for discursively negotiating local and regional identities and questioning hegemonic values (Alonso). Active on YouTube, Instagram, Facebook, and Twitter, young satirists accumulate significant online audiences and engage in cultural and sociopolitical debates with public figures. They not only reveal successful models for the development of Latin American independent digital media but also perform a postmodern reappropriation of transnational media languages and entertainment formats.

This chapter analyzes the cases of *El Pulso de la República* (the pulse of the republic), an independent Mexican online satiric news show à la *The Daily Show* created in 2012 by comedian Chumel Torres, who, after four years of producing his show independently on YouTube, transitioned to hosting a late-night show on HBO with a regional reach; and the case of *Cualca* (Whatever), an Argentinean satiric sketch show focused on gender issues, created by Malena Pichot, a feminist YouTube star who became famous for *La loca de mierda* (the crappy nutcase), a series of her homemade online videos about a breakup with her boyfriend that made it to MTV. These early cases are paradigmatic examples of a trend of independent Latin American digital humor born on the web that becomes popular first as alternative entertainment, and then negotiates its place in the mainstream media, aspiring to regional or international recognition. While the popularity of these types of digital initiatives varies according to the target (or niche) audience, levels of irreverence, format, quality of production, or ideological stance, new sociopolitical digital humor and online satiric shows exemplify how cultural globalization and hybridity operate in today's transnational entertainment and commercial critical humor.

Satire and Hybridity in Contemporary Globalized Media

Satire—a particular type of humor that ridicules human vices and follies through parody, irony, travesty, and grotesquery—takes an active role in the contemporary critique of "dangerous religious, political, moral, or social standards" (Cuddon 202). Television and online satiric shows have become an important part of the contemporary sociopolitical discourse in a mediascape defined by hybridization, the thorough melding of different media formats and contents. Baym called this process "discursive integration" (259), in which languages and practices of news, politics, entertainment, and marketing have grown deeply inseparable. These once-differentiated discourses have lost their distinctiveness and are being merged into previously unimagined combinations. The consequent hybrid programming also results from globalization and has a potentially wide range of implications for public information, political communication, and democratic discourse.

Scholars including Roland Robertson have argued that globalization produces the emergence of a variety of "hybrid," "creolized," or "glocal" phenomena, in which local elements are incorporated within globalized forms and other combinations. While hybridity and *mestizaje* are intrinsic characteristics of post-colonial societies, scholars such as Néstor García Canclini and Marwan Kraidy have discussed how the production and consumption of cultural products represent a struggle for meaning between classes within countries, between high and popular cultures, and among local, national, and imported cultural traditions. For Martín-Barbero, this struggle reveals the syncretic nature of popular culture that both adopts and resists the dominant culture while also transforming it. In this sense, hybridization describes a process in which elements of different cultures are synthesized together into new forms that reflect elements of the original cultures, but constitute distinct new ones, as García Canclini explores. In this scenario, global formats must tap into local culture to find audiences in new locations (see Moran; Straubhaar, *World Television*). According to the notion of "cultural proximity," audiences tend "to prefer and select local or national cultural content that is more proximate and relevant to them" (Straubhaar, "Beyond Media Imperialism" 43). The consequential process of hybridization then becomes a negotiation between structure and culture, and its success partially depends on its ability to allow space for local specificities (see Kraidy; Pieterse; Straubhaar, *World*

Television). While, as Straubhaar discusses, audience preference still largely depends on the cultural proximity of the local and the national ("Beyond Media Imperialism"), regional programming also holds significance, highlighting the relevance of Latin America as a geolinguistic market (see Sinclair). The online satire shows analyzed in this chapter are prevalent examples of hybrid products shaped by globalization and the phenomenon of discursive integration in media content. As such, they reflect the permanent tensions within local and global cultures, and their willingness to transgress positions in a particularly revealing space of glocal discursive struggles. This can be seen in their adaptation of global formats (the late-night and political satire formats for *El Pulso de la República* and the sitcom and stand-up tradition for *Cualca*) to criticize the role of local media and target specific sociopolitical tensions in their countries. Interestingly, these cases also negotiate the internationalization of their contents after successfully adapting and reinventing their global referents.

El Pulso de la República: Online Political News Satire in Mexico

In 2012, Chumel Torres, a mechanical engineer in his early thirties from the Chihuahua in northern Mexico, moved to Mexico City and created *El Pulso de la República* (*EPR*), a humorous weekly online political news show on YouTube that soon became very popular. Torres has frequently referred to *EPR* as his take on the satirical work of his American heroes—Jon Stewart and Stephen Colbert—and has declared that he wants to be "'the Mexican Seth Macfarlane'" (qtd. in Ramos). *EPR* closely follows the format of *The Daily Show, The Colbert Report,* and SNL's *Weekend Update*—a comedian host dressed in a dark, serious suit delivers sarcastic monologues about political news accompanied by images and videos that ironically illustrate his critical points, using Mexican slang and references to local popular culture. By 2020, *EPR*'s YouTube channel had more than 2.6 million subscribers; as well, millions followed Torres on other social media networks. Due to his success, Torres was hired in 2016 by HBO to write and host a show for Latin American audiences.

Before becoming a media celebrity, Torres worked for seven years in a "maquila," a border factory that assembles goods for sale in the US, and made a name as a "tuitstar" (a star on Twitter) due to his tongue-in-cheek tweets leading up to the 2012 presidential elections, and especially a controversial one about candidate López Obrador's declarations. Because he was an influencer on social media, Torres was offered a weekly column on a political blog, and then was hired as editor of a digital newspaper in Mexico City, where the idea of creating a satirical news show took shape:

I wrote columns that basically were scripts of *EPR* but without a camera. It occurred to me that we could convert them into videos. I began recording myself with the iPhone. I did different takes, because I didn't know if it'd be better to do a left-wing or right-wing character, or muppets, or a woman. I decided that later. Then I met Durden (co-writer of *EPR*), we talked, and we began to write.[1] (qtd. in Mulato)

Torres had already written several pilots in Chihuahua before he met José Alberto Sánchez Montiel—his co-writer, known as Durden, a social media specialist and a Mexican "tuitstar" himself—and they together wrote a "super-pilot" for CNN. However, the news company took too long to edit it, and Torres decided to do it by himself and release it on YouTube. He described the early stage of the project before it became a success:

We did it with a webcam and edited in iMovie, very low quality. But the script was good, and we already had our followers on Twitter, so we did not begin from zero. Then Yayo [a famous YouTuber who had more than 1,700,000 subscribers] published our shows on his channel. We had 18,000 views, but after he published our show on his channel, we reached 250,000. Then we took off.[2] (qtd. in Mulato)

In the coming years, *EPR* consolidated its style by uploading its videos consistently once or twice a week. While Torres has not disclosed revenue numbers, he said he makes money from advertising and sponsorship on his social media accounts. The production of the show has remained low-budget. Developed by a small crew, *EPR*'s production routines have been described by Torres as like *Wayne's World:* "'We are three dudes in a small room doing a good show'" (qtd. in Mulato).[3] Nevertheless, the main work was done by Torres and his co-writer Durden, and focused on developing a solid script that balanced entertainment and sociopolitical critique:

In the beginning, we argued a lot because, for example, I am more pop in my criteria for choosing stories, and Durden is more serious. I could choose the story of Justin Bieber taking his dick out at the beach, and he would choose a story about the community self-defense groups in Michoacán. But in three years we learned to balance comedy and journalism.[4] (qtd. in Mulato)

This negotiation of approaches and topics was developed in a national context shaped by corruption, violence, and concentration of media ownership. For more than seven decades (1929–2000), the Institutional Revolutionary

Party (PRI, Partido Revolucionario Institucional) ran an authoritarian regime in Mexico disguised as a democracy. Called "a perfect dictatorship," the system was sustained with the help of political repression, institutionalized corruption, electoral fraud, control of workers' unions, and a corrupt press. Journalists including Rosental Alves have written of how, during the PRI's regime, it was common for reporters to receive payola (known as "embutes," "chayos," or "chayotes") from officials or politicians to cover their versions of the news, while media owners received payments disguised as political ads, subsidies, and other fiscal benefits.

During this period, media concentration in Mexico was also incentivized through a tacit alliance between the PRI and Televisa, the largest media conglomerate in the country and one of the chief participants in the entertainment industry worldwide (see Calleja; Villamil; Trejo; Sosa and Gómez; Fernández). Thanks to this relationship, Televisa operated as a de facto monopoly for decades. Its owner and founder, Emilio "el Tigre" Azcárraga Milmo, considered himself "a soldier of the PRI." After the end of the Cold War, the implementation of neoliberal economic policies, and the wave of democratization in Latin America during the 1990s, the PRI's regime began to crumble under the weight of corruption, a result of the political system's decay. When, in 1997, an electoral reform allowed new political parties to purchase airtime from media groups for their electoral campaigns, Emilio Azcárraga Jean, Azcárraga Milmo's son, was already saying that democracy was "good business." The victory of the National Action Party (PAN, Partido Acción Nacional) in the presidential election of 2000 brought Vicente Fox to power and put an end to the PRI's 71 years of political dominance. During Fox's administration, discussions started to draft a law to put media at the service of democratic efforts; however, they resulted in the scandalous "Televisa Law" of 2006 (crafted in marathon day-long sessions and approved in fewer than two weeks), which evidently favored the media giant (see Gaytán and Fregoso).

After the polarizing presidential election of 2006, which concluded in a virtual tie, PAN candidate Felipe Calderón ascended to power, facing protests from thousands of followers of Andrés Manuel López Obrador, the candidate from the Party of the Democratic Revolution (PRD, Partido de la Revolución Democrática), who questioned the results of the election. In the midst of this political crisis, Calderón's administration launched an unprecedented war against drug trafficking. The initiative led to a countrywide bloodbath—more than 121,000 people were killed during Calderón's six years in power ("Más De 121 Mil Muertos")—without any practical results. In this violent scenario,

Mexico became one of the most dangerous countries in the world for journalists. From 2000 to 2014, Mexico's National Commission for Human Rights (CNDH) documented the deaths of 88 journalists or media workers who were allegedly killed for reasons related to their work. Eighty-nine percent of the attacks against journalists in Mexico remained unpunished, according to the Knight Center for Journalism in the Americas (Badgen).

Despite some efforts to limit media concentration and Televisa's power, Calderón ended up succumbing to the private media networks. A "factic [or de facto] power" because it influences the public agenda and political decisions (Lay), Televisa supported the PRI during the presidential election of 2012. The network's partisan coverage was for many a decisive factor in the electoral success of the PRI's candidate, Enrique Peña Nieto, the former governor of the State of Mexico. The electoral results sparked a wave of criticism and protests against the media, specifically Televisa, for misinforming its audience and not playing its democratic role in the elections (Parish). One of the consequences was the creation of the citizens' movement YoSoy132, initially integrated by Mexican students who called for the democratization of the mass media and the repudiation of the mediatic imposition of Peña Nieto as president of Mexico. After his inauguration, however, Peña Nieto approved a controversial reform to the country's telecommunications law, which was supposed to break the media duopoly of Televisa and TV Azteca, according to *El País* (Calderon). Nevertheless, some critics have described it as a political instrument that ultimately benefited Televisa and harmed América Móvil, property of multimillionaire business magnate Carlos Slim, according to the Knight Center for Journalism in the Americas (A. Martínez). These were the days when *El Pulso de la República* became a new alternative political source that resonated with a young generation fed up with the monolithic power of the giant media conglomerates and their overwhelming influence on national politics.

In this scenario, *EPR* has covered the most prominent issues on the news agenda from a critical perspective rarely seen in mainstream media. In fact, *EPR*'s most popular video (with around 2.5 million visits) has been the political scandal of then-President Peña Nieto's own "White House" ("Angélica Rivera responde")[5]—literally a large white mansion—which involved accusations of corruption and raised questions about conflicts of interest relating to the contractors who built the president's family home, which had allegedly been bought by his wife, actress Angélica Rivera. In the video, Torres caustically reframed the First Lady's explanations regarding her patrimony and the accusations against her, while mocking the soap opera actress's affected, solemn tone. The second-most-popular *EPR* episode is about Mexican business-man Carlos Slim, the second-richest man in the world in 2014, and Telmex, his telecommunications monopoly ("Carlos Slim Shady").[6] After contextual-izing the power that Slim has in Mexico, Torres explains Telmex's abusive practices. He comments on the company's poor products and customer ser-vice, its economic role in the country, and its impact on Mexican families' budgets, and compares its practices with those of telephone companies in other countries. Through jokes, Torres explains the history of Telmex and its questionable privatization to highlight the implications that the telecommu-nications monopoly has had for freedom of expression and citizens' lives.

While Torres has declared that he does not do stories about organized crime because he "'loves the fact that he has his head attached to his shoul-ders'" (qtd. in Tuckman), he has criticized the inefficacy of the government's attempts to calm violence in the country. One of his most popular videos is about the capture of the world-famous Mexican drug lord Joaquín "El Chapo" Guzmán Loera in 2014 ("Se escapó el Chapo! [Anteriormente]").[7] After ques-tioning the competence of the Mexican intelligence network, Torres not only mocked Peña Nieto's government for using the military accomplishment for political ends, but also warned that El Chapo had escaped before and could do so again. Torres even created a mock game allowing viewers to bet how long El Chapo would stay in jail before becoming a fugitive again. Months later, in 2015, El Chapo scandalously escaped from a maximum security prison, creat-ing one of the biggest political crises of Peña Nieto's administration.[8] Other important sociopolitical issues in Mexico addressed by *EPR* include inequity in the country ("México: Los más ricos y los más tontos"),[9] the political links between the PRI and networks of prostitution ("PRIstitución"),[10] the public protests and deaths in Oaxaca generated by educational reforms ("Qué pasó en Oaxaca"),[11] the case of censorship against journalist Carmen Aristegui ("Carmen Aristegui y el Pulso de los 70"),[12] the impact of drug trafficking on the lives of Guerrero's peasants ("Narcopulco"),[13] and the development of a case regarding the disappearance of 43 students in Ayotzinapa ("Ayotzinapa: Capítulo final?").[14] *EPR* has also covered international issues, creating con-nections to understand their impact on Mexican viewers: Donald Trump's presidential campaign ("Y Trump mamá también"),[15] Britain's exit from the European Union ("Brexítame"),[16] the massacre in Orlando's gay night club Pulse ("El Pulse de Orlando"),[17] and the scandal regarding fiscal havens known as the Panama Papers ("Panama Pay-Per-View").[18]

For Torres, the relevance of his show is to translate news into an appealing format and to inform people about the news that has already been published, but that the audience might not have read or understood. Despite its news coverage, he has described his show as political entertainment and distinguished his satirical takes from journalism:

> We are not a news channel; we analyze what has already happened, with journalistic rigor, because I don't lie. In other words, *EPR* has never been a show about current news. . . . I do not want to have breaking stories, because we are not protected by any huge network or TV station. We try to do a show that responds to what you have already seen.[19] (qtd. in Tuckman)

While the show is critical of how power works in Mexico, Torres rejects any type of partisan political stand, activist intentions, or militant involvement in any social movement (Ramos). To maintain this ideological independence, Torres considers YouTube the most democratic platform for developing digital projects, and treasures the freedom of expression the online medium offers: "On *El Pulso de la República* I can say whatever the fuck I want without anybody wagging a finger at me," he told *The Guardian* (Tuckman). The Internet is also the perfect medium to reach his target audience, which is between 14 and 34 years old, and who "'either don't watch the news or are sick of watching the news'" (qtd. in Tuckman). He believes that the Internet has much better content than mainstream television and is the ideal platform for the dissemination of relevant public information. For Torres, television has become obsolete: "Television treated us like idiots and we just got sick of it, so we started making something we would watch. They are paying for their sins," he told *The Guardian*. The comedian has repeated his perspectives on media in several interviews and conferences, taking a do-it-yourself message to young people who are frustrated with the coverage of politics by the major media:

> If the newspaper doesn't like you, doesn't listen to you, doesn't give you any money, doesn't offer any opportunities, well then, create your own project. Anybody can shoot a video or record a radio program and upload it to the web. The only limitation is what you have in your head. (Torres qtd. in Breiner)

In many ways, *EPR* is a reaction to mainstream media and its coverage of the news—particularly to Televisa, the country's biggest network, which has traditionally aligned with the political ruling class and has become a de facto power in the country. "For 50 years they have been censoring the news and stomping on the truth. It's a news source that nobody believes. My target audience doesn't watch it. It's on the point of dying, if not economically, then because of its content," said Torres to *News Entrepreneurs* (Breiner). Despite his critical attitude toward mainstream TV, *EPR*'s growing audience brought Torres offers to migrate his show to major channels, including Televisa. He rejected the offers and his response to the media giant was, "You're the enemy, man" (Breiner). He explained that he would not have the editorial control he wanted even if the media conglomerate offers it. "On national television," Torres said, "nobody mucks with the president" (Tuckman). Nevertheless, he agreed to do a series of *cápsulas,* or short videos, during the 2014 World Cup of soccer in Brazil for Televisa, which prompted a major backlash. "It was a really dark time for us. I had around 1,000 tweets a day saying you fucking sold out, how could you do this. I will never ever ever ever ever do it again," he said to *The Guardian* (Tuckman).

This episode shows one of the prevalent tensions between independent satirists and the mainstream media: how to deal with the attempts at co-optation while also developing a sustainable career and media project when legitimacy is built on being an alternative to corrupt or biased commercial TV. In the case of Torres, the answer was found on regional cable. In 2016, HBO hired him to write and host *Chumel con Chumel Torres,* a weekly late-night show à la *Last Week Tonight with John Oliver* targeting Latin American audiences. The comedian explained his decision to his viewers in an Internet promo: "I feel HBO focuses more on the content instead of getting along with sponsors and people."[20] The show began in July 2016 and ran till 2020.[21] Interestingly, *EPR* continues as a local satiric infotainment show that deals primarily with Mexico's national news agenda. The glocalization process of this case is also noteworthy: *EPR* adapted a global format, creating a unique hybrid product primarily targeting a national audience, and then, after significant success, the satiric show was re-elaborated for a macro-regional audience. From this perspective, successfully amplifying audiences from national to regional adds a layer to the cultural globalization phenomena of satiric shows, revealing the predominance of the genre in the Americas.

Cualca: The Feminist Humor of Malena Pichot in Argentina

In 2008, Malena Pichot, a liberal arts student in her early twenties from Buenos Aires who worked as a proofreader in a publishing house, broke up with her boyfriend. Her way of dealing with the separation was to upload a series of humorous videos on YouTube under the label *La loca de mierda.*[22] The series was based on monologues delivered by a hysterical, depressed woman going through heartbreak while questioning several clichés about women and their relationships with men. She explained her motivations to *El País:* "'The problem that women have is that we get defined by the guy we are with. I felt so embarrassed that it happened to me; it was so humiliating for me that I took it to the extreme doing the videos'" (qtd. in Suárez).[23] "'I felt like the typical 'concheta' [upper-class girl] without problems who gets depressed because a guy does not love her, and it wasn't that terrible; I was just an unsatisfied bougie girl,'" she added in an interview with *La Nación* (Pizarro).[24] *La loca de mierda* became an online success and was acquired by MTV for a second season of 29 episodes in 2009. From then on, Pichot's media career took off and has included collaborations on radio, TV, and film. While she has consolidated her name as a stand-up comedian, the Internet has remained the most constant platform for showcasing her work. Pichot has not only been a pioneer in Argentina in using social media to launch her comedy career but also quickly became a public feminist figure in the country.

While she has described herself as a "cheta" from Belgrano, an upper-middle-class neighborhood in Buenos Aires, her satiric humor frequently targets the prejudices of this social sector (Garófalo). In 2012, Pichot created *Cualca,* a series of satiric television sketches that criticized sexism, racism, homophobia, and other social prejudices through surreal, absurd, and visceral humor. The name *Cualca* comes from a colloquialism that loosely means "whatever" (Zavaley). While *Cualca* was initially included as a segment of the TV show *Duro de domar* (Channel 9), its viral videos (of around five minutes each) became especially successful online through its Vimeo and YouTube accounts. *Cualca* was written and acted by Pichot and other comedians (Julián Kartun, Julián Lucero, Julián Doregger, and Charo López) she brought together and described to *Rolling Stone* as "the most talented young actors from Argentina" (Zavaley).

"Piropos"[25] has been one of the most popular *Cualca* videos. In this sketch, Pichot sarcastically criticizes street harassment against women. She enumerates types of this sexist practice and then presents the experience from the point of view of a woman who reacts violently, killing the men who harass her on the streets. She ends the sketch by saying, "We want to be clear that we are against murdering people. But society does not seem to care that you show me your dick or that you tell me that you want to fuck me in the ass. So keep doing it. Maybe one day you might even rape me."[26] Other *Cualca* videos that deal explicitly with issues of gender are "Negación" (negation),[27] about women who live in denial as a strategy to cope with gender norms, beauty canons, sexual harassment, and domestic violence; and "Chicas inseguras" (insecure gals),[28] in which she satirizes the behavior in which young women will engage to get attention from stupid men, while at the same time mocking teen entertainment and rock TV shows. In "Entrevistando al enemigo" (interviewing the enemy),[29] Pichot parodies a TV talk show host who interviews an anti-abortion activist and a rugby player (played by other actors), who are presented as examples of the Argentinean right. She confronts the conservatism of these characters, revealing some of their most despicable moral values and prejudices, especially about gender. In a teaser[30] for the second season of the show, Pichot plays herself receiving instructions from a TV producer who announces some changes for the new season—for example, the new theme would deal with "three girls over 30 who still can." Malena asks, "Can what?" The producer responds, "Have children, be happy, have a purpose in life." Another request for the new season is that she show more skin, "taking advantage [of the fact] that she still has a few years of physical validity left." Finally, the producer asks her not to do scatological jokes—those should be left to the male actors. The sketch ends with Malena farting on the producer's face. This satirical video connects with a constant preoccupation in Pichot's humor: the way women are portrayed in the media. "It upsets me that society educates women to be dumbasses, to show their ass, and appear in Big Brother,"[31] she said to *La Nación* (Pizarro).

At the beginning of her media exposure with *La loca de mierda*, Pichot did not define herself as a feminist and playfully answered questions about her militancy: "I shave, I want to have name-brand clothes, I'm within the system. . . . I don't hate men, I don't say that they are all sons of bitches; I just say that my ex is a son of a bitch," she said to *La Nación* (Pizarro).[32] Pichot has also rejected the label "female humor" for her work:

> The category of "female humor" only exists because men cannot identify with a woman. Female humor does not exist because there is no male humor. There is only humor; sometimes it's done by men and sometimes by women. But because the hegemonic discourse is male, women have to identify with men, but it's hard for men to identify with a woman. Men need the category of "female humor" because women are always the otherness, the distinct, the different.[33] (Pichot qtd. in *La Capital*)

Pichot's rise to fame happened at a time when sexism and violence against women were much discussed in Argentina as part of a movement that reached its highest point with #NiUnaMenos (not one less), a public protest against femicides in the country that took place at the Congressional Plaza in Buenos Aires on June 3, 2015. The demonstration, publicly supported by several television personalities through media campaigns, was attended by nearly

300,000 people and backed by women's rights groups, unions, political organizations, and even the Catholic Church. As part of this movement, Pichot has frequently participated in public debates about feminism in Argentina and has strongly reacted to sexist remarks by public figures. When Argentina's President Mauricio Macri said that "women like to be catcalled, even if you tell them 'What a nice ass you have,'"[34] Pichot reacted in a column:

> No woman is going to die because someone says, "What a nice ass you have, [I'd like] to fuck it to pieces," but neither the president nor 90 percent of society understands that it is [still] wrong. And what we all know is wrong has to do with the fact that many were indeed killed because they were Black, fat, homosexual, or Jewish, and many women were mistreated and killed because they were women.[35] (Pichot)

When rock star Gustavo Cordera, former frontman of the legendary Argentinean band Bersuit Vergarabat, defended the rape of underage women by saying on a public show that "there are women who need to be raped," Pichot was clear in her accusation: "A person who says women need to be raped does so because he has raped" ("Malena Pichot: 'Una Persona Que Dice'"). Similarly, she has publicly questioned the way the media portrays cases of violence against women and has confronted conservative voices. With the same critical tone, Pichot, who does not like to be labeled an actress and considers herself primarily a scriptwriter, has frequently reflected on the state of comedy in Latin America:

> In Latin America, comedy is very underdeveloped, because the trajectory of humor is misogynistic and simplistic. I'm not saying that everything is shit; there are exceptions, but at the popular level, it is all shit. There is not a social consciousness in any sense, and I think that is the main problem of Latin American stand-up comedy and humor in general.[36] (qtd. in Suárez)

Pichot described the humor that she enjoys as uncomfortable, politically incorrect, and visceral. She has frequently revealed that most of her comedic referents are American—she has mentioned names such as Seinfeld, Sarah Silverman, Amy Schumer, Kristen Schaal, Maria Bamford, Dave Chappelle, and Louis CK; and series such as *Will & Grace, Friends, Arrested Development, Cheers, Curb Your Enthusiasm*, and, more recently, *Girls*. As for comedy in Spanish, she included shows such as *Muchachada Nui* (from Spain) and the Argentinean *Cha Cha Cha* and Juana Molina. Nevertheless, the comedian has stated that she considers most Argentinean humor of the 1990s "deplorable" ("Malena Pichot: 'Hago Humor'"), and many of her critiques about the sexist component of the entertainment industry in Argentina deal with the type of commercial TV produced during that decade that is still prevalent in the country. This is why Pichot has rejected certain offers to work in mainstream media: she wants to keep control of her creative work and does not want to be restricted in the type of content she is allowed to produce. In this sense, the Internet has remained her preferred platform.

When *Cualca*'s TV season in *Duro de domar* ended in December 2013 after 46 episodes, Pichot took her comedy back to the web. *Cualca*'s actors developed an online crowd-funding campaign (#ojalavuelvaCualca) to independently fund the show's second season. They had a goal of USD $22,995 which was exceeded by more than $5,000 through fans' donations. The second (and final) season had 10 episodes, and the last video was posted on January 16, 2015. In fact, *Cualca*'s videos have been described as "unprecedented in Argentina" (Garófalo) because of their high production quality. This slick quality has also marked other comedic projects of Pichot's, such as *Por ahora*, a comedy series for Cosmopolitan TV that was described as a spin-off of *Cualca*,[37] or *Mundillo*. In 2015, Pichot took her stand-up show to Spain, and in 2018, Netflix released her comedy special *Estupidez compleja*,[38] in which she took her feminist comedy—expanding on topics such as gender, language, and abortion—to global Hispanic audiences.

Conclusions

In times when traditional media intensely seek new formulas to make their online operations profitable, a recent wave of digital satire shows reveals successful models for independent media production and online TV to develop, consolidate, and negotiate their place with mainstream media and public debate. Their formula involves producing innovative, risqué, and high-quality audiovisual humor that fills gaps left by national mainstream TV. These online TV shows deal critically with sociocultural and political issues and have become especially appealing for young urban audiences eager for new content aligned with international (usually US) media production, but with a local flavor. While heavily influenced by the US comedy tradition (political satire such as *The Daily Show* or *The Colbert Report* for *El Pulso de la República*, and, in the case of *Cualca*, contemporary stand-up comedy—Sarah Silverman, Amy Schumer, Dave Chapelle—and series such as *Seinfeld* and *Girls*), these sorts of online productions have successfully digested their foreign influences and adapted them to the local culture, creating a unique glocal voice that has tapped into particular national tensions (the audience's frustration with the political news coverage from Televisa in Mexico and its historic relationship with the PRI; and the role of entertainment and advertising in reproducing sexist values in Argentina, a country with high rates of femicide and growing social movements for women's rights). As can be seen, incorporating foreign humor traditions and global formats to speak about local issues has become an essential part of cultural globalization, a process that is, nevertheless, always being negotiated in terms of cultural, media, and sociopolitical contexts.

As part of their core critiques, these satirists have been openly critical of national television. After becoming popular on the web with millions of subscribers, followers, and viewers on their social media platforms, they negotiated their relationship with national mainstream TV—Chumel Torres rejected the offer to take *El Pulso de la República* to Televisa, but agreed to do a series of videos for the media giant during the 2014 World Cup before transitioning to a transnational media outlet; the second season of Malena Pichot's *La loca de mierda* was broadcast on MTV, while *Cualca* was originally developed as a segment for a national TV show, and she is a recurrent radio and television personality. Nevertheless, both creators maintained the web as their main platform, citing the creative freedom that the medium offers and the possibility of reaching loyal audiences at any moment. It is important to note here their adaptability to the new social media platforms. While both initially became popular on YouTube, they also tailored their presence on Facebook, Instagram, and Twitter for different audiences, languages, and uses. In this sense, the evolution of their presence on social media also reflects how internationalization is constantly negotiated on different platforms and communications technologies.

As part of their evolution, these online satirists finally obtained a regional or international reach. Chumel Torres expanded the political satire of *EPR* by focusing on broader Latin American issues with his late-night show on HBO targeting a regional audience. Malena Pichot, whose feminist videos are already famous in various Latin American cities, has intensively promoted her comic work through shows in Spain, and released a stand-up comedy special on Netflix. This internationalization marks an interesting stage of their relationship with cultural globalization: while the cases first adapt international referents and create a distinctly unique voice at the local/national level, they then adapt this voice to reach wider regional or geolinguistic audiences, creating a new layer in their hybrid process.

The success of these online satire cases reveals their potential as critical voices in cultural, social, and political topics at the local, regional, and transnational levels, while the national context remains relevant to understanding the role of satire in negotiating the limits of dissent in media culture. The existence of other independent cases of audiovisual critical humor and digital satire in the region—such as *La Pulla* (Colombia), *El Desinformado* and *GCU* (Peru), *País de Boludos* and *Guille Aquino* (Argentina), *Enchufe.tv* (Ecuador), or *Porta dos Fundos* (Brazil), among others—confirms the increasing visibility of the genre in the age of the Internet, and its complex condition as a hybrid media text within the framework of cultural globalization.

Editors' Note

Translations from the original language in this as well as in all following chapters were done by each corresponding author.

Notes

1 "Escribía columnas que básicamente eran guiones de *El pulso* pero sin cámara. Se me ocurrió que podíamos convertirlos en videos y ya. Empecé a grabarme con el iPhone y hacía diferentes takes (tomas) porque no sabía si era mejor hacer un personaje de izquierda o de derecha, o muppets o una mujer, eso lo decidí después. Luego conocí a Durden (co-escritor de *El Pulso de la República*), platicamos y comenzamos a escribir."

2 "Lo hacíamos con una webcam y editábamos con iMovie, todo chafa. Pero el guión estaba padre y ya teníamos nuestros followers en Twitter, entonces no empezamos de cero. Luego Yayo, creador de 'No me revientes' (canal de YouTube que nació en 2010 y que cuenta con más de 1.700.000 suscriptores) publicó en su espacio nuestros programas. Teníamos 18.000 vistas, pero después de que publicó en su canal ya teníamos 250.000, ahí despegamos."

3 "Somos tres güeyes en un pinche cuartito haciendo un buen show."

4 "Antes nos peleábamos mucho porque, por ejemplo, yo soy más pop en mi manera de escoger notas y Durden, más serio. Yo podía escoger la nota de Justin Bieber sacándose el pito en la playa y él la de las autodefensas de Michoacán. Está cabrón, pero en tres años aprendimos a hacer un balance entre comicidad y periodismo."

5 www.youtube.com/watch?v=z74G7AuCVKc

6 www.youtube.com/watch?v=BoP9q-j5FhQ

7 www.youtube.com/watch?v=CIsosUPetwU

8 EPR also covered the escape of El Chapo and its implications: www.youtube.com/watch?v=ZVyWV5Gc7Fc
   www.youtube.com/watch?v=uFTN0XVpB7Y

9 www.youtube.com/watch?v=xZEN8LhUXaU

10 www.youtube.com/watch?v=mogkSr1v8UU

11 www.youtube.com/watch?v=RQLGDNrafbE

12 www.youtube.com/watch?v=DF9febPq0Xo

13 www.youtube.com/watch?v=z0KapGuJ1a0

14 www.youtube.com/watch?v=64ajZUssYQI

15 www.youtube.com/watch?v=MQ3WWj5h59A

16 www.youtube.com/watch?v=724hvmhnYIA

17 www.youtube.com/watch?v=xrUgURj-vFk

18 www.youtube.com/watch?v=URR4FB72FRs

19 "No somos un canal de noticias, somos un canal de análisis de lo que ya pasó con rigor periodístico porque no digo mentiras. Es decir, *El Pulso de la República* nunca ha sido un noticiero coyuntural, no maneja noticias nuevas. . . . No quiero tener exclusivas de nada porque no nos protege ningún tipo de aparato de noticias, canal o un network gigante. Tratamos de hacer un programa que sea como réplica de lo que ya viste."

20 The promo can be accessed at www.youtube.com/watch?v=oKbgBY-l4hA.

21 HBO decided to put the show on hold in the midst of the pandemic, because Torres was accused of using a racial slur against the son of President Andres Manuel López Obrador.

22 The first video of *La loca de mierda* was uploaded on August 30, 2008, and can be seen here: www.youtube.com/watch?v=yK5fhmOsnx8.

23 "El problema que tenemos las mujeres es que nos define el tipo con el que estamos. A mí me dio tanta vergüenza que me pasara eso, para mí fue tan humillante y tan vergonzoso, que lo llevé al extremo haciendo los videos."

24 "Me sentía la clásica concheta sin problemas que se deprime porque un pibe no la quiere, y no era tan terrible, sólo una burguesa insatisfecha."

25 "Piropos": www.youtube.com/watch?v=nXsEVOar6TA&index=33&list=PL0phEjHC eBGuxCDv1OtZnGy0jOB3j2Zt1
    Similar ideas to "Piropos" have been developed by the Spaniard Alicia Murillo, and in media campaigns against sexism, like "10 Hours of Walking in NYC as a Woman."

26 "Queremos dejar en claro que nosotros estamos absolutamente en contra del asesinato. La sociedad no está de acuerdo con matar gente. Pero a la sociedad no parece importarle que me muestres la pija o que me digas que me quieres romper el orto. Así que seguí haciéndolo, por ahí que un día te animás y me violas."

27 "Negación": www.youtube.com/watch?v=gOk7IsFziK4

28 "Chicas inseguras": www.youtube.com/watch?v=xS0DVNPJivg

29 "Entrevistando al enemigo 2": www.youtube.com/watch?v=vxFv3Vf4JlQ&list=PL0 phEjHCeBGuxCDv1OtZnGy0jOB3j2Zt1&index=43

30 Teaser: www.youtube.com/watch?v=HsCnWiB_37A

31 "Me angustia que la sociedad eduque a las mujeres para que sean pelotudas. La media es mostrar el culo y salir en Gran Hermano."

32 "Me depilo, quiero tener la ropa de moda: estoy adentro del sistema. . . . No odio a los hombres, no digo que son todos unos hijos de puta, digo que mi ex es un hijo de puta."

33 "La categoría 'humor femenino' existe porque los hombres no pueden identificarse con una mujer. No existe un humor femenino porque no existe un humor masculino. Existe el humor, a veces lo hacen hombres y a veces lo hacen mujeres. Como el discurso hegemónico es masculino, la mujer puede identificarse con el hombre pero al hombre le cuesta identificarse con una mujer. El hombre necesita crear la categoría de 'humor femenino' porque la mujer es siempre la otredad, lo distinto, lo diferente."

34 "A las mujeres les gustan los piropos, aunque les digan qué lindo culo tenés."

35 "Ninguna mujer se va a morir porque le digan 'que hermoso culo que tenés para rompértelo todo' pero ni el jefe de gobierno ni el 90% de la sociedad entienden que está mal. Y aquello que todos sabemos que está mal tiene que ver con que es real que

muchos se murieron cagados a palos por ser negros, gorditos, putos o judíos y a muchas mujeres las violentaron realmente y las mataron por ser mujeres."

36 "En América, la comedia está muy atrasada porque tenemos una trayectoria misógina y simplista del humor. No quiero que parezca que digo que todo es una mierda, hay excepciones, pero sí creo que a nivel popular es una mierda. No hay conciencia de nada, no hay conciencia social en ningún sentido y creo que ese es el problema mayor del stand up y del humor en general en Latinoamérica."

37 *Por ahora* involved the same group of actors as *Cualca*. It was ironic that Cosmopolitan TV in Latin America broadcast the series, since it is a publication that reinforces female stereotypes. In contrast to *Cualca*, the episodes of *Por ahora* were around 30 minutes, and focused more on the problems of a group of generational friends in their thirties (relationships, immaturity, insecurities) than on social issues.

38 The teaser can be accessed here: www.youtube.com/watch?v=tg-4sLzqv6M.

Works Cited

Alonso, Paul. *Satiric TV in the Americas: Critical Metatainment as Negotiated Dissent*. New York: Oxford UP, 2018.

Alves, Rosental. "From Lapdog to Watchdog: The Role of the Press in Latin America's Democratization." *Making Journalists*, edited by Hugo de Burgh, New York: Routledge, 2005, pp. 181–202.

Badgen, Samantha. "89% de ataques contra periodistas mexicanos siguen impunes, según comisión de derechos humanos." Knight Center, *LatAm Journalism Review*, 21 Apr. 2014, latamjournalismreview.org/es/articles/89-de-ataques-contra-periodistas -mexicanos-siguen-impunes-segun-comision-de-derechos-humanos/.

Baym, Geoffrey. "The Daily Show: Discursive Integration and the Reinvention of Political Journalism." *Political Communication*, vol. 22, no.3, 2005, pp. 259–276.

Breiner, James. "Mexican Blogger Builds a Business out of Political Satire." *News Entrepreneurs*, 12 Mar. 2014, newsentrepreneurs.blogspot.com/2014/03/mexican-blogger -builds-business-out-of.html.

Calderon, Verónica. "Peña Nieto promulga la reforma de telecomunicaciones de México." *El País*, 10 June 2013, elpais.com/internacional/2013/06/10/actualidad/1370885658 _536894.html.

Calleja, Aleida. "La concentración mediática en México." *Café Político*, 2012, mx.boell.org/ sites/default/files/aleida2mediatica.pdf.

Cuddon, J. A. *The Penguin Dictionary of Literary Terms and Literary Theory*. London, Penguin Books, 1991.

Fernández, Fátima. *Los medios de comunicación masiva en México*. Mexico: Juan Pablos, 1982.

García Canclini, Néstor. *Hybrid Culture: Strategies for Entering and Leaving Modernity*. Minneapolis: University of Minnesota Press, 1995.

Garófalo, Lucas. "Malena Pichot, no cualquiera." *Los Inrocks*, July 6, 2012, medium.com/ los-inrockuptibles/malena-pichot-no-cualquiera-9cc55c846623.

Gaytán, Felipe, and Juliana Fregoso. "La ley Televisa de México." *Chasqui: Revista Latinoamericana de Comunicación*, no. 94, 2006, pp. 40–45.

Kraidy, Marwan. *Hybridity or the Cultural Logic of Globalization.* Philadelphia: Temple UP, 2005.

Lay, Israel. "Medios electrónicos de comunicación, poderes fácticos y su impacto en la democracia de México." *Revista Mexicana de Ciencias Políticas y Sociales,* vol. 58, no. 217, 2013, pp. 253–268.

"Malena Pichot: 'Hago humor para molestar un poco.'" *La Capital,* 13 Apr. 2013, www .lacapital.com.ar/escenario/malena-pichot-hago-humor-molestar-un-poco-n437053 .html.

"Malena Pichot: 'Una persona que dice que a las minas hay que violarlas es porque violó.'" *El Patagonico,* 2016, www.elpatagonico.com/malena-pichot-una-persona-que-dice -que-las-minas-hay-que-violarlas-es-porque-violo-n1503739.

Martín-Barbero, Jesús. *Communications, Culture and Hegemony: From the Media to the Mediations.* Translated by Elizabeth Fox, Newbury Park, CA: Sage, 1993.

Martínez, Alejandro. "Mexican Congressmen Approve Telecom Reforms: A Summary." Knight Center, *LatAm Journalism Review,* 27 Mar. 2013, https://latamjournalismreview .org/articles/mexican-congressmen-approve-telecom-reforms-a-summary/.

Martínez, Jan. "México rompe el histórico duopolio de la televisión." *El País,* 12 Mar. 2015, elpais.com/internacional/2015/03/12/actualidad/1426124159_306125.html.

Moran, Albert. "Global Franchising, Local Customizing: The Cultural Economy of TV Program Formats." *Continuum: Journal of Media & Cultural Studies,* vol. 23, no. 2, 2009, pp.115–125.

"Más de 121 mil muertos, el saldo de la narcoguerra de Calderón: Inegi." *Proceso,* 30 July 2013, www.proceso.com.mx/nacional/2013/7/30/mas-de-121-mil-muertos-el-saldo -de-la-narcoguerra-de-calderon-inegi-121510.html.

Mulato, Abril. "Chumel Torres: 'El Pulso De La República No Es Un Noticiario. Somos Pizza, Chelas Y Muchas Risas.'" *El País,* 6 Feb. 2016, verne.elpais.com/verne/2015/12/ 28/articulo/1451341987_641339.html.

Parish, Nathaniel. "Mexico's Media Monopoly vs. the People." *Fortune,* 14 Sept. 2012, fortune.com/2012/09/14/mexicos-media-monopoly-vs-the-people/.

Pichot, Malena. "Mauricio y la violencia de todos los días." *Telam,* 25 Apr. 2014, www.telam .com.ar/notas/201404/60768-malena-pichot-macri-piropos.html.

Pieterse, Jan Nederveen. *Globalization and Culture: Global Melange.* Maryland: Rowman & Littlefield Publishers, 2009.

Pizarro, Emilse. "Loca pero no tanto." *La Nación,* 20 Feb. 2011, www.lanacion.com.ar/ lifestyle/loca-pero-no-tanto-nid1351193/.

Ramos, Arely. "'Me gustaría convertirme en el Seth Macfarlane mexicano.'" *Hora Cero,* 12 Nov 2014, horacerotam.com/espectaculos/gustaria-convertirme-en-el-seth -macfarlane-mexicano/.

Robertson, Roland. "Glocalization: Time-Space and Homogeneity-Heterogeneity." *Global Modernities,* edited by Mike Featherstone, Scott Lash, and Roland Robertson, Thousand Oaks, CA: Sage, 1995, pp. 25–44.

Sinclair, John. "Geo-Linguistic Region as Global Space: The Case of Latin America." *The Television Studies Reader,* edited by Robert Clyde Allen and Annette Hill, London: Routledge, 2004, pp. 130–138.

Sosa, Gabriel, and Rodrigo Gómez. "En el país Televisa." *Zapping TV: el paisaje de la tele latina,* edited by Omar Rincón, Bogotá: Fundación Friedrich Ebert, 2013, pp. 83–97.

Straubhaar, Joseph. "Beyond Media Imperialism: Asymmetrical Interdependence and Cultural Proximity." *Critical Studies in Mass Communication,* vol. 8, 1991, pp. 39–59.

———. *World Television: From Global to Local.* Los Angeles: Sage, 2007.

Suárez, Rebeca. "Malena Pichot: la loca de mierda quiere conquistar España." *El País,* 23 Oct. 2015, elpais.com/elpais/2015/10/21/tentaciones/1445424424_962719.html.

Trejo, Raúl. *Televisa, el quinto poder.* México DF: Claves Latinoamericanas, 1985.

Tuckman, Jo. "El pulso de la republica: Meet Chumel Torres, Mexico's Answer to Jon Stewart." *The Guardian,* 28 Aug. 2015, www.theguardian.com/world/2015/aug/28/el-pulso-de-la-republica-chumel-torres-mexico-youtube-show.

Villamil, Jenaro. *El sexenio de Televisa.* México DF: Grijalbo, 2010.

Zavaley, Emilio. "Cualquierismo en TV abierta." *Rolling Stone,* 7 Aug. 2012, www.lanacion.com.ar/espectaculos/cualquierismo-en-tv-abierta-nid1497143/.

3

Hypermediatic Humor

Some Tools for Its Analysis

DAMIÁN FRATICELLI

A Proposal for the Study of Hypermediatic Humor

This article aims to provide some tools for the analysis of hypermediatic humor in general, and satirical fake accounts in particular. I define hypermediatic humor as the device instituted within media social networks[1] that generates continuous interpretants[2] that make any social phenomenon laughable.[3] Among its properties, I find that every individual with an account can produce what is laughable and that this production presents low institutional regulation. Platforms have their rules, but there is no such thing as a style manual for mass media or effective censorship across the board—something not allowed on one platform can be uploaded to another.

One of the consequences of these qualities defining hypermediatic humor is the appearance of satirical fake accounts. They occupy an important place in the daily public debate, enriching it by incorporating meanings censored by other, more serious accounts, but also distorting it by acting like trolls and by fanning so-called hate speech. Here I propose to offer instruments for their analysis, because their study can exposes the complexity of hypermediatic humor. How does it differ from other forms of the laughable in mass media? How does it occur in social networks? What consequences does it have when it appears in fake accounts?

To address these problems, I will demonstrate the importance of focusing on enunciation to study the laughable and present a model for its analysis in the networks. I will look at the particularity of fake accounts and discuss a case study: Dra. Alcira Pignata, a fake account that between 2010 and 2017 satirized politics in Argentina, scandalizing people with its dark humor and political implications, given that its author was a government official with the city of Buenos Aires.

I argue that, through the inclusion of a theoretical model based on the theories of Eliseo Verón, Oscar Steimberg, and Mario Carlón, it is possible to unveil the different levels of significance that a meme can reach. Eliseo Verón was one of the first Latin American theorists to postulate mediatization as a field of study, and developed, together with Oscar Steimberg, a semiotics of it from an Argentinian perspective. Both authors elaborated their theories during the hegemony of the mass media. Carlón (*Circulación*, 65–98) appropriates their postulates to analyze the production of meaning in the new media system in which social media networks play a fundamental role. Based on his work, I have developed my model, which I will illustrate with an analysis of the circulation of the meaning of the memes of Dr. Pignata, a fake Twitter account that generated a formidable scandal in Argentina due to its political repercussions.

The Laughable, the Enunciation, and Their Patterns: The Comical and the Humorous

From a semiotic and communicational perspective, the laughable is a "meta-communicative" (Bateson 107) or "primary reference" (Goffman 23) framework.[4] Both notions allude to communicative procedures that refer to communication itself. The laughable is established as such at that meta-level of communication that builds a horizon of expectations between the actors in the exchange. Its appearance is an interlude in the dominant seriousness; it promotes polysemy and demands affective distance from the referent (Berger 41). If we laugh at someone who has just fallen, we do not worry at same time about his or her health. This distance does not imply there are no tensions, excitements, or feelings, but that they are not governed by the logic of the serious (Apter and Smith 112).

Like any metacommunicative framework, the laughable is built on discursivity. The metacommunicative indicators that construct it are accessible through enunciative analysis. I will follow Steimberg's definition of enunciation ("Semiotics") because it is flexible enough to apply to social media networks:

> ... enunciation is defined as the effect of meaning of the semiotization processes by which a communicational situation is *constructed* in a text, through devices that may or may not be linguistic in nature. (48–49)

Through the study of enunciation, the analyst can learn what the communicational proposal of an utterance is, from its moment of production to its moment of recognition (Verón 127).[5] At this level, I refer to it as a *meta-enunciative* framework composed of enunciative operations that project discursivity toward a laughable communicative exchange. In other words, the laughable meta-enunciative framework enables the metacommunicative framework and does so through multiple reflexive enunciative procedures: a gesture, a change in tone of voice, a double meaning, etc. It is important to emphasize that I say "enable" and not "determine" because I am far from a linear conception of the generation of meaning; that is to say, I consider that there is always a circulation of meaning (Verón 129).[6] A discourse can have a laughable meta-enunciative framework without provoking laughable recognition, as happens when someone is offended by a joke.

Within the laughable metacommunicative framework I find two great enunciative patterns: the comical and the humorous. There is an extensive bibliography on both, of which I will not be able to give an overview here, but I will present an enunciative reading of them. The comical has been characterized by two fundamentally enunciative scenes. The first is when an enunciator is a comic object and the enunciatee discovers her/him as such. This is the case of the person who, with her/his fall, makes us laugh—has a nose so long or is so badly dressed that he/she is ridiculous. In this scene, the enunciator does not appear to be aware that he/she is the target of ridicule, but instead acts as if he/she were not in any way incongruous with the usual clichés of the forms of nature, social norms, or discursive exchange. Clowns are an example of this comic enunciation because they break these norms without appearing to know that they do. For them, the enunciator maintains a superior asymmetrical relationship in which there is no identification.

The other scene that characterizes the comical presents an enunciator who makes a third party laugh with the complicity of the enunciatee. The typical genre is mockery. In it, the enunciator and the enunciatee join forces to ridicule a third party over whom they establish a relationship of superiority with no room for empathy. This type of enunciation is typical of the aggressive laugh, and it is frequently presented in satire in the networks.

As for the humorous, its enunciation is characterized by self-irony and proposing the identification of the enunciator and enunciatee with the target of the mockery. Freud (216) tells a joke that allows us to give a synthetic account of our conception of humor. A man condemned to death is warned that he will be executed on a Monday and exclaims, "What a great way to start the week!" How can anyone make a joke in the face of such terrible news? Freud postulates that it is because the "I" moves to the position of the superego, and from there the man says to himself, "I am too great for this trifle to affect me" (220). In enunciative terms, there is an unfolding of the enunciator that laughs at himself suffering.

However, this explanation implies that only the enunciator has access to humorous pleasure. But what about the receptor? And what about mediatization? Since Freud describes humor in face-to-face exchanges or in stories that imitate them, is it possible to talk about humor in mass media and social networks in these terms?

Steimberg (172) sees such a situation in the work of Robert Crumb in the *Village Voice*. The characters in his comics, and objects of his derision, were middle-class, liberal urban people who suffered from stubborn intellectual pretension and inconsistent social indifference. Their identity corresponded to the same stylistic sector as that of the type of reader at whom the newspaper was aimed, so when they were ridiculed, the enunciated reader was a victim as well. In this way, the ideal reader of Crumb's humor was the one who could identify with the character and laugh at him or her as if laughing at him/herself with his/her own moral contradictions. It was, in short, the reader capable of unfolding, a typical procedure of humor.

As we can see, the placement of the enunciator in the institutional enunciation of the media is a relevant factor to be considered when describing humor. Continuing with this approach, the mediatic comical would be present when the object of the mockery is not identified with the stylistic segment of the media. However, what happens with the laughable on social networks, where there is no institutional framework equivalent to that of the mass media?

Two Conditioning Factors of the Laughable in Hypermediatic Social Networks

To analyze the laughable in social networks, as in any other discursivity, I must attend to two factors: the enunciative matrix of the interface and the interactions of the account with its collective and the environment.

The Social Media Enunciative Matrix

As is common with any technical device that makes possible the construction and distribution of texts, the interface of social networks conditions *the ways of saying*, because saying implies a certain "mechanical" disposition and is the result of the specific components that integrate that disposition (Traversa, "Notas" 63). Therefore, it is not the same as reading a joke in a magazine or a Twitter post. To describe how the interfaces configure the enunciation in a

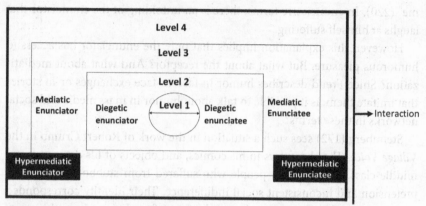

Figure 3.1. Structure of the hypermediatic social network device. Courtesy of the author.

general way, beyond the specificities of each platform, I present the model in figure 3.1.

I will start by defining the upper level and then I will deal with the rest to develop a clearer explanation. Level 4 describes the enunciative scene composed by the Hypermediatic Enunciator and the Hypermediatic Enunciated. I take the notion of hypermediatic enunciator here from Carlón ("La cultura" 119–124), who defines it as the figure discursively constructed each time an account is opened in social networks. I postulate that it constitutes the condensation of two enunciative figures: the *account's enunciator* and the *account's owner*.

The *account's enunciator* figure is the effect of the account name and other components that are permanently associated with it in each enunciation. These may range from the profile photo to the enunciative modalities that are sedimented through successive publications and build a horizon of expectations in relation to the discursive exchange. The *account's owner* figure refers to the correlation with an extra-discursive entity that is presupposed from the instance of recognition. Its materiality is found in the properties of the account's enunciator that indicate the association with a particular inter-discursive network. This is clear in the hypermediatic enunciators of public figures. Their names alone trigger the recognition of utterances produced by them in other media.

Normally, an identity is assumed between the enunciator and the owner of the account, but the accounts that are declared as laughable fakes construct an explicit dissociation between the two through different procedures: word games, thematic incongruities, ironies, etc. If a fake account does not expose this dissociation, in recognition, it can be confused with a "real" account. Finally, the Hypermediatic Enunciatee is the figure to whom the account is addressed.

In level 3 the enunciative scene composed by the Mediatic Enunciator and the Mediatic Enunciatee is displayed. Both are the producer and the recipient of each particular publication. Their properties will depend on the languages, technical devices, modalities, and discursive classifications (types, genres, styles, etc.) put into play. The Mediatic Enunciator can identify with the Hypermediatic Enunciator or not, as happens when they share a meme or any publication from an account that is not their own. A fundamental difference between the two is that while the Hypermediatic Enunciator builds a horizon of expectations in the exchange, the Mediatic Enunciator can vary in each publication. Thus, for example, an Instagrammer can become a laughable Hypermediatic Enunciator because he/she frequently publishes comic videos, but he/she can be a serious Mediatic Enunciator in a publication where he/she mourns the loss of a loved one.

Level 2 is composed of the enunciative scenes developed in the utterances of each publication. In them, multiple enunciators and enunciatees are displayed. The most evident ones are the enunciators incarnated in characters, but I also include here those produced by graphics, music, noises, etc. In the account of our laughable Instagrammer, a video can be published in which he/she interacts with another Instagrammer; both would be diegetic enunciators and enunciatees.

Level 1 consists of the enunciative scenes of the utterances produced by the diegetic enunciators. In the video mentioned above, one of the Instagrammers can quote the words of a friend. In that speech, the friend becomes a first-level enunciator.

While more could be added to these four levels regarding what happens when a Hypermediatic Enunciator shares a publication from another account, what I have outlined here will help explain the laughable production on the networks without running the risk of confusing phenomena. For example, if I take the meme in figure 3.2, I could consider it a comical joke.

Following our proposal, the meme constructs a Mediatic Enunciator who has appropriated a sequence of *Spider-Man* and assumed control by making the diegetic enunciator, Aunt May, pity Peter for being a journalism graduate. Using the incongruence between the original enunciation of the film and the intervention, the Media Enunciator does not comically mock Peter, but rather all those who have studied and are studying journalism, because they

Figure 3.2. Meme of the conversation between Peter Parker and his Aunt May in which she expresses her unease with his journalism degree.

are often poorly paid and the profession is in crisis. The problem is that this meme never appears like this on the networks. It is always in the context of an account, and this can transform its laughable nature.

I found this meme on a Facebook page called Memes de periodismo y comunicación (journalism and communication memes); its name and the regularity of its exchanges build the Hypermediatic Enunciator. Its appearance is that of a laughable representative of a group of students and graduates of journalism and in communication careers, so by sharing the meme, the joke stops being comical and becomes humorous.

The Hypermediatic Enunciator humorist invites the Hypermediatic Enunciatee to laugh at himself, as both are identified with Peter, the target of the joke.

The Interactions of the Account with Its Collective and Environment

The enunciative matrix that I have just described is not only conditioning the laughable in social networks but also the interactions that occur among the account, the hypermediatic collective[7] that they comprise, and their environment. A Hypermediatic Enunciator can post a meme and receive comments that generate new laughable productions to which it replies, and that are only interpretable in dialogue. In this exchange, its figuration can vary from comical to humorous or any other type of enunciator.

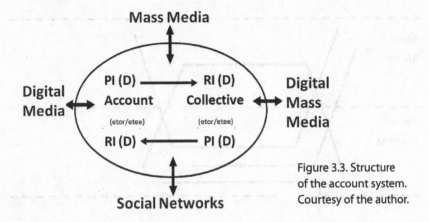

Figure 3.3. Structure of the account system. Courtesy of the author.

To this conditioning must be added that of the interactions that take place between the account and its outside. A mass medium, for example, can disseminate the production of a Hypermediatic Enunciator and make it famous by changing the symmetrical relationship it had with its collective. To approach these phenomena I will use two models, one focused on the account and the other on the hypermediatic circulation of its discursivity. The first can be represented as follows in figure 3.3.

The interactions between the account and its collective can be understood as a system of discursive production that I will call the *account system*.[8] In it, I find both the account and its collective alternately occupy the instance of discursive production PI(D) and discursive recognition RI(D). In turn, they are both enunciators and enunciatees, because the discourses exchanged construct them in this way. The system's environment is made up of other social network systems and media institutions (mass media, digital mass media, and digital media). The system maintains interpenetrative relationships with them. Why think of this relationship as a system? Because in the exchanges between the account and its collective, productive grammars are constituted; these grammars show processing logics that are different from the surrounding environment.

The other model to which I referred was proposed by Carlón ("La cultura" 46). It allows a description of the relations between the system of mass media and that of social networks in the discursive circulation that an account can generate. Carlón's research has found that four main types of circulation of meaning prevail in contemporary mediatization, which are illustrated in figure 3.4.

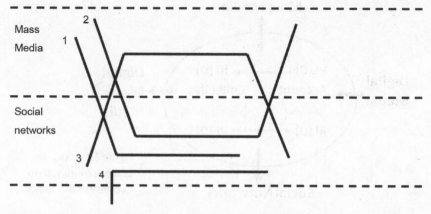

Figure 3.4. Meaning circulations diagram. Courtesy of Mario Carlón.

Carlón calls circulation 1 *descending-horizontal* because the discourse is produced in the mass media and generates new discourses that are propagated in social networks, such as the memes of the president during a nationally broadcast speech. Circulation 2 is *descending-ascending*, and it occurs when, following the above example, those memes ridiculing the president are taken up by a news program. The third circulation is *ascending-descending*, and it occurs when a comical video made on YouTube appears on television (which, in turn, disseminates it via social media). And, finally, the fourth type of circulation, ascending-horizontal, occurs when discourse is generated on the networks and propagated there without making a hypermediatic jump to the mass media.

Contemplating these types of circulations allows us to describe changes in the statutes of Hypermediatic Enunciators that affect their laughable discursivity and, at the same time, meaning twists that may occur in it due to circulation. A meme that is humorous in the account system can be transformed by hypermediatic circulation into a mockery and generate serious discursivities in which important social actors can participate, as happens in the case discussed below.

Dra. Pignata: A Case of Complex Satire

In what follows, I will analyze, according to the models presented, the satire of the fake account titled Dra. Alcira Pignata, who between 2010 and 2017 attacked the government of Cristina Fernández de Kirchner and Peronism. Her case is interesting because it exposes the complexity that the laughable nature of fake accounts can acquire and how their circulation provides input for trolls and hate speech, but also triggers collective and institutional regulation processes.

A Satire under the Cover of Comedy

As the account became popular, Dra. Pignata generated a varied satire; I will show some tweets to bring her production closer to the reader. On one hand, she published posts in which she wrote critiques within the usual limits established in media. One example was a tweet posted against Cintia García, a journalist who worked in state media and supported the government. The tweet featured an image of victims of a flood in the city of La Plata with the text, "These people say that it is very good that @cyngarciaradio earns $65,000 [Argentinian pesos] per month." The journalist's salary at the public broadcaster had recently been publicly revealed. The ironic comic enunciation exposed the contrast between those affected by a flood that the government did not prevent and the amount that the same government paid to García, far exceeding the average salary in Argentina which, in 2015, was 15,000 pesos.[9] But Dra. Pignata also produced satire unacceptable to the mass media, as can be seen in figure 3.5.

A racist post denigrated Milagro Sala, a Peronist political leader, by comparing her to an ape on account of her Indigenous roots.[10] Other publications vindicated the last military dictatorship, showing a photograph of their leader

Dra. Alcira Pignata
@drapignata

¿Ya está presa Milagro Sala?
9:15 PM - 22 Nov 2015

Figure 3.5. Tweet from Dra. Alcira Pignata: "Is Milagro Sala already in jail?" (11/22/2015)

with the ironic text, "How do I vote for the military?" (10/24/2015);[11] or used the deaths of protesters represented by state forces as political revenge, as happened with Santiago Maldonado and Rafael Nahuel with the tweet: "They wanted a dead man. I gave them two" (11/27/2017).[12] Or they directly fueled hatred, such as the publication that proposed attacking President Cristina Fernández de Kirchner: "RT if you think @CFKArgentina[13] is senile and unfit to govern. FAV[14] if it is necessary to shoot her in the face, too" (01/19/2015).

Considering these tweets, was Dra. Pignata's satire comical or humorous? Or was it simply a call for violence? Her followers, politicians, and journalists asked these same questions because of its fake nature,[15] which made possible a polysemic satire, without closure of meaning.

In the enunciative matrix I described, the Hypermediatic Enunciator of a fake account was defined by the *account enunciator*, because the figure of the *account owner* was unknown. In the case of Dra. Pignata, her profile had a photograph of Janet Reno, attorney general of the United States under Bill Clinton, accompanied by images that glorified that country or the last Argentine military dictatorship. Her utterances represented her as a retired lawyer who was also a Catholic, a Macrist,[16] a racist, a xenophobe, a homophobe, a fascist, and an anti-Peronist. The Hypermediatic Enunciator was comical because she made herself a laughable object by not censoring her fanaticism, which was inconsistent with the moral and customary norms that regulate public exchanges.

Dra. Pignata had no qualms about welcoming her new followers by saying, "Let it be known that I am against: Arabs, Hebrews, homosexuals, Blacks, Peronists, and scourge in general" (05/29/2014). Or to present as valid argument the assertion that "Blacks love Christmas and New Year's festivities because they have free rein to get drunk, shoot into the air, burn children, and gouge out their eyes" (12/23/2013). Through this comical enunciation, Dra. Pignata exhibited mockery, dark humor, and satirical attacks. It enabled her to say the most outrageous things under the guise of the laughable.

Dra. Pignata identified with a political group: the Macrists, supporters of Mauricio Macri, president of Argentina from 2015 to 209. Were they ridiculed and was there thus a humorous proposal that made them laugh at themselves? I would say that a few publications seemed to enable humor. One example was a tweet that showed an old photograph of Ku Klux Klan members with the following text: "Here, defining some names for Mauricio's cabinet" (1/23/2015). In this case, the Mediatic Enunciator included herself in the decision to define the cabinet of then candidate and later president Mauricio Macri among members of the Ku Klux Klan, identifying his political space with the violent far right. However, it is not this reflexive procedure, typical of humor, that prevailed; rather, in each enunciation, the object of satire was the political opponent of the Macrist collective as well as minorities in general. The comical framework was presented because of the exaggerations and moral incorrectness, but it did not ridicule the assumptions[17] of the utterances. What do I mean by this? To answer this question one can compare this character with another similar and very popular one in Argentina, in this case appearing on a TV comedy show: Micky Vainilla, a satirical caricature of a pop singer, a Nazi, identified with the prejudices and xenophobia of the inhabitants of the city of Buenos Aires, a district where Macrism has been winning since 2007.[18] In one of his sketches, Micky complains that the poor ask him for money in the street and accuses them of stealing from him because, in fact, they form a clandestine organization that collects alms in a common fund for drugs, alcohol, and prostitution.[19] The argument, taken to absurdity, ridicules the truism about the poor spending money on vices. This operation of ridiculing the grounds for criticism was not Dra. Pignata. In her case, the comical framework validated the attack as exaggerated and cruel, not unfounded, which safeguarded the assumptions of the Macrist identification collective in its condemnation of political opponents.

These qualities of Dra. Pignata's laughable enunciation, resistant to rapid closure of meaning, made possible the particular circulation that her discursivity had in the system of account and its environment.

The Hunt for Dra. Pignata

As described above, network accounts form systems with their collectives. In them, the continuous communicational exchanges establish productive grammars and relations of interpenetration with the environment. If we focus on the first aspect, we can outline four positions adopted by members of the collective concerning Dra. Pignata. The first one was that of someone who enjoyed the laughable, expressing it with peals of laughter or new laughable productions, often in a hostile and ironic style that might agree or not with the assumptions of the satire. The second was that of somebody who also enjoyed the laughable, although guiltily because it recognized that moral limits were being crossed. The third position agreed with the assumptions of the satire, though adding serious attacks to the target of the mockery. And the last one was the offended one, either by identifying with that target or by considering the content aggressive and in bad taste. It was this last position that provoked a drastic change in the status of the Hypermediatic Enunciatee by taking the first step toward revealing the identity of the account owner. But before tackling this issue, let us look at the system's relationship to its environment and its hypermediatic circulation.

From the beginning, Dra. Pignata established a strong link with her environment because her satire was fed by current events built by the media's agenda, participating in trending hashtags and tagging the public figures she was addressing. They, by responding to her, made her group of both followers and detractors grow. Six months after opening her account, Dra. Pignata made her first hypermediatic leap and ascended to mass media with a comedy slot on the FM Blue radio station that ran for a year. This presence, added to her growth in the networks, earned her the recognition of the mass media as a "controversial tweetstar,"[20] but within the field of the laughable, which would change drastically on April 15, 2014, with the tweet: "Impressive crowd of people to see the eclipse. @ Planetarium Galileo Galilei." The link in the tweet redirected to the account of the then minister of culture of the city of Buenos Aires, Hernán Lombardi, which revealed that the person who had composed the tweet was one of his secretaries. Dra. Pignata deleted the tweet after a few minutes, but a member of the collective managed to copy it first and it quickly spread in the networks, reaching mass media. The fact that Dra. Pignata, who was accused of fomenting hatred toward Kirchnerist militants and journalists, was an official of the Macri government moved her from the realm of the merely laughable to that of the political. The same day, Lombardi put up a funny post denying that he owned the Twitter account. However, INADI[21] began an investigation to which Lombardi responded by protecting his secretaries under the argument of freedom of expression. This episode increased Dra. Pignata's popularity by making her known to international media such as the BBC ("Why Argentines mourned"). By 2016, she had 56,600 followers and a Klout index of influence of 57/100,[22] which implied a high average of retweets.

The tweet transformed interactions within and outside the account system because Dra. Pignata's detractors identified her with Macrism and accused her of circulating propaganda and inciting hatred at the state's expense. For its part, the Macrist collective endorsed her comedy more strongly and defended her against attacks. But the transformation of the Hypermediatic Enunciator's identity would not stop there.

On June 20, 2017, Dra. Pignata published a cruel jibe against Máximo Kirchner,[23] laughing at the death of his father, Néstor Kirchner, former president and leader of Kirchnerism. In response, the Kirchnerist account @Casa-Rosada2003-2015[24] published a document showing that the alleged owner of Dr. Pignata's account worked at the Ministry of Culture of the City of Buenos

Aires and including his name, surname, salary, a photograph, and the following text: "We demand that @herlombardi make a statement about [XX],[25] a public employee of Culture who is committed to this." The tweet caused a great stir among the Kirchnerist collective, whose reactions ranged from indignation to offline physical threats, like a tweet by @Quiquin: "Piece of shit, I know you, we're going to meet, you won't know where it [the bullet] comes from!"

Neither Lombardi nor XX ever confirmed or denied the data on Dra. Pignata; the mass media did not divulge it, while the news portals did. Its propagation ended up establishing them as interpretants who acted every time Dra. Pignata engaged in some especially offensive mockery, as happened with the tweet I mentioned earlier regarding Santiago Maldonado and Rafael Nahuel in 2017. At that time, the journalist Nora Falabella tweeted the photo of XX with the following text: "Look who is behind Dr. Pignata. His name is [XX] and he works at RTA[26] as the main collaborator of Minister Lombardi. Remember this image in case you see him in the street" (11/28/2017).

This identification of the *owner enunciator* transformed the Hypermediatic Enunciator and its laughable production because it uncovered his fake account, which in turn caused the comic interpretation to compete with the cynical one when Dra. Pignata was identified as a Macrist enunciator who cruelly mocked his political opponents, but also minorities, human rights, etc.

On the Hypermediatic Laughable and Its Conditionings

I hope I have demonstrated here the usefulness of the tools proposed for the study of hypermediatic humor. The model of an enunciative matrix applied to the interfaces of social networks allow us to observe how the laughable is generated in the articulation of levels. In the case of Dra. Pignata, we were able to elucidate how the comical, at the hypermediatic level, not only covered heartless mockery and cruel, dark humor but also sarcasm and serious insults. On the other hand, we noticed that this comical level ridiculed the Hypermediatic Enunciator but not the assumptions of its satire, which allowed the Macrist collective to propagate its tweets without becoming an object of derision itself. In this way, Dra. Pignata constructed a laughable device that made hostility toward a political opponent possible without the risks associated with doing so in the realm of the serious.

To understand the meaning of her satire, it was not enough to look at the matrix and the account system. It was also necessary to address the interactions related to the experience, because they were the ones that transformed her status as a Hypermediatic Enunciator. When the owner was revealed, Dra.

Pignata stopped being a fake account, which altered her laughable enunciation.

Combining the proposed levels of analysis allows us to generate knowledge not only about what is legitimate but also about what role these publications play in public debate. With the rise of individuals and collectives to hypermediatization, a replicating democracy has been formed (Dader 48) in which a part of the citizenry, upon reaching significant scales of distribution, joins the daily political dialogue. The studied satire is established in this democracy along with the burden of information and opinion that it already had, but without its institutional regulation and leaving traces of the effects it produces. This is a novelty for studies of the laughable because previously it was difficult to know what effects it had on social life. It was only possible to carry out studies that allowed access to fragmented and laboratory-based recognition of the laughable. Today, however, every meme, comment, appropriation, etc., is accessible to the analyst and allows him/her to reconstruct which meanings are generated by its circulation and which actors involved. The analytical tools proposed here aim at creating levels of observation to take advantage of this opportunity. Perhaps they will help us to better understand the operations of hypermediatic humor, this new device that continuously frames the social in the unstable games of the laughable.

Notes

1 I give the name media social networks to the media networks that emerge from Internet-based media (Facebook, Twitter, YouTube, Instagram, etc.).

2 It is worth clarifying that when I say interpretant I am not talking about an interpreter. I am alluding to the Peircean notion that in one of its definitions understands it as a sign raised in the relationship between a sign-vehicle and an object on some basis (Peirce 1974).

3 By laughable I mean the semiotic domain that contains genres, types, and discursive procedures that promote laughter (Traversa 51). I will use the term humorous to indicate a particular way of generating the laughable—that which implies a reflexive enunciation that includes the enunciator and enunciatee in the target of the mockery. I will only use humor in a generic way when I talk about hypermediatic humor.

4 Many observations in this section and a later one are raised in Fraticelli, "El humor hipermediático."

5 Following Verón, I understand the productive conditions of the discourses as the determinations that indicate the restrictions of their generation (conditions of production) and reception (conditions of recognition).

6 Throughout this chapter I will define circulation as the difference between the moments of production and recognition (Verón 129).

7 By hypermediatic collective, I mean the grouping of individuals concentrated in a focus of interest produced by Internet-based media and telephony. For their qualities, see Fraticelli, "Los colectivos mediáticos" (47).

8 When talking about "accounts" I refer to what is usually called "user account" but, to develop an enunciative approach, I prefer to remove the term "user" because it comes from the field of computer science and is usually loaded with subjectivity in communication studies.

9 At that time, $1.00 was worth $9.20. García's salary was $7,065 while the average salary was $1,630.

10 Milagro Sala is an Argentine political, social, and Indigenous leader of the Tupac Amaru Neighborhood Organization, an organization especially known for its work in the construction of thousands of homes in the province of Jujuy. At the time of the post, she was a provincial deputy in the legislature for the Frente Unidos y Organizados de Jujuy, parties aligned with the government. The opposition was calling for her imprisonment for alleged acts of corruption.

11 The last civil-military dictatorship that ruled Argentina between 1976 and 1983. It took the form of a bureaucratic-authoritarian state and was characterized by the establishment of a systematic plan of state terrorism, which included the theft of babies (and concealment of their identity) and the many disappearances. The publication featured Jorge Rafael Videla, de facto president between 1976 and 1981.

12 Santiago Maldonado and Rafael Nahuel were two young men who died in two repressive procedures carried out by national security forces during the Macri administration. Maldonado's case had great national repercussions because he was missing for two and a half months. During that time, the opposition accused the government of being responsible for his disappearance until his body was found in the Chubut River. The day of Maldonado's wake, Nahuel was killed by a shot in the back in a repressive action by the Prefectura Naval Argentina against the Mapuche community Lafken Winkul Mapu. In the post, Dr. Pignata dedicates his death to all those who had accused the government of Maldonado's disappearance.

13 @CFKKArgentina is the Twitter account of Cristina Fernández de Kirchner.

14 FAV stands for favorite or like.

15 Examples of these questions can be found in Salinas and Mariano Suárez.

16 In Argentina, Macrists are the collective identified with Mauricio Macri, political leader of PRO and Cambiemos, president between 2015 and 2019 and main opponent of Kirchnerism, a collective identified with former presidents Néstor Kirchner and Cristina Fernández de Kirchner, vice president of the nation as of writing. While Macrism is identified with the center-right (free market, minimal state, preeminence of individual over social rights), Kirchnerism and Peronism are identified with the center-left (regulated market, strong presence of the state, preeminence of social rights over individual rights).

17 Throughout this chapter, I will deal in a broad sense with the concept of assumption, including the actual assumptions and the implicit assumptions defined by Ducrot (11).

18 In Fraticelli, "Los colectivos mediáticos," I analyze Micky Vainilla along with other characters from the *Peter Capusotto y sus videos* show and his videos.

19 The sketch can be seen at Saborido and Capusotto.
20 An example of this treatment can be found in "Quién es la Dra. Pignata."
21 National Institute against Discrimination, Xenophobia, and Racism.
22 Klout was an online tool used to measure influence in social networks. Its index ranged from 0 to 100. The service ceased operation in 2018.
23 Máximo Kirchner is a politician, son of former presidents Néstor Kirchner and Cristina Fernández de Kirchner.
24 The Twitter account @CasaRosada2003-2015 was the official account of the seat of the executive power of Argentina until Cristina Fernández de Kirchner left office. When Macri assumed the presidency, the account was not handed over to his government, but continued to publish, directed by Kirchnerism. The account has since disappeared from Twitter.
25 The name of the alleged owner of Dr. Pignata's account is not published here because it was not confirmed by Lombardi, the defendant, or any state institution.
26 RTA is the abbreviation for Radio y Televisión Argentina, an Argentine public company that manages the state-owned media that was headed by Hernán Lombardi in the government of Mauricio Macri.

Works Cited

Apter, Michael, and Ken Smith. "Humor and the Theory of Psychological Reversals." *It's a Funny Thing, Humor,* edited by Anthony J. Chapman and Hugh C. Foot, Oxford: Pergamon Press, 1997, pp. 95–134.

Bateson, Gregory. "Una teoría del juego y la fantasía." *Pasos hacia una ecología de la mente,* translated by Ramón Alcalde, Buenos Aires: Carlos Lohle, 1985 [1972], pp. 131–142.

Berger, Peter. *Redeeming Laughter: The Comic Dimension of Human Experience.* New York: Walter de Gruyter, 1997.

Carlón, Mario. "Apropiación contemporánea de la teoría comunicacional de Eliseo Verón. La dimension temporal" *Comunicación, campo(s) teorías y problemas. Una perspectiva internacional,* edited by E. Vizer and C. Vidales, Barcelona: Editorial Comunicación Social, 2016, pp. 125–140.

———. *Circulación del sentido y construcción de colectivos en una sociedad hipermediatizada.* San Luis, Argentina: Nueva Editorial Universitaria, 2020, http://www.neu.unsl.edu.ar/wp-content/uploads/2020/08/Circulacio%CC%81n-del-sentido.pdf.

———. "La cultura mediática contemporánea: otro motor, otra combustión, (segunda apropiación de la teoría de la comunicación de Eliseo Verón: la dimensión especial)." *A circulação discursiva: entre produção e reconhecimento,* edited by Paulo César Castro, Maceió: Edufal, 2017, pp. 25–48.

Dader, José Luis. "Ciberdemocracia y comunicación política virtual: el futuro de la ciudadanía electrónica tras la era de la televisión." *Comunicación política en televisión y nuevos medios,* edited by Salomé Berrocal Gonzalo, Barcelona: Ariel, 2003, pp. 309–342.

Ducrot, Oswald. *El decir y lo dicho.* Buenos Aires: Hachette, 1984.

Fraticelli, Damián. "El humor hipermediático. La nueva era de la mediatización reidera." *Arruinando chistes. Panorama de los estudios del humor y lo cómico,* edited by

Maria Burkart, Damián Fraticelli, and Tomás Várgangy, Buenos Aires: Teseo, 2020, pp.107–121.

———. *El ocaso triunfal de los programas cómicos. De Viendo a Biondi a Peter Capusotto y sus videos.* Buenos Aires: Teseo. 2019, www.editorialteseo.com/archivos/17065/el-ocaso-triunfal-de-los-programas-comicos/.

———. "Los colectivos mediáticos de las redes. Algunas observaciones desde el humor ¿y más allá?" *Inmediaciones de la Comunicación,* vol. 14, no. 1, 2019, pp. 47–61, https://doi.org/10.18861/ic.2019.14.1.2885.

Freud, Sigmund. *El chiste y su relacion con el inconsciente: Obras completas.* 1905. Translated by José Etcheverry, Buenos Aires: Amorrortu, 2006.

Goffman, Erving. *FrameAnalysis: Los marcos de la experiencia.* 1975. Translated by José Luis Rodríguez, Madrid: Centro de Investigaciones Sociológicas, 2006.

Peirce, Charles S. *La Ciencia de la semiótica.* Translated by Armando Sercovich, Buenos Aires: Nueva Visión, 1974.

"Quién es la Dra. Pignata, la cuenta más polémica de Twitter." *Perfil,* 30 June 2014, www.perfil.com/noticias/sociedad/quien-es-la-dra-alcira-pignata-la-cuenta-mas-polemica-de-twitter-20140529-0040.phtml.

Saborido, Pedro, and Diego Capusotto. "Peter Capusotto 19–07–10 Micky Vainilla." *YouTube,* uploaded by Televisión Pública, 20 July 2010, www.youtube.com/watch?v=obEdNb8Yf4c.

Salinas, Juan. "¿Reír o llorar? Denunciar ante el INADI a la Dra. Pignatta [*sic*] es un absurdo." *Pájaro Rojo,* 1 June 2014, pajarorojo.com.ar/reir-o-llorar-denunciar-ante-el-inadi-a-la-dra-pignatta-es-un-absurdo/.

Steimberg, Oscar. *Semiótica de los medios masivos: el pasaje a los medios de los géneros populares.* Buenos Aires: Atuel, 1993.

———. "Sobre algunos temas y problemas del análisis del humor gráfico." *Signo y seña,* no. 12, 2001, pp. 97–134.

Suárez, Mariano. "Polémico tuit de la Dra. Pignata generó un cruce político." *24 con,* 21 June 2016, www.24con.com/nota/149907-polemico-tuit-de-la-dra-pignatta-genero-un-cruce-politico/.

Traversa, Oscar. "Dispositivo-enunciación: en torno a sus modos de articularse." *Inflexiones del discurso.* Buenos Aires: Santiago Arcos, 2014, pp.63–86.

———. "Notas acerca de lo reidero en las tapas de revistas." *Figuraciones. Teoría y crítica de artes,* no. 5, 2009, pp. 49–63.

Verón, Eliseo. *La mediatización. Cursos y conferencias.* Buenos Aires: Universidad de Buenos Aires, 1986.

———. *La semiosis social: Fragmentos de una teoría de la discursividad.* Buenos Aires: Gedisa, 1987.

"Why Argentines Mourned the Death of a Hateful Fictional Character." *BBC News,* 7 Feb. 2015, www.bbc.com/news/blogs-trending-31131948.

4

Satire as the Voice of Resistance in Guillermo Aquino's *El Sketch*

Alberto Centeno-Pulido

According to Swiss-German philosopher Byung-Chul Han, individuals in contemporary society burn out due to an excess of positivity in their lives. When people are driven by a demand not to fail and to persevere, they become self-exploited subjugated laborers (Han, *Psychopolitics* 13). Individuals do not see themselves as subjects, but rather as projects—objects, really—and are constantly looking to reinvent themselves and show that they lead positive, happy lives. This "achievement-subject" lives in a society that is increasingly "shedding the negativity of prohibition and commandments and presenting itself as a society of freedom" (Han, *Burnout* 36). Han argues that individuals in the postmodern world, which he characterizes as a world in which subjects are not told what they can or cannot do by an external source of authority, but rather an internal one, have lost their ability to express rage, since rage is something that can only be expressed at an antagonizing Other and not at the self. Rage is fundamentally confrontational and aggressive. So is satire. Satirical humor is an attack on the status quo, aimed at highlighting problematic societal norms that audiences will reflect upon and ultimately question.

In this article, I explore the role of rage, expressed through satire, in the Argentinian context depicted in Guillermo Aquino's *El Sketch*, a series of short videos in which Aquino uses humor as a powerful tool to awaken the consciousness of the audience to the reality around them. Socioeconomic problems in the country are not a new phenomenon, and it is generally acknowledged that Argentinians are used to living in a continual state of crisis; inflation, hyperinflation, and recession—and the societal problems that they cause—seem to follow each other in an endless loop. Ideologies and discourses (Peronism, populism, religion, nationalism, etc.) that have shaped the twentieth and twenty-first centuries in Argentinian society, and their buoyancy or apparent decline, follow this same logic: initial illusion followed by generalized disappointment, then a subsequent promise of change that brings renewed illusion and inevitably gives way to more disappointment. Events that marked the beginning of the twenty-first century in the country—for example, the draconian economic measures imposed by the IMF in exchange for economic relief after the 2001 crisis—have repeated themselves fewer than 20 years later. Discourses and policies that articulate the nation are broken and ineffectual. They create pain and apathy. Arguably, in a context of constant pain—social and economic—any group of people is likely to develop a certain detachment from the surrounding reality over a period of time. It is only natural that individuals look for ways to disconnect. Coincidentally, capital is happy to provide the means for people to achieve that goal. By reframing the narrative and turning negatives into positives—the good old-fashioned spin—a new common sense is created. Lack of access to basic rights such as food, shelter, employment, or health care is glamorized and turned into lifestyle choices that individuals assume of their own free will. The illusion of freedom is very powerful from the economic standpoint because it does not present conflict, which is inefficient, as Han puts it. Thus, if rage is the way to confront this new common sense, satirists—who express this rage and at the same time create a new "common dissenting sense," which Critchley calls *dissensus communis* (19)—become crucial in postmodern society, as they are the embodiment of resistance.

Argentinian comedian Guillermo Aquino has a long trajectory of comedy writing for television and theater. He is the creator of a series of comedy sketches appropriately named *El Sketch* that began in 2017 and was aired on *La Hormiga Imperial*, a daily show of C5N, an Argentinian news network. Since then, he has produced 63 videos for this series, and maintains an active presence on social media. The main character in these sketches is Guillermo, Aquino's screen persona. This chapter analyzes two of the sketches in this series, which became a viral sensation on social media in 2018, and to this date have over one million combined views.[1] The first sketch is a review of real newspaper headlines published by major Argentinian outlets, which are presented as the ideas of an editor of a daily publication destined for mass consumption in a brainstorming session. Aquino's character presents itself as the raging voice that rejects these ideas-turned-headlines because they are essentially normalizing, and even glamorizing, manifestly unjust situations (poverty, lack of access to basic products, or downsizing—if not altogether elimination—of labor rights due to policies imposed by the IMF). These headlines make sense in a social environment in which freedom is only apparent. When individuals are expected not to be subjected to the aforementioned "negativity of prohibitions and commandments" and declare themselves free,

they are "free" to look for food in the garbage or to consider reduced working hours—and reduced earnings—as something more valuable than money;
they are even "free" to eat dirt as a way of losing weight. Guillermo reacts to all
this illusion of choice by satirically expressing outrage in the face of it.

The second sketch is set at the beginning of the year 2018 when Guillermo
receives a call from himself at the end of the year. In this call, future Guillermo warns present Guillermo of all the things that are about to happen in
the country (skyrocketing dollar exchange rates, price inflation, the passage
of an abortion law that does not ensure the right to abortion, among others),
thereby immediately killing the optimistic mood that the Guillermo of early
2018 shows at the beginning of the sketch. In this case, the rage is still there,
although it is not as dramatically displayed by the character. The overall sensation is that Guillermo awakens the consciousness of the audience by pointing
humorously at the things that the audience should feel uncomfortable about.

Guillermo Aquino's humor is used as a subversive mechanism against this
new postmodern, common-sense "freedom," the ultimate objective of which
is to turn individuals into self-exploited "projects." Critchley asserts that humor "defamiliariz[es] the familiar, demythologiz[es] the exotic and invert[s]
the world of common sense" (65). In a world where the new "familiar" and
the new "common sense" are the achievement-subject described in Han's
work, which in turn is mediated by a socioeconomic need to make sure that
this very subject is comfortable in its existence (by way of unreal—exotic,
glamorized—ideologies destined to manufacture consent, to borrow from
Chomsky), it is necessary to have someone/something that helps with the
subversion—defamiliarization, demythologization, and inversion—of this
paradigm and ultimately brings the audience back from that state of detachment from the surrounding reality, whether it is through the satirical rage
displayed in the first sketch or by compelling the audience to reassess its collective identity.

Satiric Rage

Critchley describes the physically violent nature of laughter, in the sense that
the body is subject to rather violent movement when laughter erupts. Laughter is thus a release of tension, an explosion. But a joke is something more.
The result of the joke is laughter, but that laughter brings about a change in
the perception of reality: "A true joke . . . suddenly and explosively lets us
see the familiar defamiliarized, the ordinary made extraordinary and the real
rendered surreal" (10). This *surrealization,* as Critchley puts it, is a process
by which we "become philosophical spectators upon our lives" (18). In other

words, humor has the capacity of allowing us to see what we are. Of course, being able to see what we are may also mean we do not like what we see in ourselves. This feeling can, crucially, provoke laughter because we are troubled by what we experience:

> If humor tells you something about who you are, then it might be a reminder that you are perhaps not the person you would like to be. As such, the very relativity of humor might be said to contain an indirect appeal that this place stands in need of change, that history is, indeed, . . . a nightmare from which we are all trying to awake. (Critchley 75)

The comedic voice is the voice of common sense, which reminds us of the way things are and at the same time adds a different perspective to the status quo. Satire is ideal for this, not so much because of what it does, but because of how it does it. Satire is fundamentally violent—not in the sense of causing physical harm, but in the sense of looking for a reaction caused by an attack. Political satire is described using rather violent language as "'an attack on or criticism of any stupidity'" (Cuddon 202, qtd. in Alonso 11), "'verbal aggression in which one aspect of historical reality is exposed to ridicule'" (Fletcher ix, qtd in Alonso 11); and "satire itself is intended as a form of aggression to expose . . . problems" (Paine Caufield 7). In the postmodern world, where people no longer confront external impositions that tell them what they need to do or not do but instead live by a self-imposed constant need for "achievement," the act of subversion of the status quo requires metaphorically bringing the volume to 11: "[t]o have an effect, the warning signals have to be deafening" (Critchley 36).

The Power of Negativity

As stated, Han describes postmodern society and the individual's relationship with it as the triumph of positivity (*Burnout* 1). Contrary to what one might intuit with this affirmation, Han considers that positivity is indeed detrimental to individuals, particularly those who are members of the workforce. In modern history, the relationship between the individual and capital has essentially been one of struggle: the imbalance in the power structure is conducive to permanent conflict, predicated upon a reaction to that which is different, the Other. This conflict, it turns out, is inefficient (economically speaking) in a globalized context, in which boundaries (in the sense of limitation of movement—particularly of wealth, not so much of people) tend to disappear. If conflict, as I say, is negative, and negativity is inefficient in terms of the bottom line, then it becomes necessary to change the role of individuals in their relationship to the system. People are no longer "subject" to a discipline that emanates from the unequal relationship that they may have with an outside—different, Other—force. In modern, disciplinarian society, the dialogue between master and servant (or, as Han puts it, "master and slave") is mediated by the knowledge that, for one to exercise power over the other, the freedom of the subjugated individual must be curtailed. Obedience is a necessary component of productivity, for if individuals react and defend themselves, productivity will be negatively affected.

In postmodern society, instead, the relationship between the individual and an external disciplinary force is eliminated. The individual is not bound by obedience, but by achievement. This new achievement-subject self-exploits while maintaining the illusion of freedom, since there is no perceived external oppressive force. As Han puts it:

> The achievement-subject stands free from any external instance of domination. . . . However, the disappearance of domination does not entail freedom. Instead, it makes freedom and constraint coincide. Thus, the achievement-subject gives itself over to *compulsive freedom*— that is, to the *free constraint* of maximizing achievement. Excess work and performance escalate into auto-exploitation. This is more efficient than allo-exploitation, for the feeling of freedom attends it. (*Burnout* 11)[2]

In this context, subjects see themselves as "projects [that subjugate themselves] to internal limitations and self-constraints, which are taking the form of compulsive achievement and optimization" (Han, *Psychopolitics* 1). Failure within this paradigm is perceived as a lack of drive to achieve since the individual is ostensibly free to do just that. This creates a reaction, much like it did when the oppressor was an external entity. This time, the conflict or negativity is not directed to the Other, but the self: "Under the neoliberal regime of auto-exploitation, people are turning their aggression *against themselves*. This auto-aggressivity means that the exploited are not inclined to revolution so much as depression" (Han, *Psychopolitics* 7).

The nature of work—and life—in this society, in which every activity must be perpetually optimized, becomes repetitive, mechanical, unquestioning. Optimization implies "acceleration and hyperactivity" as well as "poor[ness] in interruption" (*Burnout* 22). As a result of the ever-increasing search for optimization, Han argues, "we are also losing the capacity for rage" (*Burnout* 22). In this case, rage, which could a priori be considered a negative and undesirable trait, becomes a tool of resistance, since it "puts the present as a whole into question. It presupposes an interrupting pause in the present" (*Burnout* 22). The capacity to express rage would afford the individual an essential tool for facing a system that only gives the illusion of choice:

> Intelligence means *choosing between (inter legere)*. It is not entirely free in so far as it is caught in a *between*. . . . Therefore, intelligence does not really exercise *free choice:* it can only *select* among the offerings the system affords. Intelligence follows the logic of a system. It is system-immanent. A given system defines a given intelligence. Accordingly, intelligence has no access to what is *wholly Other*. . . . In contrast, the idiot . . . takes leave of the prevailing system—that is, abandons intelligence. (Han, *Burnout* 85)

Thus, the idiot, or the buffoon who speaks truth to power, "represents a figure of resistance opposing the violence of consensus" (Han, *Burnout* 83). Humor pulls us from this violent consensus—which equates to the common sense of this new paradigm—thus functioning as *"dissensus communis"* (Critchley 19). Through satire—and, therefore, aggressively and with rage—the idiot forces us to confront what we do not like about what we are, simultaneously revealing to us that a different way of facing reality is possible.

Guillermo Aquino and *El Sketch*

Guillermo Aquino is a comedic Argentinian actor and writer with a long career in comedy production on Argentinian television. He began his career as a scriptwriter in one of the most influential TV shows in Argentina, *Duro de domar,* in which he created the character Paco Cambiasso, a kid who hates celebrities and spends his days watching TV with a friend and criticizing them. One day, trying to fix the aerial antenna of his TV, Paco is hit by lightning. As a result, he transforms into the different celebrities that he hates so much when triggered by things he sees or hears around him.[3]

This traumatic story of the origin of Paco Cambiasso as a character is to a certain extent linked to Aquino's personal story. Explaining his decision to become a comedic actor, he recounts in an interview how his mother tumbled down a flight of stairs very late in her pregnancy with him. He equates this traumatic episode with how superheroes acquire their powers: "My mom was rushed to the hospital crying [things] like 'I destroyed my kid' [*Lo hice mierda al pibe*] and . . . well, she actually did" (*El Destape*). The interviewer retorts that it is a good story of his origins "not so much as a superhero, but because your humor has a great deal to do with laughing about how we are being destroyed [*nos estamos haciendo mierda*] every day" (*El Destape*).

After creating Paco Cambiasso, Aquino developed a theater project called *Antisocial,* which he considers the seed of his TV/Internet production called *El Sketch,* a series of sketches to which the two Aquino creations discussed in this chapter belong: "I felt it was a continuity in the style of characters, dialogue, dynamics, and the concept of the kid against the world, but [also] the world against that individual" (Provéndola, "Guille Aquino"; my translation). This is the overall feeling that viewers experience when watching these sketches. Aquino's humor is of a confrontational nature, because for him, "humor breaks limits by provoking and questioning us at a shattering pace" (Provéndola, "Guille Aquino"; my translation). The fast pace in the sketch results not only from the speed with which the dialogue is delivered but also from a masterful operation of technical elements, most notably editing. *El Sketch* presents a wide variety of topics, centered primarily around social issues: drug use, family, friendship and interpersonal relationships, sexism, sex, racism, homophobia, transphobia, the influence of social media, housing, and politics, among many others. The fast rhythm of the pieces—both in terms of dialogue and of editing—is at times of a quasi-mechanical nature that does not leave breathing room to assimilate what is being said. Thus, we witness aggression not only in terms of content but also in terms of form. I will expand more on this point later in this chapter when I analyze the sketches.

On a related note, Aquino has acknowledged the influence of satirical shows from the United States, most notably *The Simpsons.* The title of his YouTube interview for *El Destape* is "Me crié hablando en Simpson" (I grew up speaking in Simpsonese). Guehlstorf, Hallstrom, and Morris identify three types of political humor in *The Simpsons:*

> 1) humor about elites and leadership; 2) comedy targeting the irrationality of the American mass public; 3) obscure and humorous political references that are disconnected from the episode but offer gratification to politically and historically informed viewers. (212)

The first type of humor identifies and lampoons stereotypical behaviors of institutional and social leaders, such as politicians, media personalities, or educators, but also serves as a vehicle for criticism of the general public, who "usually fail to act upon the inabilities and corruption of elites, and when they do, it is rarely through political or legal avenues, but rather through individual action" (Guehlstorf, Hallstrom, and Morris 216). The second type of humor is partially related to this, since

> citizens are consistently portrayed as politically apathetic, ideologically unsophisticated, ignorant of other nations or cultures, unmotivated,

and generally disinterested [*sic*] in the . . . political process, particularly at the national level. (Guehlstorf, Hallstrom, and Morris 218)

The third type of humor consists of content-related "winks" included for the benefit of a minority of viewers who "get it," with that *it* being "yet another level of comprehension and implied intent" (Guehlstorf, Hallstrom, and Morris 224). Mutatis mutandis, a close look at the content of Aquino's sketches reveals multiple levels of similarity between them and *The Simpsons*. But the implications of these similarities go even further since they seem to place Aquino's work squarely in the middle of a framework of digital satirical content creators who "discursively negotiate local and regional identities and . . . question sociocultural values while developing a postmodern reappropriation of transnational media languages and entertainment formats" (Alonso 122). In essence, we are dealing with a hybrid, and even a tropicalized[4] (see Aparicio and Chávez-Silverman), cultural product, resulting from the adoption of referents and modalities from the North, adapted to express the idiosyncratic needs of the local South and eventually amplified to a wider *geolinguistic audience* (see Alonso 147).

The next sections offer a close reading of two of Guillermo Aquino's pieces, which appeared in late 2018 on YouTube. These two sketches encapsulate the concepts introduced in the previous sections regarding the role of the comedian as a vehicle for the expression of the rage that we all should feel when confronted with the reality in which we live, as well as, more generally, the use of satire as a mode of resistance against the consensus.

Palermo News

This sketch takes place in the meeting room of a daily newspaper/magazine at the beginning of the day.[5] The staff is meeting to decide what content will be featured in the next issue. It is, coincidentally, the first day on the job for Guillermo, the protagonist of the sketch. He sits opposite Lu (played by Lucía Iacono[6]), the editor who is chairing the meeting. Since it is Guillermo's first day, Lu asks him first to provide an idea for content and a headline:

Lu: Well, Guille, what do you have?
Guille: Umm, well, I did an Internet search. . . .
Lu: Mmm-hmm.
Guille: . . . and it turns out that the poverty indices in Buenos Aires have increased, like, a lot. . . .
Lu: And what would be the headline for you?
Guille: According to official reports? . . .

Lu: Of course, yes, obviously. . . .

Guille: OK. . . .

Lu: . . . we are reporting information, right?

Guille: "City of Buenos Aires," colon, "poverty index doubles."

Lu: Mmmm, a bit of a downer, don't you think? I don't know, I mean, that headline. . . .

Guille: OK. . . .

Lu: You have to consider that this is for people—

Guille: Yeah, well, it is a bit—

Lu:—who are reading it on the bus, I mean. Actually, these people don't really give a shit about what you're saying, you know what I mean?

Guille: So, we want kind of a more social tone, right?[7]

The intention of the entire sketch is set in this initial exchange: people are (or want to be) indifferent to the reality that surrounds them. The goal of the news is not to bring their spirits down but to offer readers a "more social tone." "Social" here cannot be interpreted as socially conscious, but rather the opposite: mindless entertainment to help readers go about their day without having to focus too much—if at all—on reality. The dominant narrative does not seek to bring the individual's spirit down by presenting reality. Reality is depressing, it is "boring," and it is also inconvenient because unmediated exposure to it can potentially create conditions in which individuals become aware that their situation is fundamentally unfair. Living in a mediated reality, provided by those who control the narrative, postmodern achievement-subjects do not consider that the system is flawed. Rather, *they* are flawed. If/when they fail, it is because they did not work hard enough on themselves—their projects. Furthermore, much like the second type of humor identified in *The Simpsons*—criticizing the citizenry's apathy—the jab works because it reflects a shared attitude and shows a side of society with which said society may not be comfortable. From the beginning, the audience is forced to examine itself and see what it may not like to see. Crucially, the "indirect appeal" that Critchley (75) mentions is about to get increasingly more direct, both in content and in form, as evidenced by the sketch's next joke:

Lu: Yeah, OK, but, I mean, these "poor" [Lu makes the gesture of air quotes] people you are talking about. . . . These people, what are they lacking? . . . Alcohol? . . . Guns? . . . Drugs? . . . A CD by La Beriso?

GA: Well, uh, food . . . basically.

Lu: And how many people are we talking about? Twenty? Thirty?

Guille: Two hundred thousand people.

Lu: OK, I've got it . . . "Argentinian Passions: The Decency of Garbage Scavengers" [A *Clarín* newspaper screenshot with that headline appears].[8]

Here many layers intersect. First, there is the assumption that the needs of poor and marginalized people are limited to stereotypically thuggish objects of consumption, such as drugs, alcohol, and guns. The addition of a CD by the Argentinian band La Beriso as one of those needs lends a local nuance to the joke, aligning with what David Critchley argues that humor manages to do: it reveals to us what we as a collective may not want to see. The band La Beriso is part of the *rock barrial* movement within Argentina's *rock nacional* scene. *Rock barrial* is characterized by themes relating to the experiences of the young people who live in working-class and impoverished neighborhoods in the Buenos Aires metropolitan area. Thus, the "need" for a recording by La Beriso is another stereotypical characterization of the poor and their non-normative wants, judged by Lu (and the people she represents) as foolish and worthy of scorn. Guille responds that what these people need is food, and he does so in a tone that indicates incredulity at what he has just heard.

Second, there is a banalization of the phenomenon based merely on the number of people who are affected by this situation. When Guillermo says that 200,000 people are affected by this poverty, the reaction that we get from Lu and the others present in the meeting is not outrage or sadness, but rather a headline—indeed, a real headline from *Clarín*, one of the country's major newspapers—that responds to a rather perverse logic: If so many people are having to go through the garbage to eat, it is not because of a systemic failure that prevents them from meeting their basic needs, but rather because they are immersed in a project, which happens to be survival, and they are fully and passionately invested in reaching that goal.

The sketch continues with a rapid succession of socioeconomic problems pointed out by Guillermo and answered in headline form by Lu. Guillermo points out that retirees will have to pay taxes on their pensions. Lu counters with a headline from *La Nación*, which suggests that the workforce should start getting used to the idea of working until the age of 80. Guillermo points out that many clothing brands are suspending operations in the country and moving elsewhere, thereby hurting the economy. The sketch continues in this way, with Lu giving another headline:

Lu: Extreme Minimalism . . . [*Clarín* headline on screen]
Man 1: Genius!
Lu: . . . people who discard almost all material things.

Guille: But who says that is necessarily a good thing?

Lu: What do you mean? The Chinese lady that teaches people how to fold shirts on Netflix—

Guille: What?

Lu: —I don't know, I mean, do you have anything against Chinese people?

Man 1: You are on a roll, Lu.

Guille: Is this real?

Woman 1: I like the human angle of that.

Guille: Are you all real?

Man 2: I know a poor person and he's going to suffer.

Guille: What the hell?[9]

All of Guille's comments in this excerpt indicate the character's attitude toward what he hears right through to the end of the sketch. Guille grows increasingly frustrated and incredulous about what he is hearing, and it only gets worse. He is, in essence, the idiot who is trying to break the accepted consensus. This is the onset of rage, which will develop as the sketch advances. Remember that, according to Han, intelligence necessarily implies that choices are limited only to those the system offers, and therefore, freedom of choice is not real. The role of the idiot—the comedic voice—is to attack that false sense of freedom. To fulfill that role, the idiot has to be aggressive if he wants to break through the barrier of common sense. Rage, as Han suggests and as Aquino's sketch demonstrates, is the fundamental element of resistance.

The sketch soon switches gears and commences an even faster-paced back-and-forth between Guille and Lu:

Lu: Ummm, shall we play a rapid-fire?

[Guille accepts.]

Lu: Breakfast. Yes or no? [headline: Pros and cons of the first meal of the day]

Guille: Yes.

Lu: No. . . . Education [headline in *La Nación*] Is attending a university worth it?

Guille: Yes.

Lu: No. . . . Health [headline in *La Nación*] How long after food is expired can you still eat it?

Guille: Truly, zero days.

Lu: Says who?

Guille: Mostly the best-by date.

Lu: Come on, think a little outside the box.

Guille: What box?

Lu: [headline in *La Nación*] The empty cardboard boxes that stimulate children's imagination.

Guille: Ah, fuck you, LinkedIn.

Lu: OK, let's go, gimme more.

Guille: Unemployment.

Lu: [headline in *Clarín*] Spare time . . . a treasure that can bring more happiness than money.

Guille: Seriously, the president wrote this one.

Man 1: Anything about the energy crisis?

Lu: [headline in *TN*] Better in the dark . . . artificial light is bad for your health.

Guille: Excuse me, what health insurance do we get here? Edenor?

Female 1: Foodstuffs?

Lu: [headline in *Clarín*] Found: the most incredible method for losing weight . . . eating dirt.

Guille: Huh?

Man 2: Eating dirt.

Guille: Publishing this cannot be legal.

Man 2: Eating dirt, dummy. You've never eaten dirt?

Guille: Are you fucking kidding?

Man 2: You know, roly polys, dirt . . .

Guille: Huh?

Man 2: Seriously, I don't know how you passed an aptitude test . . .

Guille: OK guys . . .

Man 2: . . . human resources.

Guille: . . . Seriously, I think everybody here needs a good vacation.

Lu: [headline in *Clarín*] Vacation for your head . . . how to have a mental escape.

Guille: What the fuck is a mental escape?

Lu: [addressing someone outside of the frame] Call Borda and ask. . . .

[Guille makes a frustrated gesture.]

Lu: Subject: mental escape.

Guille: I can't deal with this anymore.

Lu: [headline in *TN*] Complaining is bad for your health.

Guille: Wow.

Lu: [headline in *Clarín*] It is possible to fire people and end poverty.

Guille: How?

Lu: I don't know, but you are fired.

Guille: And what am I going to tell my family?
Lu: [headline in *Clarín*] Millennials . . . ten years working for the same
   company can be a personal failure.
Guille: But I started working here five minutes ago.
Lu: Ah, but you are a success. . . .[10]
[Guille gets up from the table, in silence, and with a clear gesture of
   defeat.]

By the end of the sketch, Guille's rage is full-blown, as his reactions demonstrate, but there is yet another layer of analysis, applicable specifically to this
final part of the sketch. The dialogue's fast pace makes it necessary to consider
all of the jokes as part of one all-encompassing unit. The feel of the dialogue
is almost automatic, a back-and-forth full of points and counterpoints that
are lobbed quasi-instantaneously, almost mechanically. Critchley (56) states
that humor "consists in the momentary transformation of the physical into
the machinic." Granted, Critchley here is talking about characters or individuals who acquire a machinic nature (think, as Critchley himself suggests,
Charlie Chaplin in *Modern Times*). However, I would argue that the idea of
the transformation of the physical into the machinic can also be applied to
the nature of language itself. The characters that transition to this new nature
are characterized by rigidity and repetition, described by Critchley as "a certain stiffness or inflexibility which is emphasized through an absentminded,
almost unconscious, mechanical repetitiveness" (56). This compulsive repetition is what makes something funny, but also makes viewers feel troubled by
the very thing we laugh at. Suddenly, it dawns on us that what we are witnessing is a representation of the reality in which we live, a reality to which we
often turn a blind eye due to the intense discomfort produced by considering
and acknowledging it. For example, the headline that questions the value of
higher education is from an article in *La Nación* (Vázquez), which discusses
the apparent disconnect between the skills acquired in higher education and
the skills that employers are seeking in graduates. The underlying criticism
in the dialogue is clearly aligned with a vision of higher education that goes
beyond a purely utilitarian view. However, one would have to consider that
a few months before this sketch's release on YouTube, María Eugenia Vidal,
then governor of the province of Buenos Aires, had expressed the view that
it was unnecessary to have so many public universities in the province, as everyone knew that people born in poverty did not attend institutions of higher
education ("Vidal").

Another example of this phenomenon is the joke about Edenor, the company holding a monopoly over the provision of electricity services to the

northwest part of the city of Buenos Aires and the northwest sectors of Greater Buenos Aires. Notorious for their deficient customer service and interruptions of service, Edenor is also known for an early-2000s judicial sentence that found that the company had acted with negligence by placing substations that were linked to cases of cancer in surrounding neighborhoods. The joke, then, is the suggestion that a company that was linked to this kind of harmful and profit-driven practice would provide health insurance in the workplace.

The rest of the headlines in this excerpt from the script (eating dirt as a method for losing weight; substituting a "mental escape" for actual vacation time, a hard-fought labor right; the negative health effects of complaining—arguably because of an unfair workplace situation; the notion that being unemployed does not necessarily condemn workers to poverty) are thrown at Guillermo, and by extension, at the audience, as a barrage of ideas that can only be confronted, as I stated before, with dissenting rage. This rage, as mentioned, builds up and reaches the highest volume at the end, when Guillermo asks what he is going to tell his family after he is fired. Critchley says that to be effective, the warning signals that make satire work "have to be deafening" (36). There is a clear connection between this idea and the volume that Guillermo uses to denounce all these issues. But, interestingly enough, this high volume works better when we consider the counterpoint offered by Lu throughout the sketch. Lu's attitude all along is calm and tempered. It is the attitude of somebody who holds all the cards and knows that no matter what the other says or thinks, their worldview will eventually be triumphant. For each protest that Guillermo offers, there is a perfectly reasonable answer—within the dominant narrative—matter-of-factly proposed by Lu. Eventually, Lu manages to annul Guille's voice, causing him to get up from the table with an expression of defeat and leave the room. That is also a deafening signal, since it signifies that even for those who see reality for what it is and point it out for everyone else to see, it is still an uphill battle.

"2018 en 3 minutos"

The sketch "2018 en 3 minutos" was released in the last days of 2018.[11] The premise is rather simple. Guillermo Aquino starts a workday, which is set at the beginning of 2018, and receives a phone call from his future self in December of that same year. The entire sketch is a summary of all the relevant events in Argentina during the year. All the jokes in the script are accompanied by graphic inserts—newspaper headlines or television images—that contextualize the joke. The speed of the dialogue and the rage of the comedic voice are still present, although the overall feeling when watching the sketch is that they are somewhat more subdued than in "Palermo News." The following are a few examples:

Guille 1: OK, you know what? I have a lot of faith in this year. Seriously, I feel that this can be my year. I even like the sound of it: for real . . . 2018.
[PHONE RINGS]
Guille 1: Hello?
Guille 2: OK, shut your mouth, stop smiling, drop that *mate* [Guille had just picked up a *yerba mate* gourd to take a drink] and listen to me. Twenty-eighteen is going to be the worst year in history. It is going to be the worst year of your life, and you are going to be very unhappy, and you are going to have a really rough time.
Man: Who is it?
Guille 1: I don't know. I think it is the president.[12]

——

Guille 2: OK, well. Here it's the end of December 2018. So, I'm you, but at the end of the year. And right now, there's a guy right behind you who is going to drop a folder in 4 3 2 1 . . .
[SOMEONE DROPS A FOLDER BEHIND GUILLE 1]
Guille 1: OK, that was really scary.
Guille 2: Yep, and you still haven't watched Gisela Barreto's show on cable (insert with images from Barreto's show) . . . Listen, you lost a pen drive, right?
Guille 1: Yes.
Guille 2: Good. Look under the keyboard.
Guille 1: [finds pen drive] Ha! Great! I can't believe it was right there all this time and I didn't see it!
Guille 2: (insert image ARA *San Juan*) Great! Now warn those who are looking for the ARA *San Juan*.
Guille 1: Huh?[13]

——

Guille 1: Well, listen, I just went to the store and bought a Chocobar. If you want, I can murder it [eat it]
Guille 2: Errr, that sentence is going to have a very different connotation in about a month [insert images of Luis Chocobar shooting a perpetrator]
Guille 1: Ah!
Guille 2: Listen, don't spend all your money [insert headline "Gas: payable in installments"], save 200 pesos that you'll need to pay for the [natural] gas installments.

Guille 1: Gas is paid in installments?

Guille 2: In the future, everything is paid in installments. In fact, that is how we will return the money we borrowed from the IMF [insert headline "Macri and Christine Lagarde: The Head of the IMF Highlights the Reforms Already Underway in Argentina"].

Guille 1: We did a deal with the International Monetary Fund?

Guille 2: Ha! And a big one at that!

Guille 1: Wait, are you in December 2018 or December 2001?

Guille 2: Look, I'll be honest with you. Nobody here is sure about that either.[14]

—

Man: Uh, ask him how we're going to do in the World Cup in Russia.

Guille 1: How are we going to do in the World Cup in Russia?

Guille 2: [insert of an image of Lionel Messi right after the elimination of Argentina in the tournament] We didn't win; Mascherano played, and Messi didn't shine.

Guille 1: He says that we're going to do the way we usually do.

Man: Not again, Messi, fuck off!

Guille 2: Oh, also, listen. Cancel the party for the final between Boca and River for the Libertadores, because it will be useless. [insert image of Boca Juniors team bus] A kid threw a bottle at the bus, and they canceled the game.

Guille 1: Boca and River reach the final of the Libertadores Cup?

Guille 2: Yes, and in the end, the game is played in Europe.

Guille 1: Huh?

Guille 2: Yes, and Gago got injured.

Guille 1: Well, I don't have to be in the future to know that.[15]

The sketch encompasses a rather wide range of topics: the economy, both at the macro and micro level; various Argentinian public figures; social issues like abortion and police brutality. Unlike the previous sketch, in which the rage level rises in a crescendo to the climactic end, in this piece the level of rage is maintained from the beginning, which may be why it feels considerably more subdued. Not all the puns show the same level of emotional charge, it is true; however, the overall delivery of the lines conveys the character's excited state. For example, at the beginning of the sketch, when future Guille tells past Guille to drop everything and pay attention to what he is about to tell him, the series of commands is delivered by Aquino in a demanding tone that does not leave room for any other interpretation. So is the tone with which future Guille confirms that the deal Argentina struck with the IMF is indeed big. We can infer from how Guille expresses the importance of the deal that it will be something that will probably further deepen the economic problems of the country, much as it did after the economic crisis of 2001. The fact that at the end of 2018 future Guille says that people do not know whether the year is indeed 2018 or they are back in 2001—implying that the country is back to square one in its race to get over its systemic economic problems—is a denunciation of the situation and an invitation to the audience to be outraged.

The humor in this sketch is generally directed at a national—Argentinian—audience. And even for this audience, the degree to which someone would have to be aware of the details surrounding the events, and the jokes that ensue, varies. These puns may be considered examples of that type of humor addressed to a specific part of the audience that "gets it." But beyond that, these jokes have one thing in common. They can put the audience "back in place in a way that is powerfully particular and recalcitrantly relative" (Critchley 74). The national sense of humor can be demonstrated in two ways, as Critchley suggests—either triumphantly, with the implied consequence that to be triumphant as a group, some other group has to be looked down upon, or "with the anxiety, difficulty and indeed, shame of where one is from" (Critchley 74). This way of dealing with these issues still seeks to subvert the social paradigm in which said issues occur. The same people or institutions that have a vested interest in transforming individuals into achievement-subjects have an interest in making sure that the ideas that are used to convince the individuals are perceived as sound, solid, and solemn. With the jokes in this sketch, Guillermo Aquino is rejecting that solemnity and vindicating humanity. Aquino himself expresses this idea:

> I don't trust people who tell you things very seriously and without any doubts. That does not have anything to do with humanity, because being human is doubting, failing, and contradicting yourself all the time. Nobody should be too convinced about anything, and, to a point, the code is to laugh at those people, even when those people are also ourselves. (Provéndola, "El rock"; my translation)

When the Guille of December 2018 tells the Guille of the 2018 New Year to drop everything and listen to him, when he talks about the ARA *San Juan* or Gisela Barreto, or Messi's performance in the World Cup, or the return of the IMF to Argentinians' daily lives, or any of the other jokes that appear in this sketch, he is waging war against the complacency that has invaded the national psyche and that facilitates the control of society by the elites. All this commentary present in the jokes is also a set of deafening signs, like those I referred to in the previous sketch, but here they play a somewhat different role. These jokes compel audience members to look at themselves critically. Why are they willing to accept yet another intervention of the IMF in the national economy after the disastrous precedent of the 2001 crisis? Why do they keep placing their hopes of achieving a certain degree of happiness in the hands of international soccer stars who have proven disappointing time and time again? Why do they give visibility to individuals with staggeringly reactionary opinions in this day and age? The adage "Fool me once, shame on you; fool me twice, shame on me" underlies this idea. There is a moment in which one—as part of a larger collective—must acknowledge a share of responsibility for the factors that caused the situation the collective is in.

Conclusion

In the postmodern world, individuals are subject to very efficient market logic, by which, instead of producing as a result of external pressures (the classic distinction between capital/master and worker/slave), they internalize that pressure—effectively becoming master and slave at the same time—and tell themselves that they are freer and that the only limits they have in their development are those that they impose on themselves. This gives people an illusion of freedom. Byung-Chul Han argues that when individuals realize that this is indeed the case—that freedom is illusory—they become burned out and depressed. People cannot escape this condition because they have lost their ability to express rage. Rage, like satire, is fundamentally aggressive. The satirist is thus uniquely equipped to express rage, and, in doing so, awaken the consciousness of his audience. By exercising the role of the idiot—the unintelligent individual—the satirist shatters the illusion of freedom that postmodern society has set in place. The satirist must produce deafening, impossible-to-ignore signals to get the audience to reflect upon its reality. This reality is mediated by a dominant narrative that causes the satirist to express rage increasingly, even as—at the end of the first sketch—he is forced to admit that opposing that narrative is an uphill, albeit necessary, battle. Alternatively, the satirist uses the signals to compel audiences to examine their individual and collective reactions—or lack thereof—to events that shape their immediate reality—reactions with which they may not be necessarily comfortable.

Notes

1 This represents the number of views of Aquino's YouTube channel as of November 12, 2020. However, some of these videos are hosted on other YouTube channels as well as in other media (Facebook, Instagram, and Twitter), which presumably makes their impact even greater.

2 Here and elsewhere in this chapter, emphasis is in the original unless otherwise stated.

3 The name of the character—Paco Cambiasso—may be a play on words with the meaning of the verb *cambiar* (to change) with the augmentative -*azo* (something along the lines of big—dramatic, traumatic—change) and the rather dramatic effects used in the show to represent such transformation, even though the result is just the actor with a paper cut-out of the celebrity's face covering his own face. This idea goes beyond the scope of this article, but it seems interesting from the point of view of the symbolic intersection between humor and violence.

4 Considering that this article deals with an Argentinian, maybe a better term, geographically speaking, would be *Australization* or even a more general *Latinization.* That being said, the point made by Aparicio and Chávez-Silverman is that Latin American and Latinx artists internalize, appropriate, and transform hegemonic Anglo cultural discourses and disseminate the resulting product back to the global centers of hegemony.

5 www.youtube.com/watch?v=zvg1CxZ4N5k.

6 Many of the actors who appear in Aquino's sketches did not have any acting experience before their participation in *El Sketch,* which is the name of the series to which the two pieces I analyze in this article belong. Lucia Iacono, for example, is a TV producer who had worked with Aquino on a previous TV show. Aquino mentions that the participation of individuals like Iacono, with no acting experience, "gave sketches an uncomfortable vibe that ultimately makes them more real . . . ending with a more sincere representation" (Provéndola, "El rock"; my translation).

7 All excerpts from the sketches are my own translation. I include the original transcripts.

> Lu: Bueno Guille, ¿qué tenés?
> GA: Eh nada estuve como buscando en Internet.
> Lu: Ajá.
> GA: . . . y resulta como que los índices de pobreza en capital federal subieron como muchísimo . . .
> Lu: ¿y para vos cuál sería el título de esa noticia?
> Guille: ¿según los informes oficiales?
> Lu: Claro, sí, obvio . . .
> Guille: OK . . .
> Lu: . . . estamos buscando informar, ¿no?
> Guille: Capital federal, dos puntos, se duplicó el índice de indigencia.
> Lu: Mmmm, como muy para abajo ¿no? No sé, digo, la noticia así . . .
> Guille: OK . . .
> Lu: Como que vos pensá que esto es para gente . . .
> Guille: Si bueno es un poco . . .

Lu: Que lo está. . . . O sea que lo consume en el colectivo. En realidad, como que le chupa un huevo lo que vos decís, ¿entendés?

Guille: En realidad es como una nota un poco más social, ¿no?

8 Lu: Sí, OK, pero digo, a esta gente "indigente" [Lu hace el gesto de 'entre comillas'] de la que vos hablás qué es lo que le estaría faltando . . . ¿Alcohol, armas . . . ? ¿droga? ¿Un CD de La Berisso?

Guille: No, sí, comida . . . más bien.

Lu: ¿Y de cuánta gente estamos hablando? ¿Son 20, son 30 . . . ?

Guille: 200.000 personas.

Lu: OK, ya lo tengo . . . Pasiones argentinas: la decencia de los que buscan entre la basura [aparece una captura de pantalla con el titular del diario *Clarín*].

9 Lu: minimalismo extremo . . . (foto titular *Clarín*).

Chico 1: ¡Qué genia!

Lu: . . . los que se despojan de casi todo lo material.

Guille: Pero ¿quién dice que eso es necesariamente algo bueno?

Lu: ¿Cómo que quién dice? La china que te enseña a doblar las camisas en Netflix . . .

Guille: ¿Qué?

Lu: . . . No sé, digo, ¿tenés algo contra los chinos?

Chico 1: La estás rompiendo, Lu.

Guille: ¿Esto es real?

Chica 1: Me gusta el enfoque humano de eso.

Guille: ¿Ustedes son reales?

Chico 2: Yo conozco un pobre y la va a sentir.

Guille: Pero, ¿qué verga?

10 Lu: Emmm, ¿vamos con un ping pong mejor?

[Guille acepta]

Lu: Desayuno. ¿Sí o no? (foto titular: Pros y contras de la primera comida del día)

Guille: Sí

Lu: No . . . Educación (foto titular *La Nación*) ¿Vale la pena ir a la universidad?

Guille: Sí

Lu: No . . . Salud (foto titular *La Nación*) ¿Cuánto tiempo después de vencido se puede comer un alimento?

Guille: De verdad, cero días.

Lu: ¿Quién lo dice?

Guille: Más que nada la fecha de vencimiento.

Lu: A ver, pensá un poquito fuera de la caja.

Guille: ¿Qué caja?

Lu: (foto titular de *La Nación*) Las cajas de cartón vacías que estimulan la imaginación de los chicos.

Guille: Ah, LinkedIn y la puta que te parió.

Lu: OK, dale vamos . . . Dame más.

> Guille: Desempleo.
>
> Lu: (foto titular *Clarín*) Tiempo libre . . . un tesoro que puede dar más felicidad que el dinero.
>
> Guille: En serio esto lo escribió el presidente.
>
> Chico 1: ¿Algo de crisis energética?
>
> Lu: (foto titular *TN*) Mejor a oscuras . . . la luz artificial afecta la salud.
>
> Guille: Sí, perdón, ¿qué obra social nos dan acá? ¿Edenor?
>
> Chica 1: ¿La canasta básica?
>
> Lu: (foto titular *Clarín*) Hallaron el método más increíble para adelgazar . . . comer tierra.
>
> Guille: ¿Eh?
>
> Chico 2: Comer tierra.
>
> Guille: No puede ser legal publicar eso.
>
> Chico 2: Comer tierra, boludo. ¿Nunca comiste tierra?
>
> Guille: ¿Me estás jodiendo?
>
> Chico 2: Bichito bolita, tierra.
>
> Guille: ¿Eh?
>
> Chico 2: En serio que no sé cómo pasaste un psicotécnico . . .
>
> Guille: OK chicos . . .
>
> Chico 2: . . . recursos humanos.
>
> Guille: . . . en serio, me parece que necesitan todos tomarse unas buenas vacaciones acá.
>
> Lu: (foto titular clarín) Vacaciones para tu cabeza . . . cómo tener una escapada mental.
>
> Guille: ¿Qué mierda es una escapada mental?
>
> Lu: [hablando con alguien fuera de cámara] Llamá al Borda y preguntá . . .
>
> [Guille hace gesto de frustración]
>
> Lu: Asunto: escapada mental.
>
> Guille: Bue, yo no puedo seguir con esto.
>
> Lu: (foto titular *TN*) Quejarse y protestar es malo para la propia salud.
>
> Guille: Wow
>
> Lu: (foto titular *Clarín*) Se puede despedir y terminar con la pobreza.
>
> Guille: ¿De qué manera?
>
> Lu: No sé, pero estás despedido.
>
> Guille: ¿Y que le voy a decir a mi familia?
>
> Lu: (foto titular *Clarín*) Millennials . . . diez años en la misma empresa puede ser un fracaso personal.
>
> Guille: Pero yo empecé a trabajar acá hace cinco minutos.
>
> Lu: Ah, pero vos sos un éxito [Guille se levanta de la mesa, en silencio y con claro gesto de derrota].

11 www.youtube.com/watch?v=grKgzLiFiA4.

12 Guillermo is referring to Mauricio Macri, president of Argentina from 2015 to 2019, whose neoliberal policies failed to achieve the economic reform of the country that he campaigned on. Toward the end of his term, the slogan *Mauricio Macri la puta que te parió* became a very popular chant in football stadiums around the country.

Guille 1: OK ¿Saben qué? Le tengo mucha fe a este año. En serio, siento que este puede ser mi año. Hasta me gusta como suena: posta . . . 2018.

[SUENA EL TELÉFONO]

Guille 11: ¿Hola?

Guille 2: OK, callate la boca, dejá de sonreír, soltá ese mate [el Guille de enero justo acaba de agarrar un mate para tomar] y escuchame. El 2018 va a ser el peor año de la historia, va a ser el peor año de tu vida y vas a ser muy infeliz y la vas a pasar pésimo.

Chico: ¿Quién es?

Guille 1: No sé, creo que el presidente.

13 Gisela Barreto is an Argentinian TV host, famous for her strong ultraconservative religious views. She has been a vocal opponent of abortion and has expressed polemic views on vaccines, the LGBTQ+ community, and the COVID-19 pandemic. The ARA *San Juan* was an Argentinian naval submarine that was lost at sea after participating at an exercise in Tierra del Fuego in November 2017. The wreck was finally found a year later.

Guille 2: OK, bueno acá es finales de diciembre de 2018. O sea, yo soy vos pero a fin de año. Y ahora hay un chabón detrás tuyo que se le va a caer una carpeta en 4 3 2 1.

[A ALGUIEN SE LE CAE UNA CARPETA DETRÁS DE EL]

Guille 1: OK, eso me dio muchísimo miedo.

Guille 2: Sí, y eso que todavía no viste el programa de cable de Gisela Barreto . . . (insert fragmento programa Barreto) . . . Escuchame, vos perdiste un pendrive, ¿no?

Guille 1: Sí.

Guille 2: Bien. Fijate abajo del teclado.

Guille 1: [lo encuentra] Ja, ja. No, tremendo, no puedo creer que estuvo todo el tiempo ahí en el mismo lugar y nunca lo vi.

Guille 2: (insert imagen ARA *San Juan*) Genial, ahora avisales a los que estaban buscando el ARA *San Juan*,

Guille 1: ¿Eh?

14 Luis Chocobar was a police officer in Avellaneda, a municipality in the Greater Buenos Aires metropolitan area, who appeared in recorded footage shooting down an unarmed robbery suspect who was running away from him. Later in the year, the federal government issued a decree regulating the use of firearms by police in these situations. The decree essentially legalized Chocobar's action retroactively. The joke hinges on a play on words between the last name of the agent and a chocolate candy bar, as well as the metaphorical use of murder in the sense of devouring food.

The joke about the IMF draws from what is arguably one of the most traumatic moments in Argentinian society in recent history—with the obvious exception of the military dictatorship in the 1970s. The 2001 economic crisis, which resulted from the neoliberal policies implemented mostly by President Menem in the 1990s, is still a hot topic of debate in Argentinian society.

Guille 1: Bue, pará, escuchame, recién fui al kiosco y me compré un Chocobar. Si querés me lo bajo a los tiros.

Guille 2: Ahhh, esa frase va a tener una connotación muy distinta en un mes (insert imágenes Chocobar disparando a un ladrón).

Guille 1: ¡Aaah!

Guille 2: Escuchame, no te gastes todo, (insert gráfico Gas: se podrá pagar en cuotas) separá 200 pesos que los vas a necesitar para pagar las cuotas del gas.

Guille 1: ¿El gas se paga en cuotas?

Guille 2: En el futuro todo se paga en cuotas. De hecho, así es como le vamos a devolver la plata que le pedimos al FMI (insert gráfico Macri y Christine Lagarde: La titular del FMI destacó las reformas puestas en marcha en la Argentina).

Guille 1: ¿Hicimos un acuerdo con el fondo monetario internacional?

Guille 2: ¡Ja! ¡Y uno grande!

Guille 1: Pero pará, ¿vos estás en diciembre de 2018 o en diciembre de 2001?

Guille 2: Mirá te voy a ser honesto, nadie está muy seguro de eso acá tampoco.

15 The joke about Messi is less obscure than that about Fernando Gago, if only because Messi is a global football icon and the World Cup arguably the biggest sporting event in the world. It is a widely shared opinion—both in Argentina and around the world—that Messi's performance with the national team is not as good as it is with his club, and that this fact has prevented Argentina from achieving victory even when they were clear favorites. On the other hand, knowing that Fernando Gago, the Boca Juniors player, is prone to injuries is something that only people who follow Argentinian football (i.e., not only, but mainly, Argentines) would know.

Chico: Uh, preguntale cómo nos va a ir en el mundial de Rusia.

Guille 1: ¿Cómo nos va a ir en el mundial de Rusia?

Guille 2: [insert imagen de Messi después eliminación de Argentina] No ganamos, jugó Mascherano y Messi no se lució.

Guille 1: Dice que nos va a ir como en todos los mundiales siempre.

Chico: Otra vez Messi, la concha de tu madre.

Guille 2: Ah, otra cosa, escúchame. Suspendé la picada de la final de Boca y River en la Libertadores, porque es al pedo. (insert imagen autocar de Boca Jrs.) Un chabón le tira una botella del micro y nada, suspenden el partido.

Guille 1: ¿Boca y River llegan a la final de la Copa Libertadores de América?

Guille 2: Sí, y al final se juega en Europa.

Guille 1: ¿Eh?

GA2: Sí, y Gago se lesionó.

GA1: Bueno, no tengo que estar en el futuro para saber eso.

Works Cited

Alonso, Paul. *Satiric TV in the Americas: Critical Metatainment as Negotiated Dissent.* New York: Oxford UP, 2018.

Aparicio, Frances R., and Susana Chávez-Silverman, editors. *Tropicalizations: Transcultural Representations of Latinidad.* Hanover, NH: Dartmouth College Press; University Press of New England, 1997.

Critchley, Simon. *On Humour.* London: Routledge, 2002.

"Guille Aquino en El Destape 'Me crié hablando en Simpson.'" *YouTube,* uploaded by El Destape, 27 Aug. 2019, www.youtube.com/watch?v=yUPRrKHY_KY.

Guehlstorf, Nicholas, Lars Hallstrom, and Jonathan Morris. "The ABCs of the *The Simpsons* and Politics: Apathy of Citizens, Basic Government Leaders, and Collective Interests." *Laughing Matters: Humor and American Politics in the Media Age,* edited by Jody C. Baumgartner and Jonathan S. Morris, New York: Routledge, 2008, pp. 211–228.

Han, Byung-Chul. *The Burnout Society.* Stanford: Stanford UP, 2015.

———. *Psychopolitics: Neoliberalism and New Technologies of Power.* Brooklyn: Verso Books, 2017.

Paine Caulfield, Rachel. "The Influence of 'Infoenterpropagainment': Exploring the Power of Political Satire as a Distinct Form of Political Humor." *Laughing Matters: Humor and American Politics in the Media Age,* edited by Jody C. Baumgartner and Jonathan S. Morris, New York: Routledge, 2008, pp. 3–20.

Provéndola, Juan. "Guille Aquino: 'Es increible que aún exista gente capaz de ofenderse con el humor.'" *La izquierda diario,* 15 Aug. 2019, www.laizquierdadiario.com/Guille-Aquino-Es-increible-que-aun-exista-gente-capaz-de-ofenderse-con-el-humor.

———. "El rock entretiene y editorializa." *Página 12,* 19 Apr. 2019, www.pagina12.com.ar/188353-el-rock-entretiene-y-editorializa.

Vázquez, Luciana. "Educación: ¿Vale la pena ir a la universidad?" *La Nación,* 18 Mar. 2016, www.lanacion.com.ar/sociedad/educacion-vale-la-pena-estudiar-una-carrera-en-la-universidad-nid1880841/.

"Vidal: 'Nadie que nace en la pobreza llega a la universidad.'" *La voz de Tandil,* 31 May 2018, www.lavozdetandil.com.ar/2018/05/31/video.-vidal---nadie-que-nace-en-la-pobreza-llega-a-la-universidad-.

5

Political Cartoons and Memes

Artifacts of Discourse Subversion through Humor

ALEJANDRA COLLADO

The cultural units of information better known as memes are defined as semantic memories that refer to cultural references, with humorous criticism
as a necessary variable. This humorous criticism seeks to confront official
speech through memes that become historical memory by taking particular
moments of political reality that are the object of indignation or discontent
and endowing them with another meaning. The memory remains not only in
the minds of those who understand the cultural reference and the political
context of the meme, but also on the Internet: it is a type of permanent digital
memory that may reappear countless times with a single-word input into a
search engine.

Since the political cartoon is an identifiable visual reference in memes, this
article proposes a balance between both forms of expression, listing their differences and similarities to understand the implications of the political meme
for other manifestations of opposition to hegemonic political discourse.

In Mexico, we have the example of former president Enrique Peña Nieto,
a political figure who during his presidential term, and even as a candidate,
became the protagonist par excellence of many political memes that circulated in the country between 2012 and 2018; this is due to his performance
as president—he remains the least-popular and worst-rated president in the
history of Mexico as of time of writing (Mitofsky)—his public actions, and
his failures as a media political figure. A pair of those memes is discussed in
this text.

Peña Nieto's six-year presidential period coincided with the growth in the
popularity of social media, in particular, that of Facebook (*Forbes*), which so-
lidified its position as an entertainment channel, a tool for work, and a place

for communication and organizing among activists. This happened at a time when the distance between civil society and the political class was growing and a crisis of trust and legitimacy was developing (Nateras, Schmidt).

In terms of methodology, I will embrace an analysis proposal by McLuhan and Powers—the tetrad model as a scientific instrument to analyze technological artifacts, with four basic questions that serve as orientation:

A. What does any artifact enhance? / Law of Expansion
B. What does it wear out or make obsolete? / Law of Obsolescence
C. What does it retrieve that had fallen into disuse? / Law of Retrieval
D. What does it reverse or flip into when pushed to extremes? / Law of Reversal

These questions can be answered through "observation, experience, and ideas" (McLuhan and Powers 43). Following what these authors propose—as do, in different contexts, Castells, Debord, Virilio, Lipovetsky, Negroponte, and Sosa—our way of communicating personally and the way we interpret and appropriate political discourse are modified by the arrival of technology and its corresponding advancement. In this sense, political cartoons and memes are technological artifacts contributing to such transformation.

The application of this model makes it clear that the political memes that circulate in Facebook and WhatsApp communities have the potential to re-signify political discourse as humor through the parodic and satirical deconstruction of the figure of the president. Here the concept of carnival, proposed by Mikhail Bakhtin in 1936 to define key aspects of popular culture, comes in handy, as it also involves saturation with grotesque and masked characters, buffoons, laughter, and fools. In carnival, authorities are always overthrown and hierarchical structures are diluted, revoking distances, classes, and positions that are replaced by collective laughter.

The object of study introduced here is important to analyze because we are at a point when communication processes as well as the roles of the medium, the message, the audience, and general meaning have been significantly re-vamped as the result of technological advances in communication, as studied by Castells, Reguillo, Sartori, Van Dijk, and others. In this context, scenarios are being engendered in which the role of users occupies a fundamental place, not only because of their active modality and their character as consumers, but also because of the possibility of appropriation, resignification, and production of content and discourses.

The term *meme* was coined by Richard Dawkins to name a "unit of cultural transmission, or a unit of imitation" (218), with the idea of designating the cultural equivalent of a gene. Although the conceptual debate had

Table 5.1. Comparison of political cartoons and memes

TRAIT	POLITICAL CARTOONS	POLITICAL MEME
NEWS FEATURE	Editorializes a news item: this requires analysis, deep reflection, and knowledge of a current issue	Synthesizes a news item: it takes a headline, a phrase, a journalistic image, a photograph, or an element that has generated impact and disseminates it
AUTHORSHIP	Created by a cartoonist working for a periodical; cannot be modified without her/his permission	Created by one Internet user and, in many cases, modified by multiple others without permission; it has no established authorship
PROFESSIONALIZATION	Requires professionalism and technique both in drawing and knowledge of politics	Primarily requires basic handling of image-editing techniques through software or apps, and knowledge of the context and cultural references
TECHNIQUE	A variation of the hand-drawn portrait. Exaggerates features to ridicule, criticize, or emphasize certain aspects of the character	Variations on digital portraits. Features or expressions can be exaggerated using digital image-editing software and apps
CREDIT	Gives the author and the medium prestige	Gives prestige (in the form of likes and hearts) to whoever shares it and to the platform where this happens
MEDIUM	Published in hard copy (magazines, newspapers), and on websites and social networks of the publication in question or of the cartoonist	Published digitally through social networks, websites, or in the image results of any search engine
PUBLIC TO WHICH IT IS ADDRESSED	Addresses a private audience that consumes political periodicals	Addresses a general public that has access to the aforementioned platforms and apps
INTERACTION WITH THE PUBLIC	The author delivers the message without interaction with or feedback from the audience[a]	The message is known, but not the author. The message and the meaning are frequently modified
TYPE OF WORK	Individual	Collective
TYPE OF HUMOR	Humor, derived mostly from the political context	Humor from popular culture of various eras, recovery of cultural references from other times, such as songs, advertising, and other popular expressions in combination with current events in the political context

Note: a. The Internet has modified this aspect, since some cartoonists publish on their personal social network accounts and interact with the public. Even so, there is no intervention or modification of the images.

already begun with the exploration of the correlation between biological and cultural evolution (Popper, White, Campbell), it was Dawkins who deepened the theorization of the concept. Thus, he first thought of *mimeme,* a word with a Greek root that means "imitation, imitate, imitable"; however, Dawkins was looking for a term that was also monosyllabic like the word gene. In the end, he shortened *mimeme* to meme, arguing that another possible interpretation could be its relationship to the word "same" in French: *même* (218).

Memes transfer information and reproduce in a certain medium, transforming themselves during the process and spreading like a virus. Following Pérez, Aguilar, and Guillermo, unlike genes and viruses, a meme does not self-replicate but requires a group of subjects to carry out its retransmission (83). Lull and Neiva explain it in this manner: "Genes replicate. People imitate. Genes don't think about what they are doing. People, presumably, do think . . . cultural choices are motivated from the start" (26).

Susan Blackmore recognized what the Internet meant for the idea of the meme (295–298), while Vélez has proposed new categories of memes to do justice to the specific Internet context (132). He has proposed the alternative concept of "imemes," which he defines as "what is retransmitted and modified by the users. They constitute one of the easiest forms of retransmitting social critique via humor" (130).

The first Internet memes, which appeared between the mid- and late 1990s, were mostly GIFs propagating through email. With the advent and full development of social media, memes composed of one fixed image—modified or not with Photoshop or created with the help of an app—began to proliferate. The image modifications generally involved superimposing text, dialogues, faces, and other elements to decontextualize the original image by giving it a new meaning.

Humorous Media Expressions against the Discourse of Power

In Mexico, political cartooning in the press has provided a graphic representation of characters, institutions, and situations of political life for humorous as well as critical purposes. Fernando Ayala explains it as "a graphic representation in which the characteristic features or vices of a person, institution, situation, or idea are exaggeratedly deformed, indicating a marked humorous and critical intention" (63). For the author, images can be powerful political weapons that "contain a double-edged sword within their satirical logic, since they can be used politically by both progressive and reactionary movements" (Ayala 64). Gantús describes it as "a symbolic satirical form of interpretation and construction of reality, a strategy of action—of individuals and groups—in the struggles for the production and control of collective imaginaries" (14).

Political memes, as the equivalent of political caricature for digital times, are reproduced and transformed from wall to wall and provide in a few seconds an update on the week, day, or last-minute events. In memes, "humor is used as a form of protest, a counter-discourse against power and institutionalized figures" (Romero 16). Memes are graphic representations that, using diverse digital strategies, exaggerate the physical traits and marks, and the character or behavioral faults, of political figures to criticize them.

Following this description, we can similarly define a political meme: it is a graphic representation that, with different digital strategies, exaggerates physical, character, and behavioral traits and defects of certain political figures to criticize them. According to Ayala, ever since the first political cartoon was recorded in Mexico in 1826—a lithograph that spoke out against tyranny (65)—numerous political publications have included the political cartoon, which over time became a sort of meticulous and critical record of the history of Mexico: assassinations, abuses of power, presidential impositions, elections, reelections, and political and social events carried out by Mexican political figures (81).

Schmidt claims "political humor is a form of participation that, by destroying the seriousness, solemnity, pomposity, and ritualism that surrounds politics, results in loss of respect or fear for politics" (58), reducing the degree of obedience to power. With the use of humor, a tension may surface between power and citizens: it subverts, in the realm of the symbolic, the formality and solemnity of politics through irreverence. It is a way of contesting hegemony by interrupting official truths and questioning the established order, claiming differences with the ruling class.

Under the premise that "our idea of reality is shaped by the experience we receive from our media . . . [and that this] largely determines our beliefs and habits of action" (Elizondo 84) I analyze some Mexican political memes as specific examples of the transformation of technology through political culture and vice versa, as well as a transition of political phenomena in the digital realm.

Application of the Tetrad Model

This section seeks to account for the transformations and coincidences between one and another medium. In the political cartoon, for example, the images of good and evil are clearly perceived; binaries such as powerful-oppressed, corrupt-honored, victim-perpetrator, and dominator-dominated

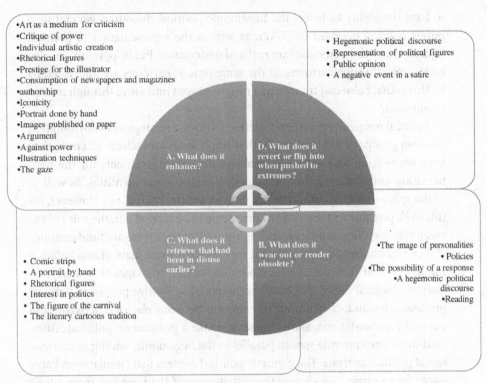

Figure 5.1. Tetrad model of a political cartoon. Courtesy of the author.

can be distinguished. Ideas are shown that do not allow power relations from another angle, that is to say, there are no mid-points or gray areas between these binaries. In addition to the centrality of the artistic and the iconic, various rhetorical figures can be identified in the cartoon's structure: hyperbole, ironies, touches of sarcasm, metaphors, comparisons, ellipses, metonymies, and euphemisms, among others. All these are strategies of resistance that, according to Scott, are not limited to the linguistic, but apply to a vast field of resources with which the discourses of the powerful seeking hegemony can be subverted (80–81). Following Bakhtin's idea of carnival, this resistance to power through critical discourse arises from the people, especially from those citizens who can use "the flattering self-portrait of the ruling elite" (Scott 80) as a political instrument to put on view their resistance.

The figure of the Bakhtinian carnival is recovered insofar as the cartoon represents a space of celebration and criticism of power, in which there is no solemnity due to conjunctural issues or political characters. It refers to a carnival in which grotesque representation is not frowned upon, and laughter is the main tool to expose poorly exercised power. The cartoon continues to have the ability to invert the hegemonic political discourse, generating a public opinion opposed to power, as well as the representation of political figures whose characteristics are real and undesirable. Public opinion can also be inverted through cartoons, at the same time as cartoons are nourished by it. This artifact also can transform a negative event into satire through its representation.

Political memes have several functions: they are strategies of confrontation between groups of different types; they imply tools for collective action; they have scope from and within journalism; they are instruments for the reaffirmation and conformation of collective and personal identities, as well as of the space in which collective imaginaries are configured, etc. However, for this to be possible and the cycle of the meme to be carried out, the roles of the creator, re-signifier, producer, and reproducer of the meme are fundamental.

For Heiskanen (20–21), political memes have three main characteristics: the first is that they are specific and summarized messages that merely illustrate electoral issues and have the potential to involve people in political processes. Second, they are an intersection between electoral activism and cultural representations, allowing users to take a position on political issues. And third, they provide speech parallel to the hegemonic, adding to conventional political analysis. The memetic political content that circulates on Facebook, for example, can change the distribution of the locations from where the discourse is created, equalizing its place with a power that was always in a higher and more distant position in the structure and thus reconfiguring the digital environment in which it develops in a process of subjectivation, which is to say Facebook modifies characteristics and tools based on the use made of them by members of its virtual communities.

If at first they were reviled for their content, form, or apparent simplicity and superficiality, political memes have recurred as a way to criticize power due to some of their fundamental features, including their replicability, adaptability, and modifiability, as well as their usefulness as a way of "deepening knowledge of political topics and events, and grounding citizens' critique of the political class" (Martín and González 130). In this way, memes have gained centrality in the formation of popular discourses of citizenship regarding politics and its actors, as studied by Harlow, Häkkinen and Leppänen, Milner, Burroughs, Adegoju and Oyebode, Rowan, Romero, Vélez, Huntington, Martínez and Piñeiro, McClure, Vaz, Tolentino, Moody-Ramírez, Chagas, Freire, Ríos and Magalhaes, and González and Rivera.

The dynamics of the existence of the political meme enhance the participation of users in the creation of its content. The root image generally comes from an official and/or specialized medium in the representation of a politi-

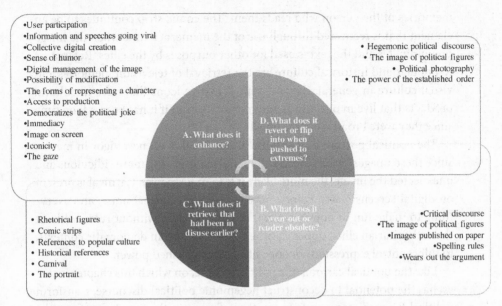

Figure 5.2. Tetrad model of the political meme. Courtesy of the author.

cal figure, which in the meme is modified over and over again by every other user. The meme amplifies the virality of information and speeches, and they then reach more recipients, not only through social networks but through interaction with family and friends. In this manner, the meme promotes collective digital creation, in such a way that each work may reflect the thinking of a community.

A sense of humor and the creativity to generate and continue to generate laughter grow, as do the digital handling of the image and the possibility of modifying an image/speech through applications or editing programs. The forms of representation of a character as well as access to the production of this representation are enhanced. The political joke is also democratized, making it more accessible to audiences of different ages, social classes, and occupations. It amplifies immediacy, the image on the screen, and iconicity.

The political meme erodes the artistic creation of the political cartoon, although it replaces it with another type of technique, now focused on the digital. Authorship ceases to exist in memes, and critical discourse, as well as a political argument, can disappear in the funny image, catchy phrases, and amusing gestures. The rules of spelling do not matter; there are no such rules in memes.

The rhetorical figures continue to be retrieved: popular songs, sayings, verses, and elements of orality that can even be read to the rhythm of the memories of the person who reads them. The comic strip continues to be an element that is recovered through use of the meme, at a time when the image predominates and the text is used for other purposes by the elites. References to popular and historical culture are the retrieval of television memories and visual culture in general: they are representative icons that refer to cultural products that live in our minds and memories even if it has been a long time since they were broadcast/consumed.

The political portrait as a critique of power takes on new vigor in memes since these images can be successful meme material: the more ridiculous and unexpected the image, the more likely it is to mock power. Carnival is present on digital screens: party, colors, masks, anonymity, visual noise, and everything to make fun of power, make it see its mistakes, without rules, without the authoritarian elitist upper class being able, at least in democratic contexts, to fully control expressions of opposition to established power.

Like the political cartoon, the political meme, on which this chapter focuses, has the potential to deconstruct hegemonic political discourse, transform political figures' image, and change those figures in the imaginary: from the pedestal to the asphalt, from the president extolled by the media to the most vilified president. Political photography, generally used to present a pristine image of figures of power in the official media, political parties, and other high spheres, can be turned into the opposite and applied to the destruction of a public image, for total discredit or the most absurd ridicule when these characters are captured in everyday moments such as a yawn, a facial expression, or any uncomfortable gesture.

Analysis of Memes with the Tetrad Model

The meme in figure 5.3[1] shows an image divided into four quarters, each representing a six-year presidential term; in each quarter is the face of the president in office for that term. Each leader and his six-year period are assigned a color and some text, in a parody of an image promoting the *Star Wars* films. In each case, the visual reference is to the publicity posters for this saga, which explores the struggle between "the Force," represented by the Rebel Alliance—embodying good, right, truth, perseverance, love, and rebelliousness—and the tyranny of the Empire. The latter is a monarchic and absolutist power that embodies the "dark side": fear, hatred, animosity, betrayal, and sadness in a galaxy full of symbols and power struggles.

In this meme, Vicente Fox's six-year period (2000–2006) is equated with Episode IV of the saga, a film called *A New Hope,* in which the Rebel Alliance seeks to destroy the Death Star, the main imperial space station, and deepen

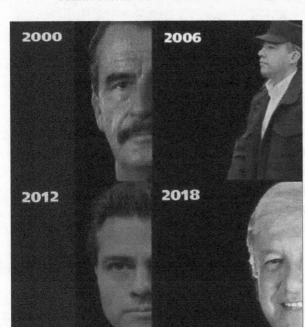

Figure 5.3. "Return of the Jedi" meme. Source: twitter.com/ tatclouthier/status/ 973528484646674433

the galactic civil war. An analogy with the Mexican context in 2000 could cast the Empire in the role of a corrupt government ignoring its people. The Death Star here is the Mexican Partido Revolucionario Institucional, or PRI, which is defeated by a Rebel Alliance that could be either Fox's Partido de Acción Nacional or the electorate, which finally rebelled against what it had endured during so many decades of oppression.

The six years of Felipe Calderón's administration (2006–2012) are presented as *Episode II: Attack of the Clones*, in which the galaxy is about to explode into civil war under the command of Count Dooku, threatening, in a context of violence and crime, the sovereignty and freedom of most of the galaxy. The parallel here is drawn to Calderón's war on drugs ("Guerra contra los narcos," or war against drug traffickers), which began in 2006. The campaign included a series of violent confrontations between the Mexican armed forces and drug cartels, as a result of which many communities and the Mexican population in many regions were negatively affected. The campaign was part of the president's fight against drug trafficking and for the "common good," but ended up producing 64,744 deaths by the end of his six years, along with many disappeared and displaced people (Meyer 16–44).

Enrique Peña Nieto's period (2012–2018) is in this meme identified with *Episode V: The Empire Strikes Back.* Years after the destruction of the Death Star, the Empire chases the rebels: "It is a dark age for the Rebellion." Speaking one's mind can result in death, as many people are captured in confrontations with the Empire and revelations of abuse multiply. In the Mexican context— as if time had stopped during the twelve years in which Fox's and Calderon's PAN (Partido Acción Nacional) governed—the Empire struck back by way of the PRI's return to power for six years full of arrests, vandalism, corruption, and crimes that are still being uncovered.

At the time this meme was first circulated, the last of the four presidents had not yet been elected. However, the meme suggested that *Episode VI: The Return of the Jedi* would be heralded by Andrés Manuel López Obrador (known as AMLO). In this film, light and darkness return to equilibrium, after the new space station planned by the Empire is destroyed by the rebels, who also win several battles against it. With the death of Darth Vader upon his return to light, the Force is re-established, and the Empire is finally defeated.

Analyzing this meme using the tetrad model and its four questions, the following emerges.

A. *What does the discursive content of this meme enhance?* It increases the scope of the iconic and symbolic representation of a popular culture product through the participation of users who viralize an oppositional discourse.

The forms of representation of each character and his political positioning are spread out by giving each of the political leaders and their respective six-year terms a specific color and relating it to the name of a movie in the *Star Wars* saga, applying this not only to the then-current president but also to earlier presidents and even to a then-presidential candidate, Andrés Manual López Obrador (Mexico's president at time of writing). Political criticism is extended to previous governments, political parties, and government strategies, and each character and his six-year term are endowed with a particular personality.

The sense of humor, the digital management of the image at an intermediate level, the access to discourse production, the democratization of the political joke, and the cultural referents that can be understood by many are all amplified in this meme.

B. *What wears out or becomes obsolete?* Now obsolete are the hypermediated representations of Enrique Peña Nieto (EPN) when he was a pre-candidate and at the beginning of his term in office, as well as the solemnity with which politics was often represented. The strategies of naturalization and hiding that were used by media for years to legitimize the behavior of the political class are also obsolete when they are re-signified through parody. In each of the six-year periods referred to in this meme, the hegemonic mass media have tried to hide what the meme shows: the struggle among political parties, the dominant governing force and its power in naturalizing corruption, inequality, abuses of power, and domination, and the concealment of all this through qualifications and distractions. At the time the meme was shared, the EPN's government was also about to be obsolete, and with it, political hegemony in Mexico.

C. *What is retrieved that may have not been in use?* The meme retrieves what had happened in each presidential term. It is a reminder that the National Action Party (PAN) and the Institutional Revolutionary Party (PRI) made mistakes during their terms. This representation seeks to recuperate the idea that hope and change are possible. The meme also seeks to recover a history that denounces corruption and violence during those periods, using a recognizable narrative: the war waged by the Empire and its leaders in *Star Wars* against the common people of the galaxy, who are always the ones suffering the negative consequences of incompetent and dishonest governments. The voice, which had been monopolized by certain social groups, is also recovered for others, while the reality concealed and naturalized in hegemonic representations is revealed. Creativity is also recuperated for political critique. Rhetorical forms such as comparison, allusion, metaphor, and synecdoche, as well as the use of parodic satire and graphic forms like cartoons, are also all recovered.

D. *What is reversed or changed when pushed to the limit of its potential?* What is inverted is the symbolic order of what each six-year political period represents. The inversion is accomplished through a parodic deconstruction of the discourse each one of those administrations deployed, as can be seen in the initial description of this meme above.

As this brief analysis reveals, the creators of these memes invert power relations through their discursive interpretations, reusing elements of popular culture that fit the message they are trying to convey, thus affecting the cultural and political referents of those who receive the message. The hegemonic political discourse and the image of political figures are inverted, and the sense of political photography as well as the way to approach the political life of the country are also changed.

The meme in figure 5.4 was published in the context of preparation for the World Cup of soccer in 2018, in which the Mexican national team participated. Before traveling to Germany, the players visited EPN at the presidential palace of Los Pinos. During the official visit, the team gave a jersey to the then-president with his name and the number 1 printed on the back. Within hours, multiple modified version of the original image circulated across Facebook—in this case with allusions to a sensitive topic in Mexican politics: the 43 students who disappeared in Ayotzinapa in September 2014 in the Iguala mass kidnapping.

A COPA DEL MUNDO RU

d de México, mayo de 20

PEÑA NIETO

43

Figure 5.4. "Los 43" (The 43) meme. Source: www .facebook.com/AltezaEPN/ photos/a.1226596487483825/ 1314799688663504/?type=3 &theater

A. *What is enhanced by any new artifact?* What is extended and widened are the two contexts required for comprehension. The first is the fact that the 43 students disappeared on September 26, 2014, in Guerrero, a case that, even as I write, remains unsolved and has remained in the public's awareness thanks to the strategies of civil society on the Internet (see Torres-Nable).

The other enhanced context is that of Mexican soccer, an activity that is only recreational, but has also grown over the years as a strategy used by "political and economic elites to reconstruct or create spaces that are useful to their hegemonic class interests" (Montero and Celis 2). Therefore, in addition to reinforcing a sense of nationalism, soccer reconfigures hegemonic power at both local and global levels.

It is again confirmed that what is extended through this meme is immediacy, participation, the virality of information and discourses, iconicity, and the forms of representation of public figures. Critique extends to humor and humor extends to critique.

B. *What wears out or becomes obsolete?* The legitimacy of official discourse as manifested, for example, in political acts loses some power at the hands of sarcasm. What becomes obsolete is the habit of the hegemonic power of entertaining the people with soccer to keep them quiet. In this case, while the people keep on re-appropriating their soccer identity, they also use it as a form of critique.

In both the first and second memes discussed here, one can sense how the image of the authority of these public figures is dissolved. They are turned into carnival buffoons; their arguments and discourses are turned into jokes. In both cases, unlike what happens with a political cartoon, there is no artistic creativity or authorship, only people capable of using certain editing software or apps, who leave no traces or signatures and allow their image production to circulate collectively on the web.

C. What is retrieved that may have not been in use? What is recovered is something power would rather see not used: memory. This is a reminder that the people have not forgotten the Ayotzinapa case and continue to demand justice. It is a message emphasizing that Peña Nieto's smile is not a sign of happiness, as the official media attempt to portray; it is, instead, a cynical smile, and an insensitive gesture that reminds viewers that he is responsible for what happened on that 26th of September. Again, popular culture, historical references, and portraits are recovered to be re-signified.

D. What is reversed or changed when pushed to the limit of its potential? The hegemonic strategies inverted here are concealment and spectacularization. In this case, one strategy is part of the other: the concealment is carried out through the spectacularization of the characters and actions in a form of pseudo-politics that hides its workings vis-à-vis citizens, offering instead infotainment. Both forms are inverted and transformed in this meme—from concealment to visibilization and from spectacularization to what power would prefer to hide.

The analyzed meme shows a scene that was minimally modified from its original version: instead of the number one on the soccer shirt Peña Nieto holds, there is the number 43. Peña Nieto's facial expression, which originally showed Mexican pride, becomes with this change of jersey number one of cynicism.

General Observations on These Technological Artifacts

Beyond the already mentioned characteristics of political cartoons and political memes, the former seeks to produce opinions, debates, and reflections against dominant powers, while in the latter that may or may not be a political intention, as it may simply seek to become viral, promote a campaign or a web-page, or generate buzz about something. This is accomplished through humor, which can be more complex or simple, depending on the fan page, website, social network, or person who shares it and on what its place of origin may be. Political memes also require certain social, cultural, economic, and technical characteristics to generate interactivity. Their existence is determined by the nature and capabilities of Internet platforms such as Facebook and Twitter. Thus, we should not underestimate the power such platforms may have in determining memes' content. While we may think that memes—to the extent that they are created by users who express their opinions autonomously—are free of determinations, they only exist as technically allowed by the platforms and their convenience and interests. For such platforms—which, after all, are businesses—memes are tools for generating traffic and consumption. Unlike political cartoons, memes do not have one single author but are, instead, a collective creation open to limitless modifications and appropriations.

Moreover, in Internet memes, spelling is not always perfect, something that would be unthinkable in the case of political cartoons, generally associated with an established journalistic medium, where grammatical competence and syntactic rules are strictly observed. Spelling in memes, state Pérez and Hernández, is sometimes used ex professo in clear contravention of spelling norms, to distinguish such memes, created by certain groups, from so-called normies, which more closely follow standard linguistic structures. The goal in this case is to provoke and create a specific audience for certain cultural products understood only by their target group (24).

The culture of political memes represents a tension between official knowledge and the type of knowledge produced by users who appropriate the technological tools they have handy on their computers and mobile phones: apps and websites. Each user, with their way of appropriating media content, actively participates in the transformations, changes, inversions, recuperation, enhancement, and other forms of actions through technologies, such as those mentioned here. Users are the continuity and extension of each artifact, and the latter is an extension of the users' practices, ideas, preferences, and positions.

From communication studies and their combination with other disciplines, it is possible to understand that structures of communication have an impact on structures of power. Thinking about the new forms of digital and interactive communication leads us, inevitably, to rethink how we used to conceive of these processes. To do so, we must think of media as environments. This, in turn, allows us to see an ecology of media as something that "can be synthesized in one basic idea: technologies—in this case, communication technologies, from writing to digital media—generate environments that affect the subjects who use them" (Scolari 29).

Both in memes and political cartoons, the image is central. Both types of artifacts coexist without replacing each other. If anything, each one represents a form of an extension of the other. The flow of information and knowledge they produce is immersed in iconicity; these artifacts use what scholars like Jacques Ellul defined as "the persuasive power of images instead of the more traditional forms of communication based on the word and discursive confrontation" (Scolari 20).

Conclusions

It has become imperative to look at contemporary media processes, such as the circulation of political memes, from an ecological viewpoint. As McLuhan put it, "'[H]umans shape the instruments of communication but, at the same time, they reshape us without us being aware of this'" (qtd. in Scolari 23). McLuhan's ecology of media perspective focuses on the perceptions of subjects and the way the media interact with each other (McLuhan 78). When we think of the way memes affect TV, newspapers, radio, language, and humor, we can see a sort of species interaction. We can then conclude that both political cartoons and memes can be considered media that "create an environment that involves the subject and models its perception and cognition" (Scolari 29) while they circulate rapidly (Bauckhage 42). In the specific case of Mexico and the presidential figure of the 2012–2018 period, we saw such memetic development, as Peña Nieto lost popularity.

In the digital sphere carnival memes return to the iconic place of things, to the representations and codes known by the majority of us. They allude to the popular, ludic, laughable, appealing to social disorder and transferring it to a place for the representation of our times: screens. Memes adapt to hegemonic discourse, and also constantly transgress it in a never-ending process. They are forms of contemporary literacy that communicate and negotiate thought and critique while developing the necessary skills for the elaboration and transformation of memes (Shifman 2).

The constant surveillance of official culture is modified, mocked, and parodied by popular culture, which uses the view of the world and life that stems from the public square or market to laugh at it through a re-signified discourse. In this regard, Bakhtin points to such subaltern and dominant processes as dynamic, always engaged in mutual influence, and in relations of borrowing, resistance, and domination. Since media operate as environments, "once a new technology has penetrated a social milieu, it does not stop impregnating such context until all its institutions are saturated" (McLuhan 189).

Marshall McLuhan thought these communicational technologies could control the content of the message, and its structure or nature. In the case of political cartoons, the message could be more or less limited by the iconic nature of the cartoon itself. In the case of memes, however, there must be a simplification of information for the artifact to be understood, and be capable, to the highest possible degree, of fidelity, fecundity, and longevity. This point connects with the adaptation process political cartoons have undergone to persist, now in the form of the meme. The cartoon had to become wider to evolve, losing some properties in the process while gaining others, as is posited by the tetrad model used here.

The creation and proliferation of these types of memes promote a participatory, communal power, not based on the intellectual and private property of any one person but, in this case, the property of Mexicans. Political memes belong to creative and unsatisfied users and all those who want to reappropriate them. This is the type of power lodged in the minds and forms of thinking of users/consumers.

In the context of democracy and power relations, the cases here analyzed generate debate, discussion, and laughter that defy the hegemonic discourse and liberate citizens, at least for a moment, from their regular apathy when it comes to politics. As amplifications proper to the technological environments that generate and transform them, political memes evolve as a form of critique previously delivered by political cartoons.

We must not forget, however, that the media, technologies, and culture are recreated, reconstructed, and reinterpreted to legitimize an idea. The idea behind the present analysis is that technology has an impact on users, on their thoughts and ways of thinking as extensions that themselves affect the technologies. Following McLuhan, then, we could understand memes as an extension of our capacity to criticize power.

Communication media and their technological artifacts can alter the cultural practices of their audiences and users, while the latter are capable of generating their meanings from laughter and the resignification of hegemonic discourses. Such results depend on collective elaborations and cultural exchanges, bidirectional effects in the relations of audiences and technologies. The intersections of politics, technologies, creativity, and knowledge are key to questioning power structures.

Finally, it is important to resume the critical reflection on the political discourse that, through memes, circulates in the public square. According to Zizzi Papacharissi, "a virtual space improves the discussion; a virtual sphere improves democracy" (11). As she also notes, the proliferation of political discussion does not necessarily imply that such discussion is more democratic.

By the same token, a higher level of participation in political discussion does not automatically produce a debate that promotes democratic ideals. What matters, then, is to understand where we find political memes and how they act within those spaces, political culture, and our everyday lives.

It is clear that the destabilizing capacity of the meme is not absolute. It is also clear that its potential does not depend on the meme itself, but, instead, on an actor who can use the meme as a tool for debate, expression, presence, and critique of political power. The meme, then, is not a miraculous solution to disarticulate in a permanent way hegemonic discourses that are constantly adapting to the resistances they elicit.

Note

1 Because of copyright issues, the text used in these memes, with its distinctive font, has been removed here. However, the link included in the caption displays the complete version of the meme, linking each image with a particular chapter in the *Star Wars* saga.

Works Cited

Ayala, Fernando. "La caricatura política en el Porfiriato." *Estudios Políticos,* vol. 9, no. 21, 2010, pp.63–82, www.redalyc.org/articulo.oa?id=42643954200.

Adegoju, Adeyemi, and Oyebode Oluwabunmi. "Humour as Discursive Practice in Nigeria's 2015 Presidential and Election Online Campaign Discourse." *Discourse Studies,* vol. 17, no. 6, 2015, https://doi.org/10.1177/1461445615602378.

Bakhtin, Mikhail. *La cultura popular en la Edad Media y el Renacimiento. El contexto de François Rabelais.* Madrid : Alianza Editorial, 2003.

Blackmore, Susan. *La máquina de los memes.* Paidós. 2000.

Bauckhage, Christian. "Insights into Internet Memes." *Proceedings of the International AAAI Conference on Web and Social Media,* vol. 5, no. 1, 2021, pp. 42–49, https://doi.org/10.1609/icwsm.v5i1.14097.

Burroughs, Benjamin. "Obama Trolling: Memes, Salutes and Agonistic Politics in the 2012 Presidential Election." *The Fibreculture Journal,* Dec. 2013, pp. 257–276, www.researchgate.net/publication/274697390_Obama_Trolling_Memes_Salutes_and_an_Agonistic_Politics_in_the_2012_Presidential_Election.

Campbell, Donald. *Evolutionary Epistemology.* Lasalle, IL: Open Court, 1974.

Castells, Manuel. *La sociedad red: una visión global.* Madrid: Alianza Editorial, 1999.

Chagas, Viktor, et al. "Political Memes and the Politics of Memes: A Methodological Proposal for Content Analysis of Online Political Memes." *First Monday,* vol. 24, no. 2, 2019, https://dx.doi.org/10.5210/fm.v24i2.7264.

Consulta Mitofsky. "Evaluación final del gobierno de Enrique Peña Nieto." México, 2018, www.mitofsky.mx/post/ev-epn.

Dawkins, Richard. *The Selfish Gene*. New York: Oxford University, 1976.

Debord, Guy. *La Sociedad del Espectáculo*. Rosario, Argentina: Kolectivo Editorial Último Recurso, 2007.

Distin, Kate. *The Selfish Meme: A Critical Reassessment*. Cambridge UP, 2005.

Martín, Victoria, and Rubén González. "Los memes como entretenimiento político. Recepción, usos y significados." *Revista Mexicana de Opinión Pública*, vol. 14, no. 27, 2019, https://doi.org/10.22201/fcpys.24484911e.2019.27.66001.

Elizondo, Jesús. *La escuela de comunicación de Toronto*. Coyoacán, Mexico: Siglo XXI, 2009.

Gantús, Fausta. *Caricatura y poder político. Crítica, censura y represión en la ciudad de México, 1876-1888*. México: El Colegio de México/Instituto Mora, 2019.

González, Gabriela, and Sergio Rivera, editors. "Los memes de Internet en la campaña presidencial." *Las benditas redes sociales digitales. El uso de internet en las elecciones presidenciales en México, 2018*. Quito: FLACSO, 2019.

Häkkinen, Ari, and Sirpa Leppänen. "YouTube Meme Warriors: Mashup Videos as Political Critique." *Texts and Discourses of New Media*, edited by Jukka Tyrkkö and Sirpa Leppänen. Helsinki: University of Helsinki, 2013, varieng.helsinki.fi/series/volumes/15/hakkinen_leppanen/.

Harlow, Summer. "It was a Facebook Revolution: Exploring the Meme-Like Spread of Narratives During Egyptian Protest." *Revista de comunicación*, no. 12, 2013, pp. 59–82, dialnet.unirioja.es/servlet/articulo?codigo=4508756.

Heiskanen, Benita. "Meme-ing Electoral Participation . . ." *European Journal of American Studies*, vol. 12, no. 2, 2017, pp. 12–21, https://doi.org/10.4000/ejas.12158.

Huntington, Heidi. "Subversive Memes: Internet Memes as a Form of Visual Rhetoric." *Selected Papers of Internet Research*, vol. 3, 2013, journals.uic.edu/ojs/index.php/spir/article/view/8886.

Innis, Harold. *The Bias of Communication*. Toronto: University of Toronto Press, 1951.

Knobel, Michele, and Colin Lankshear, editors. "Online Memes, Affinities, and Cultural Production." *A New Literacies Sampler*, edited by Michele Knobel and Colin Lankshear, New York: Peter Lang, 2007, pp. 199–217, www.researchgate.net/publication/283968435_Online_memes_affinities_and_cultural_production.

Lipovetsky, Gilles. *El imperio de lo efímero. La moda y su destino en las sociedades modernas*. Barcelona: Anagrama, 1990.

Lull, James, and Eduardo Neiva. "Hacia una nueva conceptualización evolutiva de la comunicación 'cultural.'" *Comunicar*, vol. 36 no. 18, 2011, https://doi.org/10.3916/C36-2011-02-02.

Martínez, Xabier, and Teresa Piñeiro. "Los memes en el activismo feminista en la Red. #ViajoSola como ejemplo de movilización transnacional." *Cuadernos.info*, no. 39, 2016, pp. 17–37, https://doi.org/10.7764/cdi.39.1040.

McClure, Brian. "Discovering the Discourse of Internet Political Memes." *Adult Education Research Conference*, 2016, newprairiepress.org/aerc/2016/roundtables/12.

McLuhan, Marshall. *Comprender los medios de comunicación. Las extensiones del ser humano*. Translated by Patrick Ducher, Madrid: Editorial Paidós, 1996.

McLuhan, Marshall, and Bruce Powers. *La aldea global*. Translated by Claudia Ferrari, Barcelona: Gedisa, 2005.

Meyer, Lorenzo. "Felipe Calderón o el infortunio de una transición." *Foro internacional,* vol. 55, no. 1, 2015, pp. 16–44, https://www.scielo.org.mx/pdf/fi/v55n1/0185-013X-fi -55-01-00016.pdf.

Milner, Ryan. *The World Made Meme: Discourse and Identity in Participatory Media.* 2012. University of Kansas, PhD dissertation.

Montero, Jonathan, and Dante Celis. "El futbol mexicano como instrumento de poder económico y político. El control del espacio y los espacios de control." *III Coloquio Internacional de Geocrítica. El control del espacio y los espacios de control,* Barcelona, 5–10 May 2014, www.ub.edu/geocrit/coloquio2014/Jonathan%20Montero%20Oropeza.pdf.

Moody-Ramírez, Mia, and Andrew Celis. "Analysis of Facebook Meme Groups Used During the 2016 US Presidential Election." *Social Media & Society,* vol. 5, no. 1, 2019, https://doi.org/10.1177/2056305118808799.

Morales, Carlos. "Facebook cumple 5 años de conectar a los mexicanos." *Forbes,* 19 Dec. 2017, www.forbes.com.mx/facebook-cumple-5-anos-de-conectar-a-los-mexicanos/.

Nateras, Alfredo. "Sentimiento de representación política en los mexicanos." *Opinión pública, representación política y democracia en México.* Centro de Estudios Sociales y de Opinión Pública, CDMX, 2013.

Negroponte, Nicholas. *Ser digital.* Bueno Aires: Editorial Atlántida, 1995.

Papacharissi, Zizzi. "The Virtual Sphere: The Internet as a Public Sphere." *New Media & Society,* vol. 4, no. 1, 2002, pp. 9–27.

Pérez, Gabriel, Andrea Aguilar, and María Guillermo. "El meme en internet. Usos sociales, reinterpretación y significados, a partir de Harlem Shake." *Argumentos,* vol. 27, no. 75, 2014, pp. 79–100, www.redalyc.org/articulo.oa?id=59533233004.

Pérez, Gabriel, and Carlos Hernández. "Expresiones de racismo y discriminación en grupos *autistas* en Facebook." *Comparative Cultural Studies: European and Latin American Perspectives,* vol. 4, 2017, pp. 21–33, https://doi.org/10.13128/ccselap-23179.

Popper, Karl. *The Logic of Scientific Discovery.* Vienna Verlag von Julius Springer, 1934.

Reguillo, Rosana. *Paisajes insurrectos.* Madrid: NED Ediciones, 2017.

Romero, Lucano. "Memes y opinión pública ¿una relación posible?" *Diálogos de la comunicación,* no. 91, 2015, dialnet.unirioja.es/servlet/articulo?codigo=6845112.

Rowan, Jaron. *Memes: Inteligencia idiota, política rara y folclore digital.* Ártica, Spain: Capitán Swing, 2015, biblioteca.articaonline.com/files/original/65216af72e0119b2077af48e 1785baf4.pdf.

Sartori, Giovanni. *Homo Videns.* Madrid: Taurus, 1998.

———. *¿Qué es la democracia?* Mexico City: Nueva Imagen, 1997.

Schmidt, Samuel. *En la mira. El chiste político en México.* Mexico City: Santillana Ediciones, 2016.

Shifman, Limor. "An Anatomy of a YouTube Meme." *New Media & Society,* vol. 14, no. 2, 2011, https://doi.org/10.1177/1461444811412160.

———. *Memes in Digital Culture.* London: MIT Press, 2014.

Shifman, Limor, and Mike Thelwall. "Assessing Global Diffusion with Web Memetics: The Spread and Evolution of a Popular Joke." *Journal of the American Society for Information Science and Technology,* vol. 60, no. 12, 2009, https://doi.org/10.1002/asi.21185.

Scolari, Carlos. *Ecología de los medios.* Barcelona: Gedisa, 2015.

Scott, James C. *Los dominados y el arte de la resistencia. Discursos ocultos.* Mexico City: Ediciones Era, 2000.

Sosa, Gabriel. "Medios electrónicos, democracia y elecciones." *El Cotidiano,* no. 155, 2009, pp.13–17, redalyc.org/articulo.oa?id=32512745003.

Torres-Nable, Luis César. "Redes sociales y marcos cognitivos. El caso #YaMeCansé y el conflicto de Ayotzinapa en México, 2014." *International and Multidisciplinary Journal of Social Sciences,* vol. 4, no. 2, pp. 175–193, http://doi.org/10.17583/rimcis.2015.1570.

Tolentino, Alexandre. "Memetáfora: Análisis del papel de las metáforas meméticas en la lucha de clases." *Discursos contemporáneos bajo estudio,* vol. 3, no. 1, 2018, pp. 167–196, https://doi.org/10.26512/discursos.v3i1.2018/8647.

Van Dijk, Teun. *La cultura de la conectividad. Una historia crítica de las redes sociales.* Coyoacán, Mexico: Siglo XXI, 2016.

Vaz, Gabriella. "Eles sabiam de tudo: o enunciado verbovisual em memes da capa da Revista Veja sobre as eleições 2014." *Revista Prolíngua,* vol. 12, no. 2, 2018, https://doi.org/10.22478/ufpb.1983-9979.2017v12n2.38240.

Vélez, José. "Influyendo en el ciberespacio con humor: imemes y otros fenómenos." *Versión. Estudios de comunicación y política,* no. 35, 2015, https://versionojs.xoc.uam.mx/index.php/version/article/view/602.

Virilio, Paul. *El cibermundo. La política de lo peor.* Madrid: Cátedra, 1997.

White, Leslie. *The Science of Culture: A Study of Man and Civilization.* 1949. Clinton Corners, New York. Eliot Werner Publications/Percheron Press, 2005.

6

Cutting through Layers of Brazilian Humor

Sampling the Past, Commenting on the Present, and Perhaps Creating the Future

EVA PAULINO BUENO
AND FÁBIO MARQUES DE SOUZA

This essay proposes to reflect upon Brazilian humor using multimodal texts composed of many languages that require capacities and practices of understanding and production of each one of them (a multiliteracy) to make themselves understood. As Roxane Rojo and Eduardo Moura have argued, texts like these are interactive, collaborative, and transgressive with their resources and language. Therefore, they are situated on the frontier of different forms and modes and are inescapably hybrid. To think about humor in multimodal texts involves the consideration of issues related to the production of each text, as well as the time and space that constitute a fundamental unity, exactly as in the human perception of daily reality.

In this essay, we are going to center first on two different times and their historic and cultural space in Brazilian humor as embodied by two goats: *Bode* (Goat) *Francisco Orelana*, created by the cartoonist Henrique de Souza Filho—Henfil (1944–1988)—and *Bode Gaiato*, Naughty Goat, created by Breno de Melo. Next, we are going to discuss the character Concessa, created and interpreted by the actress and comedian Aparecida Silva Mendes (Cida Mendes, or simply Cida), who currently appears on a YouTube channel and uses a distinctively Caipira regional accent while she comments, gives advice, and criticizes, always using humorous forms of expression.[1] The term "Caipira" is used here to refer to simple country dwellers, even though, as Antonio Cândido amply demonstrates in his *Os parceiros do Rio Bonito* (the partners of Rio Bonito), it also represents a culture in Brazil. But, depending on the circumstances, to call someone a Caipira in Brazil may be offensive, indicating a shy person without formal education and knowledge of more "sophisticated" urban life. Concessa's voice, however, is not the "generic" voice of a Brazilian woman that many foreigners imagine. She dresses modestly and casually, a far cry from the girl-from-Ipanema type in minuscule bikinis or "dental floss" bathing suits, showing off their youthful bodies. Concessa wears house dresses, makes no secret of the fact that she has reached menopause, and constantly refers to her adult sons. Concessa is, in other words, an adult woman from a specific culture that formed her and informs her opinions and attitudes. And she is a woman who mostly addresses other women. Like other Caipiras before her, she speaks not just with the accent but also with the authority of her culture, the product of negotiations, accommodations, struggle, and knowledge produced in the encounter between the white colonizer and the local Indigenous people who lived in the area comprising parts of the state of Minas Gerais and São Paulo.[2] But this culture is also an integral part of the enormous cultural tapestry that makes up Brazil.

Brazilian Humor across Time

The explosive mixture of humor and politics is nothing new in Brazil. Over the centuries, Brazilians have found humor to be a way to comment on and criticize the powerful through several means. Perhaps the first time Brazilians and resident Portuguese expressed the desire to mock established power was when the royal Portuguese court, fleeing Napoleon's invading army, arrived in Rio de Janeiro in 1808. Because the more than 15,000 arriving members of the court and other officers needed somewhere to stay, the most desirable houses were marked with the letters "P. R.," which meant "Príncipe Regente" (Prince Regent). The local residents, unable to oppose the regal orders, decided to interpret the two letters, P. R., to mean *Ponha-se na Rua,* meaning: "You are evicted," or "Get yourself to the street" (Meirelles 11; Saliba).

Did the mockery solve the problem? No. The best houses were still occupied by the new arrivals, and their owners moved to other parts of the city, had new houses built by their slaves, and life went on, with little consolation brought by the fact that the prince regent soon became King Dom João VI (1767–1826), who eventually returned to Portugal after the Napoleonic danger was over. But Brazil gained something, although the rich in Rio de Janeiro were inconvenienced: ports were opened to commerce with different countries, schools were founded, factories and roads were built, and a nascent press was allowed to exist. Perhaps that "P. R."—"Ponha-se na Rua!" was the first sign of how the written press was going to behave.

Later, during the reigns of Dom Pedro I (1798–1834) and Dom Pedro II (1825–1891), with the few newspapers in existence (and with at least putative

Figure 6.1. Satirical caricature of the emperor Dom Pedro II as a *manipanso,* an African idol. Each portfolio in his hands represents a ministry. Source: *O Mequetrefe,* 10 Jan. 1878.

"freedom of the press"), cartoonists used their work to publish commentaries, to express dissatisfaction with the situation, and to stand against slavery, as well as to criticize one or another political figure, including the emperors. No one was spared, as we can see in figure 6.1.

Here the emperor is represented as a *manipanso,* a Quicongo word used to designate an ancestor in the clan.[3] It is interesting to observe the contrast between the seemingly calm, grandfatherly figure and his muscular arms, which hold portfolios (the ministries), while he wears a necklace of skulls and politicians bow in front of him. From this one example (among many that could be used), it is clear that the press did not hold the emperor in great esteem and did not appreciate his absolute control of the country. But the emperor was not the only target. The following image was also originally published in the magazine *O Mequetrefe,* a Brazilian magazine published between 1875 and 1893, known for its great artistic quality and its sharp and recurrent criticism against the Brazilian monarchy and the exploitation of slave labor in the country. It outlines the Brazilian "nobility" by portraying a generic count as a rhinoceros, and an equally generic marquis as an elephant in an audience with Dom Pedro II (figure 6.2).

Dom Pedro II em audiência com o Conde de Rhinoceronte e o Marquês Masthodonte. "O mequetrefe" 1880.

Figure 6.2. Satirical representation of an audience with Dom Pedro II, the emperor. The animalized humans represent the aristocracy, pachydermic and backward. Source: *O Mequetrefe,* 1880. ·

In 1889, Brazil finally expelled the imperial family and founded the Brazilian republic, bringing with it fresh subject matter for cartoonists, who continued working and voicing their opinions even during the several harsh dictatorships the country lived through during the Getúlio Vargas era (1937–1945), as well as the military dictatorship (1964–1985). It is noteworthy that during the last dictatorship, large contingents of Brazilians moved from the countryside to the large urban centers, especially São Paulo and Rio de Janeiro, thus transforming them into enormous and complex cities. São Paulo, for instance, is among the five largest cities in the world, with a current population of more than 22 million people.[4]

It is important to keep in mind, however, that Brazil is far more than just the big urban centers with splendid houses that the court wanted to occupy during the colonial period, or the touristic spots featured in travel brochures that the rich of our time enjoy. Brazilian culture encompasses much more than what can be seen in the best-known newspapers and magazines, or on television. What accounts for this diversity? For Darcy Ribeiro, the different types of development that occurred at different times and with different ethnic and cultural components gave rise to what he calls "Brasis." Ribeiro divides the country into five types: 1. Crioulo (a child of Black and white parents); 2. Caboclo (a person of mixed Indigenous Brazilian and European background); 3. Caipira (as discussed by Antonio Cândido); 4. Sertanejo (people who come especially from the arid Northeast backlands); and 5. Sulino (a person from the southern region of the country, encompassing the states of Paraná, Santa Catarina, and Rio Grande do Sul).[5] Each of these types refers to a moment in the occupation of the territory by the Portuguese, and the land use in each period. At one point, we can say that each one of these "Brasis"—the plural of Brasil, the spelling used in the country—also had a different cultural substratum, that this substratum manifests itself on the national surface at different times, and that each of these substrata is responsible for the variety of Brazilian culture. Here we are considering culture as Clifford Geertz defines it, "a historically transmitted pattern of meanings, embodied in symbols, a system of inherited concepts expressed in symbolic forms by means of which men communicate, perpetuate, and develop their knowledge about and attitudes toward life" (89).[6]

And yet, culture is not a static reality. The Brazil of the twenty-first century is becoming quite different from the Brazil of the late twentieth century, for instance. This change is neither a preventable nor a singular occurrence. Indeed, on pace with a phenomenon that has happened all over the world, in Brazil, the rural population started moving toward the large urban centers in search of jobs, allied to the development of radio, then television, and then the Internet, which have contributed to, in some cases, the disappearance of several regional cultural aspects. But do these cultural aspects disappear forever? And if they do not disappear, how can they return without being seen only as quaint or meaningless?

In this essay, we are going to work with two examples of cultural "resurfacing," that is, the reappearance of an older cultural trait/system/belief/linguistic variant that remains alive under the layers of more recent developments in a country or a community.[7]

One of the examples we use here focuses on the cartoon character Bode Gaiato—Naughty Goat—which can be found on Facebook, and which is endlessly shared and multiplied across several platforms, including email, WhatsApp, Instagram, Twitter, and others. Bode Gaiato, as we will see in the next segment, is the heir of a previous goat, which appeared on the Brazilian cultural scene during one of the harshest periods of our history, the last military dictatorship (1964–1985). The second example is character in a YouTube show called *Tecendo prosa* (chit-chat),[8] in which the actress Aparecida (Cida) Silva Mendes appears as a housewife, sometimes wearing an apron, and always having her hair up in curlers covered with a colorful scarf. The character's name is Concessa, a fifty-ish-year-old woman who speaks with an unmistakable Caipira accent and comments on events, gives advice, scolds, and tells stories. But a character like Concessa is not a new creation in Brazilian culture. She descends from several examples, such as the poet, writer, folklorist, public speaker, and showman Cornélio Pires (1884–1958), who was renowned for his storytelling style, and wrote several books, including *Conversas ao pé do fogo* (chatting by the fire), and the film character Jeca Tatu, created by Monteiro Lobato and later embodied by actor, businessman, director, and producer Amácio Mazzaropi (1912–1981). That means that Bode Gaiato and Concessa both evoke something earlier, tapping into the knowledge, understanding, and humor available to all Brazilians, while at the same time using contemporary means and techniques. This sampling of the past and commenting on the present may be the reason why their popularity has become so great. They are both very funny, but they also make their audiences think, reflect on the current situation, and perhaps act on their futures. The COVID-19 pandemic has given both of them a lot of material, especially at a time when a large percentage of the Brazilian people feel that the government has failed to protect them against the ravages of the virus and instead has used the opportunity to conduct itself in less-than-honest ways.

The First Goat

Among Brazilian cartoonists, we want to stress the work of Henfil (Henrique de Souza Filho, 1944–1988). Henfil's political commentary was particularly important during the last military dictatorship (1964–1985), especially for his character *Bode Orelana* (Orelana Goat) and those who appeared in his stories: the stand-in for Henfil, the bird "Graúna," and the man Zeferino Ribamar das Mercês, a man who appears dressed in *jagunço*—Northeastern outlaw—clothes and speaks as a representative of "the people." With these characters, Henfil directed his sharpest criticism against the Brazilian intelligentsia, whom he saw as passive and incapable of articulating themselves and fighting against the abuses of dictators.[9]

Bode Orelana was part of the "Grupo do Alto da Caatinga" (group of the High Caatinga), a group of characters who dwell in the general area of the Northeast of Brazil. The Grupo was created by Henfil in the 1970s. The stories were published daily in the *Jornal do Brasil* and monthly in the magazine *Fradim*. Orelana appears as an intellectual who believes in the proletariat and historic action, and acts as a reinvigorating function of civil society and as a

Figure 6.3. Bode Orelana, by Brazilian cartoonist Henfil, is a goat that gets its culture by devouring books. Source: M. Pires (129).

social agent favorable to the democratization of social and political institutions.[10]

Henfil's stories and cartoons were humorous, political, critical, and satirical, always speaking through typically Brazilian characters. Henfil was responsible for the renovation of the national cartoon, fulfilling a decolonizing role at a moment in which Brazilian production was being suffocated by the distribution of American cartoons in the country.[11]

Orelana is, then, the intellectual of the Caatinga. He is responsible for transmitting knowledge and culture to the other members of the group, who do not have either formal education or proximity to sources of knowledge. According to Henfil, the inspiration for the creation of this character, who develops a peculiar reading practice, came from stories the artist Elomar used to tell about experiences and people living in the Caatinga.[12] Elomar told Henfil about a goat that used to eat books, so Henfil concluded that the goat was an intellectual, and thus the character Bode Orelana was born. However, eating newspapers was always risky for the goat, because they could put it in a state of shock.

In her study of Bode Orelana, Maria da Conceição Francisca Pires stresses that the goat represents the image of the intellectual in the Caatinga, an arid place for the production of ideas, absolutely bereft of material means, punished by the sun, which in this case represents the oppression of the dictatorship. For Orelana and his friends, the only form of accessing information and acquiring knowledge is through the consumption of reading material available to them, although in a very precarious form. Since they cannot not read, Orelana simply eats the material and "digests" it for the others.

In sum, Bode Orelana, as well as other characters created by Henfil, personified resistance against the military dictatorship. Both in their dialogues

Figure 6.4. Bode Orelana, named after the Amazonian explorer Francisco de Orellana, complains about the lack of freedom of speech.
He is saying, "Do you mean that we have to acquire culture with our mouths shut?" Source: M. Pires (130).

and his sharp, distinctive drawings, Henfil discussed the current situation; at the same time, he also criticized other intellectuals who were reduced—like Orelana—to simply eating, digesting, and defecating (figure 6.4).

The New Bode in a New Time

Brazil no longer lives under an open dictatorship (so far), and the ways of transmitting information, knowledge, and commentary are not restricted to newspapers, books, and magazines. Contemporary digital culture presents itself as multimodal and demands multiple literacies to create meaning; that is, contemporary digital culture expresses itself, produces, and distributes concepts through paper, cellular telephones, and computer screens; furthermore, it employs different types of technology, as well as different formats and representational languages: written text, visual material, audiovisual languages, and hypertexts.[13]

With the advent of the Internet, especially with the creation of Facebook, artists were able to experiment with different formats to once again criticize through humor, using different forms. Raquel Recuero discusses how danah boyd's essay "Social Network Sites as Networked Publics: Affordances, Dynamics and Implications" presents social media as hybrid spaces, exemplified by the mixture of characteristics that show communicative exchanges within the public space. As we see it, social media like Facebook and Instagram simultaneously support, modify, and amplify typical interactions among social groups. YouTube also has become one of the most important channels for new verbal and non-verbal interactions, which can be seen as very close to oral/ informal conversation, but which are also different from daily conversation.

Among the newest expressions of how humor has evolved or changed, we will focus on Bode Gaiato (Naughty Goat), a meme created in 2013, mentioned above. In these memes, the characters appear dressed mostly in t-shirts or plaid shirts, or in a flowery house dress to signify a female goat. Perhaps this choice of informal clothing seeks to lead the viewer to identify with the character. And the audience is very large indeed: on Facebook, Bode Gaiato has about nine million followers. But this number does not represent the real number of people who follow the series, because many people view the Facebook page without officially following it, and Bode Gaiato memes are frequently shared as forwarded messages. Since its inception, as we can see on Facebook, Bode Gaiato has commented on the news and scandals of the day. Since early 2020, although Bode still comments on other matters, the coronavirus pandemic has taken center stage. We will focus on this because we believe those comments contain echoes of other urgent political and social issues.

But before we start discussing this new goat in Brazilian culture, we need to discuss the genre of the meme itself. Carlos Mauricio Castaño Díaz gives an authoritative view of the development of the concept "meme," which, he writes,

> Is an academic concept coined by the biologist Richard Dawkins in his book *The Selfish Gene*. He proposed the term *meme* as a Darwinian, gene-centred approach to cultural evolution, defining it as "the unit of cultural transmission." Nevertheless, nowadays it is possible to find the concept of meme almost everywhere on the Internet, not alluding to the concept created by Dawkins, but relating to certain kinds of images, jokes or trends popular within the cybernauts [sic]. (Castaño Díaz 83)

Castaño Díaz goes on to explain how the concept has evolved within academic confines, but, as he states, due to the expansion of computer usage and the Internet itself, "the concept of meme has gone beyond the academic definition. …. Meme is now, somehow, related with what Dawkins defines as a meme, but with some special characteristics due to their way of transmission and speed of replication" (Castaño Díaz 83).

Currently, Internet memes can be considered cultural artifacts, and they are usually created by cyberspace users who try to reframe daily subjects, or subjects occurring in the news or social and political discourse. Luana Inocêncio and Camila Lopes discuss memes as an evolution of traditional games and jokes that permeate people's imaginary; for this reason, memes constitute a kind of postmodern folklore.

The characters of the memes we are focusing on in this segment are all goats, which, like Bode Orelana, are still much identified with the Northeast Region of Brazil. Bode Gaiato's themes center on the daily lives of Brazilians.[14] It is humorous because, as the name "gaiato" (naughty or mischievous) suggests, the goat likes to tell jokes, play tricks, tell stories, and amuse everybody. Because Bode usually dresses in t-shirts and other items of clothing that are commonly worn by Brazilians, the audience can immediately identify with him and his companions.

What interests us particularly is how Bode Gaiato uses several resources, such as the *remix*—the use of an element and its presentation in a different form—and the *mashup*, characterized by Araújo as more accentuated *remixes* of a hybrid nature, and that combine elements from several sources. In the case of Bode Gaiato, the images combine a human body and the head of a goat.[15] Although the image itself is funny because it is so incongruent, we think we can look at Bode Gaiato beyond the mere surface. In this part of our essay, we want to ask questions about the use of this specific animal as well as the references to the culture of the Northeast Region of Brazil, where the animal is appreciated for its milk and meat. In addition, we want to propose a look at some of the memes themselves, to reflect on the linguistic and political reach of this character.

We can see an example of remixing in figure 6.5, in which the first picture shows a universe as the background image, whereas the last scene uses the image of the frozen screen, something very common in the soap opera *Avenida Brasil*. Soap operas—or *telenovelas*—have been a mainstay of Brazilian life since 1952, when the first telenovela (*Sua vida me pertence* ["Your life belongs to me"]) aired on TV Tupi (Pessoa). Many iconic characters have graced Brazilian tv screens since then, ever since the large television networks invested heavily in them, mainly during the military dictatorship (1964–1985).[16] In this case, we observe the convention by which some characters' images would be frozen at the end of each chapter, as a suspenseful soundtrack rose.[17] This was a way of defining a scene that would be continued in the subsequent chapter of the soap opera. It was a way to create suspense and ensure the viewer would tune in the next day.

In figure 6.6, we can see the technique used with the character Carminha in *Avenida Brasil*. And, as we can see in figure 6.7, Bode Gaiato echoes the television image to create a part of the multimodal text that appears on the

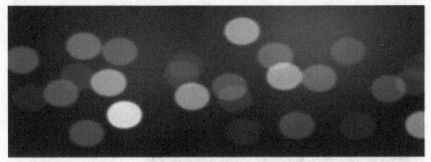

Figure 6.5. A freeze-frame of the final image from an episode of the soap opera *Avenida Brasil*. Source: gshow.globo.com/novelas/avenida-brasil/.

Figure 6.6. A freeze-frame of Carminha's dismay at the end of an episode of the soap opera *Avenida Brasil*. Source: gshow.globo.com/novelas/avenida-brasil/.

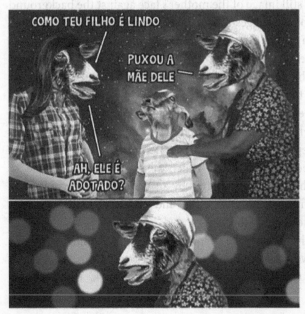

Figure 6.7. A sarcastic exchange in Bode Gaiato alluding to a compliment on a child's good looks. Man: "How beautiful your son is!" Mother: "He takes after his mom." Man: "Oh, so he's adopted?" Source: www.facebook.com/BodeGaiato.

TENHO CERTEZA QUE QUEM VAI DESCOBRIR A CURA PRO VÍRUS VAI SER UMA MÃE

DESESPERADA COM OS FILHOS 24 HORAS DENTRO DE CASA E SEM IR PRA ESCOLA

Figure 6.8. A meme on who will be most likely to discover the cure for the coronavirus. The figure is saying, "I am sure that whoever discovers the cure for this virus will be a desperate mother, with her children at home 24 hours a day and unable to go to school." Source: www.facebook.com/BodeGaiato

Internet. In this figure (episode) we see a common situation in which a man (a male goat) praises the looks of a woman's (female goat's) child. The mother, feeling that the man is complimenting her on her physical appearance, replies, perhaps a bit jokingly, "He looks like his mother." She is of course implying that she is beautiful, since her son is beautiful. But the man then asks, "Oh, he is adopted, then?" The still image of the mother's face against the background taken from the soap opera suggests that something else may happen next. In this case, the meme makes fun of very common interactions and exposes what people sometimes think about other children's and their parents' appearance. What could be the mother's reaction to an insinuation both that her son is not her son and that she is ugly? Tune in!

Bode Gaiato's memes can also be extremely topical, and lately, the meme has concentrated on what we can call "pandemic humor" related to COVID-19. There are many "episodes," but we will concentrate on just a few. One example is what we see in figure 6.8, in which the goat (a nanny or doe, of course) refers to the challenge encountered by all the mothers living in confinement with their children 24 hours a day and makes a prediction about who is going to find the cure for the virus.

Indeed, one can only imagine the desperation of a mother having to take care of all her usual work—sometimes working remotely from home—and then also take care of the children, oversee their homework, arbitrate their

PRIMEIRO ANO QUE EU NUM VOU VIAJAR PRA FORA POR CAUSA DO CORONA

NOS OUTROS ANOS EU NUM IA POR FALTA DE DINHEIRO MERMO

Figure 6.9. A meme satirizes the idea of traveling as an escape, as the poor are unable to do so. The figure is saying, "This is the first year I'm not traveling abroad because of the coronavirus. Other years I didn't go because I didn't have any money." Source: www.facebook.com/BodeGaiato

fights, etc. It is no wonder Bode Gaiato proclaims that one of these mothers will be the first to discover the cure for the virus, so the children can return to school and life can go back to what it was before the pandemic.

Several situations of life in society and the popular imaginary are transformed into memes which, once published, are commented on, "liked," shared, and reworked. Figure 6.9, for instance, refers to a situation in which a great part of the population finds itself—that is, being unable to travel abroad due to a lack of financial resources. This meme is a commentary on that reality—but at least with COVID-19 such people were able to say that the pandemic was the reason they did not travel. Indeed, according to the Brazilian Statistics Agency (IBGE), about 90 percent of Brazilians earn less than $1,000 a month, barely enough to cover most necessities (*Rendimento*).

Still commenting on the pandemic, the next meme (figure 6.10) reflects the kind of conclusion Bode (and many people, including important political figures) reaches regarding a solution for the public health emergency.

It is clear, then, to judge from Bode Gaiato's thoughts, that the cure for the virus can be something as simple as injecting alcohol into people. Indeed, this is not too far from the idea of injecting chlorine, since chlorine kills the virus on surfaces. For obvious reasons, Gaiato's idea is far from original, and this meme reflects, comments on, and criticizes something that everybody who has access to the Internet has seen: influential political figures dissemi-

Figure 6.10. A meme mocks a simplistic understanding of vaccines. The figure says, "Today I am going to sleep early." At 3 a.m. he says, "If hand sanitizer kills the coronavirus, why don't they make an alcohol-based vaccine?" Source: www .facebook.com/BodeGaiato

nating lies and peddling crazy ideas about how to cure the illness caused by the coronavirus. One such political figure was the (now former) president of Brazil himself, Jair Bolsonaro, who, at various phases of the pandemic, despite the mounting numbers of dead, called those calling for help "sissies" and "whiners" who should just shut up and go back to work. He fired his health minister, Luiz Henrique Mandetta, in 2020 when Mandetta did not agree with the president's prescription of chloroquine for the treatment of the virus (Bolsonaro is not a physician, it should be noted), and the president did not agree with Mandetta's prescription of social distancing and closing of non-essential businesses.[18]

The creator of Bode Gaiato is very well-acquainted with what is going on in Brazil and the world, not just in the political arena, but also in popular culture, and lately in people's reactions to daily struggles related to a lack of money and pandemic-related problems. Each one of the memes is not just published on Facebook, where it originally resides, but is disseminated through means such as WhatsApp (which is widely used in Brazil) and email.[19] In a sense, Bode Gaiato has become a funny and sharp commentator, and the memes have been incorporated into just about every Brazilian's life and have commented on the state of affairs in various parts of the world. In every aspect, this meme is a worthy heir to Henfil's Bode Orelana, and perhaps someday it will generate heir or heirs, who will continue the tradition of commenting on life in general and politics in particular through humor.

Tecendo prosa (Chit-Chat)

The next character is a Caipira from the state of Minas Gerais who inhabits the YouTube universe. Someone who is not from Brazil may ask how we know that the character Concessa is a Caipira. For us Brazilians, her accent is the first indication of her culture. The differentiating sound is the "r" before consonants or at the ends of words. Claudia Mehler Bot writes that the language that developed in this region is an amalgamation of the Portuguese brought by colonizers and the Tupi-Guarani language of the Indigenous peoples of the region.[20] Although Brazil, a country the size of a continent, has many accents, this specific "r" sound in the Caipira accent is understood as perhaps its most noticeable characteristic, though not the only one—the Caipira dialect includes vocabulary differences, intonation, and changes in the positions of letters. One very common example is the word "porque" (because) or "por que" (why), which becomes "proque" in both cases.[21] In every one of Concessa's videos, this changed word appears, alongside other, less-common ones. But more so than these merely linguistic aspects of her speech, other features make Concessa appealing to many Brazilians.

The actress Aparecida Silva Mendes—Cida—who plays Concessa, is herself from the state of Minas Gerais, where a large percentage of the population speaks Caipira Portuguese. Concessa appears mostly from her own house, especially from her kitchen, which is simple but well-furnished. In Brazilian terms, this is a house of the lower middle class, with a resident who dresses as a lower-middle-class woman and speaks as a person from the interior of São Paulo. In other words, Concessa is an everywoman, and she is very popular. Her videos are sometimes viewed up to a million times. And, once again, they are also shared through WhatsApp many more times.

As figure 6.11 shows, Concessa is making coffee using a traditional cloth filter, which is still widely used in the rural areas of Brazil. She has her hair in curlers and receives a phone call from her friend Jandira, her most frequent caller. The conversation between the two friends can focus on a wide range of subjects, including the news, family business, women's business, clothing, raising children, hygiene, COVID-19, and even rape, sexual abuse, and politics. We see Concessa at home, wearing a housedress, referring to her friend on the phone as "Coisinha" (little thing). The show is seemingly unaware of or uninterested in acknowledging the incongruence of the proximity of a rustic

Figure 6.11. An episode of *Tecendo prosa* with Concessa offering advice from the kitchen. Episode: "No bule" (in the kettle) (July 5, 2018). Source: www.youtube.com/watch?v=MmeMnvET_h0.

coffee contraption to a twenty-first-century cell phone. It is not lost on many Brazilians her age that not long ago—until the early 2000s at least—there were very few telephones in Brazil, and most residents of rural towns had to wait in line to use the only *Orelhão* (big ear), a payphone operated by tokens. The fact that Concessa, although living in a house that is obviously "in the country-side," has access to a cell phone with apparently unlimited minutes (for long and repeated calls to Jandira) does not seem to provoke any surprise, to judge from the comments on the YouTube page, which every viewer can access and to which any viewer can add. Indeed, what the comments written by viewers on the different episodes of "Concessa's" YouTube page reveal is that she has a loyal and thankful following—both women AND men—who admire her humor as well as her courage in speaking of the difficult things that can occur in people's lives—divorce, loss of friends and relatives, lack of money, domestic violence, and the political situation at the moment the video is created.

To our knowledge, there are as yet no scholarly essays about the artist or her character, so most of the information about her work comes from interviews and a Wikipedia entry.[22] In an interview she gave to fellow comedian Geraldo Magela, she recalls their experience working on TV shows, and makes fun of the rivalry between Paulistas (people from the state of São Paulo) and Cariocas (people from Rio de Janeiro), while stressing that "everyone likes *mineiros*—people from Minas Gerais." Cida's state of origin is a point of great importance, both for herself and for an understanding of the Caipira philosophy of the character.[23]

Dupla receita pra tempos de confilhamento...Frita no 180

Figure 6.12. An episode of *Tecendo prosa* in which Concessa addresses domestic abuse while pretending to share a recipe. Episode: "Dupla receita pra tempos de confilhamento . . . Frita no 180" (double recipe for quarantine times . . . fry at 180) (May 21, 2020). Source: www.youtube.com/watch?v=Tdz3eQ0bcCl.

Her conversation covers a wide range of subjects. She attracts such a devoted audience because she speaks directly to people "like her," who may need an encouraging word, so she talks about the need to take depression seriously, about the importance of having friends. She also touches on other thorny issues, such as the usual humiliations Brazilians who want to travel to the US have to go through, speaking of her refusal to travel to the United States because of the visa requirement. But besides being an artist, Cida Mendes is also a businesswoman who uses the interview with Magela to promote her recently opened restaurant "off BR 040, km 49."[24] Later, she devotes a full episode on YouTube to speaking about the restaurant, inviting her "friends" to "come over."

At this point, it is impossible not to remember another artist, Amácio Mazzaropi, who spoke from within that same culture, used his wildly popular movies to comment on Brazilian matters—political, social, religious, and popular culture icons of the time—and, although not considered worthy of critical acclaim after he started making money with his films, who never shied away from making sure the commercial side of his films was taken care of.[25] As an entertainer, Cida knows that an artist needs to use several methods to keep afloat. Considering that the food from her home state of Minas Gerais is highly appreciated in Brazil and that her show always portrays her at her home, it would seem natural for her to open a restaurant—Casa de Concessa (Concessa's house)—where, besides serving traditional food cooked in traditional ovens, there is also a performance space. Cida says that she invites fellow comedians and other artists to present there. When there are no entertainers, the space is used as a children's play area.[26]

But Concessa's talks are not just about food or chit-chat with her friend Jandira. As we can see in the episode titled "Dupla receita pra tempos de confilhamento. Frita no 180" (double recipe for quarantine times . . . fry at 180), Concessa uses the occasion of teaching her viewers how to make a soy and manioc dish to send a message to women who may be suffering domestic violence during the pandemic. The episode starts in the usual fashion, with her addressing the "Coisinha" who is one of her interlocutors.

The scene is set with the stove in the background, where she is cooking. In the foreground, there is an easel with a written greeting reminding viewers that Concessa is there to help them. In the sequence, she speaks directly to the camera about the recipe she is using while flipping the pages of the easel pad, which explains the increase in domestic violence during quarantine, and urging her viewers to seek help by calling 180 (the direct number for the Centro de Atendimento à Mulher [women's service center]) if they are being mistreated or threatened. But Concessa never says out loud any of the things written on the easel pad; she simply continues talking about the recipe she is making, while pointing at the written message. As research shows, victims of domestic violence are often afraid to seek help because they feel unworthy or guilty. The message Concessa gives her viewers is direct, but she delivers it indirectly, perhaps because she knows that an abuser may overhear the audio. This is a powerful example of the kind of techniques that need to be used to help victims of domestic abuse, whose tormentors may be standing right by their sides.

There are several other examples of Cida's use of voice and image to reinforce her message. We must point out that Concessa does not speak only to her friends, her "Coisinhas." Sometimes she addresses the viewer directly and, one time, in a special episode called "Jornal Concessa Edição 01" (Concessa's journal, first edition), which aired on June 27, 2017, she informs the viewer that she is going to speak directly to the president "Mickey Donadi Trump," and "as make possible I will speak in English with you" (if possible I will speak in English with you) (figure 6.13).

Then she says that she is speaking for "all the cucarachas [cockroaches] of South America, for Brazilian women, and mainly for the people of Pará de Minas, Parati, and Paracatu." At this point, she shows a video of Trump speaking in his rallies, insisting that from that time on, it is going to be "America

Jornal Concessa - Edição 01

Figure 6.13. The first edition of *Concessa News,* in which Concessa addresses the US president (June 17, 2017). Source: www.youtube.com/watch?v=a5DTDFis-t8.

first." Then Concessa tells Trump, "Don't worry, be happy! You are number one, but Brazil is number two." She proceeds to inform Trump that the Brazilian system is different from the American system because even though she went to school for only four years, she can read, write, and do math. "One thing I don't understand," she concedes, "is how American elections work. . . . But then, it doesn't matter anyway, because elections don't work in Brazil either. The last election here was not worth it." She is clearly referring to the political turmoil in Brazil at the time, when a right-wing movement staged a coup that knocked President Dilma Rousseff from power through a rigged impeachment, and persecuted (and then jailed without any proof) former president Lula da Silva to prevent him from running for president against Bolsonaro.[27]

Unlike other shows, Concessa's is interspersed with videos of Trump rallies, as well as images of Brazil, especially the Amazon—"which is ours [Brazil's], you know," she says—along with the "thousands of kilometers of beaches," as well as the "greatest lesser-known historic city of Minas Gerais, Paracatu."[28] At this point, she shows images of a very small town with old houses and cobblestone streets. Minas Gerais is well known for its famous historic cities such as Ouro Preto and Mariana, cities located in the southwest area of the state, which attract thousands of tourists. So Cida Mendes is making fun of the *mineiro* penchant for claiming certain cities as the best in the country even when the city they come from lacks great historical importance.

Jornal Concessa - Edição 01

Figure 6.14. A parodic coat of arms describing the US/Brazil relationship, according to the first edition of *Concessa News* (June 17, 2017). Source: www.youtube.com/watch?v=a5DTDFis-t8.

Continuing her dialogue, she tells "Mickey Donadi Trump" that Brazil is the number two country in world importance—behind the USA—because "we have a lot of corruption. You like it, I know!" In addition, she says, "We have another thing you are going to like: an unprecedented environmental disaster. Can't you understand what I am saying? You like it, I know!"

To close, she tells her putative viewer "Donadi" that European countries such as Switzerland, Holland, Portugal, and Germany may want to be number two, but that position belongs to Brazil, "because those Europeans are too fine to deal with you." The closing shot is a picture of a seal with the American and Brazilian flags together on it. On top, there is the label "America First," and on the bottom, "Brazil Second." Considering the then-current situation with the COVID-19 pandemic, this could be seen as prophetic, as, indeed, the US ranks first in deaths globally, while Brazil is second.[29] Life imitating art.

Concluding Thoughts

It is always dangerous to try to reach "conclusions" based on examples of phenomena that some may consider as transitory as the Bode Gaiato memes and Concessa's "Tecendo prosa." But—full disclosure—we may be speaking as people of the last century, the last millennium, educated at a time in which the printed word mattered more, simply because it only became a deciding factor in the last decades of the twentieth century. Neither Bode Gaiato nor Concessa inhabits the printed world. For us, they may seem always already on the verge of disappearing into the ether of forgetfulness or lack of Internet connections.

But for the people called "digital natives," this is their reality: it is much more common for them to acquire knowledge and make sense of the world through what they see on the screen. We can safely say memes operate in Brazilian culture today the same way that older forms of political humor operated in the past, through magazines, newspapers, and books. It is important to keep track of these changes and this continuity in different media both within the humoristic tradition and in the political system that provokes such responses on the part of humorists and artists. Maybe Bode Gaiato will someday have the same feeling of permanence as Bode Orelana had for the generation coming to adulthood in Brazil in the 1970s. Maybe Concessa will continue filtering centuries-old Caipira knowledge through her YouTube program in the same way that, from time immemorial, humans have gathered around a storyteller to hear the news, the jokes, the stories that helped them make sense of their lives and their places in the world. Once again recalling John Thompson's work, we can agree that the new media, instead of disrupting the transmission of the stories and wisdom of a culture, instead serve to make it more available to a wider audience. And yes, humor is the best way to "sweeten the pill" of hard truths that both Bode Gaiato and Concessa have to serve to their audiences: lack of money, problems at home, depression, domestic violence, hunger, and political oppression. In Brazil, a country where there are enormous regional linguistic, racial, and cultural differences, the two characters analyzed here can be seen as a kind of "cultural glue" which— like other humorists, writers, and filmmakers did in the past and are still doing today—will continue helping the country make sense of itself as a diverse, rich, and ever-evolving culture with a complex and sometimes disturbing political history.

Notes

1 The fact that the actress hails from the state of Minas Gerais is crucial to the character because this region and part of the region now encompassed by the state of São Paulo are the cradle of Caipira culture.

2 Antonio Cândido published the first full study of Caipira culture, *Os parceiros do Rio Bonito*, in 1964. In that book, Cândido studies the development of the culture and its main characteristics, and presents a culture that is both strong and fragile, resilient and about to be wiped out by incoming technologies and roads.

3 For more information on the African languages spoken in Brazil and how they influenced Brazilian Portuguese, see John M. Lipski's *A History of Afro-Hispanic Language:
Five Centuries, Five Continents,* and Esmeralda Vailati Negrão and Evani Viotti's "Epistemological Aspects of the Study of the Participation of African Languages in Brazilian
Portuguese."

4 For a more comprehensive study of when, how, and why Brazilians moved from the
countryside to urban centers, see Wilson Cano, *Raízes da concentração industrial em
São Paulo.*

5 See Ribeiro's full discussion of this division in *O povo brasileiro.* The whole book is a
detailed presentation of the ways in which the different patterns of colonization, ethnic
groups, agriculture, and commerce determined not just the occupation of the land, but
also how the language itself changed.

6 Geertz himself concedes that, even by 1973, when his book was first published, the
term "culture" had fallen into "ill-repute." However, we have not found a better term to
account for the phenomena produced within a society or group, and which have deep
roots in the knowledge, taste, ways of speaking, ways of seeing the world and society
shared by the group and transmitted to the new members (children or newcomers).
For Geertz on this subject, see pages 89 and following of his book.

7 The idea of "resurfacing" was much discussed during the heyday of the postmodernist
debate, as Stephen Cumming's essay "Back to the Oracle: Post-Modern Organization
Theory as a Resurfacing of Pre-Modern Wisdom" shows. There are also other works
that explore the different ways "resurfacing" can occur, and one good example is John
Thompson's *The Media and Modernity,* in which he states that, although current media
forms can disrupt the traditional transmission of wisdom, they can also, perhaps para-
doxically, help maintain it by making this wisdom (and art forms also) available to a
wider audience. Another important discussion comes from Lisa-Jayne Linton, who, in
her MA thesis, uses Thompson's theory (among others) to discuss how media were an
important factor in the resurgence of traditional Irish dance.

8 The name of the show, "Tecendo prosa," is difficult to translate into English. The first
word, "tecendo," means "weaving," and "prosa" means "brief and friendly conversation." "Weaving" may point to a recognizable feminine activity in Brazil, where a large
portion of women learn early in life to do needlework, crochet, etc., at least as a hobby.
Men have also begun participating in these hobbies, but they are still considered more
"feminine" pastimes.

9 In his 1984 book, *Como se faz humor político* (How to do political humor), Henfil
explains in an extended interview with journalist and music critic Tárik de Souza his
relationship with the censorship put in place by the military dictatorship, and how he
continued working despite many pressures.

10 Although "Caatinga" is usually associated with the Northeast of Brazil, it refers to the
semi-arid region that occupies about 11 percent of the national territory and appears
in states such as Alagoas, Bahia, Ceará, Maranhão, Pernambuco, Paraíba, Rio Grande
do Norte, Piauí, Sergipe and the north of Minas Gerais. In total, the Caatinga covers
about 850,000 square kilometers.

11 For an in-depth analysis of how Henfil helped shape Brazilian cartoon culture during the military dictatorship, see Mariana Virginia Moretti Carvalho's bachelor's thesis

Quando os quadrinhos viram história: uma análise das charges de Henfil e o contexto da educação no regime militar brasileiro. As for the American colonizing presence in Brazil and how it affected Brazilian cartooning, one good example is Walt Disney's creation, the parrot Zé Carioca, born after Disney's Good Neighbor visit to South America in the early 1940s. For an in-depth discussion of the creation of this character and of Disney's position on the inclusion of Brazilian music and environment in the films in which Zé Carioca appeared, see Andrew Kelly Nelson's 2017 thesis *José, Joe, Zé Carioca: Walt Disney's Good Neighbor's Colonial "Monument" in Brazil.*

12 This is a reference to the singer, guitar player, and composer Elomar Figueira Mello.

13 Melissa Grolund's 2016 book *Contemporary Art and Digital Culture* provides an insightful discussion of how the Internet and digital technologies have affected our current cultural and social environments, and how these new systems have transformed the creation and the reception of art since the end of the twentieth century. Grolund asks important questions about the market for art, and the issues around art and ownership.

14 The Bode Gaiato Facebook page shows a number of the characters that appear in the series. Available at www.facebook.com/BodeGaiato/.

15 In *Remix Theory: the Aesthetics of Sampling,* Eduardo Navas acknowledges that much has already been published about remixing under the umbrella of remix culture, and how issues of intellectual property are always a concern. He emphasizes in the Introduction to the book that "remix culture is a global cultural activity often linked with copyright" (3). For Navas, "Remix is not an actual movement, but a binder—a cultural glue" (4). Farther on in the text, he proposes that remix is "more like a virus that has mutated into different forms according to the needs of particular cultures" (4). For this reason, Navas continues, remix is "meta, always unoriginal," and it "needs cultural value to be at play" (4).

16 Victor Andrade de Melo and Mauricio Drumond provide an in-depth analysis of the development of the involvement of TV Globo (the main producer of telenovelas in Brazil) with the military dictatorship in their essay "Globo, the Brazilian Military Dictatorship and the 1970 FIFA Football World Cup: Ambiguous Relations."

17 The soap opera *Avenida Brazil,* written by João Manuel Carneiro and others, aired on TV Globo from March to October 2012. It was extremely successful, reaching large audiences. Its last chapter is said to have been seen by more than 50 million people.

18 As the Brazilian media amply illustrated on screens and in the pages of newspapers, during the height of the pandemic, when hospitals and clinics were collapsing under the weight of thousands upon thousands of daily deaths from COVID, Bolsonaro promoted large gatherings of unmasked people, and to this day claims he has not taken the vaccine, even though he himself did contract COVID. See *Jornal do Brasil, O Globo,* and other news outlets during the period ranging from March 2020 to June 2022.

19 We must point out, however, that our affirmation is based purely on anecdotal evidence and on our experience with Brazilian friends, acquaintances, and family members. The interesting thing is that sometimes we received a new Bode Gaiato installment from different sources almost at the same time, thus showing (at least to us) that many people were attuned to the latest commentary provided by Bode.

20 Claudia Mehler Bot says of Caipira culture that "A língua falada era uma variante do idioma dos índios Tupis, que mais tarde em decorrência das ordens da coroa portuguesa a exigência foi de se abrasileirar, se utilizar do português"—"The spoken language was a variant of the Tupi language; later, due to demands from the Portuguese crown that it be Brazilianized, they used the Portuguese." There are several articles on this subject available on the Internet, written both by professional linguists and by Brazilians who are intrigued by the accent, especially the very varied "r." One such article is by Pâmela Carbonari and Tiago Jokura, in which both authors clearly enjoy themselves trying to understand how geography and history affected this one phoneme in Brazilian Portuguese. The "r" sound occurring before other consonants sounds like the "r" in "more."

21 Amadeu Amaral's book *O dialecto caipira,* first published in 1920 and now freely available online, with the new spelling as *O dialeto caipira,* contains very detailed descriptions and explanations of the changes occurring in this dialect. Amaral's study includes lists of Tupi words, and his analysis goes beyond the few examples that we choose to discuss here because they are salient to Concessa's speech. Amaral's book pessimistically predicts that the Caipira dialect "will disappear soon." But such predictions do not always foresee the strength of a language, especially when its usage is fortified and celebrated by users like Aparecida Silva Mendes, the actress who plays Concessa, and technological changes. Amaral would never have been able even to imagine the existence of the powerful tool that is the Internet, which now enables a speaker of the Caipira dialect to have her own YouTube channel.

22 We acknowledge the issues associated with using only a source such as Wikipedia; however, despite Concessa's large audience (as witnessed by the number of viewers of her channel), there are as yet no scholarly essays about her. It is not difficult to see that, just as happened with filmmaker Amácio Mazzaropi's work in the past, the Brazilian critical establishment takes some time to give due credit to cultural manifestations that do not come from the mainstream cultural scene of the major urban centers. Perhaps in the near future there will be more interest in studying the episodes of *Tecendo prosa* and writing about Concessa.

23 The episode can be found in Geraldo Magela's "Tecendo prosa: Entrevista com Concessa," 3 June 2019, www.youtube.com/watch?v=HL59lkIfPUs.

24 BR 040 is an important road connecting Rio de Janeiro to Brasília, going through the state of Minas Gerais.

25 Although Mazzaropi was first hailed as a kind of Brazilian Chaplin, once he created his own cinema company (PAM Filmes), the established cinema critics started either ignoring his work or criticizing him. Mazzaropi neither participated in film festivals in Brazil or abroad nor sought the approval of other filmmakers. Instead, he made films that attracted a wide public to his yearly movies. See a full study of his work in *Amacio Mazzaropi in the Film and Culture of Brazil: After Cinema Novo.*

26 This episode is called "BR 040, KM 49 . . . nóis num tem praca, mas tem ocêis pra divurgá"—"BR 040, Mk 49 . . . We don't have signs, but we have you to promote us." She goes through parts of the restaurant, showing the food they serve, and touting the little souvenirs they sell to travelers who stop by to eat, rest, and use the facilities. Available at www.youtube.com/watch?v=KvLElhXxIiY.

It is interesting to point out that, besides inviting people he met in his many trips to the interior of the country to appear as extras in his movies, Mazzaropi also used his films to launch the careers of several artists who went on to work with other directors and in theater.

27 There have been a few books written about the Lula presidency (2003–2011) and his politics, which tried to remedy centuries of oppression of the poor and non-whites. We especially recommend Joseph L. Love and Werner Baer's *Brazil Under Lula: Economy, Politics and Society Under the Worker-President* (2009), and John D. French's *Lula and His Politics of Cunning* (2020). We believe that an understanding of Brazil's political culture of corruption and exclusion of the lower classes is necessary to comprehend the reasons behind Lula's imprisonment (in 2017) as well as Dilma Rousseff's impeachment in 2016 (in her second term). We suggest also perhaps flawed and self-serving *Truth Will Prevail: Why I Have Been Condemned*, written by Lula himself and published in English in 2020 (although no translator is identified). It is important to stress that the sentencing judge in Lula's case was Sérgio Moro, who was soon rewarded with a ministerial post by the new president, Jair Bolsonaro. Rousseff was impeached thanks to the arrival in the Brazilian Congress of a new right-wing group led by Eduardo Cunha and financed thanks to "illegal campaign financing and the influence of money in Congress. Together, the opposition and the conservative block of the PMDB blocked every move of Dilma Rousseff's administration and proposed moral and economic conservative legislations" (Avritzer 353). See more on the subject in Leonardo Avritzer's "The Rousseff Impeachment and the Crisis of Democracy in Brazil." From this point to the proposal of Rousseff's impeachment was one simple step, especially considering Rede Globo's televising of the impeachment trial and subsequent show of politicians lining up against Rousseff. What followed her presidency was the concerted dismantling of most of the progressive and inclusive policies proposed during Lula's and Rousseff's governments and, in 2018, the election of ultra-right-wing Jair Bolsonaro, who proceeded to dismantle even further what was left of the progressive governments' attempts to address centuries-old inequality in Brazil.

28 Paracatu is the place where Cida was born. It is a city of fewer than 100,000 people located in the western part of Minas Gerais. Although Paracatu has some historic buildings from the colonial period, it really cannot compete in importance with more famous places such as the storied Ouro Preto and Mariana.

29 Although at the moment of writing—the summer of 2022—the total number of COVID deaths is still far from final, the site for the World Health Organization shows that in Brazil, from January 3, 2020 to June 23, 2022, there were 31,890,733 confirmed cases of COVID-19, with 669,530 deaths. By comparison, the number of deaths in the United States by the same point was 1,005,025, thus really making the US number one and Brazil number two. However, Cida released the Concessa episode in 2019, before the pandemic. She was referring there solely to the issue of corruption.

Works Cited

Amaral, Amadeu. *O dialeto caipira.* (*O dialecto caipira*). São Paulo: Casa Editora O Livro, 1920.

Avritzer, Leonardo. "The Rousseff Impeachment and the Crisis of Democracy in Brazil." *Critical Policy Studies,* vol. 11, no. 3, 2017, pp. 352–357.

Bot, Claudia Mehler. "A multiplicidade dos Brasis na versão de Darcy Ribeiro." *Brasil Escola—Sociologia,* meuartigo.brasilescola.uol.com.br/sociologia/a-multiplicidade-dos -brasis-na-versao-darcy-ribeiro.htm.

boyd, danah. "Social Network Sites as Networked Publics: Affordances, Dynamics and Im- plications." *Networked Self: Identity, Community and Culture on Social Network Sites,* edited by Zizi Papacharissi, Routledge, 2010, pp. 39–58.

Bueno, Eva P. *Amácio Mazzaropi in the Film and Culture of Brazil: After Cinema Novo.* New York: Palgrave Macmillan, 2012.

Cândido, Antonio. *Os parceiros do Rio Bonito.* Rio de Janeiro: José Olympio Editora, 1964.

Cano, Wilson. *Raízes da concentração industrial em São Paulo.* 2nd ed., São Paulo: TA Queiroz, 1977.

Carbonari, Pâmela, and Tiago Jokura. "Sotaques do Brasil: como a geografia molda nos- so jeito de falar." *Revista Super interessante,* 25 July 2018, super.abril.com.br/cultura/ sotaques-do-brasil/.

Carvalho, Mariana Virginia Moretti. *Quando os quadrinhos viram história: uma análise das charges de Henfil e o contexto da educação no regime militar brasileiro.* 2016. São Paulo State University, Bachelor of pedagogy thesis, repositorio.unesp.br/bitstream/handle/ 11449/155736/000888724.pdf?sequence=1&isAllowed=y.

Castaño Díaz, Carlos Mauricio. "Defining and Characterizing the Concept of Internet Meme." *CES Psicología,* vol. 6 no.2, 2013, pp. 82–104.

Cummings, Stephen. "Back to the Oracle: Post-Modern Organization Theory as a Resur- facing of Pre-Modern Wisdom." *Organization,* vol. 3, no. 2, 1996, pp. 249–266.

French, John D. *Lula and His Politics of Cunning: From Metalworker to President of Brazil.* Chapel Hill: University of North Carolina Press, 2020.

Geertz, Clifford. *The Interpretation of Cultures.* New York: Basic Books, 1973.

Grolund, Melissa. *Contemporary Art and Digital Culture.* London: Routledge, 2016.

Henfil (Henrique de Souza Filho), and Tárik de Souza. 1984. *Como se faz humor político: Depoimento a Tárik de Souza.* São Paulo: Editora Quarup, 2017.

Inocêncio, Luana, and Camila Lopes. "'Brace Yourselves, The Zueira Is Coming': Memes, interação e reapropriação criativa dos fãs na página *Game of Thrones* no Facebook." *Per- iferia,* vol. 11, no. 2, 2019, pp. 153–177, www.redalyc.org/journal/5521/552159358013/ html/.

Intercom—Sociedade Brasileira de Estudos Interdisciplinares da Comunicação. *Proceed- ings of the XVIII Congresso de Ciências da Comunicação na Região Nordeste,* vol. 18, 2015. Natal: RN, pp. 01–15.

Linton, Lisa-Jayne. *The Resurfacing of Traditional Feet. The Role of Media in the Renewal of Traditional Cultural Forms. The Example of Irish Dance.* 1997. University of Natal, Durban, MA thesis, ccms.ukzn.ac.za/Files/articles/MA_dissertations/linton.pdf.

Lipski, John M. *A History of Afro-Hispanic Language: Five Centuries, Five Continents.* Cambridge: Cambridge UP, 2005.

Londoño, Ernesto, and Letícia Casado. "Ex-president 'Lula' Is Freed from Prison in Brazil After Supreme Court Ruling." *The New York Times,* 8 Nov. 2019, https://www.nytimes.com/2019/11/08/world/americas/lula-brazil-supreme-court.html.

Love, Joseph L., and Werner Baer, editors. *Brazil Under Lula: Economy, Politics and Society Under the Worker-President.* New York: Palgrave, 2009.

Meirelles, Juliana Gesuelli. *A família real no Brasil: política e cotidiano (1808–1821).* São Bernardo do Campo: Editora UFABC, 2015, https://doi.org/10.7476/9788568576960.

De Melo, Victor Andrade, and Mauricio Drumond. "Globo, the Brazilian Military Dictatorship and the 1970 FIFA Football World Cup: Ambiguous Relations." *Television and New Media,* vol. 15 no. 8, 2014, https://doi.org/10.1177/1527476414535956.

Navas, Eduardo. *Remix Theory: The Aesthetics of Sampling.* New York: SpringerWien, 2012.

Negrão, Esmeralda Vailati, and Evani Viotti. "Epistemological Aspects of the Study of the Influence of African Languages in Brazilian Portuguese." *Portugais et langues africaines: Études afro-brésiliennes,* edited by Margarida Maria Taddoni Petter and Martine Vanhove, Paris: Éditions Karthala, 2011, pp. 13–44.

Nelson, Andrew Kelly. *José, Joe, Zé Carioca: Walt Disney's Good Neighbor's Colonial "Monument" in Brazil.* 2017. Brigham Young University, MA thesis, https://scholarsarchive.byu.edu/cgi/viewcontent.cgi?article=7246&context=etd#:~:text=Within%20Brazil%2C%20Jos%C3%A9%20Carioca%20was,to%20be%20seen%20as%20native.

Pessoa, Maria Eduarda. "70 anos de telenovelas no Brasil: Relembre personagens políticos mais marcantes." *O Povo,* 22 Dec. 2021, opovo.com.br/noticias/politica/2021/12/22/70-anos-de-telenovelas-no-brasil-relembre-personagens-politicos-mais-marcantes.html.

Pires, Cornélio. *Conversas ao pé do fogo.* São Paulo: Companhia Editora Nacional, 1938.

Pires, Maria da Conceição Francisca. "Bode Francisco Orelana: uma representação humorística da intelectualidade brasileira entre patrulhas ideológicas, autocensura e odarização." *TOPOI,* vol. 8, no. 14, 2007, pp. 114–145.

Recuero, Raquel. "Discurso mediado por computador nas redes sociais." *Redes sociais e ensino de línguas: o que temos de aprender?,* edited by Julio Araújo and Vilson Leffa, São Paulo: Parábola, 2016, n.p.

Rendimento de todas as fontes 2019 *(Pesquisa nacional por amostra de domicilios continua contínua).* IBGE (Brazilian Institute of Geography and Statistics), 2020, biblioteca.ibge.gov.br/visualizacao/livros/liv101709_informativo.pdf.

Ribeiro, Darcy. *O povo brasileiro. A formação e o sentido do Brasil.* 2nd ed., São Paulo: Companhia das Letras, 1995.

Rojo, Roxane, and Eduardo Moura, editors. *Multiletramentos na escola.* São Paulo: Parábola Editorial, 2012.

Saliba, Elias Thomé. *Crocodilos, satíricos e humoristas involuntários: ensaios de história cultural do humor.* São Paulo, Brasil: Intermeios Casa de Artes e Livros, 2018.

Thompson, John. *The Media in Modernity.* Cambridge, UK; Malden, MA: Polity Press, 1993.

World Health Organization. "Coronavirus disease (COVID-19) pandemic," www.who.int/emergencies/diseases/novel-coronavirus-2019.

7

Humor and Nationalism in Bolsonarist Far-Right WhatsApp Memes in Brazil

Viktor Chagas

Brazilian far-right groups have been gaining prominence in recent years, particularly since the election of Jair Bolsonaro as president in 2018 (Solano; Penteado and Lerner; Santos and Chagas). Composed of several different hues, the far-right in Brazil brings together mainly nostalgic fans of the authoritarian military regime, conservative neo-Pentecostals, anti-communist conspiracists, monarchists, and several other collectives that had been in the shadows for years due to the advance of leftist governments' progressive agendas that preceded the impeachment of Dilma Rousseff in 2016.

Nationalist in character, this rightist movement has been distinguished by unusual rhetoric invested in justifying its acts with non-threatening discourse, a tactic that combines forwarding and rewinding—that is, attacking and then apologizing immediately once the public pushes back (Chagas, "Dolce farmeme"). A result is a form of humor that extols freedom of expression, to the detriment of conditions of social justice. This becomes especially evident on issues related to minorities, particularly those involving gender and ethnicity, in various aspects of daily life in Brazil. This is not, of course, an exclusively Brazilian issue. Sue and Golash-Boza discuss similar cases in the Latin American context, more precisely in Mexico and Peru, based on a framing operation that justifies racist jokes as "just a joke," and therefore, "softens" the racism. Something similar is described by Weaver and also by Billig regarding supremacist humor in the United States. And, although Brazil has a tradition of anti-racist satires that have gained some media notoriety, as highlighted by Gillam regarding a satirical TV series produced by Afro-Brazilian actors, it somehow became routine to hear from public authorities in Brazil that interpretations of their acts were wrong because it was only a joke (Chagas, "Dolce farmeme"; Chagas, "Making Amends"). Far-right supporters of the government not only rejoice in each of these discourses, but celebrate, episode after episode, the peculiar characteristics of their nationalist humor with jokes that build up the figure of Bolsonaro as a national hero of freedom, or, in their own words, a myth. These jokes are often circulated on social media as user-shared memes. At the same time, the ups and downs in the circulation of this content suggest that nuanced historical analysis may help one learn about the Brazilian political situation. Understanding, for example, how these Internet memes reflect political events can help to map the climate of opinion among users of a given platform and simultaneously capture readings of the public image of a particular actor or institution.

In instant-messaging applications, like WhatsApp, memes and viral contents are circulated with mythological and biblical motifs, references to the national flag and the army, or simply references to characters from pop culture, such as Bolsonaro dressed as Captain America, giving the figure of the president superhuman elements. Bolsonaro appears as a comic-book superhero fighting evil or holding hands with Jesus in a crusade against infidels. There are also references with a more misogynistic tone, whether attacking political opponents and former allies, such as former ally and right-wing federal representative Joyce Hasselmann, or other enemies of Bolsonaro. In all cases, the playful and diversionist character of the images stands out, although, especially to a progressive observer, they are not always, and sometimes not at all, funny.

At the same time, the fact that, in recent years, WhatsApp has become one of the main social platforms in Brazil, with a base of more than 120 million active accounts (Santos), has greatly contributed to the spread of a peculiar type of humor and communication. Since the platform is built in an opaque mode, for relatively restricted groups and with a network topology that is often described by experts as an echo chamber (Resende et al.; Caetano et al.; Evangelista and Bruno), it is possible and even likely that this structure has favored the spread of a barely acceptable humorous style that would be criticized in other spheres more open to the public (see Pérez). Thus, WhatsApp architecture and social affordances[1] may also play an important role in this landscape.

There is an intense correlation between the conversations held in these WhatsApp groups and the political situation in the country. One can find several hypotheses, for instance, regarding the political use of misinformation, ranging from the smokescreen effect, used to deflect controversies in which the government is involved, to the harsh political climate and moral and cultural backlash, which supposedly favor the president and his allies. It is not much different with humorous content. Posting memes can be understood as a strategy for distracting audiences, but also for cultivating a strong sense of identity and belonging—a reactionary identity, based on classist, sexist, and supremacist stereotypes (Phillips and Milner). For this reason, nationalism, digital folklore,[2] and religious traditions are strong motives for the creators of this image-based content. We call image memes iconographic user-generated content circulated on social media. This definition encompasses not only the so-called image macros—that is, image memes with juxtaposed subtitles—but other forms of visual jokes and still images, funny or not, that constitute disseminated and shared material as an online socialization and public discussion experience. Understanding, therefore, what the characteristics of these jokes are and evaluating how conservative humor is built within audiences' imaginary has become a relevant analytical challenge.

This chapter investigates the humor in Internet memes circulated in WhatsApp groups of Bolsonaro supporters for a six-month period during his presidential term. We are guided by the following hypotheses in this study:

H1. Memes shared by Brazilian far-right supporters on WhatsApp are highly ideological and present the image of President Bolsonaro associated with positive archetypes.

H2. Humor in these memes relies on several nationalist rhetorical elements and antidemocratic characteristics.

H3. The circulation of these memes closely reflects political events in the country's daily life.

This investigation was developed with a methodological approach combining ethnography, content analysis, and quantitative analysis of data extracted from a sample of content circulated in public political discussion groups on WhatsApp. Content from approximately 150 different groups was gathered and monitored, comprising the sample built by the Research Laboratory for Communication, Political Cultures, and Economy of Collaboration (coLAB) at Fluminense Federal University since the first semester of 2018. The image memes referring to Bolsonaro were selected from a set of messages and were evaluated according to axes that seek to measure the incidence of rhetorical elements such as the presentation of national symbols, reference to folk and religious myths, and other characteristics. We also identified which character archetypes were most often attributed to the president, such as hero, martyr, savior, warrior, and so on. Then, we sought to detail which aspects of memes could represent aggressions against minorities, such as women, Black people, or LGBTQ people. Finally, we tried to map a historical series of recent political events to trace correlations between the peaks present in each of these moments and archetypes triggered in memes. The research is expected to shed light on some characteristics present in the far-right humor of Bolsonaro's supporters in Brazil and draws special attention to the extent to which the opaque environment of WhatsApp is capable of favoring an atmosphere not prone to democratic values.

Humor in Brazilian Far-Right Networks

Humor assumed a fundamental role in Jair Bolsonaro's victory in the 2018 Brazilian presidential elections. Not only did the then federal representative gain enormous visibility on humorous and popular talk shows, but he also took advantage of a certain aura he possessed as a folkloric politician that guaranteed him a free pass to utter offensive things and defend controversial ideas with a strong antidemocratic character. He embodied a caricature most common to underdogs in Brazilian politics: the candidate who knows how to laugh at himself.

Brazil has always been rich in folksy characters in politics. Its most prominent politicians have always had a quaint or extravagant side. In the 1960s, for example, even before the military dictatorship that lasted until the mid-1980s, Jânio Quadros was elected after a notoriously populist campaign, in which he wielded a broom in his hands and said that he would sweep away the country's corruption (Queler). The pun was also used in his campaign jingle at the time, and Quadros distributed among his voters a kind of promotional kit with a glass vial containing a miniature broom, which he called Broomcillin, a pun on the antibiotic Penicillin. At the end of the elections, he was victorious by a significant percentage, but resigned in the first year of his presidential term—a fact that did not prevent him from continuing to occupy a place in the pantheon of national political exoticism, with weird phrases and images that guaranteed him enormous notoriety.

During the period of re-democratization,[3] Leonel Brizola, a politician from a labor tradition,[4] aroused the ire of his opponents by satirizing them through humor. In debates and interviews, Brizola coined numerous nicknames for his rivals (Abreu). One of the most famous ones, the "bearded frog," was applied to then candidate for the presidency of the republic Luís Inácio Lula da Silva. When announcing his support for Lula in the election's second round in 1989, Brizola said that "Politics is the art of eating a live frog. Wouldn't it be fascinating now to make the Brazilian elite eat Lula, this bearded frog?" (Abreu).[5] Other nicknames given to opponents, such as "Turkish Angora cat," attributed to the former governor of the state of Rio de Janeiro, Moreira Franco, and "dictatorship puppy," given to the former governor of São Paulo, Paulo Maluf, were also among Brizola's bitter inventions.

Still, in the 1989 elections, another little-known politician ended up surprising at the polls, reaching an unforeseen third place in the presidential race with a campaign that had virtually no resources and very little television time: Enéas Carneiro. With a nationalist, conservative platform, so-called Dr. Enéas was chosen by part of the electorate for his outsider profile. He used to speak quickly and incisively for little more than a minute in electoral television ads, always ending his speeches with the catchphrase "My name is Enéas" in an angry tone. Although there was no humor involved, Enéas's approach marked a whole generation and led the politician to be elected later by a wide margin as a federal representative for the state of São Paulo, after which he assumed a permanent folkloric status (Caldeira Neto).

Since then, with each new electoral cycle in Brazil, it has been common for a little-known politician to occupy this seat. In 1998, it was José Maria Eymael, from the Christian Democratic Party, with a jingle that incorporated kitsch elements and aesthetics (Miguel). In 2010, left-wing candidate Plínio de Arruda Sampaio, from the Socialism and Liberty Party, became a darling of the Brazilian memesphere by calling for *tweetazzos*[6] and participating in parallel debates on social media, while other candidates debated on television (Boechat). In 2014, the Green Party candidate, Eduardo Jorge, took up this position after appearing on television performing exaggerated and comic gestures and improvised soundbites (Freire). Having seen that he had become the star of a series of memes, the candidate not only had fun with them, but ended up incorporating humor in his campaign, and created a slogan that mixed his catchphrase in one of the debates ("Quero!," i.e., I want!) with the motto of Barack Obama's campaign in 2008, giving rise to humorous pieces with the phrase "Yes, We Quero!," instead of the world-famous "Yes, We Can."

In the following cycle, everything indicated that the baton would be passed to Cabo Daciolo, a candidate from a very small party. He gained notoriety for his religious statements, with references to parables of the Bible, which were soon ridiculed in memes. However, Jair Bolsonaro also emerged, not only as a candidate who could take a joke about himself but also as someone who laughed at and satirized his opponents with childish jokes that favored popular sensibility.

Bolsonaro became a favorite in the 2018 elections as a result of a controversial political scenario in Brazil that developed after a series of mass demonstrations in June 2013. These protests were initially described as poorly targeted, but they found common ground in autonomist practices and the criticism of inequalities (Mendonça and Bustamante). Subsequently, however—as a result, in part, of dwindling left-wing participation in the demonstrations—several right-wing and far-right movements co-opted the media agenda and staged mass protests against President Dilma Rousseff in 2014, 2015, and finally in 2016 (Rocha). Rousseff, who was re-elected by a small margin against her main opponent at the time, in the 2014 elections, saw her popularity plummet overnight and her second term was in question from the beginning. The opposition did not accept the result of the vote and set the country on fire during the first years of Rousseff's second term, which, together with a series of other factors, such as an intense economic crisis, ended up leading to impeachment in 2016. Add to that the fact that the main left-wing candidate, former president Luís Inácio Lula da Silva, was tried in an equally controversial process in which he was accused of corruption and arrested, making it impossible for him to run for president again. This left the path largely open to an antipolitical candidate who had been growing in political stature—Jair Bolsonaro (Avritzer).

Bolsonaro was an forgettable representative for seven terms in the Lower House, but, since the beginning of the last decade, he had started to appear on television talk shows. In 2011, Bolsonaro answered questions from ordinary people on a talk show called *CQC* and had an unexpected impact due to his homophobic and racist statements. At the time, when asked what he would do if his son fell in love with a Black woman, he replied by saying he would not discuss promiscuity. And, when asked what he would do if his son came out as gay, he replied that he educated his children very well to respect morality and good manners.[7]

In numerous similar controversial shows, such as *Superpop,*[8] *Raul Gil,*[9] *Ratinho,*[10] *Datena,*[11] e *Pânico,*[12] Bolsonaro accumulated a portfolio of statements that, despite resulting in extrajudicial notices and lawsuits, never had any truly serious consequences.[13] On the contrary, the politician ended up benefiting enormously from the media visibility acquired on tabloid television, and was always portrayed as a conservative but simple and good-humored person.

The fact that talk shows like *Pânico* and *CQC* enjoyed, for many years, a large audience among the younger population in Brazil quickly made Bolsonaro tremendously popular among a specific portion of the electorate. In addition to his appeal to more conservative segments, such as the military and neo-Pentecostal evangelicals, the candidate quickly became the one to beat in the electoral race because of his social media popularity. Named "the Myth" by his supporters, a reflection of the folkloric character he assumed in the face of all this media exposure, he repeatedly used misogynistic, racist, and homophobic expressions not only during the campaign but afterward, as an incumbent. At one of his rallies, held at a Jewish club, Bolsonaro criticized *quilombolas,* referring to a Black-movement leader as weighing "eight arrobas,"[14] a derogatory expression that compared him to a fat ox.

Bolsonaro's humor is questionable and aggressive, but to a large extent, it is his populist appeal that legitimizes him as an actor who says what he thinks, speaking his mind without social constraints. Bolsonaro's crusade against the so-called politically correct is notorious. Already in his inaugural speech as president, he said that he would free Brazil from the politically correct (Gulino). In several instances, when confronted by negative public reaction to his provocations, Bolsonaro has stepped back and justified himself by stating that he was simply joking. This artifice can be identified as a reactionary rhetorical strategy, in addition to the three theses posited by Hirschman, which not only the president but a significant number of his admirers and supporters have used (Chagas, "Dolce farmeme"). Hirschman makes use of a sociohistorical model in which every time a democratic reform is put on the agenda, a reactionary segment insists on its infeasibility by employing a specific rhetorical strategy. According to Hirschman, there are three common rhetorics of reaction: the rhetoric of perversity (according to which every change will have an opposite effect from what is expected); the rhetoric of futility (according to which any yearning for change is inconceivable, since everything will always remain the same); and the rhetoric of threat (according to which change can lead to chaos and disorder).

To those three I have suggested adding the rhetoric of play, which often consists of using an argument that covers the antidemocratic and reactionary character of another argument with a veil of playfulness, usually applied *a posteriori*, to avoid responsibility for the consequences (Chagas, "Dolce farmeme"). Thus, humor has been incorporated by conservative and even extremist segments interested in preempting criticism from their political opponents.

The critical literature that studies the intersection between humor and politics has been, to a fair extent, mostly concerned with the subversive uses of humor. Especially concerning sociability in the digital environment, the metaphor of carnivalization employed by Bakhtin in the context of the Middle Ages has been frequently revisited by researchers dedicated to studies of online communities and Internet memes (Milner; Beyer). Many of them allude to the satirization of public authorities in social media from the dimension of polyphony and extol the use of humor as an instrument to criticize power. No wonder the concept of political play developed by Bennett (see also Chagas and Fonseca) assumes that play is often performed by marginalized groups. However, rather than a natural occurrence, this condition is the result of an analytical bias to which historians and social scientists have been led by privileging the analysis of the behavior of progressives to the detriment of conservatives, as if the latter group did not have its own unique humor.

Only recently have studies recognized cultural backlash and troll activism as tactics assumed by right-wing activist political groups (Norris and Inglehart; Phillips and Milner). Critical humor studies, however, have emphasized for some time that racist and misogynistic humor, for instance, can help build prejudices and reinforce oppressive stereotypes (Billig; Weaver). The humor employed by Jair Bolsonaro and his supporters can be classified as a type that reproduces these stereotypes, applying a nationalist varnish to them and diluting cultural identities. Its objective is to disseminate a populist image that refuses to demonstrate respect toward minority agendas, and praises, as is typical in authoritarian regimes, the figure of the leader as a metonymic expression of the nation itself.

Most Bolsonarist memes, therefore, present Bolsonaro as their protagonist, whether as a hero, savior, or victim of a perverse society divided by the progressive field. Many of these memes attack political opponents or the media, facilitating an apocryphal negative campaign environment, executed not by political agents but by ordinary users, which to some extent makes it difficult to enact sanctions against them (Tsai and Chagas). In addition, the relationship between political events and the circulation of user-generated content like that found on social media is quite evident. In periods of greater social turbulence and crises in government, there is often an intensification in the production and sharing of these pieces, so studying memes allows one to understand, to some degree, the reflection of political conjuncture in the networks and to capture the climate of opinion among a certain portion of the population.

WhatsApp and Internet Memes

In Brazil, the Regional Center for Studies on the Development of the Information Society (Cetic.br), under the auspices of UNESCO, reports that the use of communication services with an emphasis on private messaging has increased substantially from 2012 to the present. In 2012, when asked about what uses they made of online communication services, 59 percent of respondents said they used instant-messaging applications. In comparison, 73 percent of respondents said they used online social networks. In 2019, the most recent update of the survey, the use of online social networks remained at a 76 percent adherence level, while messaging applications had reached 92 percent.

In the 2018 election, Jair Bolsonaro's electoral strategy was based to a large extent on an integrated ecosystem of political discussion groups on WhatsApp, responsible for disseminating information about the campaign, mobilizing voters for rallies, and selling t-shirts and stickers, among other actions.

Although other candidates also had groups and broadcast lists on the app, the Bolsonarist network on WhatsApp benefited from pre-existing articulations and structures of groups from different right-wing movements that had already been organizing themselves through the platform. As a result, Bolsonaro support groups were part of a network of near-ubiquity, which became one of their main assets in the electoral race. In addition to the intense exchange of messages, these groups were notable for spreading disinformation, often with a conspiratorial tone, and with a remarkable appeal to humor, as often happens with Internet memes (Chagas, "WhatsApp and Digital Astroturfing").

Patrick Davison describes memes as a digital piece, typically a joke, that gains influence through its online broadcast (144). Although there are questions about the status of these memes as humor content, this chapter is anchored in Davison's definition. Taking it into consideration, we analyze the images circulated in Bolsonarist groups on WhatsApp.

According to Chagas et al., whose taxonomic proposal is based on categories previously defined by Shifman and other researchers, Internet memes can (a) play a persuasive role in attracting supporters to a certain ideological current; (b) encourage grassroots action collectively performed in the digital environment; and/or (c) foster a regular process of socialization with politics and public debate. This can help with the understanding that political memes that circulate on WhatsApp are in some ways different from memes that circulate on other platforms, especially due to the architecture with which WhatsApp presents itself to the user.

WhatsApp is characterized as a private messaging platform. There is no public profile for users, and there are no social metrics, such as the number of likes or shares. No information available on the platform allows the identification of the content dissemination circuit, and the application is based on an end-to-end encryption system, which—in the same proportion that guarantees the system's inviolability—favors opacity in the exchange of messages. Roughly speaking, while it is virtually impossible to identify the trajectory of the contents and the network affiliation of other users, as the application does not provide this information clearly, one can easily notice a strong ideological tone in shared messages, in which any tendencies to dissonance are summarily eliminated or silenced. Memes reflect these settings. On Brazilian WhatsApp (and more specifically in Bolsonarist groups), it is common and to some extent routine to find memes that favor a persuasive message, to the detriment of situational humor. Many of these memes, while playful, cannot be clearly defined as a joke.

In addition, WhatsApp often seems to serve as a kind of hub for other social platforms, so the content shared by political groups has different sources, such as YouTube and blogs with a conservative bias or that openly disseminate misinformation and conspiracy theories. Image memes circulated in these groups often resonate with this hub condition, with trends such as spreading screenshots of other social media like Twitter in private groups. Another aspect that draws attention is the repeated use of colors and national motifs in shared memes as a way to characterize the environment as one of unrestricted support for the government. All of these factors contribute to the idea of WhatsApp memes constituting a particular memesphere in relation to those constituted in other environments and on other matters.

In the following pages, we discuss how Bolsonaro memes articulate humor and nationalism in their messages and how they portray Jair Bolsonaro. The discussion is based on a data set extracted from continuous monitoring of public political discussion groups on WhatsApp, and tries to illustrate how these memes create a snapshot of the political moment in Brazil.

Methodology

This chapter analyzes a set of images circulated in Bolsonarist groups on WhatsApp. These images were gathered upon systematic monitoring of public political discussion groups available in the application. The continuous monitoring started during the first half of 2018 in 150 groups of supporters of Jair Bolsonaro, but for this investigation, we used a randomly reduced sample of about 40 groups out of the whole base and reduced the analyzed period to the first six months of 2020. The groups have a maximum of 256 users each, a limit established by the platform itself, and an average of around 120 users. The reduced network consists of approximately 5,400 users associated with these groups.

WhatsApp encompasses a structure of groups and broadcast lists. In the latter case, only administrators can publish content, whereas in the former, the discussion is open and horizontal among members. According to the literature (Resende et al.; Santos; Chagas, "WhatsApp and Digital Astroturfing"), groups are divided into public and private. Public groups are those whose invitations circulate publicly on the platform and allow the indiscriminate entry of any user.

Groups are volatile in composition and see a constant flow of users and moderators. In addition, new groups are created constantly while others may die out or have their names and descriptions changed. These issues make the long-duration monitoring of this environment difficult. In addition, it is important to consider the fact that the Bolsonarist network is recognized as a hostile environment for research. For this reason, we employed a methodology known as covert research, in which the researcher does not present himself as such to the observed subjects. This method is supported by previous decisions of the Brazilian National Council of Ethics in Research, whose board granted permission to the present research project (Chagas, "WhatsApp and Digital Astroturfing"; see also National Health Council).

To compose a sample of the images that circulated in these groups, we chose the first six months of 2020 as the time frame for this study, considering not only that it is a sufficiently distant period from the electoral race, and therefore a moment of supposed political calm, but also that it covers recent events related to the unprecedented COVID-19 pandemic. In practice, when it comes to Brazil, the pandemic ended up driving successive crises in government, including the departure of at least four ministers—two of them in the health portfolio.

After defining the scope of the analysis, the next step was to collect the images that circulated during this period. A total of 11,374 images was shared in these groups. However, this chapter analyses only the ones that visually represent or make direct mention of Jair Bolsonaro. Screen captures and images that only served to spread statements or call individuals to demonstrations in favor of the president, or that used his image simply as a way to draw users' attention, were also excluded from the sample.

In the end, a corpus of exactly 200 image memes was analyzed. A content analysis of these images was carried out, considering four main variables, as follows.

The first variable of analysis concerns the class or genre of the memes. Four values were established for this variable. Memes could be categorized alternately as persuasive, grassroots action, or public discussion, according to the taxonomy defined by Chagas et al. in previous studies. A fourth class applied to cases in which some ambiguity or ambivalence among the other genres was noticed. The purpose of this variable is to allow one to assess whether the content that circulates through WhatsApp is more often than not of a persuasive and markedly ideological character, as it is commonly supposed.

The next variable deals with the way Bolsonaro is represented visually and semantically in the analyzed memes. Categories were defined to account for all the representations triggered in the images. Bolsonaro was represented as:

- *Hero or leader*—a subject who expresses superior strength and will, who opposes a villain, or who is simply capable of leading the masses.
- *Victim*—a subject who suffers attacks, or is injured or mistreated by someone else.

- *Martyr*—a subject who is tortured or executed for refusing to renounce his faith or principles.
- *Savior or anointed*—one who has received a blessing, was chosen by a deity, or can be recognized as the deity itself and is therefore capable of working miracles.
- *Warrior or punisher*—a person who does justice rigorously, who fights and applies sanctions in an often-ruthless manner.
- *Honest or selfless*—a subject endowed with a unique morality, who does not seek to accumulate material assets and is incorruptible.
- *Picaresque character*—an intelligent subject endowed with good humor and capable of arousing laughter from the situations he stages.
- *Ordinary person*—a citizen like any other, one of the people, in opposition to the elites.
- *Father of the poor*—one who represents the underprivileged; a charitable and beneficent figure.

The third variable is an objective one and seeks to understand whether the content visually presents any reference to Brazilian national colors (green and yellow), the coat of arms and presidential sash, the national flag, the map of Brazil, imperial or republican historical motives, the nation's armed forces, Brazilian natural resources, or some evocation of patriotism, Brazilian people, or national idols.

The fourth and final variable sought to identify antidemocratic values expressed by the images analyzed, such as misogyny, homophobia, racism, tributes to military dictatorship and restriction of freedoms, gun rights discourse, anti-communism and anti-terrorism rhetoric, anti-drugs rhetoric, attacks on political actors and institutions, or attacks on the media. Data were also analyzed according to the date of circulation of the images. It should be noted that this investigation takes into account only unique images—that is, it does not consider content that is repeated over time.

For the analysis of the circulation of the historical series of memes, data related to the images' original date of publication were considered. These data make it possible to establish a comparison between some of the crises that the Bolsonaro government experienced, reflected in the main media of the country at the time, and the data extracted from WhatsApp, to assess whether the frequency of sharing Bolsonaro memes in any way mirrors these events. With this information in hand, outcomes are discussed.

Discussion

The first issue we intend to address in our analysis is whether there is any predominance of an ideological rhetorical appeal in WhatsApp memes on the far right. To address this discussion, we quantitatively measured the extent to which these memes serve a persuasive function—that is, to what extent their goal is mainly to convince the interlocutor and not just to amuse or to call for political action. Persuasive memes have a strong propaganda tone, and therefore are good vehicles for ideological language.

As expected, Bolsonaro memes in WhatsApp primarily serve a persuasive function, to the detriment of an expression of grassroots action or public discussion. Of all analyzed memes, 54.5 percent (N=109) were framed this way, which implies that the vast majority of these memes retain propaganda characteristics in relation to the figure of the then president of Brazil.

Also notable is the incidence of representation of Bolsonaro in these images as a hero or leader (13 percent), with personal virtues such as courage and strength of character often attributed to him. Bolsonaro is also recurrently represented as a victim (11.5 percent) or a martyr (10 percent), as shown in table 2. However, it is important to note that persuasive Bolsonaro memes are generally more frequently associated with other roles, such as that of the warrior, the savior, or the selfless character. This finding suggests that memes are not only markedly ideological but also apologetic—they exalt the figure of the president using benign archetypes. Bolsonaro is invariably presented as an extraordinary character, for his prowess, his masculinity, or his honesty—the last in contrast to the accusations of corruption usually leveled against his political opponents. Memes reinforce this language and contribute to building the president's public image.

The canonical correspondence analysis (CCA) shown in figure 7.1 indicates that Bolsonaro's representation as a hero or leader is generally more associated with grassroots action memes, involving images that usually contain second-person exhortations and calls to action directed at the recipient. Public discussion memes are usually more strongly associated with picaresque or ordinary-person representations and are in direct opposition to the construction of persuasive images.

This finding corroborates our first hypothesis (H1), according to which far-right memes on WhatsApp are strongly ideological. They also endeavor to present the figure of Bolsonaro mainly through the filter of a positive archetype, such as a hero, a warrior, or a martyr. In addition, there is a close association between some roles and framings associated with Bolsonaro and the functions performed by some memes. Thus, whenever an element of the

Table 7.1. Functions of analyzed memes

Function	N	Percentage
Persuasive Memes	109	54.4
Grassroots Action Memes	41	20.5
Public Discussion Memes	46	23.0
Ambiguity or Ambivalence	4	2.0
Total	200	100

Source: coLAB/UFF

Table 7.2. Archetypal representations

Representations	N	Percentage
Hero or Leader	26	13.0
Victim	23	11.5
Martyr	20	10.0
Savior or Anointed	16	8.0
Warrior or Punisher	15	7.5
Honest or Selfless	14	7.0
Picaresque Character	16	8.0
Ordinary Person	6	3.0
Father of the Poor	12	6.0

Source: coLAB/UFF

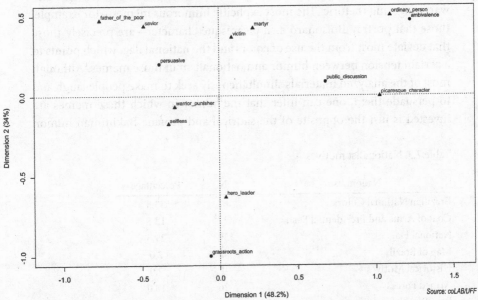

Canonical correspondence between functions of memes and Bolsonaro's representations

Figure 7.1. Canonical correspondence between functions of memes and Bolsonaro's representations. Courtesy of the author.

comic or of playfulness is more intensely evident in the meme, the character therein is also less persuasive, since Bolsonaro is portrayed in a picaresque way and not in a heroic or masculine one. On the other hand, Bolsonaro's representations as a savior or as a warrior are usually the most triggered when it comes to defending the government, which suggests that jokes associated with these representations are generally more strongly linked to an attempt to advocate for the government and, in this case, they blur the line between humor and propaganda.

Regarding nationalist motifs, national colors (33.5 percent) and the Brazilian flag (29.5 percent) are the elements most frequently used in memes. But the coat of arms of the Federative Republic of Brazil (13.5 percent) and references to the armed forces (13 percent) also draw attention (table 7.3). Once again, the correlation between this variable and representations of Bolsonaro elucidates interesting points. For example, the figure of the hero or leader, as well as that of the warrior or punisher, is more often associated with the armed forces, whereas the martyr, the savior, the selfless figure, and the victim are more often associated with visual references to the national flag and/or coat of arms (figures 7.2 and 7.3). Correlations show once more that memes in defense of the Bolsonaro government often evoke nationalist and warmongering rhetoric. The most explicitly humorous memes—for example, those that portray Bolsonaro as a picaresque character—are precisely those that deviate most from the use of colors and the national flag, which points to a certain tension between humor and nationalism in those memes. Although most of the analyzed materials simultaneously seek to make people laugh and to persuade them, one can infer that the humor in which these memes are invested is just the opposite of the satirical and profane Bakhtinian humor.

Table 7.3. Nationalist motives

Nationalism	N	Percentage
Brazilian National Colors	67	33.5
Coat of Arms and Presidential Sash	27	13.5
National Flag	59	29.5
Map of Brazil	4	2.0
Historical Motives	4	2.0
Armed Forces	26	13.0
Brazilian Natural Resources	1	0.5
Evocation of Patriotism	5	2.5
Evocation of Brazilian People	13	6.5
National Idols	4	2.0

Source: coLAB/UFF

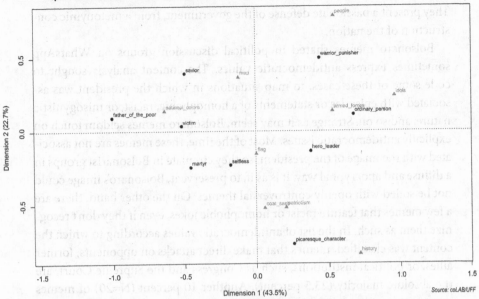

Figure 7.2. Canonical correspondence between Bolsonaro's representations and nationalist motives. Courtesy of the author.

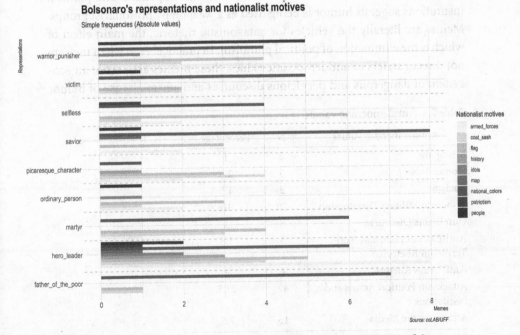

Figure 7.3. Bolsonaro's representations and nationalist motives. Courtesy of the author.

They present a passionate defense of the government, from a metonymic construction of the nation.

Bolsonaro memes shared in political discussion groups on WhatsApp sometimes express antidemocratic values. The content analysis sought to code some of these cases, to map situations in which the president was associated with episodes or statements of a homophobic, racist, or misogynistic nature, and so on. Strange as it may seem, Bolsonaro memes seldom touch on explicitly antidemocratic issues. Most of the time, these memes are not associated with the image of the president, so they circulate in Bolsonarist groups in a diffuse and apocryphal way. It is as if, to preserve it, Bolsonaro's image could not be soiled with openly controversial themes. On the other hand, there are a few memes that feature racist or homophobic jokes, even if they don't recognize them as such. In the list of antidemocratic values according to which the content was classified, memes that make direct attacks on opponents, former allies, or political institutions, such as Congress and the Supreme Court, are the absolute majority (23.5 percent). Another 10 percent (N=20) of memes support the military dictatorship of 1964–1985. And 7.5 percent (N=15) attack the media.

The high incidence of memes that pay admiring tribute to the military dictatorship and/or that launch virulent attacks against opponents and political institutions suggests humor is being used as a weapon by Bolsonarist groups. Memes are literally the vehicles for antagonistic rhetoric, the main effect of which is the elimination of political pluralism. In practice, even when they are not direct carriers of antidemocratic values, these memes are part of an ecosystem of dangerous and pernicious discourses and affirm a sense of humor

Table 7.4. Antidemocratic values

Antidemocratic Values	N	Percentage
Misogyny	2	1
Homophobia	5	2.5
Racism	3	1.5
Tribute to Military Dictatorship	20	10
Gun Rights Discourse	8	4
Anti-Communism and Anti-Terrorism Rhetoric	3	1.5
Anti-Drugs Rhetoric	4	2
Attacks on Political Actors and Institutions	47	23.5
Attacks on the Media	15	7.5

Source: coLAB/UFF

that oppresses, typically associated with the Hobbesian perspective of humor as a form of domination.

One can thus identify a bundle of nationalist and antidemocratic motifs shared by these memes, as H2 advocates. Among these, we find the appeal to militarism and gun rights, as well as attacks on opponents, an embrace of antidemocratic aspects, and the prevailing use of an aesthetic that refers to national colors, the country's flag, and, once again, the armed forces, as nationalist elements.

An additional aspect of the analysis concerns the relationship between the circulation of Bolsonaro memes and certain political events. It is noteworthy that the content circulated by users on WhatsApp peaked during specific weeks, such as week 17 (April 20, 2020, to April 26, 2020) and week 21 (May 18, 2020, to May 24, 2020). It can be inferred from figure 4, below, that the period between these two weeks corresponds to intense activity within the Bolsonarist network in WhatsApp groups. It is also a period of increasingly tense institutional relations that begins with the resignation of then Minister of Justice Sérgio Moro on the morning of April 24, 2020. Moro gained notoriety for being the judge who, after a controversial trial, sentenced former president Lula to prison, preventing him from running in the 2018 presidential elections. When Bolsonaro won, Moro was sought out by the then president-elect at the end of 2018 and, soon after, formally nominated as minister. Upon resigning from the government, Moro accused Bolsonaro of interference in federal investigative agencies and cited a ministerial meeting that had taken place a few days earlier as evidence. The video recording of the ministerial meeting was made public, authorized by Supreme Court Minister Celso de Mello, on May 22, and gave rise to a new peak in messages on social media.

Thus, as H3 proposes, whenever there is an acute crisis faced by the president, the circulation of Bolsonaro memes in pro-government groups (darker line in figure 7.4) on WhatsApp intensifies. Some of these crises are directly related to statements made and initiatives taken by the president himself or his supporters, as one can see in the meme peak in week 12 (March 16, 2020, to March 22, 2020), which covers not only the day after pro-government demonstrations in different cities in the country (on March 15) but also the president's birthday (March 21).

Figure 7.4 also shows that, in some instances, the president's tactic is to remain silent after certain events. The information presented in the chart also compiles data from a fact-checking project called Aos Fatos, which gathers Bolsonaro's statements to the media (lighter line in figure 7.4). As one can see,

Historical series

Bolsonaro memes vs. Bolsonaro's statements

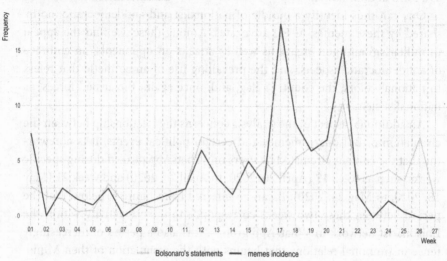

Figure 7.4. Historical series. Courtesy of the author.

in the episode in which Moro leaves government, the president appears just a few times in public, allowing, in a way, the memes to speak for themselves.

Considering other variables' co-occurrences, one can identify that, in week 17, Bolsonaro is represented most of the time as a martyr or a hero, while in week 21, when the video of the ministerial meeting revealed to the public a president who hurled profanities and behaved hysterically and aggressively, the most mobilized representation is that of the warrior or punisher. It should be noted that attacks against opponents and political institutions rise in all crisis episodes that the government goes through. Another constant of far-right groups on WhatsApp is admiration for the military dictatorship, which appears prominently in several weeks, such as week 17. In week 21, due to Bolsonaro himself extolling gun rights in the video of the above-mentioned meeting, some memes also highlight this agenda. The data draws attention to the extent to which the circulation of political memes in Bolsonarist groups on WhatsApp is aligned with events taking place in parallel on the national political scene.

What this close parallel to political events tells us about humor in Bolsonaro memes on WhatsApp is that these kinds of jokes are generally contextual and situational, even when imbued with a largely moral tone. Although there are intertextual references to episodes that are very different from one another and sometimes historically distant, there is always a close relationship with

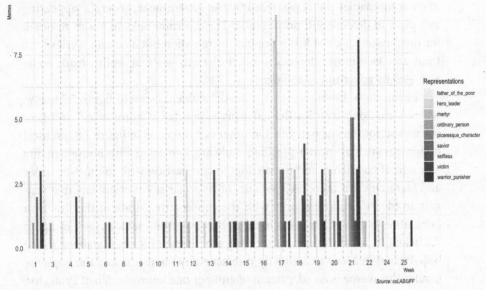

Figure 7.5. Bolsonaro's representations per week. Courtesy of the author.

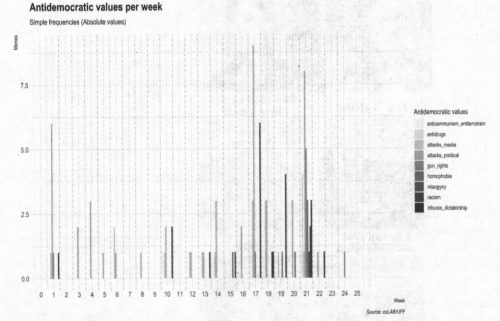

Figure 7.6. Antidemocratic values per week. Courtesy of the author.

the event at hand, so that the timing of the humorous memes is fleeting and often accompanies the crises faced by the government, generally appearing as a piece of defense and propaganda. These memes help, in a way, to build, for their audiences, not just a popular imagination but a certain spirit of the time, a collection of references—often distorted—about reality, ready to be activated by government apologists.

The humor of these memes is often debatable, as seen in figure 7.7 below, where a caption identifies the left-wing supporter as homosexual and Bolsonaro's supporters as patriots. On other occasions, as in figure 7.8, political opponents such as former president Lula are associated with homosexuality as a sign of bad habits and perversion, in comparison with militaristic order and hierarchy. But there are elements of Bolsonarist environments that suggest an identification not only with the conservative strata of the Brazilian population but with a transnational right-wing movement, as seen in figure 7.9 below, in which Bolsonaro, wearing a military uniform, is stabbed in the back by Sérgio Moro and directly threatened by the media and the Supreme Court. This meme is an adaptation of another one known as Silent Protector,

Figure 7.7. Humor and a far-right meme.

Figure 7.8. Humor and a far-right meme.

Figure 7.9. Humor and a far-right meme.

Figure 7.10. References to pop culture in a Bolsonaro meme.

which has been circulating since 2016, in different versions, always featuring a soldier, to honor the armed forces.[15]

References to pop culture, notably Hollywood movies, are common—either as the vigilante John Rambo or a virtuous hero from the Avengers, or sometimes a picaresque villain like Felonius Gru (see figures 7.10 to 7.12).[16] And occasionally there are still less comical but visually witty references to episodes in national history, such as the independence of Brazil or different religious interpretations (see figures 7.13 to 7.15).[17]

In all these cases, the humor of Bolsonaro memes on WhatsApp effectively incorporates different shades of the social segments that support him, such as the military, monarchists, and neo-Pentecostal religious groups, among others. In this way, the mythical imaginary constituted around the figure of the president can mobilize common-sense elements, references to pop culture, and nationalist values as a backdrop for the construction of the public image of Bolsonaro. The fact that many of these memes circulate primarily through WhatsApp allows users to benefit from certain freedom granted by the private character of the instant-messaging tool, and favors the flattering content of

Figure 7.11. References to pop culture in a Bolsonaro meme.

Figure 7.12. References to pop culture in a Bolsonaro meme.

1 janeiro
2º Independência do Brasil!

Figure 7.13. Historical and religious reinterpretations.

Figure 7.14. Historical and religious reinterpretations.

Figure 7.15. Historical and religious reinterpretations.

memes, without the presentation of any kind of counterpoint to official discourse and government actions.

Final Remarks

The Brazilian far-right turn has been discussed lately from several angles (Gomes; Nicolau). Some research projects emphasize social and economic aspects, and others focus on social media and digital campaign models adopted by Bolsonaro, but there is a lack of studies concerned with understanding how humor has played such a relevant role in this scenario.

Brazilian identity is largely built on a unique sense of humor, which makes intense use of self-deprecation, as if fun resides in laughing at one's misfortune (Lunardi and Burgess). This shared misfortune has fueled national pride for a long time. But recently, Brazil has also experienced a turnaround in its collective sense of humor. Far-right humor is marked not only by a strong tension between freedom of expression and antidemocratic manifestations but also by an exacerbated nationalist appeal, which often ends up turning humor into mere political proselytism. Nationalism obscures social differences and divides and drowns out the identity struggle that has become a successful part of the progressive repertoire. Thus, humor and nationalism together are a weapon in this cultural backlash.

Bolsonarist memes have played an important role in this ecosystem, as they are material and iconographic vehicles for this far-right humor. They work to shape an audience that is not only subject to this rhetoric daily but reiterate it in environments that have been described by experts as echo chambers, such as political discussion groups on WhatsApp (Resende et al.; Caetano et al.; Evangelista and Bruno). Thus, humor has served to normalize extremist discourses, and private communication platforms have been the stage for the dissemination of these discourses to broad sections of the population through memes.

This chapter has sought three main goals. The first was to understand whether Bolsonaro memes on WhatsApp can be perceived as ideological vehicles circulated by far-right supporters. The second goal was to explore the main elements of the nationalist and antidemocratic rhetoric in these memes. Finally, this chapter highlighted how far-right memes on WhatsApp were directly connected to contemporary political events, especially ones in which Bolsonaro's government was concerned. Thus, peaks in the sharing of image memes corresponded to episodes of acute government crisis, in such a way that these memes offer substance to and guide the positioning of far-right supporters.

There is an important set of limitations that do not allow, at this point, the generalization of conclusions to other scenarios. First, the corpus examined here is relatively small, corresponding to just six months of activity in these groups, and during a public health crisis caused to an unprecedented pandemic, which can result in some relevant bias. In addition, due to the private nature of the data and a series of technical limitations concerning the methods employed, as well as the length of this chapter, this study does not analyze any relational data, which could, for example, elucidate issues such as the coordinated action of some users in these groups regarding the sharing of memes. And finally, research on political memes requires different approaches, which often blur the conceptual frontier of some of its premises, such as the definition of humor, since much of this material is of a markedly ideological nature and is not deeply comic, but rather in a witty vein.

Despite the limitations, however, the chapter may represent the first step toward a more accurate understanding of how Jair Bolsonaro has been represented by groups of government supporters on WhatsApp. In this sense, as this study has tried to emphasize, the Brazilian political scene, especially regarding the use of mobile instant messaging by a large portion of the electorate, is unique. If Facebook, Twitter, and YouTube are often accused of promoting hate speech and valuing extremist and overtly nationalist messages, WhatsApp clearly represents an escalation in the harmful potential of these tools, given the opacity on which it is based. In this sense, it is urgent to encourage broad media literacy education capable of advising and alerting ordinary citizens to the effects of communicational environments that favor the distribution of word-of-mouth content and the constitution of network homophily that refuses diversity. WhatsApp memes have been blamed for fostering a radicalized political environment, but they are just an expression of the audiences that make them up. What a study like this observes is that, although there are many forms of humor in dispute by different sectors of Brazilian society, the political far right has appropriated private communication networks to carry a message that, when incorporating humor and nationalism, excludes struggles for recognition and adopts a flattened and dangerously simplified national identity.

Notes

1 Affordance is a concept coined by psychologist James J. Gibson in his book *The Ecological Approach to Visual Perception* (1979), and it refers to the possibilities for actions or relational properties in an ecological environment. It is mostly used to define technological responses through social interaction.

2 Digital folklore can be understood as a vernacular expression that helps to build imaginaries and sociocultural representations native to the digital environment. Email chains, memes, and other common practices and behaviors on the Internet can be understood as part of digital folklore. For more details, see Blank. Throughout this text, when we refer to digital folklore or political folklore, we are describing practices concerning the construction of cultural representations from specific audiences.

3 Brazil experienced a military dictatorial regime between 1964 and 1985. The military government was established, initially as a provisional military junta, in the 1960s, under the pretext of an alleged communist threat personified by then president João Goulart, who took office in 1961, after the resignation of the right-wing populist Jânio Quadros. For more than twenty years, Brazilians saw successive generals in the main executive posts, including the presidency of the republic. Despite this, a popular movement in the early 1980s emerged with force, demanding a return to direct elections. In 1985, the first civilian government was indirectly elected after the dictatorship. And, in 1989, Brazilian citizens were able to vote once again to elect their president. This period, which begins in the late 1980s and continues through the early 1990s, and which also saw the emergence of the Sixth Republic in the country after an exclusive constituent assembly in 1988, is known as "re-democratization."

4 Between 1937 and 1945, Brazil experienced its first dictatorship, after a coup d'état promoted by the then-president Getúlio Vargas, which dissolved the parliament and

promulgated a constitution that gave Vargas full powers. At the end of this period, Vargas himself was in charge of leading a democratic transition and created the basis for the Brazilian multiparty system, founding what would become the then-Brazilian Labor Party (PTB), which brought together a series of developmentalist left-wing politicians. The PTB was extinguished by the Brazilian military dictatorship in 1965, along with other parties, and several of its party cadres were exiled from the country until the end of the regime. After the death of João Goulart in 1976, Leonel Brizola, who had been governor of the state of Rio Grande do Sul, became the main leader of the Brazilian Labor Party, and, consequently, of the political left in the country. He returned to Brazil from exile in 1979, and became, in 1982, governor of the state of Rio de Janeiro, and one of the main voices of opposition at that time.

5 In the original, "A política é a arte de engolir sapos. Não seria fascinante fazer agora a elite brasileira engolir o Lula, este sapo barbudo?"

6 *Tweetazzos* are online demonstrations that consist of a coordinated collective action of people tweeting on a specific subject. Individuals are called on to participate in tweetazzos, for instance, during televised debates in order to show support for a candidate.

7 www.youtube.com/watch?v=Z4CoY_82LAQ.

8 tv.uol/17UhV.

9 www.youtube.com/watch?v=Znb957Gqwz8.

10 www.youtube.com/watch?v=TWq-BuJUfW4.

11 bit.ly/34ZT5Ad. .

12 www.youtube.com/watch?v=xpqgmnhmJao>.

13 Bolsonaro has already been the target of a large number of lawsuits. In one of the most consequential episodes, he was forced to publicly apologize and pay a fine to federal deputy Maria do Rosário, after having said in plenary that he would not rape her, "because you don't deserve it." As a deputy, he faced numerous impeachment attempts for breach of decorum. In general, however, most of the decisions were reversed, or, at most, he was forced to pay fines, without major consequences.

14 *Quilombolas* are Afro-Brazilian residents of *quilombos,* which are settlements that were established by escaped slaves. Brazil's 1988 constitution granted remaining *quilombolas,* descendants of enslaved people, the collective ownership of their occupied lands. In 2017, during one of his rallies, Bolsonaro said that quilombos were unproductive, and compared quilombolas to fat oxen, saying that they weighed "eight arrobas," an arroba being a unit of weight used by ranchers in evaluating cattle. He was initially sentenced by the court to pay a fine for moral damages to quilombola communities and the Black population in general. But, despite the speech's clearly racist tone, Bolsonaro won a reversal of the decision.

15 Translation for figure 7.7: "The guy you hate / His girlfriend / His sons / His classmates / His gang / You." Translation for figure 7.8: "Your president [*the image is of former president Lula watching a theater spectacle featuring two men kissing*] / My president [*image of Bolsonaro sitting with military officers*]."

16 Translation for figure 7.10: "Bolsonaro 2022 [*the then-next presidential elections*] / We are only beginning." Translation for figure 7.11: "[*Thor:*] I'm sure it must be here / Hey, man! / You dropped this thing [*Bolsonaro is holding the mythological hammer Mjölnir, which supposedly cannot be held by a person unworthy of it*] / Take your weapon! /

What!? / Thank you, Myth! / I knew there was still someone worthy!" Translation for figure 7.12: "I say dirty words but I am not fucking corrupt / Uncivil Me [*a pun on the movie title* Despicable Me]."

17   Translation for figure 7.13: "January 1st: Second Independence of Brazil [*Bolsonaro is portrayed as Emperor Pedro I, proclaimer of Brazilian independence in 1822*]."

Works Cited

Abreu, Alzira Alves de, et al., editors. "BRIZOLA, Leonel." *Dicionário Histórico-Biográfico Brasileiro—Pós-1930,* CPDOC, 2010, cpdoc.fgv.br/acervo/dicionarios/dhbb.

Avritzer, Leonardo. *Política e antipolítica: a crise do governo Bolsonaro.* São Paulo: Todavia, 2020.

Bakhtin, Mikhail. *A cultura popular na idade média e no renascimento: o contexto de François Rabelais.* São Paulo: Hucitec, 1987.

Bennett, W. Lance. "When Politics Becomes Play." *Political Behavior,* vol. 1, no. 4, 1979, pp. 331–359.

Beyer, Jessica. *Expect Us: Online Communities and Political Mobilization.* Oxford: Oxford UP, 2014.

Billig, Michael. "Humour and Hatred: The Racist Jokes of the Ku Klux Klan." *Discourse & Society,* vol. 12, no. 3, 2001, pp. 267–289.

Blank, Trevor J. "Toward a Conceptual Framework for the Study of Folklore and the Internet." *Folklore and the Internet: Vernacular Expression in a Digital World,* edited by Trevor J. Blank, Logan: Utah State UP, 2009, pp. 1–20.

Boechat, Yan. "Punk aos 80." *IstoÉ,* 18 Aug. 2010, istoe.com.br/95210_PUNK+AOS+80/.

Caetano, Josemar Alves, et al. "Analyzing and Characterizing Political Discussions in WhatsApp Public Groups." *CoRR,* abs/1804.00397, 2018.

Caldeira Neto, Odilon. *Nosso nome é Enéas!: Partido Da Reedificação da Ordem Nacional (1989–2006).* 2016. UFRGS, PhD dissertation, lume.ufrgs.br/handle/10183/148426.

Chagas, Viktor. "Dolce Farmeme: a retórica da brincadeira política." *Revista Brasileira de Ciências Sociais,* vol. 38, no. 111, 2023, pp. 1–15 (e3811008), https://doi.org/ 10.1590/ 3811008/2023.

———. "Making Amends with Memes." *Commonplace,* 10 Aug. 2020, https://doi.org/10 .21428/6ffd8432.ac155a53.

———. "WhatsApp and Digital Astroturfing: A Social Network Analysis of Brazilian Political Discussion Groups of Bolsonaro's Supporters." *International Journal of Communication,* no. 16, 2022, pp. 2431–2455.

Chagas, Viktor, and Vivian Luiz Fonseca. "Faster, Higher, Stronger: Sports Fan Activism and Mediatized Political Play in the 2016 Rio Olympic Games." *Journal of Transformative Works and Culture,* no. 32. 2020, https://doi.org/10.3983/twc.2020.1707.

———, et al. "Political Memes and the Politics of Memes: A Methodological Proposal for Content Analysis of Online Political Memes." *First Monday,* vol. 24, no. 2, 2019, https:// doi.org/10.5210/fm.v24i2.7264.

Davison, Patrick. "A Linguagem dos memes de Internet: dez anos depois." *A Cultura dos memes: aspectos sociológicos e dimensões políticas de um fenômeno do mundo digital,* edited by Viktor Chagas, Salvador, Brazil: EdUFBA, 2020, pp. 139–156.

Evangelista, Rafael, and Fernanda Bruno. "WhatsApp and Political Instability in Brazil: Targeted Messages and Political Radicalisation." *Internet Policy Review,* vol. 8, no. 4, 2019.

Freire, Fernanda de Alcântara. *Eleições da Zueira: memes, humor e política nas eleições presidenciais de 2014.* 2016. Universidade do Estado do Rio de Janeiro, MSc thesis, www .bdtd.uerj.br:8443/handle/1/9030.

Gomes, Wilson. *Crônica de uma tragédia anunciada: como a extrema-direita chegou ao poder.* Salvador, Brazil: Sagga Editora, 2020.

Gulino, Daniel, and Carolina Brígido. "'Vamos libertar o povo do socialismo e do politi-camente correto,' diz Bolsonaro." *O Globo,* 1 Jan. 2019, oglobo.globo.com/brasil/vamos -libertar-povo-do-socialismo-do-politicamente-correto-diz-bolsonaro-23339518.

Lunardi, Gabriela M., and Jean Burgess. "'É Zoeira:' as dinâmicas culturais do humor brasileiro na Internet." *A cultura dos memes: aspectos sociológicos e dimensões políticas de um fenômeno do mundo digital,* edited by Viktor Chagas, Salvador, Brazil: EdUFBA, 2020, pp. 427–458.

Mendonça, Ricardo F., and Marcio Bustamante. "Back to the Future: Changing Repertoire in Contemporary Protests." *Bulletin of Latin American Research,* vol. 39, no. 5. 2020, pp. 629–643.

Miguel, Luis Felipe. "Falar bonito: o kitsch como estratégia discursiva." *Revista brasileira de ciência política,* vol. 6, no. 6, 2011, pp. 183–202.

Milner, Ryan. *The World Made Meme.* Cambridge, MA: MIT Press, 2016.

National Health Council (Brazil). Resolution No. 510, 7 Apr. 2016, conselho.saude.gov.br/ resolucoes/2016/Reso510.pdf. DOU 98, 24 May 2016, section 1, 44–45.

Nicolau, Jairo. *O Brasil dobrou à direita.* Rio de Janeiro: Zahar, 2020.

Norris, Pippa, and Ronald Inglehart. *Cultural Backlash: Trump, Brexit, and Authoritarian Populism.* Cambridge: Cambridge UP, 2019.

Penteado, Claudio, and Celina Lerner. "A direita na rede: mobilização online no impeach-ment de Dilma Rousseff." *Em Debate,* vol. 10, no. 1, 2018 pp. 12–24.

Pérez, Raúl. "Learning to Make Racism Funny in the 'Color-Blind' Era: Stand-up Comedy Students, Performance Strategies, and the (Re)Production of Racist Jokes in Public." *Discourse & Society,* vol. 24, no. 4, 2013, pp. 478–503.

Phillips, Whitney, and Ryan Milner. *The Ambivalent Internet: Mischief, Oddity, and Antago-nism Online.* Cambridge, MA: MIT Press, 2017.

Queler, Jefferson José. "Quando o eleitor faz a propaganda política: o engajamento popular na campanha eleitoral de Jânio Quadros (1959–1960)." *Tempo,* vol. 14, no. 28, 2010, pp. 28–84.

Resende, Gustavo, et al. "(Mis)Information Dissemination in WhatsApp: Gathering, Ana-lyzing and Countermeasures." *WWW'19: Proceedings of the ACM, San Francisco, USA, 13–17 May 2019,* people.mpi-sws.org/~johnme/pdf/resende_www2019_whatsapp.pdf.

Rocha, Camila. *"Menos Marx, Mais Mises": uma gênese da Nova Direita Brasileira (2006–2018).* 2019. Universidade de São Paulo, PhD dissertation, https://doi.org/10.11606/T.8 .2019.tde-19092019-174426.

dos Santos, João Guilherme Bastos. "Mobile Networks and the Brazilian 2018 Presidential Election: From Technological Design to Social Appropriation." *Brazilian Studies Pro-*

gram One Pager, no. 2, 2019, pp. 1–2, www.ou.edu/content/dam/International/brazil
-studies/docs/one-pager-2.pdf.

dos Santos, João Guilherme Bastos, and Viktor Chagas. "Direta transante: enquadramen-
tos pessoais e agenda ultraliberal do MBL." *MATRIZes,* vol. 12, no. 3, 2018 pp. 189–214.

Shifman, Limor. *Memes in Digital Culture.* Cambridge, MA: MIT Press, 2014.

Solano, Esther. "Crise da democracia e extremismos de direita." *Análise,* no. 42. 2018 pp.
1–29.

Sue, Christina A., and Tanya Golash-Boza. "'It Was Only a Joke:' How Racial Humour
Fuels Colour-Blind Ideologies in Mexico and Peru." *Ethnic and Racial Studies,* vol. 36,
no. 10, 2013 pp. 1582–1598.

Tsai, Yi Jing, and Viktor Chagas. "Apocryphal Gospels: Political Memes and Memes on
Politics Used as Resource for Negative Campaigns Anchored in Anonymity and Personal Offenses." *#AoIR 2nd Flashpoint Symposium 2020,* Porto Alegre, Brazil / Online,
3–4 Sept. 2019. Unisinos, 2019, proceedings.science/aoir-2nd/trabalhos/apocryphal
-gospels-political-memes-and-memes-on-politics-used-as-resource-for-ne#.

Weaver, Simon. "Jokes, Rhetoric and Embodied Racism: A Rhetorical Discourse Analysis
of the Logics of Racist Jokes on the Internet." *Ethnicities,* vol. 11, no. 4, 2011 pp. 413–
435.

8

Barbie Votes for Bolsonaro

How an Instagram Account Satirized
the Brazilian Middle and Upper Classes

ULISSES A. SAWCZUK DA SILVA
AND MÉLODINE SOMMIER

Barbie Gets Political

Shortly before Brazil's 2018 presidential election, a political meme gained considerable popularity in the country. Known as Fascist Barbie, it consisted of images of the Barbie doll—originally produced by Mattel—that were accompanied by captions in which the character expressed racist, classist, homophobic, and sexist views, as well as her support for far-right candidate Jair Bolsonaro. The meme, which criticized white, conservative middle- and upper-class Brazilian voters, was popularized on digital platforms such as Facebook, Instagram, WhatsApp, and Twitter.

Created by left-wing voters who opposed Bolsonaro and supported the Workers' Party candidate, Fernando Haddad, Fascist Barbie was a direct descendant of another meme: Sexist Ken. In 2017, inspired by Mattel's hipster-looking revamp of the male doll, Brazilian Internet users employed the character to mock middle- and upper-class men who, despite looking trendy and claiming to be progressive, displayed traditional sexist attitudes (De Mingo).

The metamorphosis of Sexist Ken into Fascist Barbie was aligned with the emergence of anti-Bolsonaro social movements that started as hashtags and online groups such as #EleNão (#NotHim) and #MulheresUnidasContraBolsonaro (#WomenUnitedAgainstBolsonaro).[1] Due to its comic character, the meme, unlike the other initiatives, did not result in large street protests. However, it was subjected to many reinterpretations, such as those by individuals who, wearing blonde wigs and other props, recorded videos parodying right-wing Brazilians (Lellis). Moreover, Fascist Barbie became a popular costume during the 2019 Brazilian Carnival, and many party-goers attended the traditional festivities dressed up as the character (Phillips).

Interestingly, Fascist Barbie ended up being adopted by Internet users from other Latin American countries, gaining a Chilean version—with a Facebook fan page named Barbie y Ken Ciudadanos de Bien—as well as Colombian and Salvadoran adaptations. These reinterpretations were perhaps facilitated by the similarities among racist and elitist discourses prevalent in Latin America (Van Dijk 83–85).

One of the most famous Brazilian social media profiles to publish the meme was the Instagram account Barbie Fascionista—a portmanteau of the words *fascista* ("fascist") and fashionista (Barbie Fashionistas being a line of Barbie dolls launched by Mattel)—which was active between October 2018 and March 2019. The profile, which parodied Brazil's conservative social media influencers, quickly garnered more than 100,000 followers and received coverage from important Brazilian and international news outlets such as *Folha de S.Paulo* (Fioratti and Moura) and *Le Monde* (Gatinois).

Barbie Fascionista resembled a blog—each memetic image was accompanied by a short essay in which the character expressed her prejudiced and retrograde political views. Its humor relied on the contradiction between the doll's idealized and glamorous world—which is shown in the images, originally produced by Mattel, that illustrate the profile—and the character's shockingly prejudiced statements. In a non-satirical post that was published by the account between the first and second rounds of the 2018 presidential election (which took place, respectively, on October 7 and October 28), the profile declared support for Fernando Haddad—the Workers' Party candidate—which highlighted Barbie Fascionista's connection of humor and political activism. Furthermore, the post explained that the profile's goals were to criticize elitist and prejudiced discourses, foster debates about relevant social themes, and help promote sociocultural changes. The text also mentioned that several conservative Brazilians interpreted the profile's posts as an endorsement of racist, classist, and sexist discourses—rather than criticism of them—and went as far as to compliment Barbie Fascionista and say that the account represented their views. In this post, the creator(s) urged the profile's followers to take its content as irony.

In displaying many of the key characteristics of memes—particularly their intertextuality and link to participatory online practices and popular culture—Barbie Fascionista offered insights into the use of memes as a form of political commentary. The account engaged with race, class, and gender in-equalities that are widespread in Brazilian society (Layton and Smith 53; Re-iter 27), as well as reproduced many of the symbolic roles—both conservative and subversive—associated with the Barbie doll (Lord 217; Toffoletti 60–62). Additionally, Barbie Fascionista shed light on the relationship between Brazil and the US by tapping into the cultural (colonizing) repertoire attached to the doll. Through its satirical use of the character, the account simultaneously ap-propriated, criticized, and subverted US consumer culture.

Our study explores how the Brazilian middle and upper classes were por-trayed in the memetic images and texts published by the Instagram account between October 11 and December 24, 2018. Because the posts published by Barbie Fascionista blend visual content and written texts, our investigation relies on a multimodal approach that combines two complementary research techniques: semiotic analysis (Rose 74) and critical discourse analysis (Wo-dak 64–65). The results show that many of the criticisms conveyed by the ac-count echo scholarly interpretations that denounce the widespread presence of exclusionary discourses in Brazilian society. In doing this, Barbie Fascioni-sta relies heavily on sophisticated rhetorical devices to powerfully articulate its critique. Nevertheless, the subtlety of its criticisms might cause audiences to interpret its content differently from what its creators expected.

Brazil, Barbie, and Memes: Drawing the Contours of a Sociocultural Critique

Racism and racial inequalities are major issues in Brazilian society. White Brazilians—who make up the bulk of the country's affluent classes—have, on average, better income and education and tend to be viewed more favor-ably than individuals perceived to be Black (Reiter 26–27). Afro-Brazilians, in turn, often live in the poorest areas of Brazilian cities and comprise the majority of victims of criminality and police brutality (Santos 157). White Brazilians are also overrepresented in the media (Van Dijk 134), their visibil-ity being a fundamental asset in maintaining their dominance and setting the norm against which racialized minorities are evaluated (Dyer 2, 44).

Despite this reality, white Brazilians do not often acknowledge being racist and frequently argue that, because the population of Brazil is predominantly racially mixed—including most of the individuals who are considered white—the country is a "racial democracy" where prejudice is exclusively class-based (Layton and Smith 54). The denial of racism by Brazil's white privileged classes echoes similar practices in the US and Europe, where pretenses about living in post-racial societies are intertwined with covert and depoliticized expressions of racial prejudices (Bonilla-Silva 1362; Lentin 495–496).

Social inequalities are frequently justified in Brazil with the argument that the lower classes are in a subordinate position due to their inferior morals and values (Souza 17). This notion is connected to contemporary neoliberal ideas such as the concept of meritocracy. Nowadays, it is not uncommon for members of the Brazilian middle and upper classes to justify their privileges in terms of meritocracy, emphasizing their hard work and diligence while omitting the structural causes of inequity (Cavalcante 109–114; Souza 77).

Besides espousing classist views, many affluent Brazilians have anti-leftist feelings that, several scholars have argued, are connected to their fear of losing their privileges (Bähre and Gomes 15; Souza 104; Teshainer et al. 12). Although not a homogeneous group, considerable tranches of the Brazilian middle class have far-right or fascist leanings (De Jesus 14; Souza 98–99). The expression *cidadãos de bem* (upstanding citizens) is often used to describe people from these social groups. Originally a positive—often self-identifying—term applied to white, middle-, or upper-class conservative Brazilians, the meaning of the expression has been subverted and it is now also used to denote people who are racist, classist, misogynist, and nostalgic for the country's military dictatorship (1964–1985) (De Jesus 12–13). As such, the term *cidadãos de bem* illustrates the way classist and racist systems of domination are intertwined with sexism and patriarchy in Latin America (Van Dijk 84).

Throughout Brazil's history, its society—particularly the affluent classes—has recurrently adopted dominant foreign values and ideologies—a trend that is connected to the country's colonial past (1500–1822). Between the late nineteenth and early twentieth centuries, the Brazilian middle and upper classes embraced a project of Europeanization of the country marked by promotion of European immigration and miscegenation, the rejection of African and Indigenous traditions, and the adoption of European cultural values and institutions (Reiter 25–26; Skidmore 6). This changed in the 1940s, a decade in which the United States consolidated its role as the main foreign source of cultural and economic influence on Brazil—as well as other Latin American countries—in line with the geopolitical rearrangement engendered by World War II (Tota 197). Since then, most Brazilians have been heavily exposed to US-produced cultural and media artifacts, to such an extent that Brazilian society has experienced significant changes in its consumption habits (Alves 26) and Brazilian Portuguese has been increasingly influenced by the English language (Alves 24–25; Assis-Peterson 331). Nevertheless, it is worthy of note that some of these influences have given rise to creative forms of hybridization, cultural resistance, and appropriation (Alves 92; Assis-Peterson 338–339).

It is in this context that Barbie, the most famous US doll, has become one of the most popular toys in Brazil. Significantly, emphasizing Barbie's strong presence in Latin America, Lord defines the doll as a cultural colonist (170). This is because Barbie is not only a highly commercially successful toy but also a powerful cultural icon that has helped propagate imperialist and capitalist North American values globally (Lord 170; Steinberg 262). On multiple occasions, Barbie has been criticized for reinforcing values such as materialism and consumerism (Steinberg 254), whiteness, heteronormativity, and conservatism (Toffoletti 60). If, as Barthes writes, a myth is a type of discourse that has the goal of emptying reality and often serves the interests of the ruling classes (142–143), Barbie embodies several myths that include, but are not restricted to, the myth of white/US superiority, the myth of capitalism as the path to success, and the myth of material accumulation as the key to happiness. Many of these myths are similar to the discourses employed by the affluent classes of Brazil to justify their domination over other social groups.

Sexism and patriarchy are also tightly connected to the figure of Barbie. Launched in 1959, the doll was sold as a "wholesome all-American girl" imbued with an air of middle-class respectability (Lord 23). As such, she has contributed to perpetuating old-fashioned societal views, particularly regarding the status of women (Driessen 11). Moreover, Barbie has reflected unrealistic beauty standards (Dittmar et al. 284) and beliefs such as that women always need to be well-dressed and look fashionable (Driessen 14).

However, like the material she is made of—plastic—Barbie's symbolic power is flexible and subject to different interpretations (Lord 24). Some contend that Barbie was revolutionary for her time. Aligned with the protofeminist developments of the late 1950s and early 1960s, the doll was independent, unmarried, had her career, lived by herself (Lord 58), and, as stated by Barbie's creator, did not engage in domestic chores (Pearson and Mullins 236). If, during the 1950s and 1960s, women were expected to be subordinate to men, that has never been the case for Barbie. Unlike the biblical story of Adam and Eve, Barbie was created before her partner, Ken, and remains far more charismatic than he is (Lord 79). Additionally, the character's independence is reflected by her professional versatility. Throughout the years, Barbie has had a plethora of jobs, including many traditionally associated with men, having been a businesswoman, a NASCAR racer, an astronaut, and a presidential candidate (Steinberg 255–256). More recently, Mattel has created a line of Barbie dolls that praises female scientists of different ethnicities and nationalities who have played important roles in the fight against COVID-19—including Brazilian biomedical researcher Dr. Jaqueline Goes de Jesus (Nuñez). This shows how Mattel has attempted to keep the character current with sociohistorical developments, such as demands for more diversity in the media and toy industries.

Furthermore, although the extreme materialism of Barbie's universe can be associated with the commodification of women—after all, she represents a woman who can be purchased, consumed, manipulated, and discarded (Lord 86; Toffoletti 60)—the character's symbolic flexibility has allowed for critical reinterpretations, including alternative narratives that challenge gender stereotyping, colonialism, and consumer culture (Lord 221). In line with this perspective, Barbie Fascionista can be understood as a creative and subversive reshaping of a US-originated artifact that, critically, blends the meanings associated with Barbie with the discourses and practices of the Brazilian middle and upper classes. The dual status of the doll—being at the same time familiar to Brazilians and foreign—is an important aspect on which Barbie Fascionista relies to satirize the high level of Americanization of the country's privileged classes. This way, Barbie Fascionista demonstrates that the Americanization of Brazil has not always been negative, because Brazilians have also managed to reinterpret North American cultural influences in creative, irreverent, and syncretic ways (Alves 117–18; Tota 210–11). Therefore, the doll illustrates how the reception of cultural artifacts is a complex phenomenon that can vary significantly according to the diverse contexts and audiences these objects have been exposed to.

Considering her popularity and polysemy, Barbie is an ideal object for remixes, reinterpretations, and recreations of various types, including memes. The Instagram account Barbie Fascionista indeed embodies many of the typical characteristics of memes, particularly regarding its intertextuality, political resonance, and connection to popular culture as well as to local and global discourses.

According to Shifman, memes can be defined as fast-spreading and dynamic cultural artifacts created and transformed by multiple Internet users (41). Notwithstanding the close connection of memes to Web 2.0 and participatory culture (Marwick 12), these highly intertextual objects are also linked to broader cultural, historical, and aesthetic dynamics that transcend the Internet (Shifman 34). The relationship between memes and specific sociocultural and political contexts beyond social media—exemplified by the connection between Barbie Fascionista and the 2018 Brazilian presidential election—reveals the extent to which these artifacts have become an essential part of popular culture as well as powerful agents of globalization. Although memes have the potential to reinforce local cultures and identities (Monteiro Lunardi 16), they also have the power to transmit dominant US and Western values, often in invisible ways (Shifman 161). The Barbie Fascionista account draws on and plays with this dynamic through the duality of its lead character, Barbie, who, as discussed above, signifies both familiarity and exoticism to its Brazilian audience, hinting at the critique of elitism and cultural colonialism.

Initially dismissed by some as nothing more than trivial entertainment, memes are attracting increasing scholarly attention regarding their political relevance (Mina 74; Ross and Rivers 2–3; Shifman 120). Memes are extremely versatile and can take different shapes such as remixes, parodies, and mashups (Shifman 2). This flexibility allows political memes to take on different roles. They can be used by people to simultaneously create a sense of collectivity and participate in political campaigns in more personalized ways (Shifman 129), elude censorship by conveying subversive messages (Mina 46), or as counter-discourses propagated by powerful corporations or dominant political groups (Shifman 130, 149). Drawing on Shifman's work, Chagas et al. have identified three overarching roles played by memes circulated on Twitter during the 2014 presidential elections in Brazil—namely *persuasion, grassroots action,* and *public discussion.* The authors argue that changes in political campaign regulations in Brazil have left more room for online communication, thereby increasing the popularity of political memes and turning Brazil into an "impressive meme distributor."

Although memes are frequently associated with progressive movements such as Black Lives Matter, *Los Indignados,* and We Are the 99%, they have also been extensively used by conservative and authoritarian groups (Mina 100). In Brazil, several anti-leftist memes have been published by right-wing social media profiles such as *Socialista de iPhone* (iPhone socialist) and *Movimento Brasil Livre* (Free Brazil movement). Moreover, public figures such as former president Lula have been attacked with memes that blend anti-leftism with negative class and ethno-regional stereotypes (Bähre and Gomes 11–12).

Analyzing Barbie Fascionista

The data for this study consists of 45 memetic images[2]—as well as the short texts that accompany them—that were published by the Instagram account Barbie Fascionista between October 11 and December 24, 2018. We decided to exclude two posts that had been published in March 2019 from the analysis because, by the time they were made available, Jair Bolsonaro had already been the president of Brazil for two months and, in our view, this content was not directly connected to the sociopolitical context of the 2018 elections. Significantly, the Instagram account was deleted in March 2019—which seems to suggest that, to its creator(s), Barbie Fascionista was intrinsically related to the electoral atmosphere.

The distinct identity and discursive unity of Barbie Fascionista stem from the complex and multilayered content produced by the anonymous owner(s) of the page. The account consisted of four different semiotic modes: the original images (produced by Mattel); the memetic captions (apparently added to the original images by the owner[s] of the page); the short essays that accompany the images; and the hashtags that follow the texts.

Considering this textual intricacy, we have opted for a multimodal analysis that combines semiotic analysis and critical discourse analysis (CDA). The two methods complement each other to illustrate which discourses were (re)produced and contested, and how. The semiotic analysis has paid particular attention to myths—connotative signs that attribute subjective and broad values to objects/subjects, emptying them of their history—and the collective systems they are part of, which are known as mythologies (Rose 96–97). Both the Barbie doll and the elitist and prejudiced discourses that are connected to her in Barbie Fascionista are myths—and because myths serve ideological purposes (Barthes 142), the analysis has sought to reveal how the account attempted to contest the ideologies behind these mythologies.

The set of tools for visual analysis proposed by Machin and Mayr was used to identify the ideas and values represented by objects and the role that salience and settings play in the creation of meaning (51–52, 54). Drawing on Wodak's discourse-historical approach and the multilayered attention it gives to the context that surrounds the texts (67), the analysis focused on the linguistic and textual aspects of the memetic images and satirical texts published by Barbie Fascionista; the connections between the content and the prejudiced/elitist discourses it parodies, as well as its references to Barbie and other cultural artifacts; the sociocultural and political context of contemporary Brazil; and historical dynamics of class and race in Brazil and their relation to racist and classist ideologies present in other countries.

In practice, the analysis consisted of three main steps. First, visual and critical discourse analyses were conducted by focusing on all visual and textual elements as well as their interplay. For each of the 45 posts, Author 1 wrote a critical interpretation and assigned keywords. Second, three overarching themes (i.e., privilege, prejudice, and conservatism) were identified, based on the in-depth initial analyses of each post. This second phase of analysis consisted of a thorough iterative process of navigating back and forth among individual posts, full datasets, critical interpretations and keywords, and literature. Third, depth and details were added to the three themes by editing, condensing, and merging the preliminary analyses of each post to answer the research question: How do the memetic images and texts published by the Instagram account Barbie Fascionista portray the Brazilian middle and upper classes?

A Privileged, Prejudiced, and Conservative Doll

We have identified three overarching themes in Barbie Fascionista's content, which permeate the way the Brazilian middle and upper classes are portrayed in the account: privilege, prejudice, and conservatism. While some of these individual themes might be more clearly identifiable than the others in certain posts, the three of them are, for the most part, interconnected and present in most of the account's content, revealing the intersection of these categories.

When it comes to privilege, Barbie Fascionista suggests that the Brazilian middle and upper classes are composed of wealthy individuals who espouse neoliberal, capitalist, and materialistic values. Both the texts and images depict the main character as a rich woman who owns an incredible number of material goods, often travels abroad, is always elegantly dressed, and places great importance on fashion. This relates to the interpretations of scholars who view the original Barbie doll as a symbol of economic status and capitalism (Driessen 12; Lord 247; Steinberg 262).

If meritocracy is one of the main values for members of the Brazilian middle class—who attempt to legitimize their privileges by claiming that they have worked hard to obtain them (Souza 85)—Barbie Fascionista is no different. The character often describes herself as a "hard-working entrepreneur" who has had to struggle to achieve and maintain her socioeconomic status—something contradicted by the images that illustrate the posts, which often show her traveling or indulging in consumption and leisure activities. However, as we will see below, meritocratic discourse is used by the character not only to justify her wealth but also to legitimize her cultural capital.

In figure 8.1, the character's support of meritocracy is evidenced by the caption featured in the memetic image, as well as the "Meritocracy School" badge on her sleeve—which was Photoshopped in by the profile's authors. Here, the character not only reproduces discourses that are commonly used by middle- and upper-class Brazilians, but also alludes to the ideals of self-empowerment that are connected to the original Barbie doll—particularly the slogan "You can be anything," which has been used by Mattel to promote the toy (Driessen 22).

Barbie's high social status and privileged conditions are shown by visual markers. While the leather backpack worn by the doll suggests elegance and

Figure 8.1. Screenshot of the Barbie Fascionista page with a conservative critique based on meritocratic legitimation. *"If there is something I know, it is that crying won't take you anywhere!! #Enough #YouJustHaveToWantIt #Merit."* The accompanying caption reads: "Oi, fascimores!! Vocês sempre me pedem para falar um pouco sobre como vencer na vida e dicas de coach!!! Então, citarei algumas aqui!! A primeira, é a conduta de não se vitimizar!! Vou contar uma história pra vocês . . . Fiz vestibular em Boston, sabe??! Mas juro que analisei a dura realidade dos vestibulares no Brasil!!! Ouvi relatos da Melanie e da Sarah, minhas melhores amigas, e aí percebi o quanto esse governo daqui puxava sardinha para os menos favorecidos. Aquela síndrome de cachorro abandonado, sabe??! 'Mas Barbie, como isso é possível??' GENTE, PENSEM COMIGO: acham que é fácil fazer aulas gastronômicas, balé, natação, ginástica, hipismo, francês e ainda estudar o dia inteiro numa escola gringa???! NÃO!! É pesado, sabe??!" [Translation: "Hello, Fasci-lovers!! You always ask me to speak a little bit about how to win in life and also give you some coaching tips!!! So, I'm going to shed light on a few things!! Firstly, we must adopt the attitude of not playing the victim!! I am going to tell you a story . . . I applied to a university in Boston, you know??! But I swear I've analyzed the harsh reality of college entrance exams in Brazil!!! I've heard stories from my best friends Melanie and Sarah, and that's how I realized how much our government would manipulate the system in favor of the less privileged. It's clearly a case of the White Knight Syndrome, you know? 'But Barbie, how is that possible?' PEOPLE, THINK ABOUT IT WITH ME: do you think it is easy to take classes in gastronomy, ballet, swimming, gymnastics, horse riding, and French while also studying all day long at a foreign school???! NO!! That's a heavy load, you know?"]

luxury, the Apple logo on her computer—which was inserted by the post's authors—is a reference to the fact that, in Brazil, the US tech company's products are sold at extremely high prices. Because Apple devices are inaccessible to the majority of the Brazilian population, they are often viewed in the country as symbols of status, wealth, and snobbery.

The longer text, located on the right side of the image, highlights how the doll's privileges are not only economic but also associated with her cultural capital. In it, the character reveals that she has attended university in Boston (likely an allusion to Harvard). Barbie's connection to a highly ranked US university is a reference to the important role education plays for the Brazilian upper and middle classes. According to Souza, cultural capital allows the affluent to differentiate themselves from the lower classes, obtain better-paying jobs as well as prestigious social positions, and legitimize their privileges—after all, education is used as a justification for higher socioeconomic standing (54–56).

It must be stressed that the vast majority of Brazilians cannot afford to study abroad. Moreover, although Brazil has a sizable network of state-funded, tuition-free universities, these institutions have historically been attended largely by white, middle- and upper-class students. This is because Brazilian public universities are generally considered to be of better quality and more prestigious than private institutions, and the selection processes to enter them are very competitive. In an attempt to reduce these inequalities, the Workers' Party government (2003–2016) implemented affirmative action quotas for Afro-Brazilian, Indigenous, and public-school students in the country's public universities.

These measures have been highly criticized by conservative segments of the country's population (Magnoni 308), and, in line with their views, Barbie Fascionista is heavily opposed to affirmative action policies. Alluding to the fact that conservative Brazilian whites often describe affirmative action policies as unfair and discriminatory, Barbie Fascionista's authors have created, in this post, a parodic concept that could perhaps be defined as "reverse privilege."

In the text accompanying the image, Barbie argues that lower-class Brazilians are privileged because they have the "freedom" to study at public schools and do menial jobs at the same time, while upper-class youths are "overwhelmed" by their French, gastronomy, and private ballet lessons, and activities such as gymnastics, horse riding, and swimming.[3] Moreover, the doll claims that poor students are better prepared for the admission exams for public universities because the tests take place at rundown and uncomfortable facilities—circumstances that are unknown to her because she has had the "disadvantage" of attending a private high school.[4]

By creatively employing parodic devices such as irony and exaggeration, the authors of the text have created an absurd situation in which Barbie victimizes herself, claiming that her multitude of privileges has hindered her progress. This inversion satirizes meritocratic discourses that, while hiding structural and social inequalities, claim that every individual has the same conditions of access to good educational and career opportunities.

It is worth mentioning that, if taken out of context, the post might be understood as an actual defense of meritocracy—because it reproduces, literally, several elements of a meritocratic discourse. For this reason, Barbie Fascionista's type of satire can be classified as what Ross and Rivers have defined as delegitimization through moral evaluation (6). Frequently used in online environments, this rhetorical strategy makes extensive use of irony and can be found in multimodal texts such as memes that subtly criticize value systems and ideologies (Ross and Rivers 6–7). However, because this type of criticism is often made obliquely and indirectly, audiences might misinterpret it and end up taking literally content that is meant to be ironic.

Prejudice—the second theme we discuss in our study—is often alluded to in Barbie Fascionista's content, and the character espouses discriminatory views against many of Brazil's underprivileged segments. In multiple instances, the doll is shown to be racist, homophobic, classist, and sexist. Besides reflecting the various intersectional prejudices that are present in Brazilian society (Layton and Smith 54), these attitudes refer to the conservative values associated with the original Barbie doll (Steinberg 259).

Despite her backward views, the character often attempts—unsuccessfully— to mask her prejudices, in a parody of discursive strategies that are used by Brazil's middle and upper classes (Van Dijk 134). Typical examples of these practices include instances of colorblind racism—when someone claims not to see color while still discriminating against people of other ethnicities (Bonilla-Silva 1364)—and new racism, which consists of phrases employed by whites to disguise their prejudiced views, such as "I am not a racist" or "Some of my best friends are Black" (Bonilla-Silva 1365).

The account addresses the topic of racism on multiple occasions, such as in the post that was published on November 1, 2018 (figure 8.2). The image— originally produced by Mattel—which illustrates the post shows a Black Barbie doll wearing exotic-looking clothes and jewelry as well as an Afro hairdo. The profile's authors have likely chosen this picture because it highlights some of the stereotypes that are present in Mattel's non-white dolls. According to

Steinberg, Mattel has created several international versions of Barbie—such as Jamaican Barbie, Polynesian Barbie, Puerto Rican Barbie, and Indian Barbie—that portray other nationalities in a caricatured fashion (257–258). In this particular case, the Black doll seems to represent an African tribeswoman.

Written in English, the first part of the caption is a Halloween greeting, underscoring Barbie Fascionista's foreignness and obsession with US culture. The remainder of the caption claims that the image is intended to promote the appreciation of "exotic beauty." To fully understand the criticism conveyed by the post, however, we must analyze the longer text that accompanies it.

In the short essay, the character writes that she put on blackface to celebrate Halloween and praise "exotic" and "tropical beauty."[5] Because the tradition of blackface is historically situated in a context of practices that have been used to caricature and demean people of African descent in Western societies (Van Leeuwen 103–105), the text implies that the middle and upper classes of Brazil are racially insensitive and promote stereotypical and prejudiced views of Afro-Brazilians. Additionally, Barbie Fascionista's allusion to blackface is possibly a criticism of the fact that Mattel has produced non-white versions of Barbie that consist merely of the original white doll tinted different colors, without any significant changes to her facial and physical characteristics (Toffoletti 60–61).

Significantly, the post was published only three days after a well-publicized incident in which a white, upper-class Brazilian woman dressed her son up as a slave for a Halloween party ("Mãe 'fantasia' filho"). Similar situations had occurred before, such as a nineteenth-century-themed party organized by a Brazilian socialite in which Black actors and actresses were hired to pose as slaves ("'Racismo é uma acusação'"). Both of the women involved apologized or denied being racist; Barbie Fascionista acts similarly because she does not see her costume as racist. Indeed, the character goes as far as to claim that what she is doing is not cultural appropriation, but rather "cultural valuation."

Moreover, the stereotypes reproduced in the text—such as the hashtags #Tanajura (big booty), #NeguinhaMaluca (crazy little Black girl), #Escrava-DeMimMesma (slave of myself), and #DaCorDoPecado (shades of sin)[6]— also allude to common media portrayals of Afro-Brazilian women as slaves, sensual mulattas, or Macumba priestesses (Van Dijk 139).

By using rhetorical devices such as exaggeration and parody, this post is a significant example of what Martins Ferreira et al. have classified, in their analysis of Barbie Fascionista, as the Instagram profile's carnivalization (212). Although this is not the first Brazilian study to link memes produced in the country to the concept of the carnivalesque (see, for example, Monteiro Lu-

Figure 8.2. Screenshot of the Barbie Fascionista page displaying the exoticization of racial difference. *"Happy Halloween. For the appreciation of exotic beauty #AfroPrincess #OfColorButElegant."* The accompanying caption reads: "Happy Halloween, fascimores!! O que acharam da minha fantasia?? Lembram das anteriores?! Ano retrasado usei aquela maravilhosa de gueixa, ano passado a de índia e agora resolvi homenagear a beleza exótica e tropical!!! Gostei muito do resultado, achei que ficou super autêntica!! E como sei que vocês vão pedir, vou explicar meio por cima: o Henry me emprestou essa peruca toda revestida de aço!! Um amigo meu que trabalha na parte de cenografia fez essa prótese pro nariz, pra alargar e ficar real!! As roupas são super tropicais também!! Já para ficar com essa cor bem acentuada, fiz várias sessões de jet bronze e na essência coloquei cacau em pó. NÃO FIQUEI LINDA??! Espero que gostem, amores!!! Sandrinha amou a homenagem e aprovou. 😎 #PrincesaAfro #Guerreira #NeguinhaMaluca #EscravaDeMimMesma #MinhaPrópriaRefém #BelezaExótica #TraçosFinos #Torradinha #CharmeAfrodescendente #PretaNãoApenasDeCor #Tanajura #DaCorDoPecado #Respeito #NãoÉApropriação #ÉvalorizaçãoCultural" [Translation: "Happy Halloween, Fasci-lovers!! What do you think of my costume?? Remember the previous ones?! The year before last I wore that wonderful geisha costume, last year I was dressed as an indigenous woman, and now I've decided to celebrate exotic and tropical beauty!!! I really like the result, I think it looks very authentic! And since I know you're going to ask me about it, I will give you a quick explanation: Henry lent me this wig made entirely of steel!! A friend of mine who works as a production designer made this prosthetic nose to make mine look wider and more realistic!! The clothes have this super tropical look as well!! In order to get this really dark skin color, I went to several spray-tanning sessions and added cocoa powder to the lotion I used. DON'T I LOOK BEAUTIFUL??! I hope you like it, my dear ones!!! Sandrinha loves and approves of the homage. 😎 #AfroPrincess #Warrior #CrazyBlackie #SlaveofMyself #MyOwnHostage #ExoticBeauty #ThinFacialFeatures #Tanned #AfrodescendantCharm #BlackBeyondTheSkin #BigBooty #ShadesOfSin #Respect #ItsNotAppropriation #ItsCulturalAppreciation"]

nardi 22–23, 27), it does elaborate on the connection. Originally developed by Bakhtin, the concept of carnivalization is understood as the appropriation, by literature and other arts, of manifestations that typically belong to comic popular culture, such as those peculiar to a carnival (Martins Ferreira et al. 205). Marked by inversion and exaggeration, carnivalesque discourse employs satire to mock authority and subvert hierarchy and tradition (Martins Ferreira et al. 206).

By exploring the relationship between the subversive aspects of memes and the tradition of carnival, the authors provide relevant insights into the connection of memes to other cultural manifestations, also addressing the role of these digital artifacts as a form of social critique (Martins Ferreira et al. 214). It must be stressed, however, that Martins Ferreira et al.'s sample consists of only two posts. Their work thus cannot be considered a comprehensive analysis of Barbie Fascionista.

Although the majority of the content published by Barbie Fascionista's profile could be classified as carnivalesque, this post is particularly allusive to carnival because of its strong connections to elements such as costumes, disguises, and performances. By engaging critically with stereotypes of Black women that are widespread in Brazilian society, the authors have attempted to subvert the caricature and turn it against the country's privileged classes.

The third theme we have identified in Barbie Fascionista is conservatism. Much of the content featured in the account depicts the doll as an ardent Bolsonaro supporter. The character expresses her endorsement of the far-right politician's presidential campaign in multiple ways, such as addressing her female followers as "bolsodivas" and constantly referring to Bolsonaro's slogan—"Brasil acima de tudo, Deus acima de todos" (Brazil above everything, God above everyone). Moreover, Barbie is depicted as nostalgic for Brazil's military dictatorship (1964–1985), and supports policies defended by Bolsonaro that include the loosening of gun ownership laws and the killing of criminals. By attributing such views to Barbie Fascionista, the profile's creators have taken considerable liberty in reinterpreting the Barbie doll, which, from a depoliticized figure who ignores the social context she lives in and is immersed in a fairytale world (Lord 66), has become heavily politically engaged. In Barbie Fascionista, conservative values that are merely suggested by the original Barbie are explicitly revealed and criticized.

The character's backward views are indissociable from her anti-leftism. Barbie Fascionista detests the left—which, for her, is an umbrella term that encompasses all sorts of politically progressive views, movements, ideologies, and particularly the Workers' Party. She justifies her radical political stance by accusing the Workers' Party of being corrupt and populist. However, the profile suggests that the character's anti-leftism is hypocritical in that she only opposes the left out of fear of losing her privileges—a criticism that has been leveled against Brazil's middle and upper classes by the progressive segments of Brazilian society (Bähre and Gomes 15).

In the post featured in figure 8.3, Barbie Fascionista is depicted as someone whose morality is selective. Although the character accuses the leftist Workers' Party of being corrupt—reproducing slogans commonly employed by middle- and upper-class Brazilians—she simultaneously downplays corruption scandals that are associated with right-wing individuals. While this is implied by the caption featured in the picture, it is more clearly evidenced by the longer text published beside the image.

Figure 8.3. Screenshot of the Barbie Fascionista page exhibiting a moral double standard. "No more corruption! No to the Workers' Party! A millionaire fraud in my family? Nonsense." The accompanying caption reads: "Quem nunca sonegou um imposto, sabe?! Quem nunca deu aquele jeitinho? A diferença é: uma coisa é você ser um sem dedo, sem berço, sem classe, sem glamour e roubar milhões. Outra coisa é você ter estilo, ser do high society, falar oito línguas e ter um pequeno desvio de caráter. Acho até cool, gente!!!! Over é quem não se aventura. Alguns têm teto de vidro, outros de cristal. É incomparável!!!!! SOMOS SERES HUMANOS!!!! TODOS ERRAM. BASTA DE TANTO DISCURSO ODIOSO. Esqueçam o passado, o que importa é o nosso país do futuro. #DeusAcimaDeTudo #PátriaAmada #MãeGentil #MotherLover" [Translation: "Who has never evaded any taxes, right?! Who has never found an alternative way to do things? But there's a difference: one thing is when you lack a finger and you didn't have a good upbringing; when you're uncultured, without any glamour, and embezzle millions. Another thing is when you have style, belong to high society, speak eight languages, and have a minor flaw in character. I even think it's cool, people! Those who don't take any risks are dull. Some people have glass houses while others have crystal houses. You can't compare it! WE ARE ALL HUMAN BEINGS!!!! WE ALL MAKE MISTAKES. ENOUGH WITH ALL THAT HATE SPEECH. Forget the past, what matters is the future of our country. #GodAboveEverything #BelovedNation #GentleMother #MotherLover"]

In that text, Barbie argues that being corrupt is not really a problem, as long as corrupt politicians possess traits associated with the upper classes, such as "being stylish," "speaking eight languages," and "belonging to high society." In contrast, the doll strongly condemns certain corrupt individuals whom she describes as "lower-class," "unglamorous," and "fingerless."[7] Apart from shedding light on the character's class prejudice and elitism, the offensive adjectives are a clear reference to left-wing politician and Brazilian president (2003–2011, 2023–time of writing) Luís Inácio Lula da Silva—a member of the Workers' Party—who lost one of his little fingers to a work accident in the 1960s. Lula is often mocked by Brazil's middle and upper classes, in everyday discourse and Internet memes, due to his lower-class origins (Bähre and Gomes 10). These derogatory jokes depict the former president as someone ignorant and vulgar who does not speak Portuguese properly and loves alcohol (Bähre and Gomes 11).

According to Bähre and Gomes, the aversion that the Brazilian middle and upper classes have to Lula stems not from the corruption attributed to him, but from the fact that they perceive the leftist politician as a threat to their privilege due to the social policies implemented during his first term, which benefited the lower classes (15).

The character also goes beyond the realm of politics to downplay corruption by businesspersons or upper-class individuals. By rhetorically asking, "Who has never evaded taxes?" and asking people to "forget the past,"[8] Barbie Fascionista implies that tax evasion is not as harmful as political corruption, which once again suggests that she is a selective moralist. Moreover, these fragments hint at the character's strong neoliberal views, since she is frequently portrayed in other posts as someone who glorifies the market while demonizing the state.

Apart from underscoring Barbie Fascionista's strong sense of moralism—which, as highlighted by several scholars, is one of the most important values for the Brazilian middle class (Cavalcante 122; Miguel 22; Souza 77)—this post sheds light on the crucial role played by structural oppositions (Machin and Mayr 39–40) in the account's content. In most of the profile's posts, the doll adopts an us-versus-them posture, which is evidenced by dichotomies such as rich vs. poor, right vs. left, honest vs. corrupt, and white vs. Black. These oppositions are used by the authors to illustrate Barbie Fascionista's moral ambiguities—invariably, she is revealed to have the exact same traits that she criticizes in her adversaries. By reproducing right-wing discourses, Barbie Fascionista's creators sought to highlight what they perceive as the oxymorons and incongruities in these ideas. As stressed by Martins Ferreira et al., the profile's content is ambivalent, simultaneously reproducing and criticizing discourses typical of Brazil's middle and upper classes, with the ultimate aim of producing social change (207). In this way, the profile works like a mirror that, despite seemingly replicating exclusionary values, is, in fact, attempting to invert them and promote opposite views.

Conclusion

Barbie Fascionista suggests that Brazil's middle and upper classes form a homogeneous reactionary bloc, composed of privileged, prejudiced, and conservative individuals. Thus, the portrait conveyed by the account is akin to a caricature because it does not take into account the ideological divisions within the country's affluent classes (Souza 98). In light of the deep political and ideological polarization experienced by Brazilian society at the time, and considering that the account was created after the first round of the presidential election in 2018—when only two candidates remained: Fernando Haddad and Jair Bolsonaro—the lack of nuance is unsurprising. Barbie Fascionista represents a protest against what its authors considered an urgent threat to Brazil's democracy, political stability, and social equality. Furthermore, many of the criticisms conveyed by the profile are aligned with the interpretations of scholars who have analyzed issues of race, class, and gender in Brazil (e.g., De Mendonça and Jordão 14–15; Layton and Smith 56; Souza 95–96).

If, as Berger puts it, a semiotician needs to pay attention to the oppositions between signs (6), we conclude that the fundamental opposition in Barbie Fascionista is between "us" and "them." By parodying classist and elitist discourses that divide Brazil between white, wealthy, religious, heterosexual, and conservative individuals and "the rest," Barbie Fascionista mirrors these discourses and becomes their inverted reflection. In this sense, the "us" conveyed by the account comprises Blacks, women, LGBTQ+ people, lower-class individuals, and progressive Brazilians, and the "them" is the country's privileged minority, which is criticized and satirized. As underscored by Martins Ferreira et al., Barbie Fascionista's subversive humor is related to the tradition of carnival, and both the meme and the popular festival are characterized by criticism of dogmatic traditions, denunciations of power, inversions of hierarchy, and challenges to social conventions (206). It must be stressed, however, that the account's content barely alludes to the fact that many of Bolsonaro's voters came from the underprivileged segments of Brazilian society (Kalil 1–2).

To subvert hegemonic discourses that are widespread in Brazilian society, Barbie Fascionista's creators largely employed the strategy defined by Ross and Rivers as delegitimization through moral evaluation (6–7). This tactic, which relies on rhetorical devices such as sarcasm and irony to subtly contest value and belief systems, demands an attentive and careful interpretation from an audience (Ross and Rivers 6–7). Thus, although the profile's discursive sophistication is one of its main qualities, it may have prevented many Internet users from understanding its message the way it was intended by the author(s). In other words, Barbie Fascionista might have suffered from what Berger terms *aberrant decoding* (30).

Overall, Barbie Fascionista is a rich, complex, sophisticated, and contradictory object of study—not unlike Brazilian society. It proves that memes deserve attention from scholars and can reveal many of the intricacies of the sociopolitical contexts in which they are produced. Additionally, by delving into the prejudiced and elitist discourses challenged—or endorsed—by memes, researchers have the opportunity to engage in ongoing political debates and shed light on contemporary exclusionary ideologies.

Notes

1 See Carranca, Adriana. "The Women-Led Opposition to Brazil's Far-Right Leader." *The Atlantic,* 2 Nov. 2018, www.theatlantic.com/international/archive/2018/11/brazil -women-bolsonaro-haddad-election/574792/.

2 The data were collected directly from the Instagram account Barbie Fascionista by Author 1 for his master's thesis.

3 In the original: "GENTE, PENSEM COMIGO: acham que é fácil fazer aulas gastronômicas, balé, natação, ginástica, hipismo, francês e ainda estudar o dia inteiro numa escola gringa???! NÃO!! É pesado, sabe??! Enquanto adolescentes que estudam em escola pública têm a liberdade de estudar e trabalhar ao mesmo tempo. Podem fazer trufas e vender livremente nas ruas!!! E ainda recebem dinheiro do governo!!"

4 In the original: "Sem contar a estrutura das escolas, já perceberam?! Alunos esquerdopatas estão acostumados com cadeiras ruins, mesas desniveladas e barulhentas, ventilação natural etc. Ou seja, têm uma grande vantagem nos ventibulares!! Já nós, PASSAMOS POR UMA PROVA DE SOBREVIVÊNCIA!!!"

5 In the original: "Ano retrasado usei aquela maravilhosa de gueixa, ano passado a de índia e agora resolvi homenagear a beleza exótica e tropical!!! Gostei muito do resultado, achei que ficou super autêntica!!"

6 In the original: #PrincesaAfro #Guerreira #NeguinhaMaluca #EscravaDeMimMesma #MinhaPrópriaRefém #BelezaExótica #TraçosFinos #Torradinha #CharmeAfrodescendente #PretaNãoApenasDeCor #Axé #Tanajura #DaCorDoPecado #Respeito #NãoÉApropriação #ÉValorizaçãoCultural

7 In the original: "A diferença é: uma coisa é você ser um sem dedo, sem berço, sem classe, sem glamour e roubar milhões. Outra coisa é você ter estilo, ser do high society, falar oito línguas e ter um pequeno desvio de caráter."

8 In the original: "Quem nunca sonegou um imposto, sabe?! Quem nunca deu aquele jeitinho? . . . Esqueçam o passado, o que importa é o nosso país do futuro."

Works Cited

Alves, Júlia Falivene. *A invasão cultural norte-americana.* 2nd ed., Brazil: Moderna, 2004, www.academia.edu/36292936/A_invasao_cultural_norte_americ_Julia_Falivene _Alves.

Assis-Peterson, Ana Antônia. "Como ser feliz no meio de anglicismos: processos trans-glóssicos e transculturais." *Trabalhos em Linguística Aplicada,* vol. 47, no 2, 2008, pp. 323–340.

Bähre, Erik, and Fabiola Gomes. "Humiliating the Brazilian Poor: The Iconoclasm of For-mer President Lula." *Anthropology Today,* vol. 34, no. 5, 2018, pp. 10–15.

Barthes, Roland. *Mythologies.* US: The Noonday Press, 1991.

Berger, Arthur Asa. *Media Analysis Techniques.* 5th ed., Thousand Oaks, CA: Sage, 2013.

Bonilla-Silva, Eduardo. "The Structure of Racism in Color-Blind, 'Post-Racial' America." *American Behavioral Scientist,* vol. 59, no. 11, 2015, pp. 1358–1376.

Cavalcante, Sávio. "Classe média, meritocracia e corrupção." *Crítica Marxista,* vol. 46, 2018, pp. 103–125.

Chagas, Viktor, et al. "Political Memes and the Politics of Memes: A Methodological Pro-posal for Content Analysis of Online Political Memes." *First Monday,* vol. 24, no. 2–4, 2019, https://doi.org/10.5210/fm.v24i2.7264.

Dittmar, Helga, et al. "Does Barbie Make Girls Want to Be Thin? The Effect of Experimen-tal Exposure to Images of Dolls on the Body Image of 5- to 8-Year-Old Girls." *Develop-mental Psychology,* vol. 42, no. 2, 2006, pp. 283–292.

Driessen, Barbie. *The Evolution of an Icon: A Comparison of the Values and Stereotypes Re-flected in the Original 1959 Barbie Doll and the Curvy 2016 Barbie Doll.* 2016. Radboud University, MA thesis.

Dyer, Richard. *White.* NY: Routledge, 1997.

Fioratti, Gustavo, and Eduardo Moura. "Em correntes no WhatsApp e redes sociais, Barbie vira sátira de antipetista." Folha de S. Paulo, 15 Oct. 2018, webcache.googleusercontent .com/search?q=cache:5LXqrbkTYlwJ:https://www1.folha.uol.com.br/poder/2018/10/ em-correntes-no-whatsapp-e-redes-sociais-barbie-vira-satira-de-antipetista.shtml+& cd=9&hl=en&ct=clnk&gl=nl.

Gatinois, Claire. "Au Brésil, Barbie vote à l'extrême droite." *Le Monde,* 24 Oct. 2018, www .lemonde.fr/ameriques/article/2018/10/24/au-bresil-barbie-vote-a-l-extreme-droite _5373591_3222.html.

De Jesus, Samuel. *A ideologia do "cidadão de bem."* Lisbon: Terra & Liberdade, 2018.

Kalil, Isabela Oliveira. *Quem são e no que acreditam os eleitores de Jair Bolsonaro.* São Pau-lo: Fundação Escola de Sociologia e Política de São Paulo, 2018.

Layton, Matthew L., and Amy Erica Smith. "Is It Race, Class, or Gender? The Sources of Perceived Discrimination in Brazil." *Latin American Politics & Society,* vol. 59, no. 1, 2017, pp. 52–73.

Lellis, Leonardo. "'Barbie fascista': esta imagem não é exatamente o que parece." *Veja,* 30 May 2019, veja.abril.com.br/blog/virou-viral/barbie-fascista-esta-imagem-nao-e -exatamente-o-que-parece/.

Lentin, Alana. "Europe and the Silence about Race." *European Journal of Social Theory,* vol. 11, no. 4, 2008, pp. 487–503.

Lord, Mary G. *Forever Barbie: The Unauthorized Biography of a Real Doll*. London: Walker Books, 2004.

Machin, David, and Andrea Mayr. *How to Do Critical Discourse Analysis: A Multimodal Introduction*. Thousand Oaks, CA: Sage Publications, 2012.

"Mãe 'fantasia' filho de escravo para festa de Halloween em escola de Natal: 'Vamos abrasileirar esse negócio.'" *Globo*, 29 Oct. 2018, g1.globo.com/rn/rio-grande-do-norte/noticia/2018/10/29/mae-fantasia-filho-de-escravo-para-festa-de-halloween-em-escola-de-natal-vamos-abrasileirar-esse-negocio.ghtml.

Magnoni, Maria Salete. "Lei de cotas e a mídia brasileira: o que diria Lima Barreto?" *Estudos Avançados*, vol. 30, no. 87, 2016, pp. 299–312.

Martins Ferreira, Dina Maria, et al. "Paródia e riso ambivalentes em memes da Barbie Fascionista: uma análise à luz da carnavalização." *Calidoscópio*, vol. 18, no. 1, 2020, pp. 202–215.

Marwick, Alice. "Memes." *Contexts*, vol. 12, no. 4, 2013, pp. 12–13.

De Mendonça, Maria Luiza Martins, and Janaína Vieira de Paula Jordão. "Nojo de pobre: representações do popular e preconceito de classe." *Contemporânea*, vol. 12, no. 1, 2014, pp. 1–18.

Miguel, Luis Felipe. "A reemergência da direita brasileira." *O ódio como política: a reinvenção das direitas no Brasil*, edited by Esther Solano Gallego, São Paulo: Boitempo, 2018, pp. 14–24.

Mina, An Xiao. *Memes to Movements: How the World's Most Viral Media Is Changing Social Protest and Power*. Boston: Beacon Press, 2019.

De Mingo, Marcela. "15 memes do boneco Ken que escancaram o machismo do dia a dia," *Super ELA*, 26 June 2017, Superela.com/Memes-Boneco-Ken.

Monteiro Lunardi, Gabriela. *"The 'Zoeira' Never Ends": The Role of Internet Memes in Contemporary Brazilian Culture*. 2018. Queensland University of Technology, MA thesis.

Nuñez, Xcaret. "Mattel's Barbie Turns Women of Science, Including COVID Vaccine Developer, into Dolls." *NPR*, 5 Aug. 2021, www.npr.org/2021/08/05/1024888880/mattels-barbie-turns-women-of-science-including-a-covid-vaccine-developer-into-d.

Pearson, Marlys, and Paul R. Mullins. "Domesticating Barbie: An Archaeology of Barbie Material Culture and Domestic Ideology." *International Journal of Historical Archaeology*, vol. 3, no. 4, 1999, pp. 225–259.

Phillips, Dom. "Rio Carnival Turns Political as 'Barbie Fascists' Defend Women's Rights." *The Guardian*, 8 Mar. 2019, www.theguardian.com/world/2019/mar/08/rio-carnival-turns-political-as-barbie-fascists-defend-womens-rights.

"'Racismo é uma acusação pesada,' defende-se mãe de debutante que usou atores negros vestidos de escravos em ensaio fotográfico, em Belém." *Globo*, 15 Mar. 2018, g1.globo.com/pa/para/noticia/racismo-e-uma-acusacao-pesada-defende-se-mae-de-debutante-que-usou-atores-negros-vestidos-de-escravos-em-ensaio-fotografico-em-belem.ghtml.

Reiter, Bernd. "Whiteness as Capital: Constructing Inclusion and Defending Privilege." *Government and International Affairs Faculty Publications*, vol. 26, 2009, pp. 19–33.

Rose, Gillian. *Visual Methodologies: An Introduction to the Interpretation of Visual Material*. 2nd ed., Thousand Oaks, CA: Sage, 2007.

Ross, Andrew S., and Damian J. Rivers. "Digital Cultures of Political Participation: Internet Memes and the Discursive Delegitimization of the 2016 US Presidential Candidates." *Discourse, Context & Media*, vol. 16, 2017, pp. 1–11.

Santos, Rita. "'Cidadãos de bem' com armas: representações sexuadas de violência armada, (in) segurança e legítima defesa no Brasil." *Revista crítica de ciências sociais*, vol. 96, 2012, pp. 133–164.

Shifman, Limor. *Memes in Digital Culture*. Cambridge, MA: MIT Press, 2014.

Skidmore, Thomas E. "Fact and Myth: Discovering a Racial Problem in Brazil." *Working Paper*, vol. 173, 1992, pp. 1–23.

Souza, Jessé. *A elite do atraso: da escravidão à Lava Jato*. Lisbon: Leya, 2017.

Steinberg, Shirley R. "The Book of Barbie: After Half a Century, the Bitch Continues to Have Everything." *Kinderculture: The Corporate Construction of Childhood*. 3rd ed., Boulder: Westview Press, 2011, pp. 249–263.

Teshainer, Marcus Cesar R., et al. "Panelaço e o estado de exceção: uma leitura psicanalítica da convulsão social brasileira dos anos 2015–2016." *Revista Subjetividades*, vol. 18, no. 1, 2018, pp. 11–22.

Toffoletti, Kim. *Cyborgs and Barbie Dolls: Feminism, Popular Culture and the Posthuman Body*. London: IB Tauris, 2007.

Tota, Antonio Pedro. "Americanização no condicional: Brasil nos anos 40." *Perspectivas*, vol. 16, 1993, pp. 191–212.

Van Dijk, Teun Adrianus. *Racism and Discourse in Spain and Latin America*. Asterdam: John Benjamins Publishing Company, 2005.

Van Leeuwen, Theo. "Semiotics and Iconography." *Handbook of Visual Analysis*, edited by Theo Van Leeuwen and Carey Jewitt, Thousand Oaks, CA: Sage, 2004, pp. 92–118.

Wodak, Ruth. "The Discourse-Historical Approach." *Methods of Critical Discourse Analysis*, edited by Ruth Wodak and Michael Meyer, Thousand Oaks, CA: Sage, 2001, pp. 63–94.

9

"Whatever . . . It's Only a Joke!"

Exploring Memes, Racialization, and Discrimination in Puerto Rico during Hurricanes, Earthquakes, and the COVID-19 Pandemic

R. Sánchez-Rivera

This article will explore how memes are used as a way of contesting "official" stories by portraying the mismanagement of "natural" disasters in Puerto Rico. I will explore how meme sharing, tagging, commenting, and reacting on Facebook and meme databases demonstrate a political consciousness that surfaces from humor to create—aside from a virtual site of contestation—a sense of identity. I will also explain the paradoxical dynamics of meme production in Puerto Rico (PR). I will focus on how they critique the political management behind crises, and are, simultaneously, developed from pre-existing racializing, gendered, and ableist notions. While much contemporary literature on PR emphasizes the role of (US) colonialism in the exacerbation of social inequalities and environmental racism, such focus invisibilizes the internal dynamics of the archipelago, which often pathologize bodies historically constructed as Other. This article explores memes' role in critiquing structures of power while strengthening forms of racialization, discrimination, and exclusion targeted at historically marginalized communities and individuals.

Puerto Rico's Debt, Hurricane Maria, and Social Inequalities

PR was colonized in 1493 by the Spanish empire. After centuries of human rights violations, it was passed as war booty to the United States in 1898 (Klein 39). The legal and political status of "colony" was removed by the UN after the creation of the Estado Libre Asociado—the Commonwealth of Puerto Rico—in 1952 (Bonilla and Lebrón 222). During the early 1970s, PR saw a budget deficit due to the structural inequalities created through colonialism and local corruption. These dynamics resulted in the systematic issuing of bonds and loans to cover its expenditures (Joffe and Martínez). In 2014, three major credit agencies downgraded PR bonds, as the government could no longer pay its US$73 billion debt. Subsequently, and as a form of reasserting colonial power, the US enacted the Puerto Rico Oversight, Management, and Economic Stability Act (PROMESA) (Jiménez 4051). This act, established by a federal control board and implemented by the US Congress, devised an aggressive austerity plan that was first implemented in 2017 and will run until 2026.

On September 20, 2017, Hurricane Maria—one of the worst natural disasters in Atlantic history—devastated the archipelago, resulting in more than 4,000 deaths and one of the largest recorded blackouts (Minet 1234–1341). Fourteen months after the passing of Maria, neighborhoods like Veguitas in the county of Jayuya still had no electricity. Thus, what occurred, and still occurs, in PR should be cataloged as an (un)natural disaster—not because of the hurricane itself, but due to the mismanagement and the exacerbation of social inequalities produced by colonialism. After Hurricane Maria, 14 to 20 percent of the population of 3.7 million left PR due to the dire conditions and mismanagement of the crisis by the Federal Emergency Management Agency (FEMA)[1] and President Donald J. Trump. Despite PR's proximity to Florida—only 1,000 miles away—Trump took two weeks to arrive in PR, arguing that "Puerto Rico is an island. Surrounded by . . . water. Big water. Ocean water . . ." in a press conference at the White House on September 28, 2017 (Shugerman). On October 3, 2017, he visited PR, where he threw paper towels at Puerto Ricans in one of the richest and least-affected counties in the country, Guaynabo, and declared his successful management of the crisis.

Recent academic and non-academic work has discussed the social inequalities produced by US colonialism in PR before, during, and after Hurricane Maria. While demonstrating the not-so-natural dynamics of a "natural" disaster, such works tend to portray the archipelago of PR as a homogeneous entity, invisibilizing the internal complexities that often work in collaboration and/or tandem with each other. In the foreword to 2019's *Aftershocks of Disaster*, published after a conference of the same name, Arcadio Díaz-Quiñones reflects on the keynote conversation between Naomi Klein and Yarimar Bonilla, arguing that "disasters open up new possibilities for critical thinking and for art as a form of intervening in politics and imagining a radically different society" (Díaz-Quiñones 133). This poses the question: Who can think critically about intervening in society and questioning politics? Who creates knowledge, and when is this knowledge legitimized? I argue that knowledge production about Hurricane Maria in PR is political, as it is often transposed to the lighter-skinned/white middle class while dismissing knowledge produced outside these margins. In this sense, I see memes as a form of knowledge production that simultaneously critiques the political management behind crises while reproducing pre-existing racializing, gendered, and ableist notions.

In *Aftershocks of Disaster*, various mentions of internal dynamics show inner racialization and discriminatory processes during the aftermath of Hurricane Maria. For instance, Giovanni Roberto recalls the university police (at both UPR-Cayey and UPR-Río Piedras) stopping or trying to impede his and his mom's efforts to a collective *comedor*[2]—mainly for students who did not have resources for food while they were undertaking post-secondary studies (Roberto 4819). Sarah Molinari also mentions these dynamics. Molinari recounts one of her interviews with a Puerto Rican FEMA worker who stated that, culturally, Puerto Ricans tended to "leave everything to the last minute" and expect everything to be "handed to them" instead of working and prepping for disaster (Molinari 4517–4522). She argues that these racist instances that invoke racializing stereotypes of Puerto Ricans as lazy and careless are used by both local and imperial factions to affect the most vulnerable (Molinari 4528).

Memes produced by Puerto Ricans are an important tool of analysis for understanding the complex internal dynamics of ableism, discrimination, and racialization in the archipelago. Due to memes' accessibility and the wide use of social media in PR (especially Facebook), these memetic processes provide a better understanding of how individuals dealt with the pernicious effects of environmental racism and "natural" disasters while making a punchline of historically marginalized and pathologized bodies. I claim that memes, as a form of artistic expression, demonstrate the complexity of diverse individuals in PR coming together in humor to critique the system, while cementing meanings used to pathologize bodies historically constructed as Other. Broadly defined, a meme can be categorized as a "unit of cultural transmission which may represent an aspect of a culture such as language, fashion, songs—things which evolve, change, and spread" (Drakett et al. 112). Internet memes come in various formats and types (113). This article examines "image macros" (i.e., images featuring a textual overlay) to observe how memes are used to critique PR's political and colonial system while using historically stigmatized, racialized, gendered, pathologized, and vulnerable bodies as a punchline. As people share, comment on, react to, and tag others in them, memes have become an enigmatic tool of resistance in PR—one that is often overlooked. This article will, first, provide an overview of the theoretical background behind humor and memes to then analyze memes produced during Hurricane Maria, and subsequently examine memes created throughout the earthquakes of January 2020 and the COVID-19 pandemic. The contradictions shown in memes come from a long history of internalized colonialism that produces and reproduces notions of identity and nationalism at the expense of reifying, excluding, and racializing Others. These "contradictions" should not be overlooked when discussing the dynamics and layers of colonialism in the archipelago, as there are different Puerto Rican experiences even inside PR. By looking only at local and federal mismanagement and PR/US relations, scholars tend to invisibilize the complicated internal dynamics that emerge when it comes to systemic and exclusionary practices in PR by Puerto Ricans.

Memes and Humor: Subversion at the Expense of the Other

Memes are produced as copies of a series of images to reflect a cultural phenomenon. The concept of the meme was introduced by sociobiologist Richard Dawkins in *The Selfish Gene* (1976), as he wanted a term that "would be parallel to 'gene' to describe the evolution of cultural phenomena, which (he argues) are subject to the same kinds of Darwinian laws of natural selection as genes proper" (Chesterman 1). Memes have changed dramatically over the past decade to reflect how a "new arena of bottom-up expression can blend pop culture, politics, and participation in unexpected ways" (Shifman 4). In Shifman's view, memes are highly regarded in the participatory culture, as their message is encoded for a context-specific audience. In this sense, Puerto Rican "meme production and sharing process works [*sic*] in a decentralized context, where content generation is not curated or created by any central page but by a plethora of users" (Rodríguez Arce 9) who are mainly from PR and the US. However, they all share the same political goals of "criticizing disaster preparedness and disaster response in the wake of one of the worst disasters in PR history" (Rodríguez Arce 9). The purpose of my intervention is to take Rodríguez Arce's work and extend it beyond meme production during the hurricane. I will first provide some contextual information on Hurricane Maria before applying my analysis to other "natural" disasters such as the 2020 earthquakes and the COVID-19 pandemic.

During the aftermath of Hurricane Maria, when people did not have electricity, potable water, or food, people were producing memes. When discussing humor in Puerto Rican literature, Reyes (2005) states that humor does "not turn a blind eye to PR's political situation but can look at it from another side and offer a new clarity" (2). I argue that meme production in PR can be seen in a similar way, as memes are used as a way of contesting and critiquing the current situation and "[t]he daily struggles of millions of Puerto Ricans who face economic exploitation, racism, political disenfranchisement, and social marginalization [even if these] are no laughing matter" (2). Due to the long history of repression and censorship in PR, new channels of critique, such as memes, and social media more generally, are used to criticize everything from corruption to US colonialism. Memes and "humor confront many of those struggles by reaffirming an incongruous national identity through the power of laughter" (2). Whereas Reyes focuses on humor through literature, I contend that humor can also be seen in the production of memes. Unlike the case with literature, meme generators, content creators, and individuals alike have more autonomy over whom they choose to tag and what they decide to share, react to, and comment on. Social media participation allows for political views to be expressed to a broader audience in an ostensibly unharmful way while at the same time asserting identity and criticizing the current political situation—allowing different/dissenting voices to be heard.

According to Drakett et al., there are three main theories of humor: superiority/disparagement theory, incongruity theory, and release/relief theory. However, these divisions are not clear-cut, and sometimes these instances are used in combination with each other. Superiority theory is based on the misfortune of the Other, incongruity theory "credits the juxtaposition of incongruent elements" (i.e., a pun), and release theory is often a stress-relief mechanism to express catharsis through laughter (110–111). In the case of PR-themed memes, these elements are present in most of the memes that I will discuss. One of the most interesting elements of these memes is how a context of crisis allows for the memetic operation and dissemination of different forms of humor simultaneously. Drakett et al. argue that, looking from a different angle, one could distinguish two types of humor: disciplinary and rebellious. In this sense, "disciplinary humor works to mock those who are outside of social norms, whilst conversely rebellious humor mocks and subverts established rules and conventions" (Drakett et al. 111). In the case of Puerto Rican memes, rebellious humor is used to critique the structural system of colonialism and the mismanagement and corruption of the colony (by both the PR and US governments), but it does so at the expense of historically marginalized and racialized groups. Thus I observe how, in the Puerto Rican case, memes have elements of both disciplinary and rebellious humor as they operate to critique the current colonial system while relegating to the margins—through mockery—individuals and communities that have been historically pathologized through coloniality.

The use of humor to express identity is recurrent in meme production in PR through a mixture of superiority, incongruity, and release humor. Mc-Glade argues that superiority humor is "often achieved by emphasizing the inferiority of the 'target' rather than the superiority of the joker[;] superiority is achieved vicariously through an exposition of inferiority" (McGlade 4). When Donald Trump visited PR, he threw paper towels as a form of "humanitarian aid" to Puerto Ricans. While this was a very disrespectful and racist act that showed which bodies mattered to him and his government, "millions of people seem[ed] more outraged by Trump's tossing paper towels at Puerto Ricans than US colonial rule in PR, the Virgin Islands, and other US territories" (Negrón-Muntaner 1897; Graham). The pictures taken at this incident were the focus of a large number of memes, which proved more intricate and subtle as time progressed. In one instance, *The Simpsons* character Ralph Wiggum, a naive outcast with learning disabilities (Applebaum 9), is portrayed wearing a Trump wig with a caption that says, "I'm Helping" (Gremore). From this meme, one can read a critique of Trump's ignorance and audacity in presenting himself as an aid provider for the people of PR, disregarding the fact that people were starving, dying, and suffering multiple human rights violations due to the mismanagement of the aftermath of Hurricane Maria. Trump is represented by Ralph Wiggum as someone "whose childish nature, diminished intellect, and linguistic struggles" (Beers Fägersten 278) do not make him a suitable leader to deal with the aftermath of a "natural" disaster. Nonetheless, this meme also shows how the "disabled subject" is seen as unproductive and, therefore, (un)able to complete simple tasks (i.e., providing emergency humanitarian aid) in a neoliberal setting (Edwards). The meme discussed previously conveys how the inferiority of the target—in this case, the president of the US—is portrayed not to show the superiority of Puerto Ricans but the absurdity of the situation. However, by showing Trump as Ralph (using incongruity humor), and therefore as disabled/inferior, ableism constructs the joke's punchline. This, in turn, shows an ableist usage of humor in which superiority humor and the references created by incongruity humor are used to express a shared experience and common trauma that creates a cohesive in-group identity (through release humor) only at the expense of bodies constructed as "not-able." This is to say, both the use of humor and the creation of a Puerto Rican in-group identity are done at the expense of the "disabled body." Following McGlade, "the expression of solidarity and in-group identity is one of the most common social functions of humor since jokes are typically based on a set of shared values that can be stressed for humorous effect" (McGlade 4). By creating the Trump memes, Puerto Ricans both patronized and critiqued Trump's heinous acts while being ableist but also, in a sense, self-critical since, implicitly, they already know how the relief mission and federal aid will play out due to the long history of human rights violations and colonialism in the archipelago.

The following meme demonstrates both racialization processes and constructions/categorizations of the "un-productiveness" of Othered bodies in PR. Puerto Rican identity is mounted on assumptions behind the myth of mix-racedness as the organizing principle of society. This creates the assumption of a "racial democracy," so that there is an underlying supposition that "Puerto Rico [is] a 'Great Family,' made up of various racial mixtures, whose racial tolerance made it distinct from the US" (Lloréns et al. 157). Nonetheless, this supposedly harmonious mixture is predominantly understood as a whitening mechanism (Rodríguez-Díaz et al. 233). The privileging of aspirational whiteness (Tate et al. 27) allows systemic racism and anti-Blackness to permeate every stratum of Puerto Rican society. These racialization processes, in turn, produce pre-existing racializing stereotypes to be memetically replicated online.

This meme is translated as "Does someone know if they will further the welfare payments [top] . . . because of the hurricane?" (bottom). Similarly to the US, there is a "widespread perception that welfare has now become a 'code word' for race" (Gilens 3). In the case of PR, people use the historically racializing term "cafre" to refer to people who receive government aid. It is important to note that the term "cafre" has racialized and religious implications, as this term comes from the racial slur "kaffir," used to refer to Black people and/or infidels (Ramírez et al. 8, 115). As shown here, Black Puerto Ricans are portrayed as not-productive, and therefore not welcome inside PR's racial democracy. Thus, memes take negative racial stereotypes produced in the off-line world to provide "a direct assessment of negative racial views that are not confounded with political ideology" (Weber et al. 64). Hence, despite the alienation from the political status of PR, racialization processes, structural racism, and anti-Blackness are untouched and uncontested organizing principles in this hypothetical racial democracy. In this sense, racialization processes, structural racism, and anti-Blackness are central to the production of politically critical humor in PR.

Puerto Ricans' racial democracy allows for critical humor to be mounted on structural racism. In this sense, aspirational whiteness, anti-Blackness, and racial democracy operate as a way of continuing the structural dynamics of racism in Puerto Rico. While this may sound somewhat paradoxical, Puerto Rican racial democracy and its assumed harmonious mixture of "races" allow Puerto Ricans to gravitate from a rhetoric of mixture equated with equality to

ALGUIEN SABE SI ADELANTARAN LOS CUPONES,

POR LO DEL HURACAN?

Esa es la pregunta 😅

Huracan Memes

Figure 9.1. Meme Monkey meme of a man asking for coupons after the hurricane (2017).

the production and continuation of racializing hierarchies. It is precisely this that allows both meme producers and consumers to make use of humor to continue cementing and structuring anti-Blackness as the organizing structure of Puerto Rican society. However, this does not come in a vacuum. Christina A. Sue and Tanya Golash-Boza explore the cases of both Mexico and Peru to observe how racial humor "provides a new window into understanding the relationship between racial discourse and ideology and offers privileged access to racial context where race-related talk is often censored or silenced" (1584). Similarly, Reighan Gillam argues that in the case of Brazil, the "ideal of racial democracy is maintained through the [silencing] or [avoidance of] discussions [surrounding] racism" (37). Thus, ideas and practices that support racial democracies and mestizo essentialism (Caldwell, qtd. in Gilliam 37) allow racial humor to pass with impunity.

#PostalesQueEnamoran: Meme Production after Hurricane Maria

In February 2018, a series of memes circulated on Facebook about making your "partner fall in love." These Valentine's-themed memes were generated to look like romantic postcards to tag, comment on, share, and react to along with your friends, family members, and loved ones. Because these memes were made to perform as romantic postcards, it is important to explore their affective charge in the process of political action. As Sara Ahmed asserts, "'figures of speech' are crucial to the emotionality of texts" (Ahmed 12). There-fore, to explore meme production as a form of political action, it is important to note the emotionality of the memes, imagery, and texts alike. In the case of these romantic postcards, it is imperative to explore not only the very naming of emotions but the critique that emerges when political and critical images are being merged with romantic imagery.

The study of these memes will show the different ways in which romantic postcards were used as affective political rhetorical tools (Rodríguez Arce 8) through a form of storytelling. Meme production in PR operates as a digi-tal and collective archive to tell the story of the exacerbation of pre-existing inequalities after the experience of Hurricane Maria. Memes are used sub-versively not only to critique and analyze the mismanagement of Hurricane Maria and its aftermath but also to contest the colonial status of PR and cre-ate a sense of in-group identity through humor. Nonetheless, this comes at the expense of pathologizing and excluding some sectors of the Puerto Rican population.

Who are these meme creators? In her article in the electronic journal *Re-mezcla,* Jhoni Jackson states that two of the leading PR-based creators, "Radi-cal Cowry and El Blogiante, have both churned out exceptionally funny ways to woo a lover, lots of them with political implications and with references to the post-Maria struggle." Even though these big meme creators, and others such as Pixel & Archi, have not yet revealed their true identities, it is believed they are a group of millennials ("¿Quién es"). Their pages have hundreds of thousands of followers who are mostly Puerto Rican, as their content is quite context-specific and very politically engaged.

As will be evident from these so-called postcards, meme creators put a humorous spin on *flirtear* or flirting. Flirting in PR is colloquially known as *romantiqueo* or *flirteo* (Spanglish). They use humor to *romantiquear* through the creation of memes on social media. However—more than a mere *romantiqueo*—these romantic postcards are memes made to scrutinize the current political climate and subvert political narratives. The creation of these memes disrupts traditional conceptions of Puerto Rican national identity as a passive colonized role. By using humorous romantic postcards, these memes encode and decode messages as a way of expressing discontent and to critique PR's current situation regarding devastation, environmental racism, and co-lonialism.

The New Progressive Party of Puerto Rico (PNP), whose main platform is the complete annexation of the island, supported military interventionism and Donald Trump's actions vis-à-vis Hurricane Maria. As a critique, we see a postcard with former governor Carlos Romero Barceló (1932–2021), who

Figure 9.2. Radical Cowry meme in the form of a gift label with Governor Roselló willing to do anything to gain state status (2018).

during his time in office was implicated in the persecution and death of two pro-independence activists in Cerro Maravilla in Ponce, PR. The original picture used for this meme was taken at the close of the 2012 PNP campaign, when Romero Barceló happened to fall during the event. The picture is used in all kinds of memes making fun of those who are pro-statehood.

The translation of this postcard is "I want statehood . . . from anywhere" (in reference to his body). Besides this being a critique of the colonial status of the archipelago of PR, it is also an appraisal of the mismanagement of aid from the federal government and of the lack of criticism of the then government of Ricardo Roselló, then governor and leader of the PNP, and how the party was complicit in the mismanagement. During Trump's visit to PR, Roselló quietly accepted mistreatment and insults from the Trump administration. For instance, when Donald Trump visited the island and declared that "this was not a real emergency like Katrina," he nodded and smiled, sparing Trump from criticism. This meme expresses the discontent of the people of PR with the management of the crisis and the fact that there was no proper appraisal of the seriousness of the catastrophe by the majority party.

The punchline of this form of superiority humor stems from the "assumption that heterosexuality is the 'normal' orientation" (Bodinger-deUriarte 1). This makes the position in which Carlos Romero Barceló happened to fall intrinsically, pathologically, and socially deviant on account of his lack of masculinity, due to his political affiliations. This form of humor is both disciplinary—since it positions and mocks homosexuality as outside of the "norm"—and rebellious—as it ridicules the establishment and the majority party which, at this point, was the PNP. Thus, similar to the memes shown above, politically charged critiques in the form of memes tend to be made on the backs of racialization processes, ableist notions, and homophobic attitudes in Puerto Rican society.

Even though a lot of progress has been made in the last decade regarding LGBTQI+ rights, "profound biases, frequently the result of intolerance linked to traditional patriarchal and sexist thinking, have hampered demands for basic civil rights" (La Fountain-Stokes 502) in PR. These homophobic and transphobic dynamics, structured by ideas of heterocentrism, are present in PR and, more importantly, reflected in the different acts of violence against people from the LGBTQI+ community. In a sense, memes can be read as yet another instrument of othering while ultimately working to promote a form of hegemonic masculinity (Drakett 116). Thus, this type of humor is not only mounted on the mere falling of Romero Barceló but it also implies the feminization of those who are uncritical of the legacies and impacts of colonization in the archipelago, and that homosexuality is something deviant, pathological, and an object of ridicule.

Earthquakes and COVID-19 in Puerto Rico: Adding a New Layer of Complexity

On January 7, 2020, at 4 a.m., an 8.1 Mw earthquake shook the entire archipelago of Puerto Rico. The most affected part was the south and southwest of the "isla grande."[3] A series of additional earthquakes was felt over the following months. Different memes made by El Blogiante and Memes de Puerto Rico show—with humor—the already dire situation of PR produced by Hurricane Maria and its aftermath, and then by the earthquakes and the COVID-19 pandemic.

The meme presents four images, and has as its main caption, "The scariest places in the world." The four images are an abandoned cemetery, Chernobyl (representing the explosion of the nuclear plant reactor in northern Ukraine in 1986), *Silent Hill* (a horror/survival game series), and, last, a picture of a sign indicating that one is entering Guánica, one of the worst-affected areas in the south, which has as its slogan, "The Paradise of Endless Summer" (a reference to Bruce Brown's 1966 surf documentary *The Endless Summer*, which attracted US tourists). By using an ironic tone, Memes de Puerto Rico shows the precarity of the Guánica municipality. This meme received a lot of criticism, especially in its comments section, as one Facebook user and page follower argued that "this is an issue that affects all of *us*, do not make fun of this" (Memes de Puerto Rico; emphasis added). It was evident that meme consumers were not happy with the use of humor in this specific case,

Figure 9.3. Memes de Puerto Rico meme listing the scariest places on Earth, including Guánica, PR (2020).

as earthquakes were seen as a widespread problem that affected all Puerto Ricans equally. However, leads to the question: Who is a legitimate citizen of Puerto Rico? Who are "us"?

Throughout the memes shown in previous sections, we have seen how racialization, gendered practices, and ableist notions are all constructed as punchlines that create a sense of in-group identity. I argue that by refusing to laugh along with the meme created by Memes de Puerto Rico, some of the audience delineated clear boundaries that would determine who should (and should not) be considered part of "us." The underlying implication here is that racialized bodies, people construed as disabled, and members of the LGBTQI+ community are not seen as legitimate citizens of the Puerto Rican nation; therefore, discrimination and racism are seen as allowed. However,

Figure 9.4. Memes de Puerto Rico meme personifying the island as a distracted boy-friend, caught between the pandemic and earthquakes (2020).

while one of the most common discourses around the COVID-19 pandemic was "We are all in this together"—despite structural inequalities and inter-secting oppressions (Sobande)—that did not stop meme producers' and con-sumers' anti-Chinese racism, as I will explore later.

On March 12, 2020, then-Governor Wanda Vázquez declared a state of emergency and martial law in PR due to the COVID-19 pandemic. COVID-19, the earthquake, and the legacies of hurricane mismanagement combined to create a state of chaos in the archipelago. The production of memes was a way of coping with the social inequalities exacerbated and produced by these "natural" disasters.

In the meme from figure 9.4, we can observe the anxiety and fatigue of Puerto Ricans dealing with these combined disasters. The original image be-came popular in 2017, but was taken in 2015 by photographer Antonio Guil-lem and is commonly known as "Distracted Boyfriend." The meme portrays PR as the boyfriend—who is wearing a pava hat, symbolizing PR as a *jíbaro* (farmer) nation—who is distracted from his current girlfriend (who symbol-izes the earthquakes) by the coronavirus. First, it is important to note how gendered considerations become part of the meme's punchline by showing the girlfriend as a current issue or problem. Second, there is the fact that the symbol used to identify the Puerto Rican nation is the pava hat—which is emblematic of the *jíbaro*.

The *jíbaro* is a cluster of imaginaries embodied in the figure of a white male peasant who has "undergone multiple historical and ideological mutations" (Ramos-Zayas 377). Scarano argues that the myth of the *jíbaro* as a symbol of national identity responds to an aspirational whitened idea of Puerto Rican nationalism in which PR culture is represented as a "repository of a higher, patriotic morality, with the very essence of a Puerto Rican nation threatened by North American economic and cultural domination" (Scarano 1404). Cristobal Borges contributes to the conversation by adding that the continual aspiration of whiteness creates the conditions for anything outside of that to be automatically cast as outside of Puerto Ricanness (Borges 2). Thus, while these memes show how meme pages on Facebook work as a site of critique, protest, and contestation against the dynamics produced by not-so-natural disasters, these memes are also made at the expense of groups historically constructed as Other. For instance, memes regarding the COVID-19 pandemic reflect anti-Chinese racism in PR as a way of creating a sense of in-group national identity despite an assumed racial democracy.

Under precarious conditions, thousands of Chinese people arrived in Latin America in the period from 1847 to 1873 to be part of the workforce after the "abolition" of slavery (Lee Borges). From 1846 onwards, there were various attempts to introduce Chinese laborers to PR and Cuba, and, by the beginning of the 1850s, this had been approved by the Spanish empire (Lee Borges). In the case of PR, however, due to various laws and the political and economic climate, Chinese migration was not steadily implemented until much later. Instead, Puerto Rico functioned as a sort of penal colony for Chinese people working in Cuba. Due to mistreatment and human rights violations that Chinese people had to endure in Cuba, some of them decided to fight back, which resulted in the incarceration of some of these workers (Lee Borges, "El gran dilemma"). Approximately 350 Chinese individuals convicted of homicide arrived in PR—from Cuba—from 1865 to 1880 (Lee Borges, "El gran dilemma"). These people were imprisoned in PR under inhumane conditions on illegal/extended sentences (Lee Borges, "El gran dilemma"). As punishment, many of them were forced to work in the construction of roads like PR's Carretera Número 1[4] (Lee Borges, "El gran dilemma"). José Lee Borges invites his readership to rethink mythical conceptions and racialization processes of Puerto Ricans to account for the migratory complexities of the nationalist tropes behind racial democracy. In his article titled "Reflexiones de un chino en Puerto Rico,"[5] he argues that racism and discrimination are very much present in Puerto Rican society. I argue that the memes produced during the COVID-19 pandemic show how racist tropes are carried from the off-line to the online.

The memes from figure 9.5 show anti-Chinese racism early in the COVID-19 pandemic. For instance, the meme on the left shows a white man holding a sign Photoshopped to say "Seeking a Chinese person to sneeze at the Capitol," implying that only Chinese people carry the virus. This meme shows Puerto Ricans' criticism of and discontent with the government mounted on anti-Chinese racism. Another instance of this is shown in the image to the right, posted as a banner image for El Blogiante, which shows a bat with a caption stating "Don't eat me" in reference to the myths pathologizing Chinese cuisine during the COVID-19 pandemic. Moreover, the comments on this same meme feature derogatory and racist remarks against Chinese people. These critiques of the government and the management of COVID-19 in PR are cemented in racist tropes that indicate there is no room for Chinese populations inside the Puerto Rican imaginary of racial democracy, as they are seen as incompatible with the desirable project of mixing, which tends to privilege a light-skinned or white outcome for mixed-racedness.

The then-governor of Puerto Rico, Wanda Vázquez Garced, decided to implement restrictive measures during PR's COVID-related state of emergency. She imposed a curfew that demanded that people remain in their homes unless going out was absolutely necessary (i.e., for grocery shopping or if people were essential workers, etc.). In the next meme, I will show how, through a critique of the ostensibly strong measures imposed by Vázquez Garced, racialization processes and racism against Indigenous people make an appearance.

The Taíno people in PR have become part of the myth of racial democracy (i.e., the supposedly harmonious mixture of Spanish, Indigenous, and Black). Drawing on ideas behind the *indigenismo* movement in Mexico, Puerto Rican intellectuals during the second half of the twentieth century tended to romanticize an Indigenous past at the expense of the systemic invisibilization of Black Puerto Ricans (Duany). In these memes, we can observe how racialization processes in PR move away from this romanticized idea of Indigenous people to portray them as "backward" and/or "savages." Additionally, it can be argued that identifying with Indigenous people served as little more than a way of invisibilizing Blackness in the late twentieth century, as many Puerto Ricans still view Indigenous people as not-quite-human. In this meme, one can observe how different racialization processes conflate in this "racial democracy" to pathologize and racialize Black and darker-skinned bodies.

The myth of racial democracy produced by the mixture of Indigenous, white, and Black still holds whiteness as its organizing principle. Through the meme in figure 9.6, we see racialized conceptions that are demarcated by a

Figure 9.5. Sinophobic memes from Memes de Puerto Rico and El Blogiante, alluding to viral contagion and Chinese cuisine (2020).

Figure 9.6. PR Memes meme of a white man trying to civilize unruly Indigenous people (2020).

white male in Western clothing trying to "civilize" the "unruly" Indigenous people who are violating the government curfew. This division tends to be organized through whiteness and is therefore anti-Black and anti-Indigenous, seeing these bodies as a by-product and factor of historical myths around racial democracy, yet not as a part of the contemporary Puerto Rican nation. This meme shows Mel Gibson wearing the appropriate protective gear (i.e., clothes, gloves, and a mask) while one Indigenous man speaks broken Spanish (the language of the colonizer), mangling the sentence "I need to buy bread," which instead appears as "I buy bread," and the other Indigenous man has a welfare card Photoshopped to his loincloth. Thus, similarly to the meme shown above (fig. 9.1), welfare aid is racialized here and, in the case of Puerto Rico, tends to target Black and dark-skinned bodies.

Final Considerations

Reyes's observation that "[h]umor allows a subject to overcome traumatic experiences and adverse circumstances, thus it is an attitude that a subject can choose or refuse to adopt in the face of adversity" (Reyes 14) can be seen in the creation of memes in PR after a series of "natural" disasters and their (mis) management. Memes help Puerto Ricans to process, negotiate, and handle not only the occurrence of natural disasters but also their aftermath. Humor is used as a tool of resistance and critique by both meme generators and Puerto Ricans, who make use of social media to share, like, react to, or comment on posts. These memes go beyond mere entertainment, operating to critique the current political situation. These inside jokes work as a unifying tool against the outrageous living conditions in PR. Nonetheless, this tool is wielded at the expense of marginalized and racialized groups. This shows how literature on PR's disasters needs to consider the internal dynamics, discriminatory processes, ableist notions, and racializing structures that organize Puerto Rican society.

While maintaining a critical standpoint, I argue that it is imperative to explore the production of memes in PR as a new form of protest. This analysis has observed the way figures of speech and humor are used to perform a sense of in-group identity and to protest the mismanagement of the aftermath of seemingly natural disasters. This sense of an in-group identity is also present in how humor is used as a rhetorical tool of contestation around PR's political status, the thousands of deaths resulting from recent disasters, massive migration, a $74 billion dollar debt, a lack of power and potable water, and the management of the series of earthquakes and the COVID-19 pandemic, among others. What makes meme production in PR so interesting is the arguably subversive acts of sharing, commenting, and reacting that social media platforms such as Facebook allow. Pages like Radical Cowry, Pixel & Archi, Memes de Puerto Rico, and El Blogiante have thousands of followers who react to content that issues constant critiques of current political events. Thus, memes go beyond entertainment to produce a sense of political demonstration that rallies different bodies and creates, simultaneously, an expression of solidarity. These memes can be considered a form of catharsis—they respond to, contest, and critique the precariousness of the current situation in PR, and the related exacerbation of social inequities on the island.

One should not be blind, however, to the racialization processes and discriminatory practices that come with the type of humor used in the creation of these memes. Historical notions that surround off-line stereotypes of anti-

Blackness, disability, racism, and misogyny are reflected in online platforms (i.e., Facebook) and meme generators alike. I argue this is a key element when exploring the contemporary impact of colonialism in PR. By using a more accessible tool—like social media—we can get a glimpse of how ableism, homophobia, and neoliberal notions around productivity and racism operate as organizing principles of Puerto Rican society that often pass uncontested. Puerto Rico organizes racialization processes through an assumed racial democracy that allows these ideas to gravitate from the off-line to the online to delimit who should and should not be part of the nation. I argue that the political critique produced through memes in Puerto Rico often comes at the expense of Others, which allows further exclusion, racialization, and discrimination of bodies that have been historically cast as deviant, in need of fixing, or pathological. I believe that further attention is needed to understand how these types of humor are in conversation with targeted violent acts, systemic racism, and colonialism.

Notes

1 The Federal Emergency Management Agency (FEMA) is an agency that was officially created in 1979 as part of the United States Department of Homeland Security under President Jimmy Carter. Its mission, according to their website, is "helping people before, during and after disasters" (www.fema.gov/about).
2 Diner/canteen.
3 "Big island" (alluding to the island with the majority of PR's population).
4 Road 1 is now a highway connecting the north and south of PR.
5 Reflections of a Chinese Man in Puerto Rico.

Works Cited

Ahmed, Sara. 2004. *The Cultural Politics of Emotion*. Edinburgh, UK: Edinburgh UP.
"Alguien sabe si adelantaran los cupones, por lo del huracán?" *Memes Monkey*, 2017. www .memesmonkey.com/topic/huracan+irma#&gid=1&pid=19.
Applebaum, Max. *Tales from the Crip: The Relationship between Stories about Learning Disabilities in Mass Media and Teacher Perceptions and Expectations of Learning Disabled Students*. 2016. University of Toronto. MA thesis.
Beers Fägersten, Kristy. "I'm Learneding! First Language Acquisition in *The Simpsons*." *Watching TV with a Linguist*, edited by Kirsty Beers Fägersten, NY: Syracuse UP, pp. 257–281.
El Blogiante. Don't Eat Me. Facebook, 31 Jan. 2020, 7:11 p.m., www.facebook.com/ elblogiante/photos/a.426106387581036/1329460330578966.
Bodinger-deUriarte, Cristina, editor. *Interfacing Ourselves: Living in the Digital Age*. New York and Abingdon: Routledge, 2019.

Bonilla, Yarimar, and Marisol LeBrón, editors. *Aftershocks of Disaster: Puerto Rico before and after the Storm.* Chicago: Haymarket Books, 2019.

———. "Introduction: Aftershocks of Disaster." *Aftershocks of Disaster: Puerto Rico before and after the Storm.* Chicago: Haymarket Books, 2019.

Borges, Cristobal A. *Unspoken Prejudice: Racial Politics, Gendered Norms, and the Transformation of Puerto Rican Identity in the Twentieth Century.* 2014. University of Texas at El Paso, PhD dissertation, scholarworks.utep.edu/open_etd/1590/.

"Carlos Romero Barceló Se Cae En La Tarima Del PNP." *Primera Hora,* 4 Nov. 2012, www.primerahora.com/noticias/gobierno-politica/notas/carlos-romero-barcelo-se-cae-en-la-tarima-del-pnp/.

Chesterman, Andrew. *Memes of Translation: The Spread of Ideas in Translation Theory.* Amsterdam and Philadelphia: John Benjamins Publishing Company, 2016.

Díaz-Quiñones, Arcadio. "Foreword." *Aftershocks of Disaster: Puerto Rico before and after the Storm.* Chicago: Haymarket Books, 2019.

Drakett, Jessica, Bridgette Rickett, Katy Day, and Kate Milnes. "Old Jokes, New Media—Online Sexism and Constructions of Gender in Internet Memes." *Feminism & Psychology,* vol. 28, no. 1, 2018, pp. 109–127. https://doi.org/10.1177/0959353517727560.

Duany, Jorge. 2001. "Making Indians Out of Blacks: The Revitalization of Taíno Identity in Contemporary Puerto Rico." *Taíno Revival: Critical Perspectives on Puerto Rican Identity and Cultural Politics,* edited by Gabriel Haslip-Viera, Princeton, NJ: Wiener, 2001.

Edwards, Mackenzie. "Screening the Slob: Neoliberal Failure, Fatness, and Disability in 'King-Size Homer.'" *Screen Bodies,* vol. 3, no. 2, 2018, pp. 1–16. https://doi.org/10.3167/screen.2018.030202.

Foka, Anna, and Jonas Liliequist, editors. *Laughter, Humor, and the (Un)Making of Gender: Historical and Cultural Perspectives.* London: Palgrave Macmillan, 2015.

Gilens, Martin. *Why Americans Hate Welfare: Race, Media, and the Politics of Antipoverty Policy.* Chicago: University of Chicago Press, 1999.

Gillam, Reighan. "Satirical Antiracism: Digital Protest Images in Afro-Brazilian Media." *Visual Anthropology Review,* vol. 37, no. 1, pp. 31–51. https://doi.org/10.1111/var.12227.

Graham, David A. "Trump's Dubious Revisionist History of Hurricane Maria: The President Grades Himself Highly for How the Federal Government Responded to the Disaster in Puerto Rico." *The Atlantic,* Sept. 12, 2018, sec. Politics, www.theatlantic.com/politics/archive/2018/09/trump-hurricane-maria-florence-revisionism/570070/.

Gremore, Graham. "These Donald Trump Paper Towel Memes Unfortunately Say It All." *Queerty,* 4 Oct. 2017, www.queerty.com/donald-trump-paper-towel-memes-unfortunately-say-20171004.

Jackson, Jhoni. "Puerto Rico Is Creating Political Valentine's Day Cards to Protest Conditions on the Island." *Remezcla,* 14 Feb. 2018, remezcla.com/lists/culture/puerto-rico-political-valentines-day-cards/.

Jiménez, Mónica. "Looking for a Way Forward in the Past: Lessons from the Puerto Rican Nationalist Party." *Aftershocks of Disaster: Puerto Rico before and after the Storm.* Chicago: Haymarket Books, 2019.

Joffe, Marc D., and Jesse Martinez. "Origins of the Puerto Rico Fiscal Crisis." *Mercatus Research,* 12 Apr. 2016, https://doi.org/10.2139/ssrn.3211660.

Klein, Naomi. *The Battle for Paradise: Puerto Rico Takes on the Disaster Capitalists*. Chicago: Haymarket Books, 2018.

———. *The Shock Doctrine: The Rise of Disaster Capitalism*. London: Penguin Books, 2008.

La Fountain-Stokes, Lawrence. "Recent Developments in Queer Puerto Rican History, Politics, and Culture." *El Centro*, vol. 30, no. 2, 2018, pp. 502–540.

Lee Borges, José. "El gran dilema: la introducción de trabajadores chinos a Puerto Rico." *80Grados*, 24 Sept. 2016, www.80grados.net/el-gran-dilema-la-introduccion-de-trabajadores-chinos-a-puerto-rico/.

———. "Los chinos de la Carretera Central." *80Grados*, 2 Dec. 2016, www.80grados.net/los-chinos-de-la-carretera-central/.

———. *Los chinos en Puerto Rico*. 3rd ed., Cayey, PR: Ediciones Gaviota, 2020.

———. "Reflexiones de un chino en Puerto Rico." *80Grados*, 26 Feb. 2016, www.80grados.net/reflexiones-de-un-chino-en-puerto-rico/.

Lloréns, Hilda, et al. "Racismo En Puerto Rico: Surveying Perceptions of Racism." *Centro Journal*, vol. 29, no. 3, 2017, pp. 154–183.

Maldonado Torres, Nelson. "Afterword: Critique and Decoloniality in the Face of Crisis, Disaster, and Catastrophe." *Aftershocks of Disaster: Puerto Rico before and after the Storm*, edited by Yarimar Bonilla and Marisol Lebrón, Chicago: Haymarket Books, 2019.

McGlade, Rhiannon. *Catalan Cartoons: A Cultural and Political History*. Cardiff: University of Wales Press, 2016.

PR Memes. Earthquake, COVID-19, Earthquake and COVID-19. *Facebook*, 2 May 2020, 8:17 a.m., www.facebook.com/prmemes2/photos/a.1566368693693981/2514889478841893.

———. Encuentra el gato. *Facebook*, 30 Apr. 2020, 4:35 p.m., www.facebook.com/prmemes2/photos/a.1566368693693981/2513398808990960.

———. Entiendan, hay una pandemia mundial. . . . *Facebook*, 3 Apr. 2020, 10:57 p.m., www.facebook.com/prmemes2/photos/a.1566368693693981/2490404051290436.

———. Lugares más tenebrosos de Puerto Rico. *Facebook*, 2 Jan. 2020, 10:59 p.m., business.facebook.com/memespr1/photos/a.292316204286699/1256052084579768/?type=3&theater.

———. Puerto Rico, coronavirus, temblores. *Facebook*, 9 Mar. 2020, 10:09 a.m., www.facebook.com/prmemes2/photos/a.1566368693693981/2468608343470007.

———. Se busca Chino que estornude en el Capitolio. *Facebook*, 5 Feb. 2020, 4:59 p.m., business.facebook.com/memespr1/photos/a.292316204286699/1285021315016178/?type=3&theater.

Minet, Carla. "María's Death Toll: On the Crucial Role of Puerto Rico's Investigative Journalists." *Aftershocks of Disaster: Puerto Rico before and after the Storm*, edited by Yarimar Bonilla and Marisol Lebrón, Chicago: Haymarket Books, 2019.

Molinari, Sarah. "Authenticating Loss and Contesting Recovery: FEMA and the Politics of Colonial Disaster Management." *Aftershocks of Disaster: Puerto Rico before and after the Storm*, edited by Yarimar Bonilla and Marisol Lebrón, Chicago: Haymarket Books, 2019.

Negrón-Muntaner, Frances. "Our Fellow Americans: Why Calling Puerto Ricans 'Americans' Will Not Save Them." *Aftershocks of Disaster: Puerto Rico before and after the Storm,* edited by Yarimar Bonilla and Marisol Lebrón, Chicago: Haymarket Books, 2019.

Office of Communications and Publishing, USGS. "Secuencia del Terremoto en Puerto Rico, 2020 (hasta enero 16, 2020)." United States Geological Survey, 16 Jan. 2020, www.usgs.gov/media/images/secuencia-del-terremoto-en-puerto-rico-2020-hasta-enero-16-2020.

"¿Quién es el misterioso Blogiante? Conoce un poco más sobre esta figura de las redes sociales." *El Nuevo Día,* 22 Nov. 2013, www.elnuevodia.com/entretenimiento/farandula/notas/quien-es-el-misterioso-blogiante/.

Radical Cowry. Quiero la estadidad . . . por donde sea. *Facebook,* 2018. [Page deleted.]

Ramírez, Rafael L., and Rosa E. Casper. *What It Means to Be a Man: Reflections on Puerto Rican Masculinity.* New Brunswick, NJ: Rutgers UP, 1999.

Ramos-Zayas, Ana Y. "Racializing The 'Invisible' Race: Latino Constructions Of 'White Culture' And Whiteness in Chicago." *Urban Anthropology and Studies of Cultural Systems and World Economic Development,* vol. 30, no. 4, 2001, pp. 341–380.

Reyes, Israel. *Humor and the Eccentric Text in Puerto Rican Literature.* Gainsville: UP of Florida, 2005.

Roberto, Giovanni. "Community Kitchens: An Emerging Movement?" *Aftershocks of Disaster: Puerto Rico before and after the Storm,* edited by Yarimar Bonilla and Marisol Lebrón, Chicago: Haymarket Books, 2019.

Rodríguez Arce, Aziria D. *Seizing the Memes of Production: Political Memes in Puerto Rico and the Puerto Rican Diaspora.* 2018. MIT. MA thesis.

Rodríguez-Díaz, Carlos E., and Charlotte Lewellen-Williams. "Race and Racism as Structural Determinants for Emergency and Recovery Response in the Aftermath of Hurricanes Irma and Maria in Puerto Rico." *Health Equity,* vol. 4, no. 1, 2020, pp. 232–238. https://doi.org/10.1089/heq.2019.0103.

Scarano, Francisco A. "The Jibaro Masquerade and the Subaltern Politics of Creole Identity Formation in Puerto Rico, 1745–1823." *The American Historical Review,* vol. 101, no. 5, 1996, pp. 1398–1431. https://doi.org/10.2307/2170177.

Shifman, Limor. *Memes in Digital Culture.* Cambridge, MA: MIT Press, 2014.

Shugerman, Emily. "Donald Trump Says Puerto Rico Is 'an Island Surrounded by Big Water': The Trump Administration Is Under Fire for Its Response to Hurricane Maria." *The Independent,* 29 Sept. 29, 2017, www.independent.co.uk/news/world/americas/us-politics/donald-trump-puerto-rico-hurricane-maria-comments-island-big-water-a7975011.html.

Sloan, Lacey M., editor. "From Backstage to Digital Front Stage: Online Queer Community, Identity, and Emotion Management." *Interfacing Ourselves: Living in the Digital Age.* 1st ed. NY: Routledge, 2019.

Sobande, Francesca. "'We're All in This Together': Commodified Notions of Connection, Care and Community in Brand Responses to COVID-19." *European Journal of Cultural Studies,* vol. 23, no. 6, 2020, pp. 1033–1037. https://doi.org/10.1177/1367549420932294.

Sue, Christina A., and Tanya Golash-Boza. "'It Was Only a Joke': How Racial Humour Fuels Colour-Blind Ideologies in Mexico and Peru." *Ethnic and Racial Studies* vol. 36, 10, 2013, pp. 1582–1598. https://doi.org/10.1080/01419870.2013.783929

Tate, Shirley Anne, and Ian Law. *Caribbean Racisms*. London: Palgrave Macmillan, 2015.

Weber, Christopher R., et al. "Placing Racial Stereotypes in Context: Social Desirability and the Politics of Racial Hostility." *American Journal of Political Science*, vol. 58, no. 1, 2014, pp. 63–78. https://doi.org/10.1111/ajps.12051.

10

HolaSoyGermán

On Global Latin American Humor on YouTube

Juan Poblete

HolaSoyGermán (HSG) can be described as a form of YouTube-based comedic vlog, or video blog, on which Germán Garmendia, a Chilean creator born in 1990—who, like some other famous YouTubers, has gone from amateur to professionalizing to full professional—addresses an audience in Spanish with original short-form comic content that by 2021 had reached more than a hundred installments.

HSG is part of a new screen ecology of "social media entertainment" (SME), and it embodies some of the new industry sector's forms, practices, and genres. It is also part of a bigger phenomenon that Nick Couldry and Andreas Hepp call the mediatization of the social: "media now are much more than centralized content: they comprise platforms which, for many humans, literally *are* the spaces where, through communication, they *enact* the social" (2).

According to data gathering company Social Blade—which tracks YouTube, among other platforms—HSG had, by 2021, uploaded 136 videos from the time the channel was created on Sept 9, 2011. It also had 42.5 million subscribers and more than 4.5 billion views. In 2019, HSG was the second-most-viewed site in Chile (the first one was JuegaGermán, a gaming series, also produced and owned by Germán Garmendia), and one of the 20 most popular on the platform worldwide. Of those 136 videos uploaded to the HSG channel on YouTube, at least 22 have more than 50 million views, constituting his most popular among a very successful series.[1] In 2022, six years after posting the latest installment of HSG, Garmendia could still be celebrated as "[w]ithout a doubt, the most popular and best-known comic in Latin America," and with 43.2 million subscribers, his was still the fifth-most-popular YouTube site in Latin America.[2]

Focusing on HSG, this chapter, first, describes its platform context, You-Tube, as part of a new media ecology. Then it analyzes HSG's defining traits: the production of high-quality everydayness, its metalinguistic and metapoetic tendencies, its pedagogical bent and structure, and its use of the Spanish language as a comedic vehicle for generating cultural proximity within a geolinguistic region thus defined. The final section of the chapter links those traits and others to the use and production of authenticity for a media-infused generation—that is, it connects those characteristics to a social and communicational economy based on the construction and exploitation of the self. Humor is here the combined result of an array of processes of self-formation and expression meta-critically represented as media formats or genres.

YouTube and Social Media Entertainment

The first systematic exploration of YouTube as a cultural and media phenomenon was Jean Burgess and Joshua Green's *YouTube: Online Video and Participatory Culture,* a book published first in 2009, when YouTube was just four years old, and then, in a second edition, in 2018, when the company had confirmed—at least by the standards of our fast-moving information-based capitalism—its staying power and astounding popularity.

As Burgess and Green make clear, YouTube matters both as a media platform in and of itself, and as a focus of social attention and anxieties. In general, they propose, the discussion about YouTube has had three dimensions: what it brings to popular culture; what it brings to media as a business and as an object of study; and, connected to both, how it taps, distorts, and maximizes people's participation in the production and circulation of culture. It has also been a site of exploration for anxieties about what fun and young people are about, and what connections the creativity and lawlessness associated with youth culture have with mainstream formal culture. As I will try to show later, the examination of HSG, to whose analysis this chapter is devoted, involves an exploration of all these issues.

YouTube was launched in 2005 by three former employees of Paypal. Jawed Karim, Steve Chen, and Chad Hurley "realized, in 2004, that there wasn't one location where videos could be shared" (Exford). A year later the company was bought by Google for $1.6 billion. This points to one additional element of the social life of YouTube: for many young people, the platform is not simply a form of common entertainment, but also a dream space in which it is possible to fantasize about untold—and, above all, fast and self-generated—fame and riches.[3]

For media studies, YouTube embodies the convergence of the logic of social media and its entrepreneurial culture of Internet-based businesses with that of entertainment media and its cultures of production, circulation, and consumption in the production of value. According to an article in *The Economist*, more people around the world used YouTube, a Google company, in 2020 (two billion) than they did the extraordinarily popular Google search engine itself (around 1.8 billion) ("Google Grows Up" 15). However, almost one hundred billion dollars of the revenue for Alphabet (Google's and YouTube's parent company) comes from the search engine, as opposed to YouTube's contribution, which is slightly more than $10 billion.

What is at stake in any discussion of the platform is also relevant to contemporary culture and social analysis in general. Its overlapping multiple corporate and cultural logics have become a central social site of creation and friction. Burgess and Green also point to the fact that YouTube is also an example of a new form of media company with a new market structure, one that is no longer just two-sided but multi-sided, as it is not just about advertisers and the public mediated by the media but, instead, multiple stakeholders with evolving interests and practices (9). In the logic of platforms, YouTube is also halfway between claims of platform neutrality, whereby amateur users produce the content and upload it to the platform—which simply acts as a venue—and being a potent media company generating its own content and circulating that of many professional producers.

In discussing the relationship between YouTube and the media, Burgess and Green state that two dominant views are attempting to explain the functioning of the platform: "YouTube as a player in the digital economy on the one hand (the top-down view), and YouTube as a site of vernacular creativity and cultural chaos on the other (the bottom-up view)" (58). But they conclude that the contrast of these two perspectives is not the best way to understand YouTube: "It is more helpful to understand YouTube as occupying an evolving institutional function—operating as a coordinating mechanism between individual and collective creativity and meaning production; and as a mediator among various competing industry, community, and audience interests—including its own" (58).

This is what Stuart Cunningham and David Craig call, in a book by that title, "social media entertainment" (SME), a new industry sector with its own forms, practices, and genres:

> We see SME as an emerging proto-industry fueled by professionalizing, previously amateur content creators using new entertainment

and communicative formats, including vlogging, gameplay, and do-it-yourself (DIY), to develop potentially sustainable businesses based on significant followings that can extend across multiple formats. (5)

YouTube is one of these SME platforms, and thus part of a "new screen ecology . . . driven by intrinsically interactive technologies and strategies of fan, viewer, audience, and community engagement" (4). Such new screen ecology is different from the previous "legacy content industries" (i.e., Hollywood, classic TV and music industries, etc.) and their one hundred-year-long model of entertainment production and consumption based on "intellectual property control and exploitation" (Cunningham and Craig 4). For Cunningham and Craig, this contrast between models is crucial: the old model, still functioning, depended, and still does, on professionally created and corporately owned content, massively distributed through broadcasts; the new model, instead, is organized around massively available content, produced by professionalizing and non-professional creators, that is shared through the affordances of a platform that both benefits from the circulation of content and makes it possible for the user-created content to remain accessible and available while a section of it reaches commercial viability status. The difference between a platform, which I just described, and a portal (often, an additional window of access to such professionally created and owned content) makes the stakes more visible: what is involved is a significant reshaping of the mass communication production and consumption process, with related changes to the legal and technical affordances grounding the model in question. In the case of the portal, the flow of content is unidirectional, while in that of the platform, it is multidirectional and involves multiple agents, including professional, professionalizing, amateur, and occasional creators and rights holders. Additionally, as Cunningham and Craig make clear, there are other big issues involved: How does this new screen ecology fit in the political economy of transnational media, if at all? What forms of labor are represented and how are they compensated (or not)? What kind of ethos and rules drive this new media culture? and how sustainable as a production model is so-called free content? Moreover, at its most fundamental, YouTube, along with other similar SME companies, places a series of propositions at the heart of contemporary social communication: it naturalizes the idea that entertainment can be free, at the same time as it turns the free time of its audiences into something commercially productive for both platform-based capitalism and occasional, amateur, and professionalizing cultural creators. It thus opens up both the ideal and the possibility of one-person production efforts and that of immediate, almost unmediated cultural intervention and relevance. In other words, it holds the promise of radical cultural democratization (see, for example, Friedman), as it also shows, very clearly, how audiences' attention, creativity, and productivity can be commodified and capitalized on (see Fuchs; Väliaho).

HolaSoyGermán

That HSG could be this popular across audience age segments—including, at least, current teenagers and youngish people under 35 (encompassing too, those who were teenagers in 2011 and have grown older with the series)—reminds us that the so-called generational divide between so-called digital natives or youth and older users when it comes to YouTube may be a fantasy, and more of a reflection of the moral panics or anxieties around the culture of youth than a reflection of who consumes what on YouTube (see Burgess).

Like YouTube, HSG depends on producing and combining two seemingly contradictory effects: first, that it is amateur, direct content produced by someone who looks like everybody else and, second, that it is the result of the high-quality work of media professionals. One could call this high-quality everydayness, and it is part of the blurring, in so-called participatory culture (Jenkins et al.), of the traditional separation between popular culture as a site of consumption and economic exploitation by big corporations, and popular culture as generated on the ground by regular people in their daily lives.

This high-quality everydayness, the user-generated ethos, involves engaging viewers in the co-production of effects. Germán explicitly develops aesthetic categories for the enjoyment of YouTube videos in "Si te ríes reinicia el video," which is part of the JuegaGermán channel on YouTube. The game works, as it had 9,975,999 views a month after it was posted on the platform, and by July 2021 it had accumulated more than thirty million views. In it, Germán insists on his game and his rules. The one rule is this: You must restart the video he is commenting on if you laugh as a result of watching it. The viewer is invited to voluntarily engage in a time-consuming dynamic (a form of freedom bounded by rules) that is likely to result in multiple restarts, generating an effect of fun and zaniness. This video, then, manifests a triple effort: it wants to be popular and it is; it wants to develop aesthetic viewing categories that viewers use as an everyday standard and mechanism for formalization; and, in a metalinguistic way, it also wants itself to be funny—and at times it manages to be so.

This metalinguistic emphasis on the rules governing media consumption, turned into an audiovisual object of wide consumption, seems paradoxical—when one considers that the younger generations are said to be instruction-allergic, always willing to go directly to the video explaining how to do anything[4]—until you realize that these rules are themselves being communicated in a short and funny video that doubles as a shared and intimate experience between the viewer and German Garmendia, one of YouTube's biggest personalities.

The heavy metalinguistic games have been a defining mark of HSG videos since the beginning, as has the speed of delivery of Germán's Spanish. The very first HSG video, "Las cosas obvias de la vida," uploaded on September 9, 2011, and now seen more than 17 million times, begins with Germán issuing a bet that viewers are watching the video on computer monitors; that is, he is making a metalinguistic reference to communication and its physical channel (something later viewers have engagingly denied by pointing out their cell phone access). This first HSG video declares its focus to be on "the obvious things in life" and even more to the point, "those people who point out the obvious things in life"—those things that go without saying and do not need to be mentioned and yet are often mentioned, of which Germán's own bet that the viewer was watching this video on a computer monitor was meant to be a perfect example. Another recurring trait of HSG, the quick dialogue between Germán as himself and Germán as a different character—here, multiple characters saying obvious things that do not need to be said but are said often anyway—also makes a first appearance. This quick dialogue mirrors the one HSG is having with his viewers through the video itself and reinforces the metapoetic and metalinguistic nature of HSG videos: they are often about the structure of the message, its channel of circulation, and the nature of the communicational act itself. They could often be said to be instances of teaching communication, a media lesson. Thus, the structure: a topic (the obvious things some people feel obligated to mention even though they should go without saying), and an order of exposition and illustrations of its main points (three examples of the problem). They are very fast and analytically focused on communication itself, and this is part of what makes them funny. In their combination of meta-reflection and instructions on the one hand, and high speed and quick editing on the other, these HSG videos could be linked to the style of classic comedians in Latin America, like Cantinflas and La India María (see Poblete). As some later user commentaries make clear, looking back, it is also easy to discern in early HSG videos both the effort to enunciate in a way that may be broadly understood, especially at that speed of delivery, and the much heavier presence of Chilean vocabulary and pronunciation at certain points of the segment.

HSG's second video, "Ebrios, ebrios, everywhere" (Drunkards, drunkards, everywhere) is a good display of the role slapstick and popular Chilean language can play in the series. Like the first video, this one also begins with a bet issued to the viewer—in this case, that they are sitting on a chair—but then goes on to show Germán's impressive acting and comic skills through a comparison of how we behave when we are sober versus what we do when we are drunk. The drunkard, as he gets drunker and more agitated about a breakup, gets more and more aggressive and sentimental and, in the process, speaks more and more like a young Chilean of the middle or working class, as if to suggest that underneath "proper" speech, there is always, for any Chilean, a deeper and more authentic way of talking, more closely connected with true affects and emotions—a deeper self. But even this Chilean Spanish is later on in the series rendered more intelligible and less offensive as an imitation of working-class speech by a certain level of formalization and optimization for its media performance, helped or hindered by Garmendia's long residence abroad.

This oscillation between a more standardized Spanish, understandable across the world-region that is Latin America and Spain, and the frequent re-emergence of a Chilean slang and prosody, relatively standardized for performance, is a natural result of HSG's effort to produce intimate communication as if it were only for a few friends while he is in fact addressing a vast audience of many millions of viewers across multiple geographical contexts.

By the third video, "Facebook," HSG had institutionalized the starting bet ("I bet you a matchbox your room has four walls"), confirmed the high speed of its delivery, and begun formalizing its appeal to viewers to "like" the videos and interact with Germán through the comments. The video ends with Germán including in the bar at the bottom of the screen the comments left by many of his viewers, including those who challenge Germán and claim to have won the previous bet. In addition to interactivity, there are also the references to how the game is played on YouTube: "You know how it works, click like it if you liked it—and if you didn't like it, click like, anyway"; the subtitling making puns on the lines Germán delivers, adding another layer of reflexivity to what is already a very self-conscious effort. The overall appeal is to some ideal viewer who is in and gets it; who understands how communicational codes can be worked on and reflected on; how effects are produced in a medium, and what is the right attitude expected of consumers. In "Celos" (Jealousy), in the final section that closes his videos (A Question), Germán asks the viewers,

If you could choose your final words before dying, what would you say? I would say something like, "The treasure is . . . [before collapsing and dying]." And then the person next to me would say "Noooo!" And while they are saying *Noooo*, very sad music would start, and then the camera would start rotating around me, and it would begin to rain, and there would be thunder everywhere.

Ceasing to act out the final moments of this scene and returning to the now of the video, Germán says, "They must have done something to me when I was a child. I cannot be this fucked up without a good reason." Humor, then, is both the intelligent, low-key and seemingly amateur deployment of media codes for the production of an affect (a positive alteration of the viewers' mood) and their knowing metalinguistic analysis for the production of some effects (the overall humor experience and the creation of a bond between the viewers as community and the performer).

A good example of how HSG taps into language, subjectivity, mass culture, and social media simultaneously as resources for the production of value is "Mi nombre (soy el hijo de Lady Gaga)" (My name [I am the son of Lady Gaga]). The episode tells, in great and pseudo-scientific detail, the story of Germán's name as pronounced and understood in English (German=from Germany) and how, in the end, he discovered that he is the lost son of Lady Gaga (his full name can be seen as an acronym of the singer's name: Gaga), and thus has managed to extract money from her. This installment, with more than 14 million views as of April 2021, functions because throughout this fast-paced display of funny Internet logic, based mostly on quick searches on Wikipedia, Germán manages to be both very professional in his performance and final product, and very down-to-earth in his asides, commenting on the main action, as if he were a one-man classic theater company, both performing and making fun of the play at the same time. The overall result, then, is that of a carefully produced authenticity and reality. What I referred to above as high-quality everydayness belongs to the user-generated ethos presiding over HSG: the idea is that Germán will act with great talent but always keep a strong connection with the real here-and-now of the viewer, suggesting that, even as a famous YouTuber, he remains a commoner; the video will be less a fully immersive experience than a hybrid and hyper-self-conscious performance of communication with a wink—perhaps what one could call the real as staged or entertainment as non- or semi-fiction. Garmendia confirmed this point in an interview with Chilean national TV (TVN) by saying he does not like to give interviews to print or TV-based journalists because he likes the idea that his viewers see him when and if they want to (the logic and function of YouTube as a platform), as opposed to the logic of unilateral broadcasting that imposes content on viewers who may or may not be ready for it. (TVN)

Situated as a "boundary object" (Hunter et al. 13–14) at the intersection of formal and informal economies, HSG highlights a series of features of information and immaterial labor-based capitalism. At the economic level, it is located at the point of contact of two models of content production, the legacy or traditional model and the user-generated content model (UGC); at the sociocultural level, it marks the point of penetration of the logic of cultural production of the self—as in producing the self as if it were a media production through a series of public and semi-public expedient self-presentations, of which selfies are the most obvious variety—by the political economy of the individualizing and privatizing logic of neoliberalism. At the political level, it announces the internalization of forms of self-exploitation, profitability, and interest, and the blurring of what is private and political, commercial or amateur, participation or exploitation, leisure or work.

HSG, while a series in a global company like YouTube, also confirms that, for verbally based humor, language itself represents a certain limitation or frictional space to globalization and the open space of possibility for more targeted audience creation within the cultural sphere of that language. By the same token, the evolution, or rather the neutralization, of Germán's Chilean accent confirms that even within the specificity of a language-based audience there is a space for globally oriented growth within a world-region.

Rethinking media imperialism theories in the late 1980s, Joseph D. Straubhaar ("Beyond Media Imperialism"; *World Television*) developed, for communication studies, what has been called the cultural proximity theory to explain why Latin American societies were producing and consuming more and more national and regional Latin American TV amid the expansion of metropolitan media around the globe. It proposes that Latin American audiences were attracted by the cultural relevance, familiarity, and comprehensibility of nationally or regionally produced TV. Cultural proximity, always mediated by technology, had two levels: the national, and the Latin American regional. Also studying Latin American TV since the 1990s, John Sinclair has proposed the complementary idea of Latin America as the paradigmatic geolinguistic region functioning as global space: "[A] geolinguistic region is defined not necessarily by its geographical contours, but more in a virtual sense, by commonalities of language and culture [often] . . . established by historical relations of colonization" (Sinclair 130).

Straubhaar's ideas about cultural proximity and Sinclair's on geolinguistic regions could be said to imply a form of natural market protection against external competition from more developed industrial actors in national and regional markets. I have elsewhere explained what I called the vernacular advantage or the advantage of the vernacular in the case of Latin American film comedies, which from the 1930s to the 1950s constituted the basis of a veritable import-substitution phenomenon in relation to Hollywood in the region (Poblete 7). The idea is that film comedies are one area in which the national product can compete with Hollywood on a much more level field than in almost any other film genre. That which in big historical dramas, action movies, or science fiction films sometimes manifests as the poverty of production values in Latin American films (at least from the viewpoint of hegemonic cinema) is compensated for, perhaps with an advantage, when it comes to comedies. In this genre, the settings are often simple, the actors are frequently already well known nationally for their work in similar comedic national radio or TV shows, and a significant portion of the primary material is itself the national situation and the national language, that is, something that Hollywood can do best only for the American context.

I propose that, like Latin American comedies, HSG has enjoyed a similar advantage, and for similar reasons. To which one should add the technological development represented by the expansion of the Internet, which has made possible a relatively sustainable explosion of platforms for regionally circulating audiovisual productions. In the case of HSG, cultural proximity, or more precisely the double (linguistic and cultural) advantage of the vernacular, has been a plus, constituting its condition of possibility.

The world-regional form of globalization HSG embodies could then be said to be the direct manifestation of the combined effect of these traits: proximity, authenticity, the new mediated realism of everydayness, tapping into the commons of language and affects, co-construction of meaning, and deepening co-production of subjectivity and capitalism.

The Use and Production of Authenticity for a Media-Infused Generation

To understand how this mix works, we need to explore the fundamental role of authenticity as a direct complement to and consequence of the new mediated realism of everydayness. On one level, HSG, insofar as it is a series on a platform like YouTube, embodies the heightened capacity of information-based capitalism to penetrate and exploit the everyday life of its users/consumers. On another, however, what HSG models is a kind of social media and entertainment hybrid capable of producing an experience of authenticity, proximity, and co-participation for the user/spectator: all takes place as if the fun were being produced by me and people like me, on a scale that suits me and within a temporality I control.

In this latter regard, Cunningham and Craig speak of the "three irreducible characteristics of SME":

The first is that the claims to authenticity that animate native SME content are established through comparisons with the presumed inauthenticity of established fictional screen formats. The second is that the distinctive mode of address of SME is constituted in the relationship *between* discourses of authenticity and community. The third is that there is a discursive logic that attempts to render brand relationships subordinate to the dominant discourses of authenticity and community. (154)

That transmitted affective experience of directness, closeness, and immediacy is, in fact, the result of what we could call carefully curated authenticity, and it is fundamental to the business and communicational model of SME. Key to authenticity itself is the self-presentation of the vlogger—in this case, Germán Garmendia himself.

According to Cunningham and Craig, "The hard to define personality of the vlogger operates at the business and cultural center of this new screen ecology" (13). First, the vlogger is a good example of the contraction of previously specialized roles in the ecology of legacy media (such as director, producer, scriptwriter, etc.) into one person endowed with both a great degree of responsibility and very high levels of agency. Instead of judging vloggers according to the criteria of that higher specialization in traditional media creation, one ought to pay attention to what is new in the vlogger: "[T]hese creators have built a media brand based upon their personalities and through the intensely normative discourses of authenticity around vlogging" (Cunningham and Craig 13). Cunningham and Craig further expand on this last by talking about "the mediated authenticity of online vlogging" (13), and point out that the vloggers depend on "a level of interactivity and viewer- and audience-centricity that is radically distinctive in screen history" (13). Fan engagement is not simply a PR move, but instead "what triggers the revenue-sharing business model that replaces IP control" (Cunningham and Craig 14). In other words, the cultivation of a fan base, of a community of viewers, is integral to the monetization agreement that allows the vlogger to provide their content for free to the audience, while also providing for the commercial exploitation of those viewers' attention by the platform (YouTube). For this model to work, there had to be technological conditions (the emergence of social media and content platforms in particular), social conditions (the vast popularity of those social media and platforms), and legal conditions (the US Digital Millennium Copyright Act of 1998) that allowed platforms and social media "'safe harbor' provisions for online service providers . . . against copyright infringement liability, provided they responsively block access to alleged infringing material on receipt of infringement claims from a rights holder" (Cunningham and Craig 15). In other words, the act allowed platforms the right to claim neutrality when their users, in their effort to generate new content, used popular culture content of all kinds (music, films, photos, text, etc.) that sometimes infringed upon IP rights.

YouTube, then, was able to become a place in which the new capitalism of social entertainment and media meet the counterculture of DIY—post what you want as if it were, un-mediatedly, a site on which what is most profitable joins what is most personal, that is, ourselves. This carefully curated and mediated self is so crucial that P. David Marshall and his collaborators have made it central to their proposal of Persona Studies in a book by that name.

> To capture this constructed, fabricated, produced, and presented public self that goes beyond our past notions of a public personality or celebrity and becomes an elemental part of literally billions of people worldwide we were drawn to a word and concept. . . . The idea of persona best articulates this new technologically mediated but naturalized identity that we inhabit individually and collectively. (2)

This persona is something we all engage in to different degrees when, to paraphrase Ervin Goffman, we present ourselves in everyday life through social media. This involves a new relation and "interplay between the understanding of public and private" (Marshall et al. 4), and, in fact, a new parsing of what used to be the clear space separating the private from the public. Through the new media, "[w]e can see the manner in which the intimate, the private, the quasi-public, and the micro-public of friends develops" (Marshall et al. 5). In other words, we can see how private/public, rather than the opposition of two fundamental and fundamentally different ontological forms of the social, become the tail ends of a continuum that increasingly connects their modes of social existence.

This new context is defined by what Marshall et al. call their version of mediatization: "Our particular application of mediatization is to express how the formation of the contemporary self is now constructed and displayed through technologies and forms of expression that resemble media forms" (2). Through social media, "playing games, texting, teleconferencing, video streaming and participating in Twitter, YouTube, Tumblr, Flickr, Pinterest, WeChat, and Reddit and a host of other forms of connecting and communicating with others" (Marshall et al. 2), those of us who participate generate elaborate versions of ourselves. The result is something that requires another new concept: intercommunication, which Marshall et al. define as "the blending of media and communication as well as the highly mediated blending of different types of interpersonal communication" (2).

"Ex parejas" (Exes), a video uploaded in October 2011 and seen by more than nine million viewers, is a good example of the functioning of persona and mediatization as key concepts in SME. In it, Germán talks about ex-lovers and what happens when you see them somewhere. For our purposes here, it is enough to highlight how Germán develops a typology of reactions and then a set of practical tips on how to behave in such a situation: you must learn to act indifferently, you must engage in seeming attracted, immediately and evidently, to any other woman near you, you must be able to notice something in your ex's current physical appearance that justifies the breakup. "One of the biggest risks," continues Germán, "is to see her Facebook profile and current status." If nothing has happened and she continues to show the same Facebook self, then there is no problem. But if she has changed her profile picture and her status talks about her new self, transformed by embracing some new philosophy, then you are in trouble. Some of these troubles seem to stem, indeed, from the fact that many young people now may know the online social codes better than they do the off-line ones, as in "Conocidos, amigos y más que amigos" (Acquaintances, friends, and more than friends) (uploaded on November 19, 2011):

> [A]t this point to communicate is already significantly different from what it once was. And many times, this may not be good. For example, who hasn't had *this* experience with someone? You meet a person with whom you spent all day chatting online, she is interesting, you have many things in common, but when you talk to that person face to face . . . [you have nothing to say to each other].

As Germán says in "La Realidad" (Reality, uploaded on June 11, 2012), "reality stinks," and it does so mostly because of the distance between our mediatized perceptions of how reality is—or, more precisely, how we expect it to be, based on the media models we have frequently consumed—and how it really is. In this context, our expectations are always disappointed by the reality we should be able to attack in the street, which is what the video recommends. In its own humor-based way, HSG is reflecting on the depth of what Couldry and Hepp, in their understanding of mediatization as an analytical category of a materialist phenomenology of the present, call "the interrelatedness" of the "material as well as the symbolic aspects of everyday practices," that is, how we must "consider media both as technologies including infrastructures *and* as processes of sense-making" (5).

The lessons in HSG are delivered with plenty of meta-critical comments about acting, reacting, showing or not showing your emotions, checking social media and finding new information about others that can help your damaged or fragile self, and multiple dramatizations of feelings and labels about types of video scenes ("video dramático") and physical descriptions of the current screen to publicize the spaces where Germán promotes his band, which provides the background music for his videos. The example clearly showcases the dual curated and media-formatted nature of subjectivity now, on and off-line. It also shows what the components of this type of short-video humor on the Internet are: the self is mediated and curated in social media that are both vehicles of self-expression and learning and quick spaces of recreation capable of seamlessly combining authenticity (self-deprecation) and self-promotion on a platform designed for the commercial and non-commercial exploitation of that purpose. Humor is the combined result of these multiple processes of self-formation and expression, analyzed meta-critically as media formats or genres (see also "¡Hollywood exagera!") through strategies that mix making oneself and others the butt of the joke.

There are throughout the series some indications of what the intended audience of this media-savvy form of humor is, and, given the degree of its professionalization, what its actual audience may look like. In "Los Saludos" (Greetings), uploaded on March 17, 2012, and with 9.4 million views by 2021, Germán announces that he will begin uploading his weekly videos on Friday: "I don't know why, but I imagine that for you [the viewers] it would be better to get out of high school on the last day of classes of the week, open YouTube, and bang! A new video, I kind of think. . . ." "Infancia" (Childhood, May 2012) is another good example of what is generational in HSG. Germán is mostly addressing an audience that is his age—people who were born around 1985 and who share a number of memories and experiences, many of which are nostalgically referred to in this episode. He is also doing the informal history of a generational relationship with increasingly sophisticated media and the way they are imbricated in the formation of affect and subjectivity for that generation and those who have come later. This history of playable media and social media as a nostalgia and humor-based strategy of reconstructing the self, infused with the new logic of lists being produced at the time through social media, works extraordinarily well for those who are in this age group. This is proven by the more than 30 million views the video had by 2021—an impressive number even for HSG's level of popularity.

During "Los Saludos," Germán also asks its viewers what social media platform they would save if they could only save one. His answer is Facebook. The

reason is simple, he says: "[B]ecause even though it may be the least entertaining, it is the most useful. After all, it is the social medium through which
I keep my contact with you [the viewers]." In "Celos" he confirms, now in a
negative way, the impact of Facebook as a social medium: "The best ally of
jealousy is Facebook. It has been breaking up relationships since 2004. Have
you ever wondered why couples of the past lasted forever? Because they didn't
have Facebook."

One important component of the functioning of authenticity in the construction of the Germán persona is its fundamentally pedagogical nature.
Like many humorists, Garmendia often uses his art to reflect on and discuss
life and its lessons. As someone who became extraordinarily popular and
commercially successful in his early twenties, Germán's natural inclination
was to address the lives of young people. That inclination coincided with his
historically and technologically conditioned natural audience, young people
who were active in what at the time was still a relatively new social medium.
Seen from this angle, it is easy to spot the multiple lessons being frequently
imparted in HSG's videos: the need to be self-critical, to reflect on life, one's
own mistakes, and other people's mistakes, and always to have sympathy for
the generationally defined awkwardness of young people, while laughing at
their defining traits—insecurity, competitiveness, failed early relationships—
through self-mockery. In fact, in a BBC Mundo segment that featured him
and his HSG show, Germán defined his humor as "simple" and "innocent"
and based on the idea of always laughing at oneself first, instead of making
others the butt of the joke. His humor, he continued, was based on a shared
experience: "I think what is funny in my videos is not that I am funny, but
instead that they refer to things we have all experienced," and then they trigger in the audience a memory or an identification process. "I think that is the
trick" ("Germán Garmendia: el chileno").

The pedagogical and psychologically positive bent of the series is made
explicit in what the author calls Germánsejos (Consejos de Germán, i.e., Germán's advice), which are the bulk of his book #Chupaelperro. Uno que otro
consejo:

The only person who can set your limits is you, and protecting your
personality must be a battle you are always willing to engage in. And it
doesn't matter how many times they want to hurt you, nor how many
times they, the damned aggressors of your self-esteem, manage to
knock you down, because you are going to get up . . . and will go on,
feeling proud of who you are, like a true MACHO WITH A WAXED
CHEST! (163)

Predictably, given HSG's status on YouTube, the advice extends to success and happiness in life. Germán formula is a simple and well-known one: sustained effort in pursuit of your dreams and a lot of work to realize them. The life-lesson message and its connection to the vlogging form of authenticity are fully developed in "Tu puedes" (You can, uploaded on April 4, 2014, and seen almost twenty million times by 2021). The video, which is not a regular HSG video but a replacement, begins:

> I have been doing videos on YouTube for over three years now, always with the intention of making you laugh or brightening your day . . . and I have always tried to be as honest as possible with you . . . I want to tell you I am not doing well; in fact, I am not doing well at all. And I don't want to stand here and pretend that nothing is going on to make you laugh when I am not well. . . . But this video is not about "I am not doing well. Feel pity for me." . . . I want to make something [useful] out of my state to give you advice: . . . first point: convince yourself; I think we can all do everything, the only thing you need is motivation, work, and belief in yourself.

In this regard, incidentally, Germán tells in #Chupaelperro the story of how, during an interview on the radio in Colombia, after he had said "how much he enjoys inspiring people to pursue their dreams and telling them that all their dreams are possible if you stop giving yourself excuses and work really hard," the interviewer had remarked "that he [Germán] was in no position to talk about effort since he only worked five minutes a day, since 'my videos only last five minutes'" (132). Germán says he wanted to kill the host on the spot for their ignorance regarding how much effort is involved in the production of a video, and adds:

> To make a HolaSoyGermán takes me approximately twenty to thirty hours. During the first two years of my [YouTube] channel, I could not sleep on Thursday; between taping and editing there was no time for that. . . . I love making videos, but nobody said that because you love doing something, it is going to be easy to do. (#Chupaelperro 133)

Indeed, it is not just the established fictional formats or genres that the SME participant rebels against, it is also the traditional form of cultural consumption that comes with professionally generated content (PGC)—the separation between fiction and cultural consumption on the one hand and "real life" on the other.

Following a format that seems almost mandatory since the arrival of cable TV and even more so now in the age of new SME, Germán Garmendia developed, early on, HolaSoyGermán 2 (HSG2) to include curated rehearsals or bloopers of many of the videos on the main HSG channel. In these videos—such as, for example, "Bloopers: Las ventajas de estar soltero" (The Advantages of Being Single) from December 7, 2011—we gain access to the alleged behind-the-scenes preparations for the video; we are invited to understand how the acting, the script, and the effects are produced, how the whole product is produced. In other words, this "making of" video can itself be a video that can be offered to the public and draw millions of views—3.1 by March 2021. What is being sold is not simply this backstage access; it is, centrally, a new effective point in the continuum of connection between fictional content and real life. The overall effect is one of doubling down—on the commercial exploitability of the spectrum going from the real to the fictional and back in new media entertainment, and on continuity itself in such a spectrum. The main video, whose preparation is said to have produced the bloopers, is itself a very successful and high-quality example of HSG humor, with almost 12 million views. Whether you think this is funny or worrisome will most likely depend on your age and the forms of attention and focus of interest your interactions with the social and technological environment of communication have developed.

Notes

1 Garmendia, full name Germán Alejandro Garmendia Aranis, has also written at least two books: #Chupaelperro. Uno que otro consejo, published in 2016, and Di Hola, published in 2018. In addition to his YouTube channels as a vlogger and gamer, he is a songwriter, musician, and aspiring actor.

2 www.infobae.com/tendencias/2017/03/14/hola-soy-german-el-famoso-youtuber-que -lucha-por-el-medio-ambiente.

3 www.cnbc.com/2019/07/19/more-children-dream-of-being-youtubers-than -astronauts-lego-says.html

4 www.pewresearch.org/internet/2018/05/31/teens-social-media-technology-2018/ pi_2018–05–31_teenstech_0–01/; www.prnewswire.com/news-releases/millennials -turn-to-video-when-making-purchases-says-new-animoto-data-300103094.html

Works Cited

Banet-Weiser, Sarah. *Authentic: The Politics of Ambivalence in a Brand Culture.* NY: New York UP, 2012.

Burgess, Jean. "Digital Media and Generations." *Communication Across the Life Span,* edited by Jon F. Nussbaum, Washington, D.C.: International Communication Association, 2016, pp. 21–26.

Burgess, Jean, and Joshua Green. *YouTube: Online Video and Participatory Culture.* 2nd ed., Cambridge, UK; Malden, MA: Polity Press, 2018.

Couldry, Nick, and Andres Hepp. *The Mediated Construction of Reality.* Cambridge, UK; Malden, MA: Polity Press, 2017.

Cunningham, Stuart, and David Craig. *Social Media Entertainment: The New Intersection of Hollywood and Silicon Valley.* NY: New York UP, 2019.

Exford, Ace. "History of YouTube." www.engadget.com/2016-11-10-the-history-of -YouTube.html.

Friedman, Elizabeth J. *Interpreting the Internet: Feminist and Queer Counterpublics in Latin America.* NY: New York UP, 2017.

Fuchs, Christian. *Social Media: A Critical Introduction.* Thousand Oaks, CA: Sage, 2014.

Garmendia, Germán. *#Chupaelperro–Y uno que otro consejo, para que no te pase lo que a un amigo.* Madrid: Alfaguara, 2016.

———. *Di Hola.* Barcelona: Planeta, 2018.

"Germán Garmendia: el chileno que arrasa en YouTube con HolaSoyGermán." *YouTube,* uploaded by BBC News Mundo, 21 Aug. 2013, www.youtube.com/watch?v= Q9P17LqkVRM.

"Google Grows Up." *The Economist,* 1 Aug. 2020, pp. 14–17.

"'Hola soy Germán': el famoso youtuber que lucha por el medio ambiente." *Infobae,* 14 Mar. 2017, https://www.infobae.com/tendencias/2017/03/14/hola-soy-german-el-famoso -youtuber-que-lucha-por-el-medio-ambiente/.

Hunter, Dan et al. *Amateur Media: Social, Cultural, and Legal Perspectives.* NY: Routledge, 2013.

Jenkins, Henry, et al. *Participatory Culture in a Networked Era: A Conversation on Youth, Learning, Commerce, and Politics.* Cambridge, UK; Malden, MA: Polity, 2015.

Marshall, P. David, et al. *Persona Studies: An Introduction.* Hoboken, NJ: Wiley Blackwell, 2020.

Poblete, Juan. "Introduction: Cinema and Humor in Latin America." *Latin American Film and Humor,* edited by Juan Poblete and Juana Suárez, London: Palgrave, 2015, pp. 1–28.

Sinclair, John. "Geolinguistic Region as Global Space: The Case of Latin America." *The Television Studies Reader,* edited by Robert C. Allen and Annette Hill, NY: Routledge, 2004, pp. 130–138.

Straubhaar, Joseph D. "Beyond Media Imperialism: Asymmetrical Interdependence and Cultural Proximity." *Critical Studies in Mass Communication,* vol. 8, no. 1, 1991, pp. 1–11.

———. *World Television: From Global to Local.* Thousand Oaks, CA: Sage, 2007.

TVN. "Hola Soy Germán habla en Informe Especial TVN." *YouTube,* uploaded by 24 Horas–TVN Chile, 24 July 2015, www.youtube.com/watch?v=gFSGHYfblkk.

Väliaho, Pasi. *Biopolitical Screens: Image, Power, and the Neoliberal Brain.* Cambridge, MA: MIT Press, 2014.

Van Dijck, José. *The Culture of Connectivity: A Critical History of Social Media.* Oxford, UK: Oxford UP, 2013.

11

La Pulla

Humor as an Instrument of Intranational Hegemony

HÉCTOR FERNÁNDEZ L'HOESTE

Launched in 2016—its first video is from April 6 of that year—out of *El Espectador*, Colombia's oldest newspaper, *La Pulla* (the taunt) is a YouTube-based satirical video blog initially operated by five journalists: María Paulina Baena, Juan Carlos Rincón, Daniel Salgar, Santiago La Rotta, and Juan David Torres. In due time, the roster expanded to include research assistants like Lina Alonso, Cindy Bautista, Daniela Córdoba, Tatiana Peláez, and Jairo Perilla (Roldán Rueda; Russell). Many people comprise *La Pulla*, but Baena and Rincón are the two visible faces on the videos uploaded regularly to YouTube—aside from serving as scriptwriters (Martínez Sánchez). Though it currently operates as a startup—with the support of entities like George Soros's Open Society Foundations or the Friedrich Ebert Foundation (Martinez)—*La Pulla* remains housed in the newspaper. At the time of writing, it has uploaded 397 videos to YouTube, the vast majority of which focus on the world of Colombian politics from a caustic perspective, though the team occasionally dabbles in Latin American and world politics and cultural affairs. Each of the videos, which appear at a rate of 1.12 per week,[1] tends to be less than 10 minutes long—although they have grown longer as time has gone by—but, according to Social Blade, they have accumulated over 164 million views, 1.32 million subscribers, and yearly earnings of up to $30,000 (Social Blade, "La Pulla"). Their style of humor highlights cultural and political commentary in a direct, no-holds-barred way that is evocative of US comedians Stephen Colbert and John Oliver, based on the sharing of information compiled by a research journalism team with a provocative bent (A. L. González).

From the start, given the language of two anchors who rely firmly on contemporary Bogotano slang, *La Pulla* was designed to appeal to millennials and Gen-Zers (Martinez), feeding on widespread discontent with and alienation from Colombia's political class. Juan Carlos Rincón Escalante was born in Cúcuta, the capital of the Andean department of North Santander, which borders Venezuela, in 1991; strictly speaking, he is not a Bogotano. He holds an MA in Legal Research from the Universidad de los Andes in Bogotá but works as a journalist. In addition to *La Pulla,* through *El Espectador,* he is linked to initiatives like Las Igualadas (on YouTube) and La Puesverdad (on Instagram). He also teaches opinion journalism at the Universidad Javeriana, the alma mater of his sidekick María Paulina Baena (also born in 1991), who holds journalism and political science degrees. In Baena's case, her professional practice is inextricably linked to her academic background. In 2022, she was one of the five winners of the One Young World Journalist Award, presented at Manchester's One Young World Summit. As part of the journalistic team, both Baena and Rincón enact intense, opinionated personalities that rant on many matters.

Thanks to its hard-hitting style, *La Pulla* earned the Simón Bolívar National Prize for Journalism in 2016, its first year of operation. Its online personae regularly channel national rage on a variety of topics: corruption, the excesses of both the left and the right, homophobia, lack of access to safe abortion and/or same-sex adoption, widespread violence and insecurity, etc. As part of its national coverage, *La Pulla* runs specials titled *La Pulla Regional*—13 in all, when videos were examined—in which it lambastes the excesses of many a provincial political dynasty. My argument is not that these videos represent a majority of the *La Pulla* productions—they do not—but that, in them, it is easier to see the distorted manner in which the *La Pulla* team approaches the country, which is also visible in other *La Pulla* videos, though to a more concealed and/or internalized extent. *La Pulla* labels "regional" a selection of videos that, for all practical purposes, is more representative of Colombia's national geography than its habitual work, usually focused on the national government based in Bogotá. Thus, *La Pulla* calls "regional" what is national and presents as "national" what is, for all practical purposes, local/regional to their location. While the humor in *La Pulla Regional* brings their approach into the open—given the effort to empathize with provincial locations—this particular type of humor underlies most, if not all, of the videos *La Pulla* has posted. Making ample use of colloquial expressions and a brazen display of *colombianidad*—a look at any of its videos will confirm this—its humor is remarkably effective yet at the same time extraordinarily regressive. On one hand, it mocks corruption; on the other, it substantiates the unequal order that benefits the team of journalists. On one end, it chastises Colombia for being a provincial and conservative country; on the other, it fails to admit how its privilege resides in the undercurrents of a capital-city-based elite that refuses to change or relinquish its position as guardian of national impera-tives. People get a kick out of how Baena and Rincón make fun of political bosses and accompanying sycophants, yet the laughter does not invite audi-ences to reflect critically on the setting's bearing on the team's point of view. Though the videos make valid points, Baena and Rincón fail to acknowledge the team's complicity in countrywide exclusionary dynamics, ratifying cen-tralism, regional stereotyping, and societal disparity. In other words, in the construction of its comedic subject, there is no inkling of an effort on the part of *La Pulla* to favor a more inclusive, all-encompassing denunciation of politi-cal corruption, acknowledging a role in inequitable politics while attempting to reflect the viewpoint of a bigger, younger nation, well beyond the voice of two personalities who every day sound increasingly detached from Colom-bia's dissent, thanks to their cushy upper-middle-class slang.

In the following paragraphs, I will explain how the humor deployed by *La Pulla* depicts the nation in videos, relying heavily on the construct of a "country of regions." This is a notion that, while internalized by most Co-lombians, is mainly the result of theorization by Andean elites from the late nineteenth century to the mid-twentieth century. When Colombians speak of regions proudly, they are reaffirming constructs based on generalizations and stereotypes designed to condone racialization. While *La Pulla* under-mines the national character of peripheral locations through its affirmation of regionalism—emphasizing the state rather than the nation—and by gain-ing the sympathy and support of provincial audiences, it contributes to the hegemonization of the population from a centralist perspective. I will discuss the videos regarding different locations around Colombia as well as responses from subscribers and fans, ultimately offering a practical counterexample.

Region, Humor, Class

Regionalism plays a preponderant role in the enactment of Colombian identi-ties, occasionally operating as a smaller-scale nationalism. In his volume for the Federal Research Division of the Library of Congress, Rex Hudson de-scribes Colombia as follows: "As a country of five distinct mainland geograph-ic regions, Colombia is, not surprisingly, highly regionalist. . . . Even with rap-id urbanization and modernization, regionalism and regional identification continue to be important reference points" (Hudson 93). Given the country's rugged topography, with shores on two oceans and three snow-capped mountain ranges crossing the national geography that thus prevented reliable communication via a highway network for decades, it is no surprise that regional affiliation is more marked in Colombia than in most Latin American nations.

This has implications for how the nation is imagined. In *Muddied Waters*, her critique of race and region in the history of Colombia from 1846 to 1948, Nancy Appelbaum correctly points out how the idea of a "country of regions" is "a spatial manifestation of a view of modernity that associates national progress with racial whitening and homogeneity" (Appelbaum 27). In this way, the racially mixed inhabitants at lower altitudes, with warmer climates, were associated with barbarism, while the whitened mestizo population of the mountains was linked to civilization. In plain terms, the notion of a "country of regions" that emerged in the nineteenth century contributed to the racialization of the population, favoring an order benefiting the Andean elites. Thus, when Colombians speak of regions and define themselves in terms of a regional construct, to a great extent they legitimize constructs based on the denial of a racially plural nation.

In 1991, thanks to the writing of a new constitution that celebrates the plural nature of Colombia's population, this notion was turned on its head— for the most part. In *Region e historia*, the volume that summarizes his role as Secretary-General of the Commission of Territorial Ordering, the body with responsibility for proposing geopolitical categories in the spirit of the 1991 Magna Carta, researcher and sociologist Orlando Fals Borda describes how part of his goal was to update the legal framework of Colombian geopolitics so departments and municipalities could unite themselves formally as regions and provinces in a way that would benefit them economically and politically, effectively co-opting constructs that for decades had worked against them and supported the centralization of government and power (Fals Borda 1996). In this way, internalized constructs that worked against provincial interests as the result of the Andean cultural establishment's stranglehold on national identity would finally favor them.

For decades, Bogotanos have operated under the notion that the presence of people from all over the country in their city means it is representative of the integration of populations from peripheral regions neglected by the central government, disregarding the distinct locations left behind (Gill). A look at the Colombian government's travel website's information on Bogotá attests to this fact, with claims like "Here, there is room for all cultures from all regions, from the gastronomy of the coffee region to the happiness of the Caribbean region, going through the artisanal legacy of Boyacá and the party spirit of the Valle del Cauca. The capital is the union of the best there is in Colombia and therefore a place you should know" (my translation, "Historia y modernidad"). In a place as geo-culturally fragmented as Colombia, this lack of self-awareness of the misinterpretation of the capital city's demographic multiculturalism (the people from all over the country living in Bogotá, now including many Venezuelans) as proof of acceptance of regional diversity (the people from all over the country who actually live all over the country) allows *La Pulla* to abet historic injustice, ultimately authenticating Bogotá's brand of humor as the decisive arbiter in the normative application and interpretation of local identity paradigms. In customary Bogo-centric fashion, *La Pulla* keeps mistaking the capital for the country, appropriating the right to name others (Gestión Digital; Perdomo Alaba). If this were the intentional target of its humor, it would be inordinately effective. Nonetheless, this breach is not only involuntary but also unacknowledged.

In *Humour,* British literary theoretician Terry Eagleton advances a lucid exploration of the role of humor in everyday life. Eagleton glosses over several popular theories on humor, all discussed more extensively in Christopher Wilson's *Jokes: Form, Content, Use and Function.* In the case of *La Pulla,* there are two theories discussed by Eagleton that are pertinent: one is the release theory, which goes back to the understanding of humor as a form of relief (Eagleton 10), as a way of releasing pent-up emotional energy; the other relates to superiority, which hints at "personal gratification emerging from someone else's frailty, obtuseness, or absurdity" (Eagleton 36). In *La Pulla,* it is possible to recognize a practice combining both, as the relief resulting from the denunciation of the excesses of Colombia's political class is accompanied regularly by the sense of moral superiority of the team behind these accusations, given its holier-than-thou attitude. The fact that the accusers fail to apply to themselves the same level of critical verve that they use against their targets certainly does not help. Colombians are traditionally aghast at the antics of their political class, so outrageous revelations are better handled with humor than with a somber tone—thus the sense of relief emanating from the woeful sharing of information. Humor has made life manageable for many Colombians through the years (Medina Cartagena; Oviedo), so to evince its potential as a measure to relieve the stress borne from living in a country engulfed in a civil conflict for over fifty years is not exactly surprising (Bejarano González).

On the other hand, the centralist nature of the project of nation supported by the constitution that prevailed until 1991 contributed to Bogotá's establishment not viewing itself in the same light as the rest of the country. Eagleton's arguments are helpful in this respect. It is important to point out how, to the British critic, taunting and humor are premised on a lack of hierarchy. When Eagleton alludes to "the frank mockery and praise, dethroning and

244 · Héctor Fernández L'Hoeste

exaltation, and irony and dithyramb" (157) in Bakhtin's notion of carnival, he also clarifies that "there is no question of superiority in its scoldings, not least since there are no spectators in the sphere of carnival to condescend to its participants" (157). Instead, he adds, "It is humanity itself that is on stage, a stage that is coextensive with the auditorium" (157–158). And so a distinction becomes apparent: when Bakhtin suggests that "'The satirist whose laughter is negative places himself above the object of his mockery'" (qtd. in Eagleton 12), it is because, to Eagleton, this underscores the fact that "at carnival time the populace taunt themselves, as subjects and objects of satire in a single body" (158). The verb points directly at the lack of egalitarian spirit in the practice of *La Pulla* (the taunt), which fails to build a position at the same level as its audience, revealing a disparity in enunciation characteristic of Colombian idiosyncrasy, time after time bent on class ethnocentrism.

From the manner of their enunciation—their antagonistic tone, pontificating language, and defiant pose before the camera ("Nos emberracamos")—it is plain that, as anchor people for *La Pulla*, Baena and Rincón fail to imagine and understand themselves at the same level as their viewers; they address their audience authoritatively, never from a lower angle. In this sense, Eagleton's critique fits them to a tee. If lack of hierarchy is a condition for the successful celebration of carnivalesque humor, *La Pulla* fails miserably. Nonetheless, there are alternative ways to enact humor. Chief among them is the superiority theory, suitable for an existence premised on the sense of inequity emanating from class differences. This attitude is not uncommon in Colombia. This is not just Baena and Rincón at work, but a good part of Colombian society. According to the World Bank, Colombia has one of the highest levels of income inequality in the world, the second-highest among 18 countries in Latin America and the Caribbean (LAC), and the highest among all OECD countries ("Building an Equitable Society"). Inequality of this caliber can only be possible in a thoroughly hierarchical society. Gustavo Petro's interest in the creation of a Ministry of Equality denotes a concern for Colombian society's failure to imagine and materialize conditions of equality when compared to other Latin American countries with lower Gini coefficients ("Gini"; "Gustavo Petro dio"; Palomino).

The Internet is packed with videos of Colombian citizens who, at the point of facing shame for some misdeed, immediately resort to the line "Ud. no sabe quién soy yo" (You do not know who I am), bringing into play their hypothetically higher socioeconomic status (Peña Castañeda). Names like Nicolás Gaviria, Melissa Bermúdez, or Hernando Zabaleta Echeverry, all virtual nobodies who wielded the hackneyed catchphrase only to be caught on video, are familiar among Colombians. The behavior is so common that in

2016 a Colombian film was released with the phrase as its title, with the main character (Ricardo Quevedo) trying to conquer a woman with lies about his social status. Classism prevails in Colombia, so humor premised on a lack of hierarchy, as preached by Eagleton or Bakhtin, is unlikely. In Colombia, class stratification is built into the way people speak and express themselves (Pardo, "Qué son"). Thus, when Baena and Rincón resort to the linguistic twists and turns of their age group and social milieu, for all practical purposes, they are reinforcing the sense of exclusion of many people. The mechanisms upon which this sense of exclusion operates are so prevalent in Colombian culture and society that a large segment of the population, personified by the many followers who celebrate and consent to the value of the work done by *La Pulla*, has espoused them.

A more practical explanation comes in handy. Thirty years ago, the government decided that every single utility bill should be identified with a number describing the value of a property. Conceived as the way to bring access to utilities to the entire population, instead social stratification according to government guidelines became pervasive. With utility bills marked according to the value of the property, determining who should pay more or less would be easier, went the idea, with people from more affluent neighborhoods subsidizing the cost of bringing services to less well-off vicinities (Pardo, "Protestas"; Pardo, "Qué son"). In due time, this numerical system permeated the culture. Unforeseen by the government, class stratification in utility bills resulted in people being described as de estrato uno, dos, tres, cuatro, cinco, or seis (stratum one, two, etc.), rather than as working, middle, or upper class (Wallace, "Estrato 1"). Thus, the national classist mindset operates as a hindrance even at the moment of revealing corruption to "fellow" nationals. When Baena and Rincón mock corrupt politicians, the way they speak and even the events and things that they allude to belong to a strongly class-determined repertoire that, rather than promoting humor based on inclusion, promotes laughter by substantiating inequity—class-wise, geographically, regionally, etc. This, I maintain, is another reason why Baena and Rincón are not able to address or relate to their audience as equals. Their humor works, but not on the more general basis celebrated by Eagleton (release through a carnival, with social barriers tending to disappear). Rather, theirs is humor firmly reliant on sarcasm and superiority. When the team at *La Pulla* lectures its audience, it bears class disparity in the back of its mind, whether it likes it or not.[2]

It is through the conjugation of the two mentioned aspects of humor and the sanctioning of the notion of "a country of regions" that I suggest *La Pulla* operates. On the whole, what I contend is that, as a practice supportive of the dynamics of intranational hegemony, *La Pulla*'s type of humor is founded

theoretically—be it through Eagleton, Bahktin, or Wilson—on the conjugation of reprieve and preeminence. First, through its many assessments of Colombian political reality, which tend to rely on exposure of corruption with a
mixture of disbelief and disdain, La Pulla builds on a notion of humor rooted
in the astonishment resulting from the excesses of Colombia's political class.
In this way, La Pulla serves as a safety valve for the stress resulting from an environment in which dishonesty appears to spread rampantly and unchecked.
Second, La Pulla also works within the framework of the superiority theory,
as even when it operates beyond its "regional" scheme, it tends to criticize
politicians from the provinces rather than focus on Bogotá's ruling political
class and/or cronies, substantiating the notion that the capital city is, more
than topographically, on higher ground.[3] This happens by way of imagery—
the graphics and scenes in videos—and language—the nicknames and slang
embraced to designate people from one or another place.

On top of this, when La Pulla does embrace its "regional" version, it becomes plain that Baena and Rincón do not regard provincials as equals. If La
Pulla covers stories from any location other than Bogotá, the videos racialize the population from the perspective of a mestizo melting pot, endors-
ing the notion of a "country of regions." In other words, when the broadcast
pertains to national coverage, they defend a hegemonic discourse, embracing
their YouTube videos as a technology of colonialism (Appelbaum 15). In this
respect, Appelbaum asserts, "the geographical categories through which Colombians located themselves within the national community were racialized,
and racial prejudices and inequalities were thus inscribed in the spatial ordering of the emerging nation-state" (11). By default, then, one can assume that
to the team at La Pulla, "national" only takes place when reporting pertains
exclusively to the central government in Bogotá. While La Pulla appears to
be indicting corruption, what it accomplishes is the validation of the right of
Bogotano culture to articulate the identities of other corners of the country,
in this way preserving the inequality of Colombia's greater body politic, nourished by the centralization of power of any kind.

It is key to note that, habitually, Bogotano voters have tended to vote in a
more progressive fashion than other sectors of the country; think of the city
as supportive of Luis Carlos Galán, Sergio Fajardo, or Gustavo Petro, even
when these figures were not nationally viable—or for that matter, the election of Claudia López, the first openly gay mayor of a Latin American capital.
Historically, election results of this nature have authenticated Bogotá's more
open-minded self-image. Thus, what may appear funny to Bogotanos is not
precisely what may appear funny to more conservative elements in the provinces, even among intended audiences. And so, while election results may

be employed to argue that much of what is wrong with the country's political class tends to come from the periphery, even though Colombia's political system has operated for over one hundred years within the tenets of rigid centralism—with Bogotá at its heart—the challenge supposedly remains in breaching the cultural gap that remains between the more hypothetically progressive leanings of the capital and the less affirmative sectors of the provincial bourgeoisie. This is not an easy task for humor, but YouTube numbers attest to the effectiveness of *La Pulla's* proposal. Baena and Rincón make fun of politicians; of their wasteful spending, which appears déclassé, vaguely reminiscent of the nouveau riche lifestyles of drug kingpins; and of how they forsake the population, ratifying the impact of difference substantiated by *estratos* (strata) in an almost brotherly spirit, rooted in theoretical class solidarity. When they embrace humor as a tool for building consensus, in truth, they are contributing to a growing sense of intranational hegemony—that is, underwriting how a medium from the capital manages to reinforce the notion that the city is, for all intents and purposes, the legitimate champion of the political interests of the entire nation.

On *La Pulla's* Videos

To explain how *La Pulla's* humor is complicit with the enactment of intranational hegemony, a look at their videos is in order. Two of the most recent presidencies (Álvaro Uribe Vélez [2002–2010] and Iván Duque Márquez [2018–2022]) have been led by individuals from Medellín, in the department of Antioquia, a place that, in terms of social investment and progressivism as well as in political conservatism, repression, and violence, has rivaled the central administration—to the point of occasionally brandishing the slogan "Antioquia federal," recalling the time of the 1863 constitution (when the country went by the name of the United States of Colombia). The depiction of Antioqueño culture and language in *La Pulla's* videos relies on customary tropes of caricaturization, like the imitation of the *paisa* accent, the local Antioqueño dialect; a persistent reference to *arepas,* or corn patties, a staple of the region; or quasi-comical allusions to Uribe's penchants (the *carriel,* a peasant briefcase; the lighter, local version of a poncho; or his daily homeopathic drops of valerian to combat stress)(*La Pulla,* "CUIDADO").

As mentioned, even when it speaks of the central government, *La Pulla* accompanies this with its views of the periphery. Its construct of Duque is firmly tinted by his connection to Uribe, underlining the Antioqueño—hence outsider—nature of both politicians. *La Pulla* includes videos on the scandal of "Ñeñe" Hernández, a drug trafficker from the Costeño department of Cesar, who purportedly died while being mugged in Brazil and was linked to both presidents, clarifying the extent of their connection (*La Pulla*, "Por esto tienen miedo"); the political situation in Antioquia, with special emphasis on Uribe, bent on coercing justice so it decides in his favor, demonizing his political rivals, and supporting violence as the only way to bring peace to the nation (*La Pulla*, "Uribe, FICO"); how Duque gradually, but autocratically and continuously, placed friends in key posts in government, including the office of attorney general, so things also evolved in his favor (*La Pulla*, "Las artimañas"); and a detailed account—decision per decision—of his failed policies, resulting in disastrous government (*La Pulla*, "Así funciona"). The last two of these segments, at the beginning and end of the video, include well-known excerpts featuring Vice President Marta Lucía Ramírez's infamous snafu, pronouncing Uribe's name instead of Duque's when referring to the president; Duque introducing Uribe as "el Presidente Uribe," when in Colombia it is not customary for former government officers to retain their title, as it is in the United States; and Duque's original minister of justice, Gloria María Borrero—she resigned after nine months—also confusing the names amid her participation in a seminar at the Colombian College of Barristers. In this way, it becomes clear that *La Pulla*'s parodic tendency to constantly mistake one president for the other is excused by reality.

The almost mandatory alternative to Antioqueño protagonism is Bogotano Juan Manuel Santos, president from 2010 to 2018. There was some criticism of the Santos administration, with ties to one of the longest lineages of power in national history—a great-uncle served as president from 1938 to 1942—but, after receiving the 2016 Nobel, Santos opted for an international focus, detaching himself from Colombian affairs. To be fair, a search for Santos on *La Pulla*'s YouTube page will locate only a few videos—seven out of 386, at time of searching—like those titled "Chao SANTOS, cinco cañonazos bailables de su presidencia" (Bye Santos, five hot dance tracks of his presidency) (*La Pulla*, "Chao SANTOS"), "Juan Manuel Santos nos cumplió todas sus promesas" (Juan Manuel Santos fulfilled all his promises) (*La Pulla*, "Juan Manuel Santos"), "Las muertes que no les importan a Duque ni a Santos" (The deaths that do not matter to Duque or Santos) (*La Pulla*, "Las muertes"), "Santos insultado, reinas trans, jugos engañosos y más" (Santos offended, trans queens, deceitful juices, and more) (*La Pulla*, "Santos insultado"), "Santos and Uribe love to play the idiot" (in English in the original) (*La Pulla*, "Santos and Uribe"), and "¿Santos corrupto?, DANE no sabe sumar, Mockus Vuelve [*sic*] y más" (Santos corrupt? DANE does not know how to add, Mockus returns, and more) (*La Pulla*, "¿Santos corrupto?"). Yet what also becomes clear is that during his presidential period the bulk of *La Pulla*'s production focused alternately on FARC (Fuerzas Armadas Revolucionarias de Colombia, or Revolutionary Armed Forces of Colombia) guerrilla leaders, Gustavo Petro, the AIS (Agro Ingreso Seguro) scandal linked to former Minister of Agriculture Andrés Felipe Arias, the scandal of the Ituango dam, the continued presence of Álvaro Uribe as senator, etc. There were targets for humor aplenty. Guerrillas are no laughing matter, but the identities of some leaders are so idiosyncratic (e.g., Jesús Santrich's pseudo-kaffiyeh-clad, sunglass-wearing, wheel-chaired persona), that they nearly immediately inspire derision. Petro's quirky speech patterns sometimes invite scorn. Arias's childish looks, which engendered the moniker "Uribito," also make for easy material. And the catastrophic boondoggle at the dam, where a landslide blocked a tunnel built to divert river waters, eventually flooding an unfinished powerhouse, is amusing, given its exposure of massive official ineptitude. In line with this trend, even when *La Pulla* chastises the central government, it is not engaging Bogotá's elite, effectively giving it a free pass in terms of responsibility for engendering the second-most-unequal Latin American society. In fact, at the beginning of his administration, Santos was still linked to Uribe—having served as his minister of defense (2006–2009)—so instead of focusing on the Bogotano president, *La Pulla* centered on Uribe. Furthermore, even during Duque's presidency, Uribe still served as a distraction as a senator.

When it comes to "regions," no place is othered in *La Pulla* as much as the Caribbean. The greatest example may be the video on the debacle of Electricaribe, the troubled electric utility of Colombia's Caribbean, which was finally dissolved in 2020 (*La Pulla*. "La costa"). To make the video, *La Pulla* invited subscribers from the seven affected departments of Colombia to submit complaints, compiling them in a single video. Unlike with other videos, Baena barely participates. Instead, viewers face a parade of racially mixed individuals speaking nasally inflected Caribbean Spanish (though a few Andean Colombians slip in). What remains clear is the association of a mess and corruption with upset people staring directly into the camera in a confrontational manner. *La Pulla* takes advantage of the fact that the utility's customers are displeased with its economic mismanagement, so producing a gathering of amusing, enraged speakers is easy. In addition, *La Pulla* embraces the stereotype of the Costeño, as Caribbean Colombians are called. According to stereotypes, Costeños are said to be more direct and franker (read, aggressive to the point of embracing foul language) than their Andean equivalents, so the straightforward manner in which people enumerate the utility's blunders makes for predictable entertainment. It is important to note that, to Andeans, the Costeño stereotype incarnates a perplexing otherness, given the Caribbean's unmistakable Black heritage, while embodying bewildering backwardness, a disdain for the status quo, modernity, and rebelliousness in a manner akin to the South's stereotype in the USA.[4] Within this perspective, Costeños exemplify a demographic minority that plays an oversized role in the construction of national identity and the circulation of colombianidad throughout the world (e.g., Gabriel García Márquez, Carlos "El Pibe" Valderrama, Shakira, Sofía Vergara, Carlos Vives, Totó La Momposina, the vueltiao hat, cumbia, etc.).

Yet *La Pulla*'s most effective stab in terms of humor while replicating a mindset of intranational hegemony is when it maps corruption throughout the country, following its "regional" propensities. In a veritable retracing of Colombian geography and accompanying stereotypes—often alluded to in the coverage—when *La Pulla* wishes to speak about the Caribbean, historically in tension with Bogotá's cultural and political establishment, it speaks with feigned admiration of Cartagena de Indias as the nation's touristic paradise, with half a million international tourists per year, the fourth-busiest Latin American port, and close to 500 years of history and cultural heritage, as well as the García, Montes, Blel, and Cáceres Leal political clans, all linked to paramilitary groups (*La Pulla*, "Cartagena"). By the end of the video, though, the mirage has faded. Juan Carlos Rincón speaks alarmingly of the city's rate of poverty and of social exclusion, with 25 percent of its population unable to make ends meet and 26,000 people without running water. Thus, the overall picture is one of dysfunction. The city is ideal as a playground for privileged Andeans, but the locals seem to be nothing more than a poor bunch, lacking any capacity to manage the finances of their city judiciously.

In Barranquilla, the nearby industrial port, the description of the city blends in with María Paulina Baena's information on the all-powerful Char political clan, so only scenarios that have to do with that family's influence are mentioned. So, while *La Pulla* sets its takes in a variety of locations around the city, any of the city's positive achievements are tinted by the debatable way in which the Char clan allegedly operates. In short, the Chars become the city, and the 2.4 million inhabitants of the metro area are portrayed in a monolithic, totalizing manner (*La Pulla*, "Los Char"). In this way, Barranquilla becomes a primary example of the autocratic demeanor with which Bogotá conceives the enactment of provincial power, though it has served as the template. In the case of the archipelago of San Andrés, the second-most-important touristic destination in the country, the way the place is introduced is even more telling: through the admission of oblivion. When Juan Carlos Rincón mentions there is a location in Colombia that is entirely forgotten, a voice off-screen lists many departments in the periphery of the country— Vichada, Guaviare, Guanía, Guajira, Putumayo, Vaupés, and Amazonas—to which Rincón responds, "That's fine. All those are f***ed up, but today we will speak of San Andrés, the island that Colombia only remembers when Nicaragua tries to take it away" (*La Pulla*, "San Andrés"). Never mind that, when the location is described as the second-most-important tourist destination in Colombia, it is mostly thanks to people from Andean urban centers—like Baena or Rincón—who frequently document vacations on Colombian shores through social media, reflecting recurrent commodification of the margin. Even so, the humor condones the notion that, for practical purposes, half of the country is irrelevant to Bogotá, a train of thought that, a century earlier, brought about Panama's independence. And so, aside from being a pretty destination for vacations, the archipelago does not feature highly in the plans of the national government, a mindset that became shamefully clear after the islands faced the fury of Hurricane Iota in November 2020. At the end of the video, as comic relief, Rincón mentions that over 60 percent of the island lacks access to running water, while sewage service only reaches 34 percent of the population. The local waste disposal plant, erected six years ago, never worked. In the meantime, the island has become a mandatory stopover on many drug-trade routes. Lastly, there is the godforsaken and poverty-stricken department of Chocó, which Baena describes ironically as "rich and rainy," with "astonishing jungle," "rivers everywhere," "gold, platinum, and silver deposits," and "sea everywhere in sight." Then she goes on to mention that 18.5 percent of the inhabitants suffer from hunger, 33 percent experience extreme poverty, and there is a general dearth of housing, running water, and good utilities. On top of that, there are the ELN guerrillas and the Gulf Clan drug cartel. Yet, ever avoiding concrete contexts, Baena omits the main reason behind such neglect: 82 percent of Chocó's population is Afro-Colombian, 13 percent is Amerindian or Mestizo, and only 5 percent is of European descent. Baena refuses to acknowledge the elephant in the room: the relevance of race in Colombian society, though in a manner undermining the glorified "country of regions" construct. This may be indicative of the denial of many Bogotanos, as the ethnic makeup of the city, even after intensive national migration due to conflict-related demographic displacement, tends to be more homogeneous than that of the rest of the country. Thus, within this representation, it is as though politicians' extensive corruption and endemic lack of ethics somehow seep into the human fabric of these enclaves—or maybe it is the other way around. In any case, what remains clear is that warmer, more sea-driven locations seem to lack the discipline and rigor necessary for sensible management of public monies. They may also lack the entire budget of the national government to fund cushy, middle-class jobs. Even in the case of Barranquilla, points out Baena, as the Chars have brought a hot streak of public works and official investment, the overall point is, most poignantly, the lack of checks and balances for these provincial bosses who act like emperors. The paradoxical nature of this assertion in the mouth of a Bogotana journalist, the likely beneficiary of a central order occasionally exempted from oversight, hints at the power of negation.

When it concerns the coffee-producing region of the country, which includes the Eje Cafetero (Coffee Alliance) and the city of Medellín, the willingness to depict the political fringes of Bogotá as backward and troublesome is no less dramatic. In Risaralda, the heart of the coffee region, where *La Pulla* makes a quick assessment of the Merheg political clan, the place is described eloquently "as another orchid blooming from this wondrous terrain," embracing the national flower in a manner evoking an imperial gaze—only intranationally. The lineage of the family is described as "a gift from Lebanon to the world," with explicitly Orientalist undertones (*La Pulla*, "Risaralda"). Risaralda is described as "having the most beautiful mountains of the coffee region, the third touristic destination after Cartagena and San Andrés, an airport with flights to Miami and Panama, and a loving, nocturnal, and tanned capital." The last part of the description, "loving, nocturnal, and tanned," plays on the stereotype of women from Pereira, the capital of Risaralda, who are routinely portrayed as licentious gold diggers—all of this coming from another woman. In the case of Medellín, thanks to its mayor Daniel Quintero, sardonically described by *La Pulla*'s team as "a prophet," "a true democrat," "a humble god," "an independent pol," "the local Elon Musk," "a Colombian Twitter star," "the one with transparency flowing through his veins," "the one who would make Medellín great again," "the one who would unmask Antioquia's corruption," "the one who does not represent any traditional party," "the politician that Colombia needs," and "the president that we will deserve," the hyperbolic acerbity blends in with the allusion to the region's legendary entrepreneurial spirit and its focus on tech-driven initiatives (*La Pulla*, "Daniel Quintero"). Baena may rightly mock Quintero as an "alternative tyrant," given his opportunism, his duplicitous flip-flopping in terms of issues, and his autocratic bent, but the entire episode on Quintero rips apart the regional fabric as though nothing good could come from it, mocking the Antioqueño work ethic to the core. In other words, the episode conjures tensions between the elites of Medellín and Bogotá. After all, Medellín incarnates the Latin American anomaly that a city that is not the capital enjoys better public transportation and infrastructure than the capital city, defying centralism's dicta through and through. To Baena, it is as though Quintero were representative of Antioquia's entire political class, despite his singularity.

When it comes to the Pacific coast, just around the corner from Antioquia, the team from *La Pulla* repeats the official assessment of the region as though it were a badge of honor, somewhat in denial about the palpable degree of social tension evident in the 2021 revolts. In the department of Valle, where Cali, the third-largest Colombian city, is located, the focus is on the positive despite the formidable political machinery of governor Dilian Francisca Toro (*La Pulla*, "Ésta es la emperatriz"). The team describes the region as "prosperous," emphasizing the strength of its economy, that it has "very little inequality," "very low poverty rates compared to other regions," and "a local industry." Never mind that even upper-class pols like Maurice Armitage, Cali's former mayor and one of the most important philanthropists in the region, underscore the city's lack of local industry and brewing socioeconomic tensions, which generate skyrocketing unemployment and dramatic inequality, according to a BBC interview (Pardo, "Protestas"). Given the 2021 protests, in which Cali was a hotbed of conflict, one would think this internalized, Bogo-centric way of imagining the province is precisely what is at the heart of the Colombian elite's denial of the country's situation. Whether the Caribbean is a mess or Valle is paradise, what is clear is that *La Pulla* reproduces a vision of the rest of the country as dictated by Bogotano creeds, never reaching beyond. In contrast, out of its many videos, I could only identify six alluding explicitly to Bogotá: one on the bombing of the police academy, another one on an assassination attempt, yet another one on taxis, one on corruption in the public transportation system, one on Mayor Peñalosa's engagement in a drug-ridden neighborhood nicknamed "The Bronx," and finally, one on Mayor López's snafu preaching xenophobia against Venezuelan immigrants. In short, *La Pulla* may travel to other corners of the country, but it seems unable to engage realities and what these suggest about Bogotá's role in the way things are in Colombia.

In more distant locations, like the departments of Caquetá and Meta, spanning from the Andean foothills to the Amazonian basin, *La Pulla* is no less reductive in its appreciation of regional identity. Caquetá is described as a site of deforestation, violence instigated by the FARC, and perverse politicians, in a fashion reminiscent of national government views, which habitually describe the place as the heart of the alternate state enacted by subversives, despite its widespread reputation for natural beauty (*La Pulla*, "Parapolíticos"). Meta is described from the start in terms of that which most Bogotanos dread about the place: the instability of the highway connecting it to the capital—the Vía al Llano (road to the plains)—which, despite repeated multimillion-dollar investments, is constantly experiencing landslides (*La Pulla*, "En el Meta").

The mention of *joropo,* the local cowboy dance; cattle, a traditional staple and former mainstay of the economy, now replaced by oil; *coleo,* the local version of rodeo; and *chigüiro,* a sizable, mustachioed rodent cherished as a delicacy, all contribute to the caricatured depiction of Meta as a Colombian wild west, where the rule of law cannot possibly prevail.

Farther to the northern end of the plains and bordering Venezuela, the department of Arauca is not even described in terms of cultural practices or nature (*La Pulla,* "Ésta es la region"). The way *La Pulla* introduces its analysis of the political situation in the place is based exclusively on news having to do with the ELN (Ejército de Liberación Nacional, or National Liberation Army), the guerrilla group that chose not to embrace the 2012–2016 peace process and instead decided to hide near (or beyond) the Colombian/Venezuelan border, where, when Colombian armed forces show up, it can seek refuge in Nicolás Maduro's dictatorship. As though this were not enough, Rincón starts the video by stating, "Arauca is a department that you perhaps hardly know anything about—that almost does not even show up in the news, and when it does, it tends to be for matters like these." Thus, the name should be added to the extensive list of places from which the central government seems to be absent. This is indeed a view of the periphery from the perspective of Bogotanos, whose vision of national boundaries is strongly determined by the extent to which incidents at these localities may affect matters in the capital (just like an empire tends to be by matters in its colonies). In a speedy sequence, the video then shows national TV news stories about the ELN calling for a 72-hour-long departmental strike, repeated denunciations of underage recruitment by guerrilla forces, the assassination of a police officer by hit men, attacks against the police, videos showing the trip from Arauca of a pickup loaded with explosives that detonated at Bogotá's police academy, etc. By the end of the video, when Rincón claims Araucanos are sick and tired of the ELN guerrillas and Bogotanos asking for war, he summarizes how the department was the second-most-successful in the country in crop replacement, exchanging coca plants for cocoa and plantains—to the point of receiving, amazingly, according to Rincón, international awards in Paris for the quality of its chocolate—and home to one of the most successful reintegration programs for ex-FARC guerrilla members, with 114 recent high school graduates. And so, it becomes quite clear that even the positive news about this location is filtered through the prism of war. To a large extent, it is this perception of the plains and the Amazon basin that has substantiated the high degree of neglect of almost half of the total area of the country—luckily, from the perspective of nature—for over two hundred years, justifying the Colombian government's lack of presence.

La Pulla even endorses Bogotá's preeminence in urban areas within the same Andean range as the capital, like the city of Bucaramanga, the capital of the department of Santander. The video for Santander lacks any description of the land or actual reference to the character of its people, effectively focusing on a group of local political bosses with ties to paramilitary groups. One of them happens to be the ex-police officer who killed Pablo Escobar and ended up—disconcertingly, given his presumed salary as a policeman—owning two Porsches and properties worth millions of dollars. In the department of Huila, another satellite of Bogotano political power, given its proximity to the capital city, the situation is analogous. Aside from alluding to the overwhelming heat of the Upper Magdalena River valley, there is no mention of the geography or culture of the region. If anything, most Colombians only recall the place as the location of the National Bambuco Music Folkloric Festival and Pageant, habitually held during the feasts of Saints Peter and Paul toward the end of June, when many Bogotanos tend to drive into Neiva, Huila's capital. The Bogotano imaginary holds such a grasp on the construction of regional identity that even the way in which one peripheral location makes fun of another peripheral location must go through Bogotá, precluding any closer contact at the expense of central hegemony.

Comments, Consent, Hegemony

The clearest way to document how consent in favor of the capital city's primacy is achieved is, without a doubt, the comments on every single video by *La Pulla*. Though handles are not included, quotes reproduce the factual language of comments, providing irrefutable evidence.[5] YouTube visitors from all over the country embrace the opportunity to try to draw attention to cases of corruption in their localities. Through their comments, *La Pulla* gains legitimacy as the champion of those who want a country free from corruption, thus pushing forward a normative mapping of Colombian politics. The tone of the responses shifts from pleading to outrage in a matter of lines. In the comments for the video on corruption in Cartagena de Indias, a visitor pleads for equal attentiveness to his Andean department: "I would appreciate speaking about Antioquia and its politicians."[6] In the same section, someone asks about Meta: "Please. Meta, here you have material for a three-hour movie."[7] Somebody else proposes going to Cúcuta, the capital city of North Santander: "Do not forget Cúcuta. Hernando and Jorge Acevedo are the most dangerous ones here."[8] And yet another Andean visitor pleads, "I would like you to unmask how politics works in Bogotá and Cundinamarca."[9] It is important to note that this particular request denotes the lack of coverage of corruption in the department surrounding Bogotá. A visitor presumably from a Caribbean location recommends, "I suggest Guajira and Cesar. . . . Good money with coal royalties."[10] Guajira and Cesar are Costeño departments where coal mining has resulted in greater political stature in recent decades. Finally, a viewer suggests exposure of the situation at the nearby Caribbean port of Santa Marta: "The Cote, Zúñiga, Vives families, Lacouture vs. Caicedo. In Santa Marta."[11] In these remarks it is possible to see how *La Pulla* garners the validation necessary to uphold its purported construct of "national reality."

When it comes to the video on the unlimited power of the Char political clan in Barranquilla, the comments are no less telling. Someone demands, "Make a video on Cesar and Valledupar. Render visible the political monopoly of the Gnecco and Ape Cuello families."[12] A viewer from neighboring Cartagena suggests, "The episode on Cartagena will need at least 3 seasons."[13] Someone reiterates, "Do one on Cartagena, please, you have great material, phew."[14] Some are more sanguine, emphasizing, "The char-latans, wake up DUMBOMBIA. Good video pulla (*sic*) thanks."[15] Some commenters compliment *La Pulla:* "I hope these people's empire ends. I love this channel, it opens our eyes [open eyes emoji]."[16] Comments like these, which legitimize *La Pulla*'s critique of political bossism, evince the degree of consent attained by their reporting, paying scant attention to the troubling implications of the news team's identity politics.

In the case of the video on corruption in the San Andrés archipelago, a visitor from Antioquia says, "I hope the one on Antioquia is two hours long :v."[17] A fan who appears to be from continental Colombia urges, "We hope you will arrive and speak of Magdalena, the land of oblivion, as Carlos Vives says."[18] Yet another fan from the southern portion of Colombia's Caribbean appeals, "For when one on SINCELEJO and MONTERÍA!!"[19] Someone who seems to be from the Andean coffee region asks, "We need one on Quindío! FULL OF CORRUPTION."[20] Somebody from the northern end of the Caribbean insists, "I am waiting for the one on Magdalena, the Cote family, and the story of the University of Magdalena."[21] A viewer from Risaralda says, "I am from Pereira. And with this content, I learned about many things I ignored. My poor Risaralda. Regards Paulina [heart icon]."[22] Another visitor from the Caribbean department of Córdoba asserts, "To account for how dirty politics is in Córdoba we need three episodes."[23] Someone from the Andean department of Tolima hints at a bigger scandal: "Tolima is close by, come and taste tamales and suckling pig corrupted by national games and politicking flavor,"[24] while a visitor from the coffee region begs, "Please, do not forget to come to Quindío . . . because if it pours there, it does not clear here."[25] From the outskirts of Cali, somebody praises the team: "I like *La Pulla* a lot. . . .

Congratulations, when will you cover Palmira and Valle del Cauca."[26] The variety of the locations referenced in these responses speaks volumes about the widespread internalization of the version of the country propounded by *La Pulla*, thus hindering new ways of imagining a more cohesive, equitable relationship between the center and its periphery.

Personalized attacks also add to the sense of support gathered by the team. The video on Daniel Quintero, Medellín's controversial mayor, sparked special attention. From a nearby suburb, a visitor concurs, "I agree, but when is it the turn for the office of Envigado? In other words: Fajardo."[27] Also referring to erstwhile presidential candidate Sergio Fajardo, someone else insists, "And if we do one on Fajardo? Will you dare? Blink, blink."[28] Yet another viewer points in the direction of another local Antioqueño politician, Federico "Fico" Gutiérrez, who stood as a right-wing presidential candidate: "I would like it if you would speak sometime about Federico Gutiérrez."[29] Going back to Barranquilla, a viewer commands, "Now a video like this one on Jaime Pumarejo, Elsa Noguera, and William Dau [grimacing face emoji]."[30] However, some insist on Fajardo, with one person asking, "Why does it seem to me you are afraid of speaking about Fajardo?"[31] while others commend and persist: "Excellent! Fajardo, when will it be?"[32]

When it comes to the video on the governor of the department of Valle, a follower is appreciative: "I was expecting it. Many thanks to *La Pulla*'s team [heart emoji]."[33] Others are wittier, praising *La Pulla*'s inventiveness: "The creole Daenerys Targaryen. HAHAHAHAHAHAHAHA Pros!!!!!"[34] Comments like this one, celebrating *La Pulla*'s allusion to the popular character from HBO's *Game of Thrones*—a series accessible only through cable or a streaming service—situate the team's humor within a specific class register. Once again, someone from bordering Antioquia recaps, "I am anxiously awaiting the one on Antioquia."[35] From the southern tip of the country, a viewer warns, "Anxiously awaiting the one on the Amazon!!!!"[36] Another viewer from the coffee region reiterates, "Quindío is a banquet for you. We are awaiting anxiously. A big hug."[37] Finally, a viewer from the northeastern department next to Venezuela declares, "*La Pulla* on mayoral and gubernatorial candidates for North Santander, a great topic."[38]

While this is just a sample of the many comments posted on *La Pulla*'s YouTube account, they are sufficient to give an idea of the degree of consent generated by its actions. In the comments, it is possible to recognize how people rejoice in *La Pulla*'s humor and envision its work as an authentic representation of provincial interests, thus condoning the vision of the country that *La Pulla* brandishes, in which, as it turns out, an utter lack of equality in expression between the population of the capital city and any other part of the country is manifest. Aside from additional suggestions, the only exception to the overall celebration of *La Pulla*'s work is the hint of a preference for Sergio Fajardo—a politician who, despite coming from Medellín, once was a Bogotá favorite, thus validating my argument that *La Pulla* sides constantly with the political views of the capital—and the request for a video on corruption in Bogotá and the surrounding department of Cundinamarca, which goes unanswered (I have searched) ("Sergio Fajardo da la lección"). *La Pulla* does have videos on former Medellín mayor Federico Gutiérrez. Nonetheless, the point here is not that there is corruption or even corruption in the provinces; political corruption is a worldwide constant. The point is that, in the way it denounces corruption—by employing humor and sarcasm to substantiate its critique of dishonesty as a consequence of an extensive lack of checks and balances—the team at *La Pulla* manages to reinforce and validate the perspective and power of the capital city over locations all over the nation.

An Amusing Alternative

This does not necessarily need to be the case. There are more effective, humorous ways of denouncing corruption in Colombia—and for that matter, in any country—without playing into the hands of a central establishment. Perhaps the best way to illustrate this is by way of a counterexample. Witness Alejandro Riaño, a renowned Colombian comedian and YouTuber (with 1.86 million subscribers and 230 million views [Social Blade; Juanpis]). He is celebrated for playing the character Juan Pablo González Pombo, also known as "Juanpis," a highly amalgamated incarnation of a wide variety of evils of the Colombian (and Bogotá's) upper class: Anglophilia, classism, conservatism, egocentrism, Eurocentrism, generalized prejudice, homophobia, nationalism, petulance, political incorrectness, racism, regionalism, and, most obviously, sexism ("Juanpis González"). To underscore his point, whenever the character is introduced formally, Riaño follows the name with the phrase "de los Pombo de toda la vida" (of the Pombo of always), alluding to the surname of a well-connected family from Bogotá's upper-class circles.

Given the politically incorrect nature of the character, Riaño can approach many hotly debated topics in Colombia and even interview many personalities and inquire about topics that would not be feasible in a more formal context, in a fashion somewhat similar to Stephen Colbert's character on *The Colbert Report*, who mimicked right-wing TV hosts to get away with criticizing conservatives. Riaño's brand of humor is so successful that what started as an experiment in social media has blossomed into separate shows (like many successful YouTube franchises, including *La Pulla*), including "JP News—

periodismo libre de mantecos" (JP News—journalism *sans* domestic help), "El Boletín del Gomelo" (The Preppie's News Bulletin), and "The Juanpis Live Show." Given his point of departure is self-critique—Juanpis behaves and dresses as what is known as a *gomelo* (a preppie, or someone who acts like a member of the upper class)—indicting the capital's elite, with its English-speaking schools, linguistic crutches, a particular way of dragging certain consonants, and Eurocentric demeanor—Riaño is better able to interact with and criticize situations from all over the country. A good example is Riaño's interview of Gustavo Petro, in which Juanpis enacts the stinginess of the national bourgeoisie, bringing into the open all the excesses that justify Petro's political proposals and thus providing an opportunity for closer examination of the politician's train of thought. Juanpis may behave as though he is hierarchically superior, but the character is so wacky that it readily becomes apparent that the playing field is quite level. In this way, Riaño can talk to characters from everywhere, even international guests, and comment on some usually barred topics, from physical appearance to sexual intimacy—and question them as would be typical for a prejudiced upper-class Bogotano. The unrelenting message is "Do not take yourself seriously," because if you do, I will exploit your sense of self-importance to make fun of you. Along the way, he dexterously dissects the implications of his guest's responses in terms of class, race, gender, etc., within the context of Colombian (and sometimes international) cultural politics.

Riaño does not take himself, or his character, very seriously when it comes to being a target of humor. He enjoys making fun of himself, which, to a fair extent, clears the way to make fun of others. On a very general basis, perhaps because of the widespread classist mindset, Colombians are not inclined to make fun of themselves. José María López Prieto, a.k.a. "Pepón," one of Colombia's most renowned cartoonists, once said, "Despite everything, Colombians still laugh, but basically at others. This isn't healthy. For the most part, Colombian people do not enjoy laughing at themselves, and I think this is why they suffer from so many psychoses, paranoia, and hysteria. People like to make fun of others, especially if they are powerful." (qtd. in Bejarano González 1999)

The hierarchical mindset built into the culture may hinder self-mockery—blame it on the oversized importance of saving face in the culture. And this is why Riaño's brand of humor is so disarming in comparison with *La Pulla*, which, though chock-full of jokes in its videos, tends to take itself too seriously. Were *La Pulla* more like Juanpis—declining to project itself as the country's redeeming grace, guiltless and with the power to indict anyone at any time with impunity—its videos would embrace a more effective tone. As it stands, *La Pulla* risks being viewed as reactionary. It also comes across as perilously binary and Manichaean. In a country where everyone appears to be guilty in the eyes of one particular party, what gives it the right to nominate itself as the definitive political judge and jury? In contrast, Juanpis's approach seems fresher and more sincere: We are all flawed; we live in a flawed society and, as such, we must learn to engage with it constructively, little by little, rather than throw up our hands in horror upon witnessing one more case of corruption—lest we end up handless. In a country like Colombia, Riaño's agenda is a risky bet. His family has already been threatened (*Tendencias El Tiempo*, "Comediante Alejandro Riaño"). For *La Pulla*, the road is not easier. If both parties wish to avoid the misfortune of Jaime Garzón, a popular comedian and pioneer of political humor in television who was assassinated on August 13, 1999 (Wallace, "El día que"), they will have to be careful. They will also need to do their best: in the case of Riaño, to contribute to the consolidation of a less reductive and literal audience and, in the case of *La Pulla*, to foster a more inclusive, generous vision of the nation, well beyond the boundaries and identitarian schemes of the Colombian capital.

Notes

1 This figure is obtained by dividing the total number of videos uploaded by the number of weeks the YouTube channel has been operating.

2 It is important to note that the members of *La Pulla* see themselves as journalists who are enraged by the excesses of the political class, so, traditionally speaking, it could be argued that their main object is not humor. However, given the ways in which they satirize politicians and reproduce regional stereotypes, their practice has gained such traction that, when Mexican comedian Chumel Torres broadcast an episode of HBO's *Chumel* from Colombia in the fall of 2018, María Paulina Baena was designated as his Colombian correspondent (despite Chumel's appearance on YouTube with *El Tiempo*'s columnist Daniel Samper Ospina). Given the brand of Chumel's humor, founded on incessant rebuke of corruption in Mexican politics, it is understandable that Baena ended up performing as associate. See #HolaSoyDanny, "Mi País."

3 I am aware of a single video in which *La Pulla* chastises the central government for its absence from the periphery, but as is customary, Baena emphasizes the physicality of the state rather than the idea of nation. See *La Pulla*, "Esto pasa."

4 This analogy is not mine. The many commonalities between William Faulkner's and Gabriel García Márquez's literature have been the subject of ample research. For more information, see Megan Barnard's "The Company We Keep: García Márquez's Literary Influences," *Ransom Center Magazine*, 22 Oct. 2015, sites.utexas.edu/ransomcentermagazine/2015/10/22/the-company-we-keep-gabriel-garcia-marquezs-literary-influences/.

5 Beaulieu and Estalella underscore the neither positive nor negative dynamic of trace-

ability and suggest providing anonymity to informants is not an achievable aim. Still, amid mediated settings well beyond research control, ethical concerns advise restraint.

6 Les agradezco que hablemos de Antioquia y sus politicos [Medellín].

7 Por favor. EL META, aquí tienen para hacer una película de tres horas.

8 No se olviden de Cúcuta, Hernando y Jorge Acevedo son los más peligrosos de acá.

9 Me gustaría que desenmascararan como [*sic*] se mueve la política el [*sic*] Bogotá y Cundinamarca, gracias.

10 Les sugiero a la guajira [*sic*] y al César [*sic*]. . . . Buena plática [*sic*] con las regalías del carbon [*sic*].

11 Los Cotes, Zuñiga [*sic*], Vives, Lacouture vs Caicedo. En Santa Marta.

12 Hagan un video sobre el César [*sic*] y Valledupar. Visibilicen el monopolio político de la familia Gnecco y Ape Cuello.

13 El episodio de Cartagena va a necesitar al menos 3 temporadas.

14 Haz uno de Cartagena por favor, tienes buen material uffff.

15 Los char-latanes, despierta BOBOMBIA. Buen video pulla [*sic*] gracias.

16 Espero que el imperio de esta gente acabe. Me encanta este canal, hace abrir los ojos.

17 ESpero [*sic*] que el de Antioquia sea de dos horas :v.

18 Anhelamos que lleguen y hablen del Magdalena, la tierra del olvido, como dice Carlos Vives.

19 Para cuándo uno de SINCELEJO y MONTERÍA!!

20 necesitamos [*sic*] el del Quindío! LLENO DE CORRUPCIÓN.

21 Estoy esperando el del Magdalena, los cotes [*sic*] y la historia de la Universidad del Magdalena.

22 Soy de Pereira. Y con este contenido me entere [*sic*] de muchas cosas que no sabía. Pobre mi Risaralda. Saludos Paulina.

23 Para contar lo sucia que es la política de Córdoba necesitan tres capítulos.

24 Les queda cerquita el Tolima vengan y prueben Tamal y Lechona corrupta con sabor a juegos nacionales y politiquerías.

25 Por favor, no dejen de venir al Quindío . . . porque si por allá llueve, por acá no escampa.

26 Me gusta mucho La Pulla . . . Felicitaciones, para cuando Palmira y el Valle del Cauca.

27 De acuerdo, pero cuándo le toca a la oficina de Envigado? Es decir: Fajardo.

28 Y si hacemos uno de Fajardo? Se le miden? Guiño, guiño.

29 A mí me gustaría que hablaran una vez sobre Federico Gutiérrez.

30 Ahora un video así de Jaime Pumarejo, Elsa Noguera y William Dau.

31 ¿Por qué me parece que aquí les da miedo hablar de Fajardo?

32 Excelente! [*sic*] Fajardo pa' cuándo?

33 Lo estaba esperando, Muchas gracias al equipo de La Pulla.

34 "La Daenerys Targaryen criolla" JAJAJAJAJAJAJAJAJAJAJA Cracks!!!!! [*sic*]

35 Estoy esperando ansiosamente el de Antioquia.

36 Espero ansioso el de la Amazonía !!!! [*sic*]

37 El Quindío es un banquete para ustedes. Se les espera con ansia. Un gran abrazo.

38 La Pulla sobre los candidatos a la alcaldía y la gobernación del N de S, un súper tema.

Works Cited

Appelbaum, Nancy. *Muddied Waters: Race, Region and Local History in Colombia, 1846–1948*. Durham and London: Duke UP, 2003.

Ayllón, Fernando, and Andrés Felipe Orjuela, directors. *Ud. no sabe quién soy yo*. Take One Productions, 2016.

Bakhtin, Mikhail. *Rabelais and his World*. Bloomington, IN: University of Indiana Press, 1984.

Barnard, Megan. "The Company We Keep: García Márquez's Literary Influences." *Ransom Center Magazine*, 22 Oct. 2015, sites.utexas.edu/ransomcentermagazine/2015/10/22/the-company-we-keep-gabriel-garcia-marquezs-literary-influences/.

Beaulieu, Anne, and Adolfo Estalella. "Rethinking Research Ethics for Mediated Settings." *Information, Communication & Society*, vol. 15, no. 1, 2012, pp. 23–42.

Bejarano González, Bernardo. "¿De qué se ríen los colombianos?" *El Tiempo*, 26 Sept. 1999, www.eltiempo.com/archivo/documento/MAM-909657.

Chumel con Chumel Torres. Directed by Eneko Obieto, Boomdog Films and HBO Latin America Group, 2016.

Eagleton, Terry. *Humour*. New Haven and London: Yale UP, 2019.

"El Boletín del Gomelo—Gustavo Petro." *YouTube*, uploaded by Juanpis González, 19 Nov. 2019, www.youtube.com/watch?v=RLmAZ22lGIE.

Fals Borda, Orlando. *Región e historia: elementos sobre ordenamiento y equilibrio regional en Colombia*. Bogotá: TM Editores, 1996.

Game of Thrones. Created by David Benioff and D. B. Weiss, HBO Entertainment, 2011–2019.

Gestión Digital. "Sobre el bogocentrismo." *El Heraldo*, 3 June 2015, www.elheraldo.co/columnas-de-opinion/sobre-el-bogocentrismo-197733.

Gill, Nicholas. "Spicing Up the Colombian Melting Pot." *The New York Times*, 2 Feb. 2017, www.nytimes.com/2017/02/02/travel/bogota-colombia-regional-food-restaurants.html.

"Gini Coefficients by Country 2023." *World Population Review*, 2023, worldpopulationreview.com/country-rankings/gini-coefficient-by-country.

González, Ana Luisa. "A Democratic Space." *Goethe Institut*, Jan. 2020, www.goethe.de/en/uun/pub/das/dgw/21743825.html.

"Gustavo Petro dio a conocer detalles de lo que sería el Ministerio de la Igualdad." *Infobae*, 22 Mar. 2022, www.infobae.com/america/colombia/2022/03/08/gustavo-petro-dio-a-conocer-detalles-de-lo-que-seria-el-ministerio-de-la-igualdad/.

"Historia y modernidad en un solo lugar." *Colombia Travel*, 2022, colombia.travel/es/bogota.

#HolaSoyDanny. "Mi País [*sic*] es más absurdo que el tuyo challenge ft. Chumel Torres." YouTube, 18 Oct. 2018, www.youtube.com/watch?v=Ove73IUUJDE.

Hudson, Rex. *Colombia: A Country Study*. Washington, DC: Federal Research Division, Library of Congress, 2010.

"Juanpis González." *YouTube* channel. www.youtube.com/channel/UC49w7S0pbX6HM JeiWibcvsg.

La Pulla. "Así funciona la cabeza del mejor presidente de la historia de Colombia" *YouTube*, 7 Aug. 2020, www.youtube.com/watch?v=KxUcZCVw-9g.

———. "Cartagena: ¿Llena de parapolíticos y corruptos?" *YouTube*, 16 Sept. 2019, www.youtube.com/watch?v=3-mdUEG39ig&t=15s.

———. "Chao SANTOS, cinco cañonazos bailables de su presidencia." *YouTube*, 2 Aug. 2018, www.youtube.com/watch?v=1J4jLTZpl4M.

———. "CUIDADO: Miles han caído en este fraude." *YouTube*, 19 Sept. 2019, www.youtube.com/watch?v=rbbHN8-SaNA.

———. "Daniel Quintero, el 'tirano alternativo' que manda en Medellín." *YouTube*, 1 Oct. 2020, www.youtube.com/watch?v=emClidVKGdU&t=2s.

———. "En el Meta estos mañosos se rotan el poder." *YouTube*, 10 Oct. 2019, www.youtube.com/watch?v=fpH1wSASaVg.

———. "Ésta es la emperatriz del Valle del Cauca." *YouTube*, 12 Sept. 2019, www.youtube.com/watch?v=M8GyM2cmt4c&t=115s.

———. "Ésta es la region donde manda el ELN." *YouTube*, 21 Oct. 2019, www.youtube.com/watch?v=1ttK4PmUlfE.

———. "Esto pasa cuando el Estado ignora su gente." *YouTube*, 4 Apr. 2019, www.youtube.com/watch?v=xL8aTa_Cuow.

———. "Juan Manuel Santos nos cumplió todas sus promesas." *YouTube*, 19 Oct. 2017, www.youtube.com/watch?v=caqbfU4hsrk.

———. "La costa vive sin luz por culpa de Electricaribe y nadie hace nada." *YouTube*, 16 Aug. 2016, www.youtube.com/watch?v=qfEzqetEeW4.

———. "Las artimañas de Iván Duque para concentrar todo el poder." *YouTube*, 6 May 2021, www.youtube.com/watch?v=JuKo-nN28ec&t=671s.

———. "Las muertes que no les importan a Duque ni a Santos." *YouTube*, 6 Feb. 2020, www.youtube.com/watch?v=QgKaejKO1eU.

———. "Los Char hacen lo que se les da la gana en Barranquilla." *YouTube*, 5 Sept. 2019, www.youtube.com/watch?v=fasE2JspSUU.

———. "Parapolíticos y tramposos mandan en Caquetá." *YouTube*, 24 Oct. 2019, www.youtube.com/watch?v=hpYhSZ3UNqA.

———. "Por esto tienen miedo Uribe y Duque | Me acabo de enterar." *YouTube*, 9 Mar. 2020, www.youtube.com/watch?v=5Wiu3o2lAyI.

———. "Risaralda está en la inmunda por culpa de estos politicos." *YouTube*, 15 Aug. 2019, www.youtube.com/watch?v=02reAZor2JQ&t=48s.

———. "San Andrés: Playa, brisa y politicos corruptos." *YouTube*, 7 Oct. 2019, www.youtube.com/watch?v=wwtBjLqjVE0.

———. "Santos and Uribe Love to Play the Idiot." *YouTube*, 30 Mar. 2017, www.youtube.com/watch?v=Zcq2Y55zm2o&t=190s.

———. "¿Santos corrupto?, DANE no sabe sumar, Mockus Vuelve y más." *YouTube*, 8 July 2019, www.youtube.com/watch?v=kJtra9bLXHw.

———. "Santos insultado, reinas trans, jugos engañosos y más." *YouTube*, 8 Oct. 2018, www.youtube.com/watch?v=TZ633iKNpEY.

———. "Uribe, FICO y otros desastres de la política en Antioquia." *YouTube*, 17 Oct. 2019, www.youtube.com/watch?v=VW3ObkjidMc&t=24s.

Martinez, Marta. "La Pulla's Wildly Popular YouTube Videos (Born at a 130-Year-Old Newspaper) Are Bringing Hard News to Young Colombians." *NiemanLab,* 7 June 2018, www.niemanlab.org/2018/06/la-pullas-wildly-popular-youtube-videos-born-at-a-130 -year-old-newspaper-are-bringing-hard-news-to-young-colombians/.

Martínez Sánchez, Nicolás. "'El periodismo prende la luz de un cuarto oscuro,' María Paulina Baena." *Conexión Externado,* 3 Mar. 2022, conexion.uexternado.edu.co/maria -paulina-baena/.

Medina Cartagena, María Alejandra. *Humor político audiovisual en Colombia: de los gloriosos años noventa en television a internet como alternativa.* Bogotá: Universidad del Rosario, 2017.

"'Nos emberracamos, pero con argumentos': La Pulla" *Semana,* 6 Oct. 2016, www .semana.com/enfoque/articulo/la-pulla-maria-paulina-baena-cuenta-como-nacio-y -polarizacion-que-genera/477235/.

Oviedo, Gilberto L. "El humor gráfico y la formación de la individualidad en la Colombia del siglo XIX." *Humor y política: una perspectiva transcultural,* edited by Jacqueline Benavides Delgado, Bogotá: Ediciones Universidad Cooperativa de Colombia, 2018, pp. 41–71.

Pardo, Daniel. "Protestas en Colombia: 'Es la primera vez que veo los estratos cinco y seis angustiados, y eso es bueno,' Maurice Armitage, exalcalde de Cali." *BBC News Mundo,* 19 May 2021, www.bbc.com/mundo/noticias-america-latina-57164377.

———. "Qué son los estratos, el sistema 'solidario' que terminó profundizando el clasismo y la desigualdad en Colombia." *BBC News Mundo,* 28 May 2021, www.bbc.com/ mundo/noticias-america-latina-57264176.

Perdomo Alaba, Juan Diego. "Diatriba contra los rolos y el excesivo bogocentrismo." *El Espectador,* 16 May 2022, blogs.elespectador.com/politica/politicamente-insurrecto/ diatriba-los-rolos-excesivo-bogocentrismo.

Palomino, Sally. "Racismo y clasismo, una herida que sangra en las protestas de Colombia." *El País,* 12 May 2021, elpais.com/internacional/2021-05-12/racismo-y-clasismo-una -herida-que-sangra-en-las-protestas-de-colombia.html.

Peña Castañeda, Camilo. "'Ud. no sabe quién soy yo,' el mal que nos aqueja como sociedad." *El Tiempo,* Aug. 31, 2018, www.eltiempo.com/vida/educacion/por-que-hay -tantos-casos-de-usted-no-sabe-quien-soy-yo-en-colombia-260872.

Roldán Rueda, Natalia. "Los secretos de la pulla." *Cromos,* 25 Aug. 2018, www.elespectador .com/cromos/vida-social/los-secretos-de-la-pulla/.

Russell, Benjamin. "AQ Top 5 Political Satirists: María Paulina Baena." *Americas Quarterly,* 11 Oct. 2019, americasquarterly.org/article/aq-top-5-political-satirists-maria-paulina -baena/.

"Sergio Fajardo da la lección y gana en Bogotá, pero no llega a segunda vuelta." *Semana,* 27 May 2018, www.semana.com/pais/articulo/sergio-fajardo-gana-en-bogota-pero-no -llega-a-segunda-vuelta/258868/.

Social Blade. "Juanpis González." Jan. 2023, socialblade.com/youtube/c/juanpisgonzalez.

———. "La Pulla." Jan. 2023, socialblade.com/youtube/c/lapulla.

"#TBT: Los casos más recordados de 'Ud. no sabe quién soy yo?'" *YouTube,* uploaded by *El Tiempo,* 26 Mar. 2019, www.youtube.com/watch?v=8p_d04JGFAg.

Tendencias *El Tiempo.* "Comediante Alejandro Riaño denuncia amenazas contra su familia." *El Tiempo,* 17 Mar. 2021, www.eltiempo.com/cultura/gente/alejandro-riano -denuncia-amenazas-en-su-contra-y-la-de-sus-gemelos-573449.

Wallace, Arturo. "El día que Colombia perdió las ganas de reír." *BBC News Mundo,* 13 Aug. 2012, www.bbc.com/mundo/noticias/2012/08/120813_colombia_jaime_garzon _impunidad_humor_aw.

———. "Estrato 1, estrato 6: cómo los colombianos hablan de sí mismos divididos en clases sociales." *BBC News Mundo,* 23 Sept. 2014, www.bbc.com/mundo/noticias/2014/09/ 140919_colombia_fooc_estratos_aw.

Wilson, Christopher P. Jokes: *Form, Content, Use and Function.* London and New York: European Association of Experimental Social Psychology by Academic Press, 1979.

World Bank Group. "Building an Equitable Society in Colombia." Open Knowledge Repository, openknowledge.worldbank.org/handle/10986/36535.

CONTRIBUTORS

Paul Alonso is associate professor in the School of Modern Languages at Georgia Tech. He is the author of *Satiric TV in the Americas: Critical Metatainment as Negotiated Dissent* and *Thirty Years of Entertainment and Politics in Peru,* among other books.

Eva Paulino Bueno is professor emerita of Spanish at St. Mary's University in San Antonio, Texas. She has published the books *Amácio Mazzaropi in the Film and Culture of Brazil: After Cinema Novo* and *Resisting Boundaries: The Subject of Naturalism in Brazil,* among others.

Alberto Centeno-Pulido is a Spanish teacher at Asheville School in Asheville, North Carolina. He is also an interpreter and translator. He is the translator into Spanish of *Comics and Memory in Latin America.*

Viktor Chagas is associate professor of political communication at the Fluminense Federal University of Brazil. He is the editor of the collection *A cultura dos memes: aspectos sociológicos e dimensões políticas de um fenômeno do mundo digital* [The Culture of Memes: Sociological Aspects and Political Dimensions of a Digital World Phenomenon], and has published several articles in scholarly journals.

Alejandra Collado is a researcher at the Centro de Investigaciones y Estudios de Género (CIEG) at UNAM (National Autonomous University of Mexico), and professor in the Facultad de Ciencias Políticas y Sociales (FCPyS) at UNAM. She is the author of, among other publications, the books *Lo digital es político: feminismos en la cibercultura* and *Las identidades ciborgs. Materialización de sujetos encarnados.*

Héctor Fernández L'Hoeste is professor of Latin American cultural studies at Georgia State University in Atlanta. He is the author of *Narrativas de representación urbana* and *Lalo Alcaraz: Political Cartooning in the Latino Community.*

Damián Fraticelli is professor of semiotics at the University of Buenos Aires and the National University of the Arts in Argentina. He is the author of *El Humor Hipermediático. Una nueva era de la mediatización reidera* and *El ocaso triunfal de los programas cómicos. De Viendo a Biondi a Peter Capusotto y sus videos.*

Fábio Marques de Souza is professor in the Arts and Languages Department at the State University of Paraiba, Brazil.

Juan Poblete is professor of literature at the University of California, Santa Cruz. He is the author of *Hacia una historia de la lectura y la pedagogía literaria en América Latina* and *La Escritura de Pedro Lemebel como proyecto cultural y político,* among other books.

R. Sánchez-Rivera is research fellow in the study of race and anti-racism in Gonville & Caius College and affiliate lecturer in sociology at the University of Cambridge. They work on the sociology of health and illness and historical sociology with a focus on scientific racism, critical eugenics studies, and reproductive justice.

Ulisses A. Sawczuk da Silva is a communication manager at the Municipality of Londrina, Brazil, and has a master's degree in media studies from Erasmus University Rotterdam.

Mélodine Sommier works as an Academy of Finland Research Fellow at the University of Jyväskylä (Finland). She has coedited the book *Interculturality in Higher Education: Putting Critical Approaches into Practice.*

INDEX

Page numbers followed by the letters *t* and *i* indicate tables and illustrations.

Abortion, the right to, 74
Affordance, 5, 10, 19–20, 24, 124, 145, 171n1, 224
Afro-Brazilian, 144, 172n14, 178, 186, 188
Agostini, Angelo, 10
Alborada, La, 10
Alonso, Paul, 3, 24
Alphabet, the, 21
Alphabet (company), 223
Alves, Rosental, 39
Amazon (company), 13
América Móvil, 40
Anointed, 155, 157t
Anti-Blackness, 204–205
Antioqueño, 247–248, 252, 257
Antisocial, 78
Aos Fatos, 161
Aquinas, Thomas, 9
Aquino, Guillermo, 6, 26, 49, 72–74, 77–88
ARA San Juan, 86, 88, 93n13
Arauca, 254
Arepas, 247
Argentina, 6, 10, 13, 16, 25, 30, 43–45, 49, 55, 64–65, 69nn11–13, 69n16, 70n24, 70n26, 77, 85, 87, 91n8, 92n12, 94nn14–15; average salary, 63; feminism in, 46; fiscal deficit, 26; *rock nacional,* 81; sexist component of the entertainment industry, 47; sexist values in, 48
Argentinidad, 6
Arias, Andrés Felipe, 249
Aristegui, Carmen, 41
Aristotle, 9
Arrested Development, 46
Attack of the Clones, 105
Avellaneda, 93n14
Avengers, the, 166

Avenida Brasil, 126–127
Avritzer, Leonardo, 141n27, 149
Ayala, Fernando, 99–100
Ayotzinapa, 41, 107, 109
Azcárraga Jean, Emilio, 39
Azcárraga Milmo, Emilio "El Tigre," 39

Baena, María Paulina, 239–241, 244–247, 249–252, 261nn2–3
Bain, Alexander, 7
Bakhtin, Mikhail, 24, 26, 97, 101, 111, 150, 158, 190, 244–245
Bamford, Maria, 46
Barbie, 7, 27, 176–178, 180–194; Indian, 188; Jamaican, 188; Polynesian, 188; Puerto Rican, 188
Barbie Fascionista, 27, 177–178, 181–183, 186, 190–194; allusion to blackface, 188; authors, 186; comprehensive analysis of, 190; connection of humor and political activism, 177; content, 187; creators, 192–193; foreignness and obsession with US culture, 188; Instagram account, 177, 184, 194n2; moral ambiguities, 192; posts, 178; screenshot of page, 185i, 189i, 191i; strong sense of moralism, 192; subversive humor, 193
Barranquilla, 250, 256–257
Barreto, Gisela, 86, 88, 93n13
Baumgartner, Jody, 3
BBC, 66, 235, 253
BBC Mundo, 235
Belgrano, 44
Benavides Delgado, Jacqueline, 13
Benjamin, Walter, 21
Beriso, La, 80–81
Bieber, Justin, 38, 49n4
Blackface, 188
Black Lives Matter, 182
Blackmore, Susan, 99

Black people, 146, 204
Black Puerto Ricans, 212
Blim, 13
Blogiante, El, 206, 208, 212, 213i, 215
Boca Juniors, 87
Bode Francisco Orelana, 122–124, 126, 130, 137
Bode Gaiato, 117, 121–122, 125–130, 136–137, 139n14, 139n19
Bogotá, 9, 240, 242–243, 246–247, 249–256, 258, 261n9
Boletín del Gomelo, El, 3, 259
Bolsonarist, 27, 151–154, 160–162, 164, 170
Bolsonaro, Jair, 7, 27–28, 130, 135, 139n18, 141n27, 145–151, 153–164, 166, 167i, 169–170, 172nn13–16, 173n17, 176, 182, 190, 193, 194n1; election of, 144; figure as national hero of freedom, 145; victory in the 2018 presidential elections, 147
Borda (hospital), 83, 92n10
Border studies, 23
Borges, Cristobal, 211
Borges, José Lee, 211
Borrero, Gloria María, 248
Bot, Claudia Mehler, 131, 142n20
BR 040, 133, 140n24, 140n26
"Brasis," 121
Brazil, 10, 12–14, 27, 117–118, 120–121, 124, 130–131, 133, 135–137, 140n25, 141n27, 144, 147–148, 158, 166, 171nn3–4, 178–183, 186, 188, 190, 193, 194n1, 248; African languages spoken in, 138n3; American colonizing presence in, 139n11; number two, 135–136; political turmoil, 135; 2014 World Cup in, 43
Brazilian Labor Party, 171n4
Brazilian National Council of Ethics in Research, 154
Brazilian Statistics Agency, 129
Brizola, Leonel, 147, 172n4
Broncano, Fernando, 22
Broomcillin, 147
Bucaramanga, 255
Bueno, Eva Paulino, 5, 26
Buenos Aires, 44, 55, 65, 79–81, 84–85, 93n14
Burgess, Jean, 169, 222–223, 225

Caatinga, 122–123, 138n10
Cabello, Marcelo, 9

Cabo Daciolo, 148
Cafre, 204
Caipira, 117–118, 121, 131, 137nn1–2; accent, 27, 117, 122, 131; culture, 140n20; dialect, 140n21; knowledge, 137; philosophy of the character, 132
Calderón, Felipe, 39, 105
Cali, 253
Cambiasso, Paco, 77–78, 90n3
Cândido, Antonio, 117, 121, 137n2
Cantinflas, 12, 228
Cantinflismo, 11–12
Capitalism, 15, 21–22, 180, 222, 224, 229–230, 232
Captain America, 145
Capulina, 12
Capusotto, Peter, 69n18, 70n19
Caras y Caretas, 10
Carlón, Mario, 55, 58, 61–62
Carneiro, Enéas, 148
Carnival, 12, 24, 26, 97, 101, 104, 109, 111, 150, 177, 188, 190, 193, 244–245
Carriel, 247
Cartagena de Indias, 250, 255
Carter, Eli, 13
Cartoons, 27, 101–103, 107, 112, 117, 119–123, 138n11, 259; political, 26, 96–100, 104, 109–112
Castaño Díaz, Carlos Mauricio, 125
Castells, Manuel, 21–22, 97
Castoriadis, Cornelius, 15
Catholic Church, 46
"Celos," 227, 235
Centeno-Pulido, Alberto, 6, 26
Center for Media & Social Impact, 14. See also CMSI
Centro de Atendimento à Mulher, 134
Cerro Maravilla, 207
C5N, 73
Cha Cha Cha, 46
Chagas, Viktor, 20, 27, 28, 182
Chanchada, 12
Chapelle, Dave, 47
Chaplin, Charlie, 84, 140n25
Chapo, El, 41, 49n8
Chapulín Colorado, El, 12
Chartier, Roger, 21
Chattoo, Caty Borum, 14
Chavo del Ocho, El, 12

Cheers, 46
Chernobyl, 208
"Chicas inseguras," 44, 50n28
Chihuahua, 37
Chile, 10, 13, 30, 221, 226–229; culture, 6; version of Barbie, 177
Chocó, 251
Chocobar, Luis (police officer), 86, 93n14
Chocobar (food), 86
Chomsky, Noah, 74
Choteo, 11
Christian Democratic Party, 148
Chumel con Chumel Torres, 43
Cida, 27, 117, 121, 131, 133–134, 135, 141nn28–29
Cidadãos de bem, 179
Cinema, 10, 12, 140n25, 230
CK, Louis, 46
Clarín, 81, 83–84, 91–92
CMSI, 14. *See also* Center for Media & Social Impact
CNN, 38
Coisinha, 131, 134
CoLAB, 146, 157t, 158t, 160t
Colbert, Stephen, 37, 47, 239, 258
Collado, Alejandra, 20, 26
Colombia, 9, 12–14, 22, 24, 30n2, 49, 236, 242–256, 258–260; Barbie, 177; news team, 9; oldest newspaper, 239; political class, 240; politics and identity, 29
Colonialism, 28, 181–182, 198–199, 201–202, 204, 216, 246
Comedic voice, 75, 82, 85
Common sense, 7, 73–75, 82
Communication technology, 12, 30n2
Concessa, 27, 117–118, 122, 131–137, 140n21, 141n29
"Conocidos, amigos y más que amigos," 233
Conservative, 27, 46, 141n27, 148–150, 179, 182, 184–186, 193, 241, 246, 258; bias, 153; humor, 146; middle- and upper-class Brazilian voters, 176; neo-Pentecostals, 144; social media influencers, 177; strata of the Brazilian population, 164; values, 187, 190
Cordera, Gustavo, 46
Cosmopolitan TV, 47
Costeño, 247, 249–250, 256
Costumbrismo, 11
Couldry, Nick, 19, 221, 233

Count Dooku, 105
COVID-19, 129, 131, 141n29, 208, 210, 212; pandemic, 93n13, 122, 136, 154
CQC, 149, 201, 210–212, 215
Craig, David, 223–224, 230–232
Critchley, Simon, 1, 5–8, 73–74, 80–81, 84, 88
Critical discourse, 101, 103; critical discourse analysis, 178, 183
Crumb, Robert, 57
Cualca, 3, 24, 35, 37, 43–44, 47–48, 51n37
Cuba, 10–11, 211
Cuenca, Enrique, 12
Cultural appropriation, 27, 188
Cultural proximity, 36–37, 222, 229–230
Culture, 3, 12, 18, 20–23, 27–28, 36, 66–67, 79, 112, 117–118, 121, 123i–124i, 126, 131, 133, 137, 138n6, 146, 188, 200, 222–223, 229, 242, 245, 255, 259; Antioqueño, 247; Brazilian, 27, 120–122, 125, 137; Bogotano, 246; Caipira, 140n20; Chilean, 6; Colombian, 245; consumer, 181–182; comic popular, 190; digital, 17, 30n2, 124, 129n13; entrepreneurial, 223; folk, 12; historical, 104; international popular, 2; local, 36, 47, 182; mass, 228; mass-mediated, 20; material, 4; media, 48, 224; national, 12, 27; of political memes, 110; official, 111; participatory, 1, 181, 201, 222, 225; political, 113, 141n27; pop, 146, 167i, 201; popular, 5, 36–37, 97, 98t, 104, 106, 109, 111, 130, 133, 177, 181, 190, 222, 225, 232; PR, 211; rural, 12; tensions within local and global, 37; US, 27, 188; US consumer, 178; virtual, 23; visual, 104; youth, 222, 225
Cunningham, Stuart, 223–224, 230–232
Curb Your Enthusiasm, 46

Daily Show, The, 35, 37, 47
Da Silva, Luís Inácio Lula, 135, 147, 149, 192
Da Silva, Ulisses Sawczuk, 7, 27
David, Larry, 8
Davison, Patrick, 152
Dawkins, Richard, 97, 125
Death Star, 104–105
Defamiliarization, 8, 74
De Jesus, Jaqueline Goes, 181
De la Torriente, Ricardo, 10
De Mello, Celso, 161
De Melo, Breno, 117
Demythologization, 74

Desinformado, El, 49
De Souza, Fábio Marquez, 5, 26
De Souza Filho, Henrique, 27, 117, 122
Destape, El, 77–78
Díaz-Quiñones, Arcadio, 199
Digital folklore
Digital Millennium Copyright Act of 1998, 231
Digital natives, 137, 225
Discursive production, 61
Discursive recognition, 61
Disney, 13, 139n11
Dissensus communis, 73, 77
Dissent, 14, 48
Dissenting, 73, 85, 202
DIY, 224, 232
Do-It-Yourself, 42, 224
Dom João VI, 118
Dom Pedro I, 118
Dom Pedro II, 118–119, 120i
Don Quijote, 10
Doregger, Julián, 44
"2018 en 3 minutos," 85
Duque Márquez, Iván, 247
Durden, 38
Duro de domar, 44, 47, 77

Eagleton, Terry, 5, 7, 243
Earthquakes, 198, 201, 208–210, 210i, 215
"Ebrios, ebrios, everywhere," 226
Economic crisis, 88, 93n14, 149
Edenor, 83–85, 92n10
Eje Cafetero, 252
ElDeforma, 3
El Espectador, 240
Ellul, Jacques, 111
ELN, 251, 254
Elomar, 123, 139n12
Empire Strikes Back, The, 105
Enchufe.TV, 49
Endless Summer, The, 208
"Entrevistando al enemigo," 45, 50n29
Enunciatee, 56, 59, 61, 68n3; hypermediatic, 65; mediatic, 59
Enunciative matrix, 57, 60, 64, 67
Enunciator, 56–57, 59–61; diegetic, 59; hyper-mediatic, 58, 58i, 59–62, 64; mediatic, 59, 64
Epoché, 6
EPR, 37–38, 40–43, 48, 49n8. See also *Pulso de la República, El*

Estupidez compleja, 47
Ethnie, 1, 6
Exchange rates, 74
Ex parejas, 233
Eymael, José Maria, 148

Facebook, 17, 30, 35, 48, 97, 102, 107–108, 108i, 121, 125, 127i, 128i, 129i, 130, 171, 198, 205, 208, 211, 227, 233–235; *Barbie y Ken Ciudadanos de Bien* fan page, 177; Blackness, disability, racism, and misogyny reflected in, 216; Bode Gaiato page, 139n14; creation of, 124; digital platform, 176; growth in popu-larity, 96; impact as a social medium, 235; Internet-based media, 68n1; media, 90n1; nature and capability of Internet platforms, 110; page, 60, 125; social media, 124; social media platforms, 215; wide use in PR, 200
Fajardo, Sergio, 246, 257–258
Fake account, 55, 59, 62–64, 68
Falabella, Nora, 67
Fals Borda, Orlando, 242
Far-right: Bolsonarist WhatsApp memes, 27; Brazilian groups, 144; Brazilian supporters, 146; Brazilian turn, 169; candidate Jair Bol-sonaro, 176; humor, 147, 169–170; leanings of Brazilian middle class, 179; meme, 164i, 165i; memes on WhatsApp, 156, 170–171; movements, 148; networks, 147; supporters, 170; women's opposition to Brazilian leader, 194n1
Fascist, 27, 64, 177, 179; Barbie, 27, 176–177
Father of the poor, 155, 157i
Federal Emergency Management Agency, 199
Federative Republic of Brazil, 158
FEMA, 200
Feminism, 46
Ferguson, Niall, 10
Fernández de Kirchner, Cristina, 62, 64, 69n13, 70n24
Fernández L'Hoeste, Héctor, 9, 29
Fierro Palas, Francisco, 10
Flickr, 232
Flirtear, 206
Fluminense Federal University, 146
FM Blue, 66
Fontanarrosa, Roberto, 16
Force, the, 104, 106
Fox, Vicente, 39, 104

Framework, 19, 25, 49, 57, 65, 79; metacommu-
nicative, 55–56; meta-enunciative, 56
Franco, Moreira, 147
Fraticelli, Damián, 15–16, 20, 25
Free constraint, 76
Freedom, 26, 72–74, 76, 82, 89, 105, 145, 155,
166, 186, 225; of choice, 82; compulsive, 76;
creative, 48; of expression, 41–42, 66, 144,
169; of the press, 119; of speech, 124i
Freud, Sigmund, 6–7, 56–57
Friedman, Elisabeth Jay, 24
Friends, 46
Fuchs, Christian, 17, 225

Gago, Fernando, 87, 94n15
Galán, Luis Carlos, 246
Game of Thrones, 257
García, Cintia, 63
García Canclini, Néstor, 36
Garmendia, Germán, 6, 28–29, 221, 223, 225–
229, 231, 233–237
GCU, 49
Geertz, Clifford, 121, 138n6
Gente Como Uno, 3
Geolinguistic audience, 48, 79
Germánsejos, 235
Germany, 106, 136, 228
Gervais, Ricky, 8
Gibson, Mel, 214
GIFs, 20, 99
Gimmick, 2–3, 20
Gini coefficients, 244
Girls, 47
Globalization, 37, 181, 229–230; cultural, 3, 24,
36, 48–49
Globoplay, 13
Goffman, Ervin, 232
Goldstein, Donna M., 14
"Graúna," 122
Green, Joshua, 222–223
Green Party, 148
Greg News, 3
Greñas, Alfredo, 10
Gru, Felonius, 166
Grupo do Alto da Caatinga, 122
Guandalini, Isabela Gama, 14
Guánica, 208–209, 209i
Guardian, The, 42–43
Guerrero, 41, 108

Guille Aquino, 49, 78
Guillem, Antonio, 210
Gutiérrez, Federico, 257–258, 261n29
Guzmán Loera, Joaquín "El Chapo," 41, 49n8

Haddad, Fernando, 176
Han, Byung-Chul, 26, 72, 89
Hasselmann, Joyce, 145
Hate speech, 54, 63, 171, 191
HBO, 13, 25, 35, 37, 43, 48, 50n21, 257
Hegemonic, 7, 9, 15, 20, 24, 90n4, 96; discourse,
45, 90n4, 96
Hegemony, 29, 55, 90n4, 100–101, 107, 255;
intranational, 247, 250
Henfil, 27, 117, 122–123, 123i, 124, 130, 138n9,
138n11
Hepp, Andreas, 19, 221, 233
Hero, 24, 145, 154, 156, 157t, 158, 166
Hidalgo, Narciso, 11
History, 17, 23, 75, 86, 93n14, 107, 121, 138n3,
140n20, 183, 231, 234, 250; Atlantic, 199;
Brazil's, 179; of Brazilian comics, 27; of Co-
lombia, 242; of human rights violations and
colonialism in PR, 204; of internalized co-
lonialism, 201; Internet, 18, 30n2; of media,
16; of Mexico, 96, 100; national, 26, 166, 248;
political, 137; of repression and censorship in
PR, 202; of Telmex, 41
Hobbes, 6, 161
HolaSoyGermán, 221, 225, 236–237
Holland, 136
Homophobia, 44, 78, 155, 160t, 240, 258
Honest, 87, 122, 155, 157t, 192, 236
Hopenhayn, Martin, 23
Hormiga Imperial, La, 73
HSG, 29, 221–222, 225–230, 233–237
Human rights, 23, 40, 67, 198, 204, 211
Humor, 1–20, 22, 24–30, 36, 44–46, 48, 55–57,
64–65, 67, 72, 74–75, 77–81, 84, 88, 90n3,
97, 98t, 99–100, 103, 106, 108–109, 111,
117–118, 122, 124–125, 131, 137, 144–148,
150–153, 155, 158, 160–162, 164, 165i, 166,
169–171, 177, 193, 198, 200–203, 206–208,
215–216, 222, 228–229, 233–235, 237, 239–
241, 243–247, 249–251, 257–259; Argentinean, 46; audiovisual, 47; Bakhtinian, 158;
Brazilian, 117; carnivalesque, 244; conservative, 146; critical, 48, 151, 204; digital, 35;
far-right, 147, 169–170; feminist, 43;

Humor—*continued*
    hypermediatic, 25, 54, 67–68; mediatic, 16;
    mediatized, 16; pandemic, 128; political,
    100, 137, 260; racial, 205; satiric, 44, 72;
    superiority, 203, 207; supremacist, 44
Hurricane Maria, 15, 198–201, 205–206
Hybridity, 3, 13, 24, 36
Hyperinflation, 72
Hypertext, 22, 124

Iacono, Lucía, 79, 90n6. *See also* Lu
IBGE, 129
Iguala, 107
Igualadas, Las, 240
IMF, 73, 87–89, 93. *See also* International
    Monetary Fund
INADI, 66
Incongruity, 1, 6–9, 202–203
Indigenismo, 212
Indigenous, 63, 69n10, 118, 121, 131, 186,
    189i, 212, 214, 214i; communities, 23;
    traditions, 179
Indignados, Los, 182
"Infancia," 234
Inflation, 4, 72; inflation, price, 74
Inocêncio, Luana, 126
Inodoro Pereyra, 16–17
Instagram, 30, 35, 48, 68n1, 90n1, 121, 124,
    176, 240; account, 177–178, 181–184,
    194n2; profile, 188
Instagrammer, 59
Institutional Revolutionary Party, 38–39, 107
Intelligence, 77, 82; intelligence network, 41
International Monetary Fund, 87. *See also*
    IMF
Internet, 1–5, 8, 10, 13, 17–18, 20, 22–30,
    30n1, 42–44, 47, 49, 78–79, 90n7, 108, 121,
    124–125, 128–129, 139n13, 140nn20–21,
    171n2, 181, 230, 234, 237n4, 244; Brazil-
    ian, 28; Brazilian users, 176; connections,
    137; exchanges, 18; history of, 18, 30n2;
    Internet-based businesses, 223; Internet-
    based culture, 2; Internet-based humor,
    2–4; Internet-based interactions, 17;
    Internet-based media, 68n1, 69n7; logic,
    228; memes, 110, 125, 145–146, 149, 151–
    152, 192, 200; platforms, 110; services, 13;
    users, 177, 181, 194

Inversion, 74, 107, 110, 187, 190, 193

Jackson, Jhoni, 206
Jagunço, 122
Jandira, 131–132, 134
Jíbaro, 210–211
Jokes, 4, 7–8, 25, 41, 45, 84–85, 88–89, 109,
    125–126, 137, 145–146, 158; childish,
    148, 162, 203, 243, 259; derogatory, 192;
    homophobic, 160; inside, 215; racist, 144;
    visual, 146
Jorge, Eduardo, 148
Juanpis, 258–260. *See also* Riaño, Alejandro
JuegaGermán, 221, 225

Kant, 6
Kartun, Julián, 44
Katrina, 207
Kierkegaard, 6
Kirchner, Máximo, 66, 70n23
Kirchner, Néstor, 66, 69n16, 70n23
Knight Center for Journalism in the Americas,
    40
Kraidy, Marwan, 36
Ku Klux Klan, 64

Lacan, Jacques, 8
Lafken Winkul Mapu, 69n12
Lagarde, Christine, 87, 94n14
Landaluze, Víctor, 10
Language, 2, 7, 36, 47–48, 59, 84, 111, 117,
    131, 138n5, 140n21, 156, 191–192, 191i,
    200, 228–231, 246; African, 138n3; Antio-
    queño, 247; audiovisual, 124; English, 179;
    foul, 249; ideological, 156; media, 35, 79;
    national, 230; of the colonizer, 214; pontifi-
    cating, 244; representational, 124; Spanish,
    222; Tupi, 140n20; violent, 75
La Plata (city), 63
La Pulla, 3, 29, 49, 239–241, 243–260,
    260nn2–4, 261n26, 261n33, 261n38
"Las cosas obvias de la vida," 226
Last Week Tonight with John Oliver, 43
Latin America, 13–15, 22, 30n2, 37, 39, 51n37,
    177, 179, 227, 244
Laughable, 6, 11, 17, 25, 54–60, 62, 64–68, 111
Leader, 63, 104, 107, 154, 156, 157t, 158, 203,
    249; black-movement, 149; of the Brazilian

Workers Party, 172n4; far-right, 194n1; figure of, 151; guerrilla, 249; Indigenous, 69n10; of Kirchnerism, 66; of the PNP, 207; political, 106; social, 78

LGBTQ, 146

LGBTQ+, 93n13, 193

LGBTQI+, 208–209

Libertadores Cup, 87, 94n15

LinkedIn, 83, 91n10

Lobato, Monteiro, 122

Loca de mierda, La, 34, 43–45, 48, 50

Lombardi, Hernán, 66–67, 70n25

Lopes, Camila, 126

López, Charo, 44

López, Claudia, 246, 253

López Obrador, Andrés Manuel, 37, 39, 50n21, 106

López Prieto, José María, 259

Loya García, Luis, 3

Lu, 79–81, 85, 91n8. *See also* Iacono, Lucía

Lucero, Julián, 44

Macri, Mauricio, 25, 46, 64–67, 69n12, 69n16, 70n24, 70n26, 87, 92n12, 94n14

Magela, Geraldo, 132–133, 140n23

Maldonado, Santiago, 64, 67, 69n12

Maluf, Paulo, 147

Mañach, Jorge, 11

Mandetta, Luiz Henrique, 130

Manipanso, 119, 119i

Manzano, Eduardo, 12

Maquila, 37

Maria, Hurricane, 15, 198–201, 205–206

María, La India, 12

Mariana (city), 135, 141n28

Marshall, P. David, 232

Martín-Barbero, Jesús, 12, 15, 20–23, 36

Martyr, 146, 155–156, 157t, 158, 162

Marx, Karl, 21

Marx, Groucho, 8

Mascarada, La, 10

Mascherano, 87, 94n15

Mashup, 126, 182

Mattel, 27, 176–177, 180–181, 183–184, 187

Mazzaropi, Amácio, 122, 140n22, 140n25, 141n26

McLuhan, Marshall, 26, 97, 111–112

Medellín, 247, 252, 257–258, 261n5

Media, 1, 3–4, 13, 16, 19–21, 23, 26, 28, 39–40, 42–46, 49, 50n25, 54–55, 57, 59, 61, 66, 68n1, 69n7, 79, 90n1, 96, 100, 104, 106, 110–111, 138n7, 139n18, 144, 148–149, 155, 161, 164, 178, 222–223, 226–227, 229, 231–233, 237; citizen, 23; combined effects of, 20; communication, 112; digital, 35; digital resistance, 23; ecology of, 110; history of, 15; mass, 1, 16, 40, 54, 57, 62, 66–67, 106; modern, 3, 20; new, 5; official, 109; portrayals of Afro-Brazilian women, 188; social, 4–5, 10, 14–15, 17–18, 24–25, 30, 38, 44, 48, 55, 73, 124, 145, 150–151, 153, 169, 177, 182, 200, 202, 215, 221–223, 228, 230–231, 234, 258; state, 63, 70n26

Media artifacts, 179

Media content, 37, 110

Media culture, 48, 224

Media expressions, 99

Media formats, 36, 234

Media industry, 181

Media languages, 35

Media literacy, 27, 171

Media outlets, 30, 48

Media ownership, 38

Media personalities, 78

Media production, 29, 47

Media professionals, 225

Media services, 13

Media space, 1, 5

Medina Cartagena, María Alejandra, 13

Meme, 55, 59–60, 62, 97, 99, 102–109, 113, 125, 128–130, 161–162, 164, 177, 182, 193, 198, 200–201, 203–204, 205i, 207–212, 214; content, 15; creators, 206; generators, 202, 215–216; political, 96, 102–103, 176; production, 198, 201, 203, 205–206, 215

Meme News, 14

Memes de Puerto Rico, 208–209, 209i–210i, 213i, 215

Mendes, Aparecida Silva, 27, 117, 121, 131, 140n21

Mequetrefe, O, 119

Meritocracy, 179, 184, 187

Messi, Lionel, 87–88, 94n15

Mestizaje, 23, 36

Mestizo essentialism, 205

Meta (Colombian department), 253–254

Mexicanidad, 26
Mexico, 11–14, 26, 30n2, 31n2, 37, 39–43, 47,
    96, 99–100, 106–107, 111, 144, 205, 212
Mexico City, 37
Michoacán, 38, 49n4
Mimeme, 99
Mina, An Xiao, 20
Minas Gerais, 118, 131–133, 135, 137n1,
    138n10, 140n24, 141n28
Mineiro, 132
"Mi nombre (soy el hijo de Lady Gaga)," 228
Mockery, 8, 11, 56–57, 62, 64–65, 68n3, 118,
    202, 243–244; offensive, 67; self-, 235, 259
Modern Times, 84
Molina, Juana, 46
Molinari, Sarah, 200
Monsiváis, Carlos, 11–12
Moreno, Mario, 11
Moro, Sérgio, 141n27, 161–162, 164
Morreall, John, 5, 7–9
Morris, Jonathan, 3
Moura, Eduardo, 117
MTV, 35, 44, 48
Muchachada Nui, 46
Mundializações, 2
Mundillo, 47

Nación, La, 44–45, 81–84, 91n10
Nahuel, Rafael, 64, 67, 69n12
Nation, 69n16, 73, 151, 210–211, 241–243
National Action Party, 39
National Commission for Human Rights, 40
Nationalism, 11, 27, 72, 108, 146, 153, 158, 158t,
    170, 201, 242, 258; Puerto Rican, 211
National Liberation Army, 254
Nation-state, 2, 20, 246
"Negación," 44, 50n27
Negro Timoteo, El, 10
Neoliberal, 18, 76, 92n12, 93n14, 179, 184, 192,
    203, 216; economic policies, 39; economy, 15
Neoliberalism, 22, 229
Netflix, 13, 47–48, 82, 91n9
Networks, 10, 21–22, 30n2, 40–41, 54, 56, 59–
    62, 66, 68n1, 171; electronic, 23; far-right,
    147; social, 25, 54, 57–58, 62, 67, 70n22, 98t,
    103, 151; social media, 37, 55; television, 13,
    126
Networld, 10
New Hope, A, 104

New Progressive Party of Puerto Rico, 206. *See
    also* PNP
New Year, 64, 88
Ngai, Sianne, 2–3, 20

Oaxaca, 41
Optimization, 76, 227
Ordinary person, 155, 157t
Orelhão, 132
Ortiz, Renato, 2
Oscarito, 12
Otelo, Grande, 12
Other, the, 8, 76, 201–202
OTT, 13
Ouro Preto, 135, 141n28

País, El, 40, 43
Paisa, 247
País de Boludos, 3, 49
Palacios, Cristian, 16
Palermo News, 79, 86
PAN, 39, 106. *See also* National Action Party;
    Partido Acción Nacional
Panama Papers, 41
Pânico, 149
Papacharissi, Zizzi, 112
Paracatu, 134–135
Pará de Minas, 134
Parati, 134
Parceiros do Rio Bonito, Os, 117, 137n2
Partido Acción Nacional, 39, 106. *See also*
    National Action Party; PAN
Partido Revolucionario Institucional, 39, 105.
    See also PRI
Party of the Democratic Revolution, 39. *See also*
    PRD
Patriarchy, 179–180
PBS, 10
Peirce, 25, 68n2
Peladito, 11–12
Peña Nieto, Enrique, 40, 96, 105–106
Pepón, 259
Pérez Firmat, Gustavo, 11
Peronism, 62, 69n16, 72
Persona studies, 232
Pertierra, Ana Cristina, 23
Peru, 10, 49, 144, 205
Petro, Gustavo, 244, 246, 249, 259
Philosophy of Laughter and Humor, The, 5

Picaresque character, 155, 157t
Pichot, Malena, 3, 24–25, 35, 43–48
Pignata, Dra. Alcira, 25, 54–55, 62–68, 69n12, 70n20
Pinos, Los, 107
Pinterest, 232
Pires, Cornélio, 122
Pires, Maria da Conceição Francisca, 123
"Piropos," 44, 50n25
Pitman, Thea, 22
Plato, 6
PNP, 206. *See also* New Progressive Party of Puerto Rico
Poblete, Juan, 6, 28, 226, 230
Política Cómica, La, 10
Polivoces, Los, 12
Populism, 72
Por ahora, 47, 51n37
Porta dos Fundos, 3, 13, 49
Portugal, 118, 136
PRD, 39. *See also* Party of the Democratic Revolution
PRI, 39–41. *See also* Partido Revolucionario Institucional
PROMESA, 199. *See also* Puerto Rico Oversight, Management, and Economic Stability Act
Puerto Rico, 15, 28, 198–199, 204, 206, 208–210, 210i, 211–213i, 214–216, 216n5
Puerto Rico Oversight, Management, and Economic Stability Act, 199. *See also* PROMESA
Pulla, La, 3, 29, 49, 239–241, 243–260, 260n2, 260n3, 261n26, 261n33, 261n38
Pulse (gay night club), 41
Pulso de la República, El, 3, 24, 35, 37, 40, 42, 47–49, 49n1, 50n19. See also *EPR*
Punisher, 155, 157t, 158, 162

Quadros, Jânio, 147, 171n3
¿Qué nos pasa?, 12
Quilombolas, 149, 172n14

Racial democracy, 178, 204–205, 211–212, 214
Racial inequalities, 178
Racism, 6, 187, 209, 212, 216; anti-Chinese, 211–212; denial of, 178; environmental, 200; systemic, 204
Radical Cowry, 207i, 215
Radio, 10, 12, 42, 44, 48, 70n26, 111, 230, 236; development of, 121; FM Blue station, 66

Radio y Televisión Argentina, 70n26. *See also* RTA
Rage, 26, 73–74, 82, 84, 87; ability/capacity to express, 72, 77, 89; capacity for, 76; dissenting, 85; national, 240
Rambo, John, 166
Ramírez, Marta Lucía, 248
Ranchera, 12
Rancière, Jacques, 21
"Realidad, La," 233
Rebamar, Zeferino, 122
Rebel Alliance, 104–105
Recession, 72
Recuero, Raquel, 124
Reddit, 232
Regional Center for Studies on the Development of the Information Society, 151
Regionalism, 241–242, 258
Relief: economic, 73, 204; humor and, 1–2, 5, 6, 7, 8, 9, 202, 243, 251
Religion, 14, 72, 93n13, 146, 148, 166, 168i, 169i, 193, 204
Remezcla, 3, 206
Remix, 126, 139n15
Reno, Janet, 64
Research Laboratory for Communication, Political Cultures, and Economy of Collaboration, 151
Return of the Jedi, The, 105i, 106
Revista Cómica, La, 10
Rhetoric, 16, 144, 155, 170, 204; anti-Communism, 160t; antidemocratic, 170; anti-drugs, 155, 160t; anti-terrorism, 155, 160t; of futility, 150; of perversity, 150; of play, 150; of threat, 150; warmongering, 158
Rhetorical: appeal, 156; devices, 178, 188, 194; elements, 146; figures, 101, 103; forms, 107; strategy, 150, 187; tool, 206, 215
Riaño, Alejandro, 258–260. *See also* Juanpis
Ribeiro, Darcy, 120
Right-wing: activist political groups, 151; character, 38; discourses, 192; federal representative, 145; groups, 28, 141n27; individuals, 191; movement, 135, 148, 152, 164; populist, 171n3; presidential candidate, 257; social media, 182; TV hosts, 258
Riley, Amy Henderson, 14
Rincón, Juan Carlos, 239–241, 244–247, 250–251, 254

Rio de Janeiro: arrival of Portuguese court, 118; governor of, 147, 172n4; people from, 132; road connecting to Brasília, 140n24; shantytowns, 15

Rio Grande do Sul, 121, 172n4

Rivera, Angélica, 40

River Plate, 87, 94n15

Roberto, Giovanni, 200

Robertson, Roland, 36

Rock barrial, 81

Rock nacional, 81

Rodríguez, Clemencia, 24

Rojas, Luis Fernando, 10

Rojo, Roxane, 117

Rolling Stone, 44

Romantiqueo, 206

Romero Barceló, Carlos, 206–207

Roselló, Ricardo, 207

Rousseff, Dilma, 135, 141n27, 144, 149

RTA, 67, 70n26. See also Radio y Televisión Argentina

Sala, Milagro, 63, 63i, 69n10

Salazar, Juan Francisco, 23

"Saludos, Los," 234

Sampaio, Plínio de Arruda, 148

San Andrés, 250–252, 256

Sánchez Montiel, José Alberto, 38

Santos, Juan Manuel, 248

São Paulo, 118, 120, 131, 137n1, 138n4

Sarcasm, 8, 67, 101, 108, 194, 258

Sarkazein, 8

Satire, 3, 36, 47–49, 56, 62–68, 72, 75, 77, 79, 85, 89, 102, 187, 190; anti-racist, 144; online, 35; parodic, 107; shows, 37, 47; subjects and objects of, 244; political, 16, 48, 75

Satiric TV in the Americas, 3

Savior, 146, 151, 155–157, 157t, 158

Schaal, Kristen, 46

Schopenhauer, 6

Schumer, Amy, 46–47

Scott, James C., 15, 101

Seinfeld (comedian), 46

Seinfeld (TV show), 47

Self-denigration, 8

Selfish Gene, The, 125, 201

Selfless, 155–157, 157t, 158

Semiotic analysis, 178, 183

Sensus communis, 6–7

Sexism, 44–45, 50n25, 78, 179–180, 258

Shifman, Limor, 4, 111, 152, 181–182, 201

Show de los Polivoces, El, 12

Silent Hill, 208

Silent Protector, 164

Silverman, Sarah, 46–47

Simpsons, The, 78–80, 203

Sinclair, John, 2, 37, 229

Sketch, El, 26, 72–73, 77–78, 90n6

Slim, Carlos, 40–41

SME, 221, 223–224, 230–231, 233, 236. See also Social media entertainment

SNL, 37

Soap opera, 40, 126–127i, 128, 139n17. See also Telenovela

Soccer, 43, 89, 107–109

Social Blade, 221, 239, 258

Socialism and Liberty Party, 148

Social media entertainment, 221–223. See also SME

Sommier, Mélodine, 7, 27

Sony, 12

Spencer, Herbert, 6

Star Wars, 104, 107, 113n1

Steimberg, Oscar, 55

Stewart, Jon, 37

Straubhaar, Joseph D., 36–37, 229

Suárez, Héctor, 12

Superiority, 1, 5–6, 9, 56, 180, 203, 243–245; humor, 203, 207; moral, 243; theory, 7–8, 202, 244, 246

Surrealization, 74

Suzina, Ana Cristina, 23

Switzerland, 136

Taíno people, 212

Targaryen, Daenerys, 257, 261n34

Tatu, Jeca, 122

Taylor, Claire, 22

Tecendo prosa, 121, 131, 132–133, 136, 138n8, 140nn22–23

Technology, 5, 19–23, 111–112, 124, 229; of colonialism, 246; and humor, 10; mass-communication, 12; transformation of, 100

Tecnicidad, 21, 23

Telenovela, 12–13, 126, 139n16. See also Soap opera

Televisa, 12–13, 25, 39–40, 42–43, 47–48

Television, 10, 12–13, 35–37, 42–43, 45, 48, 62, 73, 85, 104, 121, 126, 148–149, 229, 260; Argentinian, 77; networks, 126; satiric, 44

Telmex, 41

Tetrad, 97, 100–101, 101i, 103–104, 103i, 106, 112

Tetradic model, 26

Theory, 8, 19, 24, 26, 138n7; Bakhtin's, 26; cultural proximity, 229; of the gimmick, 20; incongruity, 8, 202; information, 9; release/relief, 7, 202, 243; remix, 139n15; of signs, 25; superiority, 7–8, 202, 244, 246

Thompson, John, 137, 138n7

Thorne, David, 3

TikTok, 30

Tin Tan, 12

Torres, Chumel, 3, 24, 35, 37, 43, 48, 260n2

Transphobia, 78

Trump, Donald, 41, 135, 199, 203–204, 206–207

Trump, Mickey Donadi, 134, 136

Tumblr, 232

TV Globo, 13, 139nn16–17

TV Tupi, 126

Tweetazzos, 148, 172n6

2014 World Cup, 43, 48

Twitter, 17, 30, 35, 37–38, 48, 49n2, 68n1, 90n1, 105i, 110, 121, 153, 171, 176, 182, 232, 252; account, 66, 69n13, 70n24; fake account, 95; post, 57

UGC, 229

Univision, 14

Upsocl, 3

Uribe Vélez, Álvaro, 247–249

Uruguay, 10

User-generated content, 146, 151

Vader, Darth, 106

Vainilla, Micky, 65, 69n18

Van Dijck, José, 17–19

Vargas, Getúlio, 120, 171n4

Vásquez Garced, Wanda, 210, 212

Verón, Eliseo, 55

Viacom, 13

Victim, 57, 63, 100, 151, 155, 157t, 158, 185i; of criminality and police brutality, 178; of domestic abuse, 134; of domestic violence, 134

Vidal, María Eugenia, 84

Videla, Jorge Rafael, 69n11

Video, 5–6, 13, 26–29, 37–38, 40–44, 47–49, 49n1, 50n22, 59, 69n18, 72–73, 90n1, 131–132, 162, 221–22, 225–228, 233, 235–237, 239–241, 244, 246–251, 253–260, 261n12, 261n15; comic, 59, 62; Concessa's, 131; homemade online, 35; HSG, 226; of Trump, 134–135; parodying right-wing Brazilians, 177; recording, 162; satirical, 45; scenes, 234; streaming, 232; viral, 44; YouTube, 225, 246

Village Voice, 57

Virtual space, 112

Vlog, 29, 221

Vlogger, 28, 231, 237n1

Warrior, 146, 155–157, 157t, 158, 162, 189i

Wayne's World, 38

We Are The 99%, 182

Web, 1, 3, 19, 35, 48; memetics, 4

Web 1.0, 17

Web 2.0, 4, 17, 181

Web 3.0, 17

WeChat, 232

Weekend Update, 37

WhatsApp, 28, 121, 130–131, 145–147, 151–156, 160–162, 166, 170–171, 176; communities, 97; memes, 27

Wiggum, Ralph, 203

Wikipedia, 17, 132, 140n22, 228

Will & Grace, 46

Wilson, Christopher, 7, 243, 246

Women, 14, 43–46, 118, 132, 134, 138n8, 146, 180, 188, 193; Black, 190; business, 131; commodification of, 181; from Pereira, 252; rights, 48; rights groups, 46; united against Bolsonaro, 176, 194n1

Workers' Party, 190–192; candidate, 176; government, 186

World Bank, 244

World Cup, 87–88, 94n15, 107; 1970 FIFA Football, 139n16; 2014, 43, 48

Yayo, 38, 49n2

Yerba mate, 86, 93n12

Yo soy Betty, la fea, 12

YouTube, 13, 17, 28, 35, 38, 42–43, 48–49, 49n1, 62, 84, 125, 132i–133i, 135i–136i, 137, 153,

YouTube—*continued*
171, 221–226, 229–232, 234, 236, 239–240,
260n2; accounts, 44, 257; channel, 3, 37,
90n1, 117, 140n21, 236–237, 237n1, 260n1;
feminist star, 35; interview, 78; page, 248; political news team, 3; numbers, 247; universe,
131; videos, 246; visitors, 255
YouTuber, 6, 29, 38, 221, 228, 258

Zancudo, El, 10
Zapatismo, 23
Zé Carioca, 139n11

Reframing Media, Technology, and Culture in Latin/o America

Edited by Héctor Fernández L'Hoeste and Juan Carlos Rodríguez

Reframing Media, Technology, and Culture in Latin/o America explores how Latin American and Latino audiovisual (film, television, digital), musical (radio, recordings, live performances, dancing), and graphic (comics, photography, advertising) cultural practices reframe and reconfigure social, economic, and political discourses at a local, national, and global level. In addition, it looks at how information networks reshape public and private policies, and the enactment of new identities in civil society. The series also covers how different technologies have allowed and continue to allow for the construction of new ethnic spaces. It not only contemplates the interaction between new and old technologies but also how the development of brand-new technologies redefines cultural production.

Telling Migrant Stories: Latin American Diaspora in Documentary Film, edited by Esteban E. Loustaunau and Lauren E. Shaw (2018; paperback edition, 2021)

Mestizo Modernity: Race, Technology, and the Body in Postrevolutionary Mexico, by David S. Dalton (2018; first paperback edition, 2021)

The Insubordination of Photography: Documentary Practices under Chile's Dictatorship, by Ángeles Donoso Macaya (2020; first paperback edition, 2023)

Digital Humanities in Latin America, edited by Héctor Fernández L'Hoeste and Juan Carlos Rodríguez (2020; first paperback edition, 2023)

Pablo Escobar and Colombian Narcoculture, by Aldona Bialowas Pobutsky (2020)

The New Brazilian Mediascape: Television Production in the Digital Streaming Age, by Eli Lee Carter (2020)

Univision, Telemundo, and the Rise of Spanish-Language Television in the United States, by Craig Allen (2020; first paperback edition, 2023)

Cuba's Digital Revolution: Citizen Innovation and State Policy, edited by Ted A. Henken and Sara Garcia Santamaria (2021; first paperback edition, 2022)

Afro-Latinx Digital Connections, edited by Eduard Arriaga and Andrés Villar (2021)

The Lost Cinema of Mexico: From Lucha Libre to Cine Familiar and Other Churros, edited by Olivia Cosentino and Brian Price (2022)

Neo-Authoritarian Masculinity in Brazilian Crime Film, by Jeremy Lehnen (2022)

The Rise of Central American Film in the Twenty-First Century, edited by Mauricio Espinoza and Jared List (2023)

Internet, Humor, and Nation in Latin America, edited by Héctor Fernández L'Hoeste and Juan Poblete (2024)